Knowledge and Space

Volume 13

Series editor
Peter Meusburger, Department of Geography, Heidelberg University, Heidelberg, Germany

Knowledge and Space

This book series entitled "Knowledge and Space" is dedicated to topics dealing with the production, dissemination, spatial distribution, and application of knowledge. Recent work on the spatial dimension of knowledge, education, and science; learning organizations; and creative milieus has underlined the importance of spatial disparities and local contexts in the creation, legitimation, diffusion, and application of new knowledge. These studies have shown that spatial disparities in knowledge and creativity are not short-term transitional events but rather a fundamental structural element of society and the economy.

The volumes in the series on Knowledge and Space cover a broad range of topics relevant to all disciplines in the humanities and social sciences focusing on knowledge, intellectual capital, and human capital: clashes of knowledge; milieus of creativity; geographies of science; cultural memories; knowledge and the economy; learning organizations; knowledge and power; ethnic and cultural dimensions of knowledge; knowledge and action; and mobilities of knowledge. These topics are analyzed and discussed by scholars from a range of disciplines, schools of thought, and academic cultures.

Knowledge and Space is the outcome of an agreement concluded by the Klaus Tschira Foundation and Springer in 2006.

More information about this series at http://www.springer.com/series/7568

Johannes Glückler • Roy Suddaby • Regina Lenz
Editors

Knowledge and Institutions

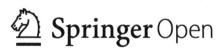 

Klaus Tschira Stiftung
Gemeinnützige GmbH

Editors
Johannes Glückler
Department of Geography
Heidelberg University
Heidelberg, Germany

Roy Suddaby
Peter B. Gustavson School of Business
University of Victoria
Victoria, BC, Canada

Regina Lenz
Department of Geography
Heidelberg University
Heidelberg, Germany

Assistant Editor
Anna Mateja Schmidt
Department of Geography
Heidelberg University
Heidelberg, Germany

Technical Editors
David Antal, Berlin

James Bell, Berlin

ISSN 1877-9220
Knowledge and Space
ISBN 978-3-319-75327-0   ISBN 978-3-319-75328-7   (eBook)
https://doi.org/10.1007/978-3-319-75328-7

Library of Congress Control Number: 2018939553

Printed on acid-free paper

This Springer imprint is published by the registered company Springer International Publishing AG part
of Springer Nature.
The registered company address is: Gewerbestrasse 11, 6330 Cham, Switzerland

Acknowledgements

The editors thank the Klaus Tschira Stiftung for funding the symposia and book series on Knowledge and Space. The team of the Klaus Tschira Stiftung and the Studio Villa Bosch have always been contributing greatly to the success of the symposia. Together with all the authors in this volume, we are especially grateful to Anna Mateja Schmidt for her superb assistance to the editors as well as to David Antal and James Bell for their tireless dedication to quality as technical editors of all the chapters and as translators for some of them. Volker Schniepp at the Department of Geography at Heidelberg University has generously helped get figures and maps into shape for publication. We also thank all student assistants and colleagues from the Department of Geography who have helped accomplish the symposium as well as this 13th volume in the Klaus Tschira Symposia book series. We are especially grateful to Katrin Janzen, Andreas Kalström, Pia Liepe, Leslie Ludwig, Florence Wieder and Hanna Wilbrand.

Contents

Contributors

Harald Bathelt Department of Political Science and Department of Geography and Planning, University of Toronto, ON, Canada

Ryan Coles ILR School, Department of Organizational Behavior, Cornell University, Ithaca, NY, USA

Nicolas Conserva Department of Political Science, University of Toronto, ON, Canada

Diego Coraiola Augustana Campus, University of Alberta, Camrose, Alberta, Canada

Riccardo Crescenzi Department of Geography and Environment, London School of Economics, London, UK

Rainer Diaz-Bone Department of Sociology, University of Lucerne, Lucerne, Switzerland

Marco Di Cataldo Department of Geography and Environment, London School of Economics, London, UK

Henry Farrell Department of Political Science, The George Washington University, Washington, DC, USA

William M. Foster Augustana Campus, University of Alberta, Camrose, Alberta, Canada

Johannes Glückler Department of Geography, Heidelberg University, Heidelberg, Germany

Andreas Hess School of Sociology, University College Dublin, Belfield, Dublin, Ireland

Regina Lenz Department of Geography, Heidelberg University, Heidelberg, Germany

Jerker Moodysson Jönköping International Business School, Jönköping University, Jönköping, Sweden

Tiina Ritvala Department of Management Studies, Aalto University, Helsinki, Finland

Andrés Rodríguez-Pose Department of Geography and Environment, London School of Economics, London, UK

Lionel Sack CIRCLE, Lund University, Lund, Sweden

Michael Storper Luskin School of Public Affairs, UCLA, Los Angeles, CA, USA

Department of Geography and Environment, London School of Economics, London, UK

Center for the Sociology of Organizations, Sciences Po Paris, Paris, France

Roy Suddaby Peter B. Gustavson School of Business, University of Victoria, Victoria, BC, Canada

Pamela S. Tolbert ILR School, Department of Organizational Behavior, Cornell University, Ithaca, NY, USA

Tammar B. Zilber The Jerusalem School of Business Administration, The Hebrew University of Jerusalem, Jerusalem, Israel

Chapter 1
On the Spatiality of Institutions and Knowledge

Johannes Glückler, Roy Suddaby, and Regina Lenz

The relationship between geography and the creation, use, and reproduction of knowledge has been at the core of this book series. The previous twelve volumes have focused, among other topics, on the role that creativity (Meusburger, Funke, & Wunder, 2009), science and universities (Meusburger, Livingston, & Jöns, 2010), power (Meusburger, Gregory, & Suarsana, 2015), culture and action (Meusburger, Werlen, & Suarsana, 2017), and networks (Glückler, Lazega, & Hammer, 2017) have in cultivating an understanding of how the social process of knowing unfolds in space. They all draw attention to ways in which this process is situated in places and how learning connects people across places. Centering on institutions, volume 13 presents yet another perspective on the spatiality of human knowledge. Across the social sciences scholars have been attributing to institutions a major part in social, political, cultural, an d economic development. Although there is agreement on the importance of institutions, there are several understandings of what institutions are and how they influence social life. The purpose of this volume is to examine a rather neglected and only recently acknowledged dimension in institutional theory: the spatiality of institutions, the spatiotemporal dynamics of institutional change, and the role of institutions in the creation and reproduction of knowledge and related social outcomes in bounded territories.

In this introduction we wish to stimulate a dialogue on the spatiality and dynamics of institutions across the boundaries of individual disciplines in the social sciences. We open the floor to such dialogue by briefly highlighting achievements of

J. Glückler (✉) · R. Lenz
Department of Geography, Heidelberg University, Heidelberg, Germany
e-mail: glueckler@uni-heidelberg.de; lenz@uni-heidelberg.de

R. Suddaby
Peter B. Gustavson School of Business, University of Victoria, Victoria, BC, Canada
e-mail: rsuddaby@uvic.ca

J. Glückler et al. (eds.), *Knowledge and Institutions*, Knowledge and Space 13,
https://doi.org/10.1007/978-3-319-75328-7_1

and challenges to both the "institutional turn" in geography and what may be an incipient "spatial turn" in institutional theory. Whereas geographical studies have offered a detailed insight into spatial differences and regional path dependencies stemming from institutional variation, they have lagged somewhat in exploring the processes of institutional dynamics, especially those of informal institutions. Institutional theory as applied in organizational institutionalism or political sciences has made important advances in this respect but has only recently entailed discussion of the spatial dimension of institutional life. With this volume we aim to bring the two strands of research together to facilitate a mutually beneficial dialogue and improve comprehension of the role that institutions play in the relationship between knowledge and space.

The Institutional Turn in Geography

A major interest in geography lies in the dynamics of economic development, and, over the years, it has led to different growth models of how to reduce the unevenness of development across regions. Regional disparities, however, have remained a fact and continue to challenge geographers, economists, and political scientists alike. Yet the approach to these issues has changed since the 1990s, when geographers began to recognize an institutional turn by attributing increased significance for economic development to institutions (Amin, 1999; Jessop, 2001; Martin, 2000). Having often concentrated on economic action apart from its sociocultural context, economic geographers then acknowledged that economic action itself is one form of social action that must be understood in its context and within a wider system of social, economic, and political rules of both formal and informal nature (Bathelt & Glückler, 2003; Gertler, 2010; Martin, 2000). This emerging institutional perspective was accompanied and facilitated by a cultural turn (Barnes, 2001) that also accentuated actors and their relations with others at the microlevel.

This change in perspective is mirrored in policy recommendations ranging from incentive-based, top-down investments in physical capital since the 1960s to endogenous growth theories for unlocking the wealth of regions through investment in education and training to mobilize their existing potential (Amin, 1999; Martin, 2000; Rodríguez-Pose, 2013). This shift thereby stressed the importance of regional specificities, path dependencies, and the social foundations of interdependent economic behaviors (Amin, 1999). Yet although statistics showed correlations between growth and particular policies, effective policies in one context could not be easily transferred to others. It remains an open question, then, how positive developmental paths can be purposively directed (Martin & Sunley, 2006). This question has led geographers to ask themselves what it is that makes it easier to unlock the potential of one region than that of another. Here is where institutions come in. They seem to be crucial in regional trajectories of social and economic development, and it has proven nearly impossible to reproduce institutions identically in other places, regions, and countries to render the same effects on social and economic outcomes (Rodríguez-Pose, 2013).

Institutions have some peculiar characteristics: As with Storper's (1997) untraded interdependencies, institutions are not tradable. Unlike real capital (e.g., assets, infrastructure), financial capital (e.g., venture capital, credits), and codified knowledge (e.g., technologies, patents, designs), institutions can be neither bought nor licensed, and they are nearly impossible to imitate (Maskell & Malmberg, 1999; Wernerfelt, 1984). This contextual and often geographical idiosyncrasy can either hamper or facilitate certain innovation and development paths, and poses epistemological challenges to universal growth models because of stubborn, unexplained residuals (Rodríguez-Pose & Storper, 2006). It is not that previous findings of positive influences on development and growth have become obsolete (e.g., investments in infrastructure, technology, or human capital). Rather, the critical aspect is the way in which these factors are combined. It is not enough, for example, just to have business associations promoting entrepreneurship within a region. The work of these organizations is shaped at least partly by expectations that are informed by past experiences, knowledge frames, policies, and established business relations and routines. These contextual settings influence socioeconomic action and economic success or failure (Amin, 2001). Even though institutions might not be the only cause of development, they enable or constrain the use of regional assets (Martin, 2000). Because it is difficult to grasp these underlying "deep determinants" (Bosker & Garretsen, 2009, p. 295) and to model them statistically (Tomaney, 2014), institutions are still hard to integrate into regional policies (Rodríguez-Pose, 2013). We identify two current challenges for institutional research in geography.

First, there is no clear definition of what an institution is. The understanding of institutions is often vague and inconsistent and can range from regulation (Rodríguez-Pose & Di Cataldo, 2015) and organizations (Amin & Thrift, 1995) to beliefs and stable patterns of practices (Bathelt & Glückler, 2014). It can even include all these phenomena. Research interest in how local characteristics determine competitiveness, knowledge creation, and growth has led to many economy-wide quantitative studies in geography, usually operationalizing institutions as formal rules and regulations (Farole, Rodríguez-Pose, & Storper, 2011; Rodríguez-Pose, 2013). Since the 2000s, studies have been characterized by opposing views and findings with regard to the primacy of institutions over geography (Rodrik, Subramanian, & Trebbi, 2004) or vice versa (Carstensen & Gundlach, 2006; Sachs, 2003). On the one hand, researchers have found, for example, that a region's quality of government matters for innovation (Rodríguez-Pose & Di Cataldo, 2015), as do the region's linkages to other countries and their institutional qualities (Bosker & Garretsen, 2009). Glaeser, La Porta, López-de-Silanes, and Shleifer (2004), on the other hand, argue that institutions can often only be poorly operationalized and that standard indicators such as human capital continue to be more important—also for developing beneficial political institutions in the first place. So far, there has been no solution to this debate, but there is certainty that more research is needed on various scales and with greater methodological variety, including microscale qualitative case studies emphasizing informal institutions that are not easily quantifiable (Bathelt & Glückler, 2014; Gertler, 2010; Pike, Marlow, McCarthy, O'Brian, & Tomaney, 2015).

Second, once "good" institutions are identified, it remains an open question how to achieve them. How do institutions manifest themselves differently in different regions, and what are the possible mechanisms of institutional change (Bathelt & Glückler, 2014; Farole et al., 2011; Tomaney, 2014)? Recent studies criticize that although institutions are seen as the causes of regional inequality, their mode of operation has not been adequately analyzed (Dellepiane-Avellaneda, 2010; Rafiqui, 2009; Tomaney, 2014). As long as the expression "institutions matter" is not verified by explanations, institutions will remain some kind of "magic dust" (Tomaney, 2014, p. 133), and the concept will become a truism by which regional disparities are explained simply by the existence of institutions (Jessop, 2001; MacLeod, 2001; Martin, 2000; Rafiqui, 2009). Only by making the processes of institutional effects and of institutional changes apparent can the problems of endogeneity between institutions and growth be addressed, as well as the possibility of the political malleability of institutions (Farole et al., 2011; Tomaney, 2014).

Drawing on Jessop's (2001) typology, we find several stages of an institutional turn that indicate to what extent a line of research becomes truly institutional. In the case of a *thematic* institutional turn (p. 1215), researchers analyze noninstitutional factors and only seek additional explanatory power in the institutional dimension of the space economy without going into further detail. In a *methodological* institutional turn (p. 1216), researchers recognize institutional aspects as a key starting point for analyzing social life even if other factors later become the main analytical interest. An example is the fact that other major streams of research within economic geography explicitly cross-reference institutions. In such cases institutions are seen as necessary underlying conditions for, say, creating capabilities in the relatedness approach (Boschma, 2017), building global production networks (Coe & Hess, 2013), and establishing national and regional innovation systems (Asheim, Lawton Smith, & Oughton, 2011). Lastly, in what Jessop (2001) calls an *ontological* institutional turn (p. 1217), geographers have spotlighted institutions as the essential foundation of social existence. These researchers inquire into aspects that cannot be covered by quantitative macroanalyses, such as the change processes of informal institutions at the microlevel. That kind of work is oriented to other disciplines and their approaches to analyzing the dynamics of institutions. Geographers can contribute their strong sense of geographical context and awareness of the role that place and space have in the formation and effect of bounded institutions. With their insight into the embeddedness of agents in regional or national territories, geography can help understand the ways in which local institutions matter (Bathelt & Glückler, 2014; Pike et al., 2015; Rodríguez-Pose & Storper, 2006; Tomaney, 2014). In sum, research in geography has been enriched by the integration of institutional theory in its various manifestations. Conversely, and basically without exchange between the two fields, institutional theorists are beginning to discuss the relevance of spatial aspects.

A Spatial Turn in Institutional Theory?

The spatial turn in organizational institutionalism is latent rather than manifest. There is neither a defined category of geographic institutionalism nor much explicit theorization of space in institutional theory. However, considerable recent work—the research now identified as neoinstitutional theory—contains an obvious subtext that is premised on axial divisions of space and the implications that such divisions hold for related divisions of meaning and time.

The construct of the organizational field may offer the most obvious illustration of how neoinstitutional concepts are built on implicit assumptions of space. The original definition of an organizational field is, "those organizations that, in the aggregate, constitute a recognized area of institutional life: key suppliers, resource and product consumers, regulatory agencies, and other organizations that produce similar services or products" (DiMaggio & Powell, 1983, p. 148). This definition's reliance on structural relationships and boundaries provides an obvious metaphorical resemblance to comparable understandings of regional clusters in economic geography.

The concept of an organizational field was developed to avoid the somewhat artificial clustering of organizations into groups based on single attributes of comparability—such as industry, which is commonly used in economics to identify organizations that produce similar products. The intent behind the concept of an organizational field is to identify "a community of organizations that partakes of a common meaning system and whose participants interact more frequently and fatefully with one another than with actors outside of the field" (Scott, 1994, pp. 207–208). Not only does this definition underline the powerful spatial elements of the construct, it also encourages institutional researchers to adopt the network as the logical method of analyzing organizational fields and introduces a host of related constructs that further reinforces the spatial elements of fields: centralization, density, and boundary (Kenis & Knoke, 2002).

In fact, these spatial subcomponents of fields have come to define much of the empirical elaboration of organizational fields in institutional research that has used the structural components of fields to explain organizational change. Because institutions are seen as cognitively totalizing social structures, neoinstitutional theory has struggled to explain how organizations innovate and fields change (Suddaby, 2010). Some studies suggest that new ideas emerge only from organizations that exist on the periphery or margins of fields (Leblebici, Salancik, Copay, & King, 1991). Other research suggests that new ideas emerge from institutional entrepreneurs or organizations because their structural position allows them to span two or more fields and move ideas from one to another (Greenwood & Suddaby, 2006). Both views partition organizations into categories of "incumbents" or "challengers" based on their spatial position—either geographically or hierarchically—within the boundaries of the field (Fligstein & McAdam, 2012).

An alternative notion that also adopts an implicit spatial perspective is "world society," which researchers use to analyze the movement of worldwide models of practice that are "propagated through global cultural and associational processes" (Meyer, Boli, Thomas, & Ramirez, 1997, p. 144). Early research in neoinstitutional theory was devoted to examining the global diffusion of management practices and ideas such as total quality management, business-process reengineering and new public management. Although the spatial boundaries of the organizational field, in this view, were expanded to the global level, this stream of neoinstitutional theory bears a strong similarity to a body of literature in economic geography that focuses on global value chains. More specifically, both the world-society concept and economic geography call attention to the observed tension between localism and globalism in the consumption of products, services, and, above all, the diffusion of ideas (Sahlin & Wedlin, 2008). Institutional accounts are thus increasingly used to analyze and understand the effects of globalization (Djelic & Sahlin-Andersson, 2006; Drori, Meyer, & Hwang, 2006; Guillén, 2001). Perhaps unsurprisingly, this literature's analytical references to the "routes" along which institutionalized ideas "travel" (Czarniawski-Jorges & Sevon, 1996) incorporates the metaphorical language of geography.

Organizational institutional theory has an aspect in common with economic geography: the understanding that the axial division of physical space is intimately associated with a corresponding division of ideational space. This correspondence is made clearest in Scott's definition of organizational fields as organizations that not only interact "frequently and fatefully" (Scott, 1994, pp. 207–208) in the same physical or communicative space but also thereby "partake of a common meaning system" (Scott, 1994, p. 207). This extension of the notion of organizational fields to ideational fields seems like a rather close approximation of Bourdieu's (1993) original notion of social fields as *champs*, or spaces, of semantic contestation. Institutional researchers have made some progress in developing the relationship between meaning and space, particularly in studies on understanding how the ability of an entity to fit into a semantic category can improve that entity's perceived legitimacy (Hsu, Hannan, & Koçak, 2009; Zuckerman, 1999). Considerably more progress on this work, however, has come from methodological insights into topic-modeling in which network-related statistical techniques, commonly used to measure interaction in space, are applied to interaction in meaning systems (DiMaggio, Nag, & Blei, 2013; Mohr & Bogdanov, 2013). Mohr and Guerra-Pearson's (2010) analysis of how organizational forms come to be differentially distributed across institutionalized spaces of meaning exemplifies this type of research.

There is a nascent line of research in neoinstitutional theory, which extends this line of reasoning to suggest that the axial division of institutional space not only impacts meaning but also alters the understanding of time and history (Suddaby, Foster, & Mills, 2013). There are two components to this emerging strand of neoinstitutionalism. First, there is the observation that institutions that emerge across different spatial contexts differ because they reflect distinct historical and cultural influences. At least one source of this insight was Westney (1987), who described how key western institutions—the police, the post office, and newspapers—were transformed after their adoption by the Japanese during the Meiji period. Dobbin (1994) then demonstrated how the emergence of government policies regulating railroads in the United States, France, and Britain varies as a result of distinctly different historically embedded assumptions of how economic activity should be organized.

Several studies have expanded on Dobbin's (1994) seminal insight that institutions vary in their expression over different geographic contexts. Meyer and Höllerer (2010), for example, investigate how the concept of shareholder value shifted as it moved from the United States and the United Kingdom to Austria. They observed that organizational practices and concepts change when they pass through culturally determined filters that are the product of a local history. The central concept that institutional pressures vary across different spatial contexts is perhaps best captured by the construct of "institutional distance" first articulated by Kostova (1999) and Kostova and Zaheer (1999). The term refers to the degree of similarity or difference between the regulatory, cognitive, and normative institutions of different geographic contexts, such as nation-states or the different units of a multinational corporation (Kostova, Roth, & Dacin, 2008).

Second, there is a growing awareness that perceptions of the possibility of change are determined by institutionalized assumptions about the objectivity or rigidity of time and associated assumptions about human agency, or the capacity to bring about change (Suddaby & Foster, 2017). Typically, such institutionalized assumptions about time are localized. Gouldner's (1954) now classic study of labor unrest in a gypsum plant, for example, observed that the strike he researched originated in bureaucratized ideas about time and efficiency that northern industrialized owners had introduced into a southern rural factory. The northern industrialists did not share the workers' assumptions of shutdowns to accommodate the hunting and planting seasons. Orlikowski and Yates (2002) summarized this thread of research with the observation that temporal structuring or assumptions about the relative objectivity or subjectivity of time and its role in standardizing organizational practices are shaped by ongoing actions of members of a spatially localized community. In combination, these assumptions reinforce economic geography's insight that institutionalized assumptions of space are invariably associated with reciprocal assumptions of time and history.

In sum, we see the threads of an emerging spatial turn in organizational institutionalism. Unfortunately, at this stage, the turn is still largely latent and is reflected mostly in implicit assumptions that belie a distinct understanding of institutions as instruments of creating, maintaining, and changing spatial boundaries (Lamont & Molnár, 2002). Indeed, the core metaphor of institutions as an "iron cage" (DiMaggio & Powell, 1983) perhaps best summarizes the implicit spatial foundations of institutions. For the spatial turn to become formalized and explicit in organizational theory, intellectual engagement with colleagues in other disciplines, particularly geography, will clearly have to intensify. This exchange will deepen the understanding of space and boundaries less as statements of physical property—as oppressive things—and more as processes or opportunities to understand the creative interaction of space, time, and meaning.

Institutions, Change, and Social Outcomes: Key Challenges

The institutional turn in geography and the incipient spatial turn in institutional theory have made the limits of disciplinary blinders visible and have helped identify a series of conceptual and methodological challenges in institutional research. These boundaries need to be overcome to improve the understanding of both the nature and processes of institutional change and the association between institutions and the creation, reproduction, and use of knowledge. Taking an explicit view from the angle of the geography of knowledge, we identify four key questions in current institutional thinking across the disciplines in social science.

First, what exactly are institutions? When Martin (2000) proclaimed the institutional turn in geography, he found no commonly accepted definition of institutions. A consensual definition is still missing today. In fact, the more institutions are claimed to be key drivers of social, organizational, and economic development, the more varied the meanings of the concept of institution have become. They range from formal rules and regulations (e.g., constitutions, laws, and directives) to different types of organizations (e.g., courts, parliaments, public authorities, and business associations) and stable patterns of interactions in recurring situations. What is critical about gathering such a variety of social phenomena under one conceptual umbrella is that each of these phenomena is affected by the others in quite complex ways (Glückler & Lenz, 2016; Helmke & Levitsky, 2004). Some studies empirically accentuate one of these concepts, others portray institutions as a complex system of rules that noncanonically encompasses all the above (Ahmadjian & Robinson, 2001; Hodgson, 2006; Rodríguez-Pose, 2013). This book presents a variety of understandings of institutions, but in every chapter the authors explicitly define theirs and thus enable the reader to learn from and compare the perspectives.

Second, what is the relation between space and institutions? This question lies at the heart of the institutional turn in geography. In order to address the overarching question of beneficial economic development, geographers have acknowledged that the "mechanisms of economic development operate unevenly across space and that those mechanisms are themselves spatially differentiated and in part geographically constituted; that is, determined by locally varying, scale-dependent social, cultural and institutional conditions" (Martin, 1999, p. 83). We contend that institutions are constituted and reproduced through repeated and ongoing social interactions and are thus confined to social context. Moreover, we argue that social context is often territorially bounded, but not necessarily so. Laws and regulations are imposed on geographical jurisdictions. Conventions and routines are created, understood, and shared in often much smaller contexts, embedded within places, neighborhoods, cities, and regions. State policies, legal regulations, and even technological standards have a certain territorial scope, as do informal habits that can be enacted only by people who know about them. Physical proximity often is a strong enabler for people to develop and sustain these practices and to sanction each other for noncompliance. Even organizations have their own rules and habits that are bound to one or more particular entities. In an effort to lessen the gap between the two fields, each of the following chapters directs particular attention to the context-specificity of institutions.

Third, how do institutions change? Theories of institutions focus on the conditions for and processes of the emergence, reproduction, and change of institutions. Unlike earlier research on reproduction and diffusion (Meyer & Rowan, 1977; Tolbert & Zucker, 1983), recent work highlights the dynamic aspects of institutions and the endogenous quality of change by focusing on the role of actors as agents of institutional change. Institutions, on the other hand, structure the expectations and actions of the actors but are themselves influenced by the actions of these agents (Greenwood & Suddaby, 2006; Heaphy, 2013; Lounsbury & Crumley, 2007). The solution to this paradox of embedded agency lies in the duality of social action (Giddens, 1984), meaning that institutions structure the expectations and actions of people and that agency simultaneously either reproduces or transforms these underlying structures of meaning. In this respect the relatively recent approaches of institutional entrepreneurship (Maguire, Hardy, & Lawrence, 2004; Munir & Phillips, 2005) and of institutional work (Empson, Cleaver, & Allen, 2013; Lawrence, Leca, & Zilber, 2013; Smets, Morris, & Greenwood, 2012) call for a comprehensive consideration of the conscious and unconscious practices of individual and collective actors in the transformation of institutions. One important step forward in this endeavor comes from a neostructural approach to institutionalization that emphasizes the impact that relational infrastructure in social networks, such as social status and niche, have on norm alignment and institutional transformation (Lazega, 2001; Lazega, Quintane, & Casenaz, 2017). Despite great advances in the general development of institutional theory, such as the exploration of institution-reproducing mechanisms (Powell & DiMaggio, 1991), institutional hysteresis (Hargadon & Douglas, 2001), and relational turnover in social networks (Lazega, 2017), mechanisms and processes of institutional change are still little understood and call for a more process-oriented empirical approach. Several chapters of this book therefore address the mechanisms of institutional emergence, change, and persistence in relation to regulation and policies designed to influence the dynamics and effects of institutions.

Fourth, what effects do institutions have on the creation of knowledge and related social outcomes? Much institutional research is dedicated to analyzing institutional effects on innovation and, more generally, on socioeconomic development in order to generalize them into action models. Empirically, most of these studies usually rest on quantitative macroanalyses (Farole et al., 2011), whose scope is often confined to the effects of formal rules, such as property rights (Acemoğlu, Johnson, & Robinson, 2005; Galiani & Schargrodsky, 2010), the rule of law (Duquet, Pauwelyn, Wessel, & Wouters, 2014), specific mechanisms of allocation and distribution (Di Tella, Galiani, & Schargrodsky, 2007), or labor market conditions (Glaeser et al., 2004). Additionally, the research on varieties of capitalism (Hall & Soskice, 2001; Streeck & Thelen, 2005), on national and regional innovation systems (Asheim &

Gertler, 2005; Cooke, Uranga, & Extebarria, 1997; Morgan, 2004), and on produc-tion systems (Hollingsworth & Boyer, 1997) is concerned with the effects of insti-tutional conditions on economic results. Whereas this kind of research is often about formal, codifiable rules, researchers using microsocial approaches have tended to investigate the institutions of daily practices, such as trust, reputation, conventions, and social capital (Farrell & Knight, 2003; Glückler, 2005; Portes, 1998; Storper, 1997), and their effects on innovation (Glückler & Bathelt, 2017) as well as on eco-nomic and organizational outcomes. Institutions frame the conditions of social actions, thereby potentially contributing to regional path dependencies (Martin & Sunley, 2006; Schamp, 2010). One part of this book is devoted to the study of both the detrimental and beneficial effects on societal outcomes, such as entrepreneur-ship, economic development, and competitiveness.

Structure of the Book

The following twelve chapters are divided into three parts. Part I highlights some of the key challenges already mentioned in this introduction and has a rather concep-tual orientation to institutions. All chapters have an explicitly spatial perspective when focusing on institutional dynamics (Part II) and their effects on social out-comes (Part III). In Part II the contributors seek responses to the question of how institutions change, and they analyze the dynamics of institutions between continu-ity and change. Part III is dedicated to the question of how institutions affect social outcomes. Its chapters center on the influences that the institutional context has on institutions and, vice versa, inquire into the effect of institutions on other phenom-ena, such as innovation, productivity, and development.

Challenges in Institutional Research

The authors in Part I consider different viewpoints on institutions and key chal-lenges that they identify for institutional research. The three chapters range from a general critique of the dominant schools of institutional theory and the conceptual challenges they face to organizational institutionalism and its problems of concep-tualizing institutions in organizational fields, and finally to the critical engagement with institutions through the economics of convention. All these conceptual takes on institutional theory suggest that institutions need to be understood in social prac-tice and within specific sociogeographical contexts.

In chap. 2, Henry Farrell discusses the major advances and shared challenges of institutional theories in rational-choice, historical, and sociological institutional-isms. He sharply analyzes some of the key theoretical problems, such as compre-hensively explaining institutional change, modeling gradual transitions, distinguishing institutions from other kinds of behavior, and, most important, demonstrating their causal force on social outcomes. He then searches for an endogenous theory of institutions that takes into account the mutual influence of institutions and the actions that they foster. Farrell concludes by outlining an alternative way of thinking about institutions as congregations of similar beliefs about specific rules, a line of thought that allows for institutions to be influenced by external factors as well as to change endogenously.

In chap. 3, Diego Coraiola, Roy Suddaby, and William M. Foster provide a novel approach for researching a core concept within institutional theory—the reproduction and change of organizational fields over time. They introduce the concept of mnemonic communities as institutionally shaped frameworks for remembering the past and making sense of the present. Rather than underscoring either the structural or ideational aspects of fields, the authors argue that seeing organizational fields as "imagined communities bounded by collective processes of remembering" hones analysis of how actors on various scales within the field attribute meaning to both structural relations and place.

The last contribution of this section, chap. 4, by Rainer Diaz-Bone, invites readers to view institutions through the lens of the French approach known as the economics of convention. Benchmarking it against a critique of transaction-cost theory, Diaz-Bone advocates an internalist concept of institutions that does not conceive of them only as external constraints. In the economics of convention, institutions are seen as incomplete on their own, without competent actors actively using them in specific situations by mobilizing conventions. Conventions, the cornerstone of this approach, are understood as the deeper culturally established knowledge frames that enable actors to interpret situations and to act appropriately. By highlighting agency, process, and situated interaction, this approach's understanding of conventions coincides and overlaps with the definition of institutions in large parts of organizational institutionalism.

Institutional Dynamics Between Continuity and Change

Part II of this book shifts the focus on institutional dynamics and examines how institutions evolve between the extremes of continuity and change. The individual contributions offer conceptualizations of change as well as empirical case studies in the regional context, which highlight the potential mechanisms and different types of institutional change (and maintenance). In chap. 5, Andreas Hess discusses a particular kind of change, institutional emergence. His case study reconstructs the formal and informal dimensions that gave rise to the institution of the *txoko* (the Basque term for a gastronomic society), a singular Basque invention and an example of a specific institution in space and time. Summarizing the *txoko*'s development and the homogenization and differentiation processes that explain cultural peculiarities of the Basque Country, Hess strives to contextualize the phenomenon of the gastronomic society, especially the unique position that the *txoko* occupies as an interface between the public and the private sphere.

In chap. 6, Johannes Glückler and Regina Lenz theorize the dynamics of institutional change in response to shifting regulations. By conceptually separating institutional form from its function, they suggest a model that identifies which part of an institution changes and which one does not. They use this model to analyze two types of rather subtle and hybrid institutional change: drift and morphosis. The first example, drift, illustrates how the centuries-old institution of the journeyman years of German artisans has sustained its form while adapting its function to an ever-changing regulatory context. Conversely, the second example, morphosis, shows how German construction firms and public administration have found ways to circumvent new regulations against traditional customs of local preference in public procurement by conforming their practices to official procedural rules while essentially retaining the institutionalized function of favoring local enterprises. Glückler and Lenz's analysis thus informs a new typology of modes of institutional change, offering a more nuanced understanding of institutional change in response to shifting formal regulations.

Similarly, in chap. 7, Jerker Moodysson and Lionel Sack analyze the possibilities for institutional change and innovation in contexts of rigid regulations that are generally hostile to change and in danger of institutional hysteresis. They assess how a protected label of origin cluster in Cognac, France, has given rise to both incremental and radical changes in recent decades even though regulation has remained the same. Their case study disentangles different types of change processes such as layering, drift, and conversion that are triggered by inefficiencies that had gradually emerged in a given institutional context. The region's entrepreneurs, increasingly pressured to reinterpret their possibilities, broke free from regulatory constraints by innovating different, yet related, products without following local regulation.

In chap. 8, Tiina Ritvala inquires into how the production of art may constitute an important form of institutional work. In a case study on the process of designing a work of art that reminds viewers of the common responsibility to protect the Baltic Sea, she illustrates how institutional change can be actively achieved. Ritvala identifies three mechanisms through which artistic institutional work takes place: creating emotional response by generating a sense of nostalgia over a lost common experience, educating by producing a mnemonic device that informs the audience and constructs the commons as a shared category, and empowering marginalized actors to help protect the commons. The chapter shows how artists assist in creating a shared material and symbolic space through art, a process that helps construct mutual responsibility over collective resources, in this case the world's seas and oceans.

In chap. 9, Tammar B. Zilber offers another example of the importance of agency in institutional work processes and situates her contribution at the very center of knowledge, space, and institutions. In her analysis of a high-tech industry conference, she focuses on how actors working in the Israeli high-tech industry use the concept of place to construct meaning and identity at field-configuring events. Beyond showing that organizational fields are largely discursive, nonspatial constructions around shared meaning systems, Zilber demonstrates specific mechanisms of how place is constructed in a discursive field through rhetorical strategies in multiple and sometimes contradictory or ambivalent ways.

The Impact of Institutions on Regional Learning and Development

Part III addresses the importance of the institutional context in shaping the economic outcomes of regions. The authors of the four contributions in this section probe the regional variation in development, production, and innovation, asking why some regions do better than others, how they can adapt to changes in their wider context, and how actors can actively shape their environment, either by adopting appropriate policies or by engaging in entrepreneurship. In chap. 10, Michael Storper investigates the uneven geography of innovation across time and places, an asymmetry that causes incomes and employment to diverge according to the innovativeness of places and to change from one period to the next. In an attempt to explain this variation, Storper carries out a detailed comparative study of two regions—Greater Los Angeles and the San Francisco Bay Area—from 1970 onward. He tests several mainstream explanatory approaches but finds that the different successes in the regions' innovation transitions can best be accounted for by various institutional factors, collectively called the "relational infrastructure." This infrastructure comprises cross-network connections that aid learning about new organizational practices, informal and leadership networks, and organizational sites that facilitate these contacts.

By contrast, the discussion in chap. 11, deals with the case in which institutions do not lead to positive regional transitions but rather to underperforming investments stemming from political interest rather than sound socioeconomic evaluations. Andrés Rodríguez-Pose, Riccardo Crescenzi, and Marco Di Cataldo show how local institutional environments shape types of public administration and rule-making and how investment decisions can contrast with the needs of and acceptance by the population. The authors illustrate their argument with several examples of prominent "prestige" investments in transport infrastructure in some European regions and contrast those investment strategies with less "glitzy," but more necessary, infrastructure projects yielding better economic results in regions with better government quality.

In chap. 12, Harald Bathelt and Nicolas Conserva pose the question of how regional production systems can adapt their institutional context to altered conditions in order to remain successful. Empirically, they analyze regional restructuring in the Italian industrial district of Canavese and its adaptability to globalization processes over the past 35 years. Canavese has been traditionally dominated by the automotive and metallurgical industries linked to FIAT and the electronics industry associated with Olivetti. The authors argue that regional production systems that are characterized by localized learning dynamics can best adapt to globalization when hybrid institutional adjustment is taking place. In such situations fundamental institutional change aimed at triggering new economic developments in certain fields is combined with institutional persistence in others to integrate established industries actively into the restructuring process.

In the final chap. 13, Pamela S. Tolbert and Ryan Coles propose a research agenda based on the premise that entrepreneurship should be viewed as an institution. Their approach rests on the assumption that typical structures and processes involved in founding new businesses reflect common social understandings that members of a group have about both the value of a given enterprise and the ways in which it should be run. The local manifestations of these behavioral patterns and social understandings often vary across regions and over time. This fluctuation explains why studying entrepreneurship as an institution entails systematically delving into the sources of such geographic and temporal variability as well as its consequences. Tolbert and Coles discuss two key dimensions of such institutional variation—modes of entry and modes of governance—arguing that such research can provide an important basis for integrating the study of institutions in the growing body of scientific literature on entrepreneurship and can yield important theoretical and policy-oriented insights.

Conclusion

This book affords an explicit look at the intersection of geography, knowledge, and institutions. It bridges disciplinary boundaries within the social sciences to explore the spatial contextuality and temporal dynamics of institutions as well as their effects on knowledge creation and regional development. The chapters cover a range of current debates and empirically illustrate the great diversity of institutions, ranging from formal regulations to regionally specific patterns of stable practices, such as corruption, the function of art, and the historical institutions of traveling journeymen and the Basque gastronomic society. Some of the chapters stress the positive effects that institutions have on the renewal of traditional industries and clusters but also examine their adverse effects on infrastructure development and environmental protection. Other chapters show how regulation and policies try to influence and sometimes prohibit established institutions and reveal the reasons and possibilities for the failure of such influences. With theoretical discussions and empirical case studies, each chapter offers a geographical perspective to shed light on the contextuality of institutions and to pave the way for new research ideas exploring the part that social institutions have in shaping contexts and creating new knowledge.

References

Acemoğlu, D., Johnson, S., & Robinson, J. A. (2005). Institutions as a fundamental cause of long-run growth. In P. Aghion & S. N. Durlauf (Eds.), *Handbook of economic growth: Vol. 1, Part A* (pp. 385–472). Handbooks in Economics: Vol. 22. Amsterdam: Elsevier.
Ahmadjian, C. L., & Robinson, P. (2001). Safety in numbers: Downsizing and the deinstitutionalization of permanent employment in Japan. *Administrative Science Quarterly, 46,* 622–654. doi:https://doi.org/10.2307/3094826

Amin, A. (1999). An institutionalist perspective on regional economic development. *International Journal of Urban and Regional Research, 23*, 365–378. doi:https://doi.org/10.1111/1468-2427.00201

Amin, A. (2001). Moving on: Institutionalism in economic geography. *Environment and Planning A, 33*, 1237–1241. doi:https://doi.org/10.1068/a34108

Amin, A., & Thrift, N. (1995). Institutional issues for the European regions: From markets and plans to socioeconomics and powers of association. *Economy and Society, 24*, 41–66. doi:https://doi.org/10.1080/03085149500000002

Asheim, B. T., & Gertler, M. S. (2005). The geography of innovation: Regional innovation systems. In J. Fagerberg, D. C. Mowery, & R. R. Nelson (Eds.), *The Oxford handbook of innovation* (pp. 291–317). Oxford, UK: Oxford University Press. doi: https://doi.org/10.1093/oxfordhb/9780199286805.003.0011

Asheim, B. T., Lawton Smith, H., & Oughton, C. (2011). Regional innovation systems: Theory, empirics and policy. *Regional Studies, 45*, 875–891. doi:https://doi.org/10.1080/00343404.2011.596701

Barnes, T. J. (2001). Retheorizing economic geography: From the quantitative revolution to the "cultural turn". *Annals of the Association of American Geographers, 91*, 546–565. doi:https://doi.org/10.1111/0004-5608.00258

Bathelt, H., & Glückler, J. (2003). Toward a relational economic geography. *Journal of Economic Geography, 3*, 117–144. doi:https://doi.org/10.1093/jeg/3.2.117

Bathelt, H., & Glückler, J. (2014). Institutional change in economic geography. *Progress in Human Geography, 38*, 340–363. doi:https://doi.org/10.1177/0309132513507823

Boschma, R. A. (2017). Relatedness as driver of regional diversification: A research agenda. *Regional Studies, 51*, 351–364. doi:https://doi.org/10.1080/00343404.2016.1254767

Bosker, M., & Garretsen, H. (2009). Economic development and the geography of institutions. *Journal of Economic Geography, 9*, 295–328. doi:https://doi.org/10.1093/jeg/lbn047

Bourdieu, P. (1993). *The field of cultural production: Essays on art and literature*. Cambridge, UK: Polity Press.

Carstensen, K., & Gundlach, E. (2006). The primacy of institutions reconsidered: Direct income effect of malaria prevalence. *The World Bank Economic Review, 20*, 309–339. Retrieved from https://elibrary.worldbank.org/doi/abs/10.1093/wber/lhl001

Coe, N. M., & Hess, M. (2013). Global production networks, labour and development. *Geoforum, 44*, 4–9. doi:https://doi.org/10.1016/j.geoforum.2012.08.003

Cooke, P., Uranga, M. G., & Extebarria, G. (1997). Regional innovation systems: Institutional and organizational dimensions. *Research Policy, 26*, 475–491. doi:https://doi.org/10.1016/S0048-7333(97)00025-5

Czarniawska, B., & Sevón, G. (Eds.). (1996). *Translating organizational change*. Berlin: Walter de Gruyter.

Dellepiane-Avellaneda, S. (2010). Review article: Good governance, institutions and economic development: Beyond the conventional wisdom. *British Journal of Political Science, 40*, 195–224. doi:https://doi.org/10.1017/S0007123409990287

Di Tella, R., Galiani, S., & Schargrodsky, E. (2007). The formation of beliefs: Evidence from the allocation of land titles to squatters. *The Quarterly Journal of Economics, 122*, 209–241. doi:https://doi.org/10.1162/qjec.122.1.209

DiMaggio, P. J., Nag, M., & Blei, D. (2013). Exploiting affinities between topic modeling and the sociological perspective on culture: Application to newspaper coverage of U.S. government arts funding. *Poetics, 41*, 570–606. doi:https://doi.org/10.1016/j.poetic.2013.08.004

DiMaggio, P. J., & Powell, W. W. (1983). The iron cage revisited: Institutional isomorphism and collective rationality in organizational fields. *American Sociological Review, 48*, 147–160. Retrieved from http://www.jstor.org/stable/2095101

Djelic, M.-L., & Sahlin-Andersson, K. (Eds.). (2006). *Transnational governance: Institutional dynamics of regulation*. Cambridge, UK: Cambridge University Press.

Dobbin, F. (1994). *Forging industrial policy: The United States, Britain, and France in the railway age*. Cambridge, UK: Cambridge University Press.

Drori, G. S., Meyer, J. W., & Hwang, H. (Eds.). (2006). *Globalization and organization: World society and organizational change.* Oxford, UK: Oxford University Press.

Duquet, S., Pauwelyn, J., Wessel, R. A., & Wouters, J. (2014). Upholding the rule of law in informal international lawmaking processes. *Hague Journal on the Rule of Law, 6,* 75–95. doi:https://doi.org/10.1017/S187640451400102X

Empson, L., Cleaver, I., & Allen, J. (2013). Managing partners and management professionals: Institutional work dyads in professional partnerships. *Journal of Management Studies, 50,* 808–844. doi:https://doi.org/10.1111/joms.12025

Farole, T., Rodríguez-Pose, A., & Storper, M. (2011). Human geography and the institutions that underlie economic growth. *Progress in Human Geography, 35,* 58–80. doi:https://doi.org/10.1177/0309132510372005

Farrell, H., & Knight, J. (2003). Trust, institutions, and institutional change: Industrial districts and the social capital hypothesis. *Politics & Society, 31,* 537–566. doi:https://doi.org/10.1177/0032329203256954

Fligstein, N., & McAdam, D. (2012). *A theory of fields.* Oxford, UK: Oxford University Press.

Galiani, S., & Schargrodsky, E. (2010). Property rights for the poor: Effects of land titling. *Journal of Public Economics,* 94, 700–729. doi:https://doi.org/10.1016/j.jpubeco.2010.06.002

Gertler, M. S. (2010). Rules of the game: The place of institutions in regional economic change. *Regional Studies, 44,* 1–15. doi:https://doi.org/10.1080/00343400903389979

Giddens, A. (1984). *The constitution of society: Outline of the theory of structuration.* Berkeley: University of California Press.

Glaeser, E. L., La Porta, R., López-de-Silanes, F., & Shleifer, A. (2004). Do institutions cause growth? *Journal of Economic Growth, 9,* 271–303. doi:https://doi.org/10.1023/B:JOEG.0000038933.16398.ed

Glückler, J. (2005). Making embeddedness work: Social practice institutions in foreign consulting markets. *Environment and Planning A, 37,* 1727–1750. doi:https://doi.org/10.1068/a3727

Glückler, J., & Bathelt, H. (2017). Institutional context and innovation. In H. Bathelt, P. Cohendet, S. Henn, & L. Simon (Eds.), *The Elgar companion to innovation and knowledge creation: A multi-disciplinary approach* (pp. 121–137). Cheltenham: Edward Elgar.

Glückler, J., Lazega, E., & Hammer, I. (Eds.). (2017). *Knowledge and networks.* Knowledge and Space: Vol. 11. Cham: Springer.

Glückler, J., & Lenz, R. (2016). How institutions moderate the effectiveness of regional policy: A framework and research agenda. *Investigaciones Regionales—Journal of Regional Research, 36,* 255–277. Retrieved from https://www.researchgate.net/publication/311652886

Gouldner, A. W. (1954). *Wildcat strike: A study in worker-management relationships.* New York: Harper and Row.

Greenwood, R., & Suddaby, R. (2006). Institutional entrepreneurship in mature fields: The big five accounting firms. *Academy of Management Journal, 49,* 27–48. doi:https://doi.org/10.5465/amj.2006.20785498

Guillén, M. F. (2001). Is globalization civilizing, destructive or feeble? A critique of five key debates in the social science literature. *Annual Review of Sociology, 27,* 235–260. doi:https://doi.org/10.1146/annurev.soc.27.1.235

Hall, P. A., & Soskice, D. W. (Eds.). (2001). *Varieties of capitalism: The institutional foundations of comparative advantage.* Oxford, UK: Oxford University Press.

Hargadon, A. B., & Douglas, J. Y. (2001). When innovations meet institutions: Edison and the design of electric light. *Administrative Science Quarterly, 46,* 476–501. doi:https://doi.org/10.2307/3094872

Heaphy, E. D. (2013). Repairing breaches with rules: Maintaining institutions in the face of everyday disruptions. *Organization Science, 24,* 1291–1315. doi:https://doi.org/10.1287/orsc.1120.0798

Helmke, G., & Levitsky, S. (2004). Informal institutions and comparative politics: A research agenda. *Perspectives on Politics, 2,* 725–740. doi:https://doi.org/10.1017/S1537592704040472

Hodgson, G. M. (2006). What are institutions? *Journal of Economic Issues, 40*, 1–25. doi:https://doi.org/10.1080/00213624.2006.11506879

Hollingsworth, J. R., & Boyer, R. (Eds.). (1997). *Contemporary capitalism: The embeddedness of institutions.* Cambridge, UK: Cambridge University Press.

Hsu, G., Hannan, M. T., & Koçak, Ö. (2009). Multiple category memberships in markets: An integrative theory and two empirical tests. *American Sociological Review, 74*, 150–169. doi:https://doi.org/10.1177/000312240907400108

Jessop, B. (2001). Institutional re(turns) and the strategic-relational approach. *Environment and Planning A, 33*, 1213–1235. doi:https://doi.org/10.1068/a32183

Kenis, P., & Knoke, D. (2002). How organizational field networks shape interorganizational tie-formation rates. *Academy of Management Review, 27*, 275–293. doi:https://doi.org/10.5465/AMR.2002.6588029

Kostova, T. (1999). Transnational transfer of strategic organizational practices: A contextual perspective. *Academy of Management Review, 24*, 308–324. doi:https://doi.org/10.2307/259084

Kostova, T., Roth, K., & Dacin, M. T. (2008). Institutional theory in the study of multinational corporations: A critique of new directions. *Academy of Management Review, 33*, 994–1006. doi:https://doi.org/10.5465/AMR.2008.34422026

Kostova, T., & Zaheer, S. (1999). Organizational legitimacy under conditions of complexity: The case of the multinational enterprise. *Academy of Management Review, 24*, 64–81. doi:https://doi.org/10.2307/259037

Lamont, M., & Molnár, V. (2002). The study of boundaries in the social sciences. *Annual Review of Sociology, 28*, 167–195. doi:https://doi.org/10.1146/annurev.soc.28.110601.141107

Lawrence, T. B., Leca, B., & Zilber, T. B. (2013). Institutional work: Current research, new directions and overlooked issues. *Organization Studies, 34*, 1023–1033. doi:https://doi.org/10.1177/0170840613495305

Lazega, E. (2001). *The collegial phenomen: The social mechanisms of cooperation among peers in a corporate law partnership.* Oxford, UK: Oxford University Press.

Lazega, E. (2017). Organized mobility and relational turnover as context for social mechanisms: A dynamic invariant at the heart of stability from movement. In J. Glückler, E. Lazega, & I. Hammer (Eds.), *Knowledge and networks* (pp. 119–142). Knowledge and Space: Vol. 11. Cham: Springer.

Lazega, E., Quintane, E., & Casenaz, S. (2017). Collegial oligarchy and networks of normative alignments in transnational institution building. *Social Networks, 48*(Suppl. C), 10–22. doi:https://doi.org/10.1016/j.socnet.2016.08.002

Leblebici, H., Salancik, G. R., Copay, A., & King, T. (1991). Institutional change and the transformation of the U.S. radio broadcasting industry. *Administrative Science Quarterly, 36*, 333–363. doi:https://doi.org/10.2307/2393200

Lounsbury, M., & Crumley, E. T. (2007). New practice creation: An institutional perspective on innovation. *Organization Studies, 28*, 993–1012. doi:https://doi.org/10.1177/0170840607078111

MacLeod, G. (2001). Beyond soft institutionalism: Accumulation, regulation, and their geographical fixes. *Environment and Planning A, 33*, 1145–1167. doi:https://doi.org/10.1068/a32194

Maguire, S., Hardy, C., & Lawrence, T. B. (2004). Instituional entrepreneurship in emerging fields: HIV/AIDS treatment advocacy in Canada. *Academy of Management Journal, 47*, 657–679. doi:https://doi.org/10.2307/20159610

Martin, R. (1999). The new 'geographical turn' in economics: Some critical reflections. *Cambridge Journal of Economics, 23*, 65–91. doi:https://doi.org/10.1093/cje/23.1.65

Martin, R. (2000). Institutional approaches in economic geography. In E. Sheppard & T. J. Barnes (Eds.), *A companion to economic geography* (pp. 77–94). Malden: Blackwell.

Martin, R., & Sunley, P. (2006). Path dependence and regional economic evolution. *Journal of Economic Geography, 6*, 395–437. doi:https://doi.org/10.1093/jeg/lbl012

Maskell, P., & Malmberg, A. (1999). Localised learning and industrial competitiveness. *Cambridge Journal of Economics, 23*, 167–185. doi:https://doi.org/10.1093/cje/23.2.167

Meusburger, P., Funke, J., & Wunder, E. (Eds.). (2009). *Milieus of creativity*. Knowledge and Space: Vol. 2. Dordrecht: Springer.

Meusburger, P., Gregory, D., & Suarsana, L. (Eds.). (2015). *Geographies of knowledge and power*. Knowledge and Space: Vol. 7. Dordrecht: Springer.

Meusburger, P., Livingston, D., & Jöns, H. (Eds.). (2010). *Geographies of science*. Knowledge and Space: Vol. 3. Dordrecht: Springer.

Meusburger, P., Werlen, B., & Suarsana, L. (Eds.). (2017). *Knowledge and action*. Knowledge and Space: Vol. 9. Cham: Springer.

Meyer, J. W., Boli, J., Thomas, G. M., & Ramirez, F. O. (1997). World society and the nation-state. *American Journal of Sociology, 103*, 144–181. doi:https://doi.org/10.1086/231174

Meyer, J. W., & Rowan, B. (1977). Institutionalized organizations: Formal structure as myth and ceremony. *American Journal of Sociology, 83*, 340–363. doi:https://doi.org/10.1086/226550

Meyer, R. E., & Höllerer, M. A. (2010). Meaning structures in a contested issue field: A topographic map of shareholder value in Austria. *Academy of Management Journal, 53*, 1241–1262. doi:https://doi.org/10.5465/AMJ.2010.57317829

Mohr, J. W., & Bogdanov, P. (2013). Introduction—Topic models: What they are and why they matter. *Poetics, 41*, 545–569. doi:https://doi.org/10.1016/j.poetic.2013.10.001

Mohr, J. W., & Guerra-Pearson, F. (2010). The duality of niche and form: The differentiation of institutional space in New York City, 1888–1917. In G. Hsu, G. Negro, & Ö. Koçak (Eds.), *Categories in markets: Origins and evolution* (pp. 321–368). Research in the Sociology of Organizations: Vol. 31. Bingley: Emerald.

Morgan, K. (2004). The exaggerated death of geography: Learning, proximity and territorial innovation systems. *Journal of Economic Geography, 4*, 3–21. doi:/10.1093/jeg/4.1.3

Munir, K. A., & Phillips, N. (2005). The birth of the 'Kodak moment': Institutional entrepreneurship and the adoption of new technologies. *Organization Studies, 26*, 1665–1687. doi:https://doi.org/10.1177/0170840605056395

North, D. C. (1990). *Institutions, institutional change and economic performance*. Cambridge, UK: Cambridge University Press.

Orlikowski, W. J., & Yates, J. (2002). It's about time: Temporal structuring in organizations. *Organization Science, 13*, 684–700. doi:https://doi.org/10.1287/orsc.13.6.684.501

Pike, A., Marlow, D., McCarthy, A., O'Brien, P., & Tomaney, J. (2015). Local institutions and local economic development: The Local Enterprise Partnerships in England, 2010–. *Cambridge Journal of Regions, Economy and Society, 8*, 185–204. doi:https://doi.org/10.1093/cjres/rsu030

Portes, A. (1998). Social capital: Its origins and applications in modern sociology. *Annual Review of Sociology, 24*, 1–24. doi:https://doi.org/10.1146/annurev.soc.24.1.1

Powell, W. W., & DiMaggio, P. J. (Eds.). (1991). *The new institutionalism in organizational analysis*. Chicago: The University of Chicago Press.

Rafiqui, P. S. (2009). Evolving economic landscapes: Why new institutional economics matters for economic geography. *Journal of Economic Geography, 9*, 329–353. doi:https://doi.org/10.1093/jeg/lbn050

Rodríguez-Pose, A. (2013). Do institutions matter for regional development? *Regional Studies, 47*, 1034–1047. doi:https://doi.org/10.1080/00343404.2012.748978

Rodríguez-Pose, A., & Di Cataldo, M. (2015). Quality of government and innovative performance in the regions of Europe. *Journal of Economic Geography, 15*, 673–706. doi:https://doi.org/10.1093/jeg/lbu023

Rodríguez-Pose, A., & Storper, M. (2006). Better rules or stronger communities? On the social foundations of institutional change and its economic effects. *Economic Geography, 82*, 1–25. doi:https://doi.org/10.1111/j.1944-8287.2006.tb00286.x

Rodrik, D., Subramanian, A., & Trebbi, F. (2004). Institutions rule: The primacy of institutions over geography and integration in economic development. *Journal of Economic Growth, 9*, 131–165. doi:https://doi.org/10.1023/B:3AJOEG.0000031425.72248.85

Sachs, J. D. (2003). Institutions don't rule: Direct effects of geography on per capita income (NBER Working Paper No. 9490). doi:https://doi.org/10.3386/w9490

Sahlin, K., & Wedlin, L. (2008). Circulating ideas: Imitation, translation and editing. In R. Greenwood, C. Oliver, K. Sahlin, & R. Suddaby (Eds.), *The SAGE handbook of organizational institutionalism*, (pp. 218–242). London: Sage.

Schamp, E. W. (2010). On the notion of co-evolution in economic geography. In R. Boschma & R. Martin (Eds.), *The handbook of evolutionary economic geography* (pp. 432–449). Cheltenham: Edward Elgar. doi:https://doi.org/10.4337/9781849806497.00030

Scott, W. R. (1994). Conceptualizing organizational fields: Linking organizations and societal systems. In H.-U. Derlien, U. Gerhardt, & F. W. Scharpf (Eds.), *Systemrationalität und Partialinteresse: Festschrift für Renate Mayntz* (pp. 203–221). Baden-Baden: Nomos.

Smets, M., Morris, T., & Greenwood, R. (2012). From practice to field: A multilevel model of practice-driven institutional change. *Academy of Management Journal, 55*, 877–904. doi:https://doi.org/10.5465/amj.2010.0013

Storper, M. (1997). *The regional world: Territorial development in a global economy*. New York: Guilford.

Streeck, W., & Thelen, K. A. (Eds.). (2005). *Beyond continuity: Institutional change in advanced political economies*. Oxford, UK: Oxford University Press.

Suddaby, R. (2010). Challenges for institutional theory. *Journal of Management Inquiry, 19*, 14–20. doi:https://doi.org/10.1177/1056492609347564

Suddaby, R., & Foster, W. M. (2017). History and organizational change. *Journal of Management, 43*, 19–38. doi:https://doi.org/10.1177/0149206316675031

Suddaby, R., Foster, W. M., & Mills, A. J. (2013). Historical institutionalism. In M. Bucheli & D. Wadhwani (Eds.), *Organizations in time: History, theory, methods* (pp. 100–123). Oxford, UK: Oxford University Press.

Tolbert, P. S., & Zucker, L. G. (1983). Institutional sources of change in the formal structure of organizations: The diffusion of civil service reform, 1880–1935. *Administrative Science Quarterly, 28*, 22–39. doi:https://doi.org/10.2307/2392383

Tomaney, J. (2014). Region and place I: Institutions. *Progress in Human Geography, 38*, 131–140. doi:https://doi.org/10.1177/0309132513493385

Wernerfelt, B. (1984). A resource-based view of the firm. *Strategic Management Journal, 5*, 171–180. doi:https://doi.org/10.1002/smj.4250050207

Westney, D. E. (1987). *Imitation and innovation: The transfer of western organizational patterns to Meiji Japan*. Cambridge, MA: Harvard University Press.

Zuckerman, E. W. (1999). The categorical imperative: Securities analysts and the illegitimacy discount. *American Journal of Sociology, 104*, 1398–1438. doi:https://doi.org/10.1086/210178

Part I
Challenges in Institutional Research

Chapter 2
The Shared Challenges of Institutional Theories: Rational Choice, Historical Institutionalism, and Sociological Institutionalism

Henry Farrell

The last two decades have seen many calls for an integration of scholarship on spatial patterns of development and scholarship on institutions. Initially, much of the literature on spatial development was defined deliberately in contradistinction to the kinds of institutionalism seen in economics and political science, while sharing significant orientations with sociology. Specifically, it rejected the overt individualism of much institutionalism in political science and nearly all institutionalism in economics. Ash Amin (1999) argued that his approach was institutionalist precisely because it was not based on the individualist assumptions of homo economicus, or economic man. While Amin had sharp differences with other scholars interested in localized economies, they all agreed that the kinds of local *thickness* that fostered economic success were inimical to the more individualist orientations that rationalist political scientists and economists saw as the basis of institutional compliance and change (Becattini, 1990; Piore & Sabel, 1984).

These theoretical battles are giving way to a more practical interest in common interchange, focusing on how institutions, however conceived, shape outcomes. Thus, for example, economic historians have claimed that countries' long term trajectories of economic growth are a product of their specific institutional endowments (North, 1990; North, Wallis, & Weingast, 2009). Political scientists have turned to path dependence to explain why welfare states have endured despite substantial changes in party politics (Pierson, 2000). Sociologists have explained long term patterns of political development as a product of path dependence (Mahoney, 2000), while social choice theorists first turned towards institutionalism in order to deal with *chaos theorems,* which predicted irresolvable instability as a likely product of even moderately complex strategic situations (McKelvey, 1976, 1979; Schofield, 1978; Shepsle, 1979). Geographers are examining how institutions mediate between regional policies and regional outcomes (Glückler & Lenz, 2016).

H. Farrell (✉)
Department of Political Science, The George Washington University, Washington, DC, USA
e-mail: farrellh@gwu.edu

J. Glückler et al. (eds.), *Knowledge and Institutions*, Knowledge and Space 13,
https://doi.org/10.1007/978-3-319-75328-7_2

However, the institutional turn has come at a cost. On the one hand, social scientists need a theory of how institutions can change, because they self-evidently do change, while on the other, they need a theory of how institutions can have material consequences for human behavior. This obliges them to steer a dangerous course between two obstacles. They need both to have a theory of institutional change and a theory of institutional effects. The former requires them to identify the external factors that lead institutions to change over time. The latter requires them to identify the causal effects that institutions have for other factors.

The problem, as Przeworski (2004) cogently described it, is that if you have a theory which does both at once, why not cut out the middle man? In other words, if Factor X leads to institutional change, which then leads to Outcome Y, why not get rid of the intermediating factor, *institutional change*, because it appears not to be doing any additional work. If institutions are mere transmission belts for other factors, they are not causally interesting. If they are more than transmission belts, one needs to say why and how. In other words, one needs an endogenous theory of institutions, something that does not properly yet exist.

The difficulties of meeting this objection helps explain the volatility of argument around institutional theory. Theories of institutional consequences, which assume that institutions are stabilizing forces that structure human behavior, beg the question of why institutions should themselves be stable, leading theorists to search for theories of what causes institutions, and hence institutional change. These theories, however, raise the question of why institutions are important if they are the mere condensate of some underlying structural force or forces, obliging a return to a proper account of how institutions have visible consequences, so the pendulum of argument swings back.

This raises salient problems for economic geographers who wish to explain, for example, economic growth or innovation. For sure, there are theories of how institutions may have effects for human behavior, and hence shape growth or innovation. Yet these theories are problematic, insofar as they often do not illuminate the underlying factors explaining why one gets one set of institutions (say—growth and/or innovation promoting) and not another. Furthermore, theories that do look to do this—by explaining why one country, or region, or locality has one set of institutions, and not another—are liable to collapse institutions into the underlying forces that are intended to explain them. This means that institutionalists need to think more carefully about what institutions actually are, and how they might have some independence both from the forces that shape them and the behaviors that they shape.

In the remainder of this contribution, I look to contribute to existing efforts to reconcile the study of knowledge in space and the study of knowledge in institutions, focusing on the latter rather than the former. I begin with a brief survey of the rationale among scholars studying knowledge in space for embracing social science accounts of institutions. I then proceed to briefly outline the three major approaches to institutions in the social sciences—rational choice institutionalism, historical institutionalism, and sociological institutionalism—outlining briefly the development of each approach, and how each has faced these enduring problems, despite their distinct origins and trajectories of development. I then, in conclusion, briefly sketch out an alternative approach, building on joint work with Danielle Allen and Cosma Shalizi, which starts to provide an alternative account of institutional change that arguably helps reframe the problem in some useful ways.

Economic Geography and Institutional Change

Prominent scholars studying spatial development have recently called for better integration of insights from social science institutionalism into their accounts. For example, Farole, Rodriguez-Pose, and Storper (2011) argued that both economic geographers (despite the centrifugal tendencies of the field) and social science institutionalists are interested in the underlying determinants of growth. Bathelt and Glückler (2014; Glückler & Bathelt, 2017) suggest that institutional theory can help economic geographers better understand the underlying dynamics of innovation. Their arguments built on earlier scholarship (e.g., Amin & Thrift, 1995), which sought specifically to understand the contribution of institutions to geographically specific economies.

As these scholars stress, the dialogue should be two-way. The study of spatial phenomena has much to offer to institutionalist theory as well as vice versa. Specifically, attention to the interaction between different scales of economic activity, at the local, regional, national, and international level, could usefully help inform social science debates about institutionalism, which often rest on indefensible and convenient assumptions, such as *methodological nationalism* (Callaghan, 2010; Farrell & Newman, 2014), to wave away such interactions. However, in this chapter, I focus on just one direction of influence—how standard approaches to institutions can inform the study of spatial development and what is currently missing from these approaches.

Social science institutionalism may offer a more systematic account of key topics of interest to economic geographers. Thus, for example, Farole et al. (2011) pointed to the burgeoning literature on the sources of economic growth. They argued that institutionalism offers multiple benefits that economic geographers ought to take advantage of.

First, it potentially provides more theoretic rigor. Specifically, it provides the building blocks for more precise models, which could not only provide a better understanding of how institutions work in practice, but also help scholars move beyond thick description toward a more analytically precise language that would better articulate the relationship between abstract models and complex facts. Second, as a result, institutionalism contains the seeds of better comparisons. If researchers have better defined accounts of institutions, and of the precise ways in which they affect, for example, economic development, they will be able to build better accounts of how (apparently) different institutions may lead to similar outcomes in some instances, while (apparently) similar institutions lead to different outcomes in other instances.

Bathelt and Glückler (2014) were more concerned with innovation than economic growth as such, but they reached similar conclusions. They cautioned that the social science literature on institutionalism is itself often riven by contradictions, for example, concerning what exactly an institution is. However, they argued that institutions provide a valuable conceptual tool for understanding the constraints on economic action. Actors respond to the institutions that they are embedded in, thanks both to broad social logics and individual self-interest.

These accounts highlight how institutions may be valuable for the study of spatial development processes. However, they also plausibly need more than existing accounts of institutions are capable of giving. On the one hand, they call for increased conceptual rigor in understanding how institutions work—it is, in part, this intellectual rigor that can help economic geographers better focus their arguments and build beyond thick description. On the other, they call for attention not only to how institutions shape economic interactions, but also to how economic interactions shape institutions. Thus, in the description of Bathelt and Glückler (2014) institutions involve relational action:

> Where real interaction is informed by historical patterns of mutual expectations (path-dependence) and where, at the same time, contextual interaction contributes to the transformation of these patterns based on the principle of contingency. The interplay between experiential action and patterns of instituted expectations drives a recursive process of correlated interactions and transformative institutionalization. (p. 344)

Similarly, Farole et al., (2011) said that:

> The relationship between institutions and economic growth is an endogenous one. Institutions and economic growth co-evolve, with changes in capacity building and improvements in governance contributing to the development of economic activity and vice versa. Institutional improvement may more often be the consequence, rather than the cause, of development. (p. 16)

In other words, researchers seek a theory of institutions that is endogenous so that it captures the ways in which institutions are imbricated with the actions that they foster. Institutions are not ahistorical constants; rather, they are themselves the product of human agency, and as humans enact institutions they correspondingly transform them.

Here, however, social science institutionalism is less useful than it might first appear. Different approaches to institutions arose in different disciplines, in response to different imperatives. Yet they all struggle with the questions of how to capture endogenous relations between expectations and action, and how to link expectations to underlying causes. In each discipline, scholars tended initially to focus on explaining stability rather than change, using institutions to explain why patterns of behavior endure under circumstances where one might expect them to change. In each, a subsequent wave of scholars has reacted against institutional determinism, looking to incorporate the possibility of change, by explaining the underlying forces that shape institutions, but creating new perplexities as a consequence.

As Riker (1980) famously argued, one cannot claim that institutions stabilize social interactions, without explaining how institutions are somehow different from the interactions that they are supposed to stabilize.

> In the end, therefore, institutions are no more than rules and rules are themselves the product of social decisions. Consequently, the rules are also not in equilibrium. One can expect that losers on a series of decisions under a particular set of rules will attempt (often successfully) to change institutions and hence the kind of decisions produced under them. In that sense, rules or institutions are just more alternatives in the policy space and the status quo of one set of rules can be supplanted with another set of rules. (pp. 444–445)

Without some clear understanding of how institutions differ from the decisions that they are supposed to structure, institutional theory is liable to degenerate into a series of just-so-isms, which posit that institutions have binding force, while providing no specific rationale for why they are binding.

The obvious retort is to turn to some external circumstance—such as power relations, the attractions of efficient outcomes, or the binding power of social ritual—to explain why institutions are enduring and how they are capable of exerting force on people's decisions. People may comply with institutions because they fear the wrath of more powerful actors, or because they recognize the benefits from coordinating on a salient solution, or because they are caught up by the demands of ritual behavior. Such arguments also provide the basis for theories of institutional change. Institutions may change when power balances shift, or when new, more attractive solutions become available, or when skilled social actors construct new binding myths.

However, as Przeworski (2004) sharply observed, it is hard to invoke such external forces to explain institutional compliance and institutional change without suggesting that institutions are epiphenomenal, and that what is doing the actual work are the external forces rather than the institutions themselves. Przeworski pointed out that most institutionalist accounts do a very bad job at showing that institutions matter in their own right—which is to say that current accounts have difficulty in theorizing how institutions have independent causal force.

It is notable that these theoretical difficulties spring up across quite different approaches to institutions, despite their various origins and emphases. In part, this reflects very broad problems in the social sciences (such as the relationship between structure and agency). In part, it reflects problems that are specific to institutional theory, and in particular to the difficulty of distilling a clear definition of institutions from the murky interactions of beliefs, decisions, and actions and the social forces conditioning all three.

Rational Choice Institutionalism

For rational choice scholars, institutions are usually either *structures*—forces which conduct actors to select one equilibrium or another, or *equilibria*—sets of strategies from which no actor has any incentive to defect if no other actor defects. Under both definitions, institutions may usually be thought of as rules—regardless of whether these rules are considered to be exogenous regularities that structure choices or enchained patterns of equilibrium behavior in which every actor will continue to behave in specific ways provided others do the same. Current rational choice institutionalism is the culmination of two distinct lines of inquiry—one in social choice theory, the other in economics—which intersected in the early 1990s. Social choice theory, building on eighteenth-century work on voting by the Marquis de Condorcet and others, gave rise to an extensive formal literature in theoretical economics in the second half of the twentieth century. Economists such as Kenneth Arrow (2012), Duncan Black (1948), and Amartya Sen (1997) arrived at basic results about the aggregation of decisions, looking to examine the strengths and limitations of various voting schemes and other schemes for collective choice, under assumptions of rationality. This literature soon discovered various paradoxes and instabilities, which began to have important consequences for political science as well as economics.

Basic results such as Arrow's Possibility Theorem (Arrow, 2012) suggested that it was impossible to universally reconcile minimal desiderata for decision making. Others, such as Downs (1957), provided a more optimistic account. For example, under Downs's *economic theory of voting*, political outcomes were likely to converge on the preferences of the *median voter*, creating a centrist equilibrium.

However, it soon became clear that the more optimistic account depended heavily on favorable assumptions, including the assumption that voters' preferences could be expressed on a single dimension (e.g., a single left-to-right scale). Work by McKelvey (1976, 1979) and Schofield (1978), among others, demonstrated that if politics had more than two dimensions, then majority rule could not provide stability. Instead, politics could end up cycling from one alternative to another, without ever necessarily gravitating towards any central solution or set of solutions.

These chaos theorems generated immense frustration among political scientists, because they not only cast doubts on the stabilizing benefits of democracy, but also suggested a degree of radical instability that seemed at odds with empirical observations. Politics appeared to be relatively predictable—so what was the root cause of stability?

The answer—according to a prominent line of argument developed in political science—was institutions. For example, one might think of the institutional structure of the U.S. Congress—which is composed of different committees, each with a specialized jurisdiction—as simplifying politics in ways that produced stability and predictability. Congressional committees could carve out specific issue dimensions, reducing the issue space so that each issue dimension was dealt with separately, and a chaotic space of social choice across multiple dimensions was transformed into a series of iterated decisions taken within discrete jurisdictions (Shepsle, 1979). Hence, institutional arrangements such as congressional committees could avoid the chaos of multidimensional voting spaces, and instead produce so-called *structure-induced equilibrium* outcomes. As scholars began to develop the structure-induced equilibrium approach further, they began to use noncooperative game theory rather than social choice theory to model decision making, seeking to capture the essential details of even quite complex institutional arrangements as game trees, in which individual strategies potentially lead to equilibrium outcomes.

This literature hence began from a puzzle—invoking institutions to explain why people's choices remained stable even under circumstances when rational choice theory would predict that they should not. As it was developing, a second body of work in economics began to confront a very different puzzle of observed stability (North, 1990). Economists studying development believed that they had a good sense of what was necessary to produce economic growth—strong markets and free enterprise. Basic rational choice theory suggested that national economies should converge over time on the practices that led to increased economic growth, because otherwise they would be leaving dollar bills on the pavement. Yet in reality, countries continued to stick to dramatically different growth paths, rather than converging on the more efficient possibilities offered by countries with free markets. What explained this anomaly, in which national economies remained stably attached to practices that made no sense?

According to the influential work of North (1990) the answer lay in the relationship between institutions and organizations. Institutions, as sets of rules, shape the incentives in a particular society. Organizations, as collective actors, pursue their self-interest within a given set of rules, perhaps changing those rules in the process. Borrowing from Arthur's (1994) work on path dependence, North argued that national societies tended to develop along specific trajectories. Societies with institutions that have appropriate incentive structures will tend to develop along a virtuous path, in which institutions and organizations reinforce each other so as to encourage growth-promoting activities. Societies with institutions that tend to promote predatory behavior by the state or other actors may find themselves trapped on long-term, low-growth trajectories, but lack the institutions and organized social actors that might allow them to escape these constraints.

Both of these accounts struggled with the question of why institutions have binding force. Riker's (1980) initial critique of institutionalism was aimed directly at structure-induced equilibrium approaches, which, he politely suggested, were less a solution to the problem of social instability than an unconvincing deus ex machina. Since institutions were themselves the product of choices (presumably made across multiple dimensions) they should be just as subject to problems of instability as the social choices they purportedly structured. Put less politely, invoking institutions as structures—without explaining the choices through which these institutions had themselves arisen and why these choices were enduring—was sharp practice.

Yet North's (1990) arguments, too, had fuzzy microfoundations. At times, North seemed to argue that actors' microlevel choices were driven by their desire to secure benefits for themselves, regardless of whether this would help or hurt others. At other times, North seemed to suggest that actors' choices were driven by the desire to find efficient arrangements (as argued by his sometime rival in the new institutional economics, Oliver Williamson [1975, 1985]). Under the one account, institutions were binding because they produced good outcomes for particular powerful individuals. Under the other, they were binding because they produced good outcomes for everyone. The failure to stick to one or the other allowed North to shift back and forth between explanatory frameworks without ever committing himself to a fully developed set of microfoundations.

These deficiencies inspired pushback. Structure-induced equilibrium accounts gave way to disagreements over whether it was better to think about institutional equilibrium or equilibrium institutions (Shepsle, 1986). The former reflected the emphasis of the structure-induced equilibrium approach on explaining how specific institutional features might produce one or another equilibrium, depending, for example, on the order within which actors made choices and had power to set the agenda. Typically, it used models based on one-shot games, treating the institutions as part of the game tree.

Equilibrium institution approaches, instead, treated institutions as the outcomes of games rather than structures within the game. Instead of looking to one-shot games with complex structures, they typically treated social interactions as indefinitely iterated games with simple structures (Calvert, 1995). These simple games, however, could give rise to quite complex and sophisticated equilibria, in which actors continued to behave in particular and sometimes quite complex ways, subject to other actors continuing to behave in the expected fashion. Under the so-called *folk theorem* an enormously wide variety of equilibria can arise in many indefinitely iterated games with reasonable parameters. Hence, the equilibrium institutions approach did not provide an account of how institutions arose or changed, so much as an account of which institutions were possible given particular parameter values. To understand how such equilibria arose, one had to turn to selection mechanisms outside the game itself.

This approach was swiftly adapted to understand the kinds of questions that North (1990) and his colleagues grappled with. Hence, for example, Greif (1994) investigated the differences between Genoese and Maghribi traders in the mediaeval period, treating both sets of traders as engaged in an indefinitely iterated *One Sided Prisoner's Dilemma* game, and looking to the ways in which different *cultures* might give rise to different sets of expectations, and hence different self-reinforcing institutions. Milgrom, North, and Weingast (1990) used a broadly similar theoretical approach to understand medieval Champagne Fairs (see also Calvert [1995] for an extensive theoretical overview and framing).

These accounts, however, continue to have difficulty (a) in distinguishing institutions from behavior and (b) in explaining when institutions might change. In the account of Calvert (1995), for example, no very sharp distinction is drawn between strategically implicated behavior, organization, and institution; each being a more or less sophisticated example of behavior conditioned on expectations of the behavior of others. For Greif and Laitin (2004), who adopted a formally similar approach, institutions consisted of factors influencing behavior rather than the behavior itself, so that an institution was "a system of humanmade, nonphysical elements—norms, beliefs, organizations, and rules—exogenous to each individual whose behavior it influences that generates behavioral regularities" (p. 635). While this definition is encompassing, it makes it difficult to capture precisely how these very different elements interact. Such a broad definition of institutions makes it difficult to be sure what—apart from behavior—is not part of the institution under examination.

Even more pertinently, equilibrium accounts of institutions almost by definition have great difficulty in explaining change. A game-theoretic equilibrium, after all, is a situation in which no actor has any incentive to deviate from his or her strategy given the strategies of others. Greif and Laitin's (2004) game-theoretic account of institutional change is less an account of change as such, than an account of how institutions may have unintended consequences for the parameters that they depend upon, leading them to become *self-reinforcing*, or *self-undermining*, depending on whether the behaviors associated with the institution become possible under a broader or narrower range of parameters. It cannot explain within its own formal framework how one institution may change into another. Yet problems of *real* institutional change are endemic in economic development.

This poses the problem of developing equilibrium-based models that can encompass institutional change. Acemoğlu, Johnson, and Robinson (2001) were forerunners in developing methodological answers to Przeworski's (2004) problem—using an *instrumental-variables* approach to argue that institutions have indeed had independent consequences for development (albeit not to Przeworski's own satisfaction). However, for just this reason, they had difficulty in explaining what factors lead to institutional change.

For example, Acemoğlu and Robinson (2006) provided a stylized account of how the transition from authoritarian regime to democracy might take place, arguing that institutional change will be the result of bargaining processes and social conflict (Knight, 1992). However, although such modeling strategies can capture transitions between different political systems that are well defined ex ante, they are poorly suited for capturing more open-ended and gradual transitions.

This shortcoming means that these scholars have difficulties in answering the crucial question posed by North (1990), Greif (2006), and others, of how mediaeval European countries with predatory elites and drastically underperforming economies were transformed into modern societies. Though there is a rich body of work that employs comparative statics (Acemoğlu & Robinson, 2012; Greif, 2006; North et al., 2009), the dynamic aspects of this question remain more or less unexplored. Existing accounts provide histories that are notably stronger at comparing systems or stages of development than at capturing the actual mechanisms of transformation. Levi (2013) noted of Acemoğlu and Robinson:

> On page 308, they write: "We saw how inclusive economic and political institutions emerge. But why do they persist over time?" This is a good question, but it rests on a problematic statement. They have shown us that inclusive economic and political institutions emerge, but not how they do. They have described the process and provided wonderful examples in which they emphasize political coalitions, interest groups, and other forms of mobilization, but they offer little in the way of a political analysis concerning how such collective actors come into being and enhance their power. The authors simply assume the existence of collective actors or portray a process of evolution over time as a consequence of small institutional advantages granted for other purposes than significant empowerment. (p. 189)

Historical Institutionalism

Historical institutionalists have similarly contradictory understandings of institutions. For one major body of work, institutions are *structures*—vast, enduring, and solid patterns of social organization at the level of the nation state, which are relatively stable over the long run, shaping more particular forms of political and social behavior. For others, they are *processes*—rules, procedures, or policies that change over time.

Historical institutionalism began with a different intent and mission—securing some space for the macrohistorical tradition of social inquiry, which was under threat both from quantitative social science, and from micro-oriented rational choice theories. Controversies between macrohistorical sociologists and political scientists and rational choice antagonists led to nervousness among young scholars in this tradition that they were in danger of extinction, leading them to coin the term *historical institutionalism* to describe an approach that would both focus on institutions, and ground them in processes of change (Steinmo, Thelen, & Longstreth, 1992).

This presented difficulties from the beginning. Macrosociological inquiry—as practiced by Theda Skocpol (1979), Tilly & Ardant, (1975), Stein Rokkan (Flora, Kuhnle, & Urwin, 1999), and others, was grounded in the role of structure—how different combinations of structural factors led to different combinations in different societies. It too, had begun in argument with an antagonist, but quite a different one: Marxism. Macrosociological approaches looked to disagree with Marxism by showing how other factors than the class struggle generated social structure.

However, other tendencies in the social sciences led these scholars to emphasize the potential for change. Thus, in Steinmo, Thelen, and Longstreth's (1992) initial introduction, the relationship between political strategies and institutional constraints was dynamic rather than fixed—actors used the opportunities that institutions provided them, but potentially changed those institutions as a result of those actions. In contrast to rational choice scholars, who tended either to see institutions as structures producing an equilibrium, or as that equilibrium itself, historical institutionalists thought of institutions in terms of processes of change, with no necessary end point.

In short then, historical institutionalists equivocated between two notions of what *history* was. One saw it as a nightmare from which we were struggling to awaken—or more prosaically, as a vast set of structural givens, which led to fixed but potentially very different outcomes in different societies, depending on which specific conjuncture of structural factors a given society had. The other saw history as a process, which was relatively open-ended, in which institutions did not squat on possibilities as stony near-immovables, but instead changed over time as they were worked on by the artful behavior of multiple actors, with the unexpected congregations of those actions leading to new institutions that presented new opportunities and new constraints in an endless dance.

Historical institutionalists were confronted with the challenge of arriving at theories that captured the relationship between structure and process in a more exacting way. The first systematic efforts looked to build on results from economics—but not the standard economics of game theory and equilibria. Instead, Pierson (2000) and his colleagues looked to mathematical work by the Irish economist Brian Arthur (1994), to come up with an account of institutional change based on the notion of *path dependence*. Arthur used so-called *Polya urn processes* to model change over time and to argue against his colleagues who insisted that actors with free choice would inevitably converge on efficient equilibria. Instead, Arthur compared the progress of markets and institutions to one in which individuals' current choices were dependent on their past ones in a self-reinforcing way. Social systems that were initially open to a variety of possibilities tended to converge rapidly on a single path, as the product of sometimes arbitrary initial decisions or interactions that led to self-reinforcing patterns. Thus, for example, patterns of product innovation built upon previous innovations, so innovators tended to get *locked in*, with actors using the same tools and becoming stuck on the same path of development, even when they would have been far better off had they chosen a different path initially.

For historical institutionalists, as for economic geographers (Grabher, 1993), path dependence appeared to offer an account of how history mattered. Paths of institutional change were tightly constrained by initial, sometimes arbitrary choices, just as, in the Polya urn processes that path dependence theory built upon, initial distributions of balls of one or the other color could lead to enduring and self-reinforcing patterns. Path dependence led to the prediction that institutional change would be a succession of *punctuated equilibria* (Gould & Eldredge, 1977; Krasner, 1982), in which long periods of stability (periods when people remained on a given path of institutional change) were interspersed with brief and sporadic moments when change was possible, perhaps because existing institutions had collapsed, providing actors with the possibility of moving towards a different path. These accounts provided a historically grounded account of institution-induced stability, allowing scholars potentially to examine how institutions could lead to continuity in policy, even under circumstances where one might otherwise have expected change.

However, for just that reason, path-dependence accounts had difficulty in explaining institutional change, which they tended to treat as the result of exogenous factors. Some institutions seemed capable of changing radically over time through processes of incremental change. Thelen (2004), for example, studied the vocational training system in Germany and other countries, and found extraordinary transformation happening over long periods of time, in which a system designed for one set of uses and external system became fully adapted to another, and yet another. Crucially, these processes of transformation were not sudden and sporadic—they were slow and incremental. This was at odds with the predictions of path dependence (which suggested that paths will quickly stabilize after an initial period of uncertainty). More broadly, path dependence offered no obvious theory of the mechanisms of institutional reproduction or change (Thelen, 1999), and, by concentrating on *critical junctures*, where anything could happen, emphasized exogenous change to the exclusion of any proper consideration of what paths actually involved

(Streeck & Thelen, 2005). This has prompted historical institutionalists increasingly to emphasize "gradual institutional transformations that add up to major historical discontinuities" (Streeck & Thelen, 2005, p. 8).

These disagreements have led to a new focus on mechanisms of institutional reproduction and change. Here, for example, Hacker's (2004) explanation of changes in the U.S. welfare state posited four plausible strategies of reform—layering, conversion, drift, and revision—that might be adopted by opponents of the existing institutional status quo.[1] It has been particularly helpful in pointing to the ways in which institutions are continually contested in their application, and how this contestation may have long term consequences. However, as historical institutionalists have moved from considering institutions to examining how agents can change them, they have effectively excluded certain research trajectories. The emerging body of work, because it focuses on the role of agents and agent strategies in incrementally changing institutions, plausibly overstates the importance of incremental, as opposed to radical, change in shaping institutional outcomes (Schmidt, 2012).

Furthermore, these accounts tend to conflate actors' strategies—that is, the specific approaches to institutional change given their specific situation—with mechanisms of change—that is, the broad social mechanisms through which one might expect to see transition from one institution to the next. In part, this is because historical institutionalists lack a good toolset for thinking about how strategies aggregate—so, for example, the efforts of actors to undermine an institution using one strategy interact with the actions of others (perhaps using different strategies towards the same or related ends), as well as with still others who are looking to defend a given institution (plausibly also via a variety of different strategies). Game theorists have their notion of an equilibrium—a situation in which no actor has any reason to change its strategy given the strategy of others—but historical institutionalism has no cognate concept to equilibrium, or competing concept either. This makes it hard to build from a theory of actors' individual strategies as prompted by their situation to a theory of how and when institutional change will occur, and what kind of change it is likely to be.

Finally, these accounts have difficulties in explaining what it is that institutions do, and how they are separate from the presumably more evanescent actions that are shaped by institutions, such as policies. By moving from a theory of institutions as structures that lead to outcomes to a theory of institutions as outcomes of agents'

---

[1] Streeck and Thelen (2005) describe five "modes of gradual but nonetheless transformative change" (p. 19)—layering, displacement, drift, conversion, and exhaustion. Most recently, Hacker, Thelen, and Pierson (2013) emphasize how drift and conversion can allow well situated actors to change policy without public scrutiny, while Mahoney and Thelen (2010) look to how different kinds of *change agents* can deploy strategies to reshape institutions. Hall and Thelen (2009) examine how institutions are continually contested by the agents applying them, with important consequences for institutional change. This new direction has surely allowed scholars to identify an important universe of new cases, which would have been invisible to researchers who assumed that large changes in institutional outcomes must be the consequences of abrupt and substantial disruptions.

strategies, the dominant approach to historical institutionalism risks failing to examine why it is that institutions are indeed consequential for political outcomes. To be clear—this is not a particular fault of historical institutionalism. Instead, it is a generic problem faced by all social science institutionalisms.

Sociological Institutionalism

Sociological institutionalism starts from the premise that institutions are organizing myths. This allows the approach to distinguish neatly between institutions and actual behavior, since the ways in which people act day to day are very often distinct from the myths through which our behaviors are legitimated. Equally, however, sociological institutionalism is the approach to institutionalism that has had the most difficulty in accommodating institutional change, in large part because of its origins in the work of Weber and Durkheim. Sociological institutionalists have typically been more interested in explaining continuity than change, and when they do address change they have typically seen it as involving propagation via isomorphism rather than transformation.

Sociological institutionalism is an offshoot of the classical sociology of the late nineteenth and early twentieth centuries. Like the great sociologists of that period—Durkheim, Simmel, Weber, its initial core focus was to explain modernity, and how it was that modern social practices reproduced themselves and spread across the world.

One key line of inquiry extends Weber's famous image of the *Iron Cage* of rationalization (Gerth & Mills, 2009). Weber depicted a world that was becoming increasingly rationalized, deflating the pneuma of prophecy, silencing the warring voices of different gods, and replacing them with a single set of imperatives based around bureaucratic and organizational rationality. Weber predicted that the result would be a more homogenous world, a prediction espoused by DiMaggio and Powell (1983) in a famous article in which they claimed that the world was continuing to become more homogenous, but not because of the mechanisms that Weber predicted. Instead, DiMaggio and Powell argued that rationalization was today being driven by *isomorphism*—the imperative for organizations to copy each other, converging on a similar set of procedures and approaches. Sometimes this isomorphism was coerced by more powerful actors, sometimes resulting merely from actors looking to copy others in an uncertain environment, and sometimes from normative pressures towards conformity.

These pressures led to worldwide convergence on an apparently similar set of institutional practices, as identified in the work of Meyer and his colleagues (Meyer, Boli, Thomas, & Ramirez, 1997), who built on Durkheim as much as Weber. Meyer and his collaborators sought to explain the lack of institutional variation across countries, as they opted to institute similar rules and organizations, despite their widely varying circumstances, adopting parliaments, ministries of education, and a host of other institutional elements. Meyer and Rowan (1977) noted that this homogeneity coexisted with a wide variety of different behaviors, which were not caused or predicted by formal institutions. Instead, there was often an effective decoupling between the institutions that powerful actors within given states adopted, and the actual practices through which everyday life was organized.

In Meyer and Rowan's (1977) description, institutions served less as structural elements than as organizing myths. While DiMaggio and Powell (1983) saw institutional isomorphism as being in part driven by institutional efficiencies (rationalized institutions sometimes worked better, leading to their adoption in competitive circumstances, Meyer and Rowan stressed the extent to which institutions often would lead to inefficiencies if they were taken seriously. Thus, institutions became ceremonies to be performed as much as structures that shaped action.

This account went together with a considerable skepticism about the notion of the *actor* (Jepperson, 2002). Actors were constructed within the broader frameworks given by institutions and culture. The individual was not a pregiven, outside society; instead, she or he largely enacted the scripts that society gave her. So too, organizations and even states, which existed within what Meyer and his coauthors described as a common *world polity* (Meyer et al. 1997).

Some scholars within this account looked to establish the processes through which institutions came into being. Thus, for example, Dobbin (1994) looked to different political processes surrounding the state to explain why France, the United Kingdom, and the United States had such different understandings of railway markets in the nineteenth century. However, the processes of institutional change were in the background, briefly adverted to; what was in the foreground were the ways in which institutions made certain ways of thinking and enacting policy *natural*, with the effect that it was extraordinarily difficult to escape one's national style of policy making. This literature in general tends to treat institutions as cultural—that is, as being important not so much because they coerce or provide information, as because they shape people's understandings of themselves, of others, and of the appropriate relations between them.

In Clemens and Cook's (1999) description, this led to a strong (and even relentless) focus on institutions as *enduring constraint*, to the extent that the *capacity* of these "institutions to constrain political action and policy variation appear[ed] to marginalize the processes of conflict and innovation that are central to politics" (p. 442). Fligstein and McAdam (2012) noted that:

> [sociological] institutional theory is really a theory of how conformity occurs in already existing fields. It lacks an underlying theory of how fields emerge or are transformed . . . Actors follow rules, either consciously by imitation or coercion or unconsciously by tacit agreement. (p. 28)

Stinchcombe (1997), meanwhile, caricatured the theory as "Durkheimian in the sense that collective representations manufacture themselves by opaque processes, are implemented by diffusion, are exterior and constraining without exterior people doing the creation or the constraining" (p. 2).

Again, different approaches within sociology have sought to react against this account in which institutions are seen as constraints rather than the product of human agency. Clemens and Cook (1999) noted that institutions can be treated either as constraints or as guiding prescriptions and that the two may combine to explain durability. They pointed to how institutions may contain cultural components—schemas, or ways of thinking about the world, which may create the possibility for institutional change. In particular, they emphasized the importance of heterogeneity of viewpoints, network fragmentation, and contradiction between institutional rules in explaining the circumstances under which change is more or less likely.

Fligstein and McAdam (2012), for their part, focused on the important role of entrepreneurs in creating and reorganizing the *fields* that constitute the *rules of the game* in a given area of activity. Here, like latter day historical institutionalists, they focused on how there may be actors who are primarily concerned with maintaining a field the way it is, so-called *incumbents*, and actors who seek to disrupt the field and replace it with a new set of arrangements—so-called *challengers*. Actors with different endowments of resources (including social skill in identifying and forming possible coalitions) vie with each other for advantage.

However, these accounts too have had difficulty in reaching generalized lessons, in part because the theoretical concepts they invoked were very often situation specific. *Skilled social action*, *robust action*, and similar concepts describe something that is real and plausibly crucial in explaining which coalitions form and which do not, but they do not lend themselves easily to the formulation of testable propositions. Social skill only reveals itself partially and indirectly, and is primarily visible through its consequences.

A second set of difficulties for sociological institutionalism lies in demonstrating its effects. To the extent that cultures and rationalism have greater consequences for ritual invocation than for real behavior, their implications for real world behavior are uncertain. As Schneiberg and Clemens (2006) described the problem:

> A second set of questions, asked only recently, appears if one looks beyond the moment of adoption of a "legitimate" policy or institutional structure to address the consequences of adoption . . . This question is often truncated by the invocation of "de-coupling," but it is worth asking "what are the substantive implications of these institutional effects?" To the extent that standard research designs fail to address questions of the consequences of institutional diffusion, they are left open to the charge that institutional effects will be most pronounced in situations that are, among other things, "of relatively little consequence." (p. 201)

Although Schneiberg and Clemens pointed out that a significant body of recent work in this approach had sought to identify important consequences, this literature still faces two important challenges. First, it does not do an especially good job at distinguishing the specific mechanisms through which institutions operate. In particular, it tends to treat any evidence for the influence of higher order institutions as being evidence of cultural effects, rather than looking to other plausible mechanisms through which institutions could have consequences. Second, because it overemphasizes the extent to which institutions provide a structuring backdrop, it underestimates heterogeneity of viewpoints and the likelihood that people will have different perspectives on institutions, and indeed perhaps sharply different understandings (or adhere to different institutions altogether). This not only means that sociological institutionalism's account of institutions themselves is too stylized, but that its account of the consequences of institutions is also over-totalizing. To the extent that people have different perspectives, institutions are more likely to be contested (potentially leading to institutional change) than sociological institutionalists surmise.

A Different Approach to Institutions

These various approaches to institutions started with different goals and have set out to analyze different phenomena, but end up in a quite similar place. Each of them has struggled to provide an account of institutions that shows (a) how institutions may be influenced by other factors and (b) how institutions can in turn influence behavior, without either reducing institutions to a mere transmission belt between external forces and human behaviors or treating institutions as coterminous with the behaviors they are trying to explain. Constructing explanations that tell us at once how institutions change and why they matter has proved to be extremely hard.

Thus, rational choice institutionalism began by arguing that institutions explained stability in situations of multidimensional choice or, alternatively, why it was that some countries prospered while others failed to grow. However, this led to the question of how institutions might change, which have been stymied in part by the difficulties of adapting a set of theories intended to explain stable equilibrium to discuss instead how things may change. Historical institutionalism similarly started from an emphasis on stability and structure, and as it has sought to explain change has found itself moving towards an imperfectly theorized mixture of mechanisms and individual action. Sociological institutionalism has been the most resistant to explaining change of all the major institutionalisms and has also tended sometimes to duck the question of institutional consequences as well, arguing instead that institutional rituals are often decoupled from what real people do. Each of these approaches faces similar conceptual problems.

In this section, borrowing from work in progress by Allen, Farrell, and Shalizi, I lay out an alternative way of thinking about institutions that may offer some clues as to a way forward. Specifically, an account of institutions that (a) stresses that institutions are built of *beliefs*, and (b) looks at how differences in individual beliefs may have consequences for institutional change may serve three useful goals. First—it can offer a clear account of how other factors than institutions may have consequences for institutions. Second, it can offer a clear account of how institutions have consequences. Third, it can do so while demonstrating that institutions are neither reducible to the forces that influence them nor to the behaviors that they influence.

Building on the work of Knight (1992) and North (1990), it is useful to think about institutions as rules, but also to consider exactly what social rules are made from. Specifically, as Knight outlines, a rule is an institution when it is known by everyone in the community to be the appropriate rule for how parties should behave in a particular situation. What this implies is that institutions are rules that are instantiated in beliefs. In other words, an institution is only an institution because everyone in the relevant community of actors believes it to be an institution. Indeed, an institution has no existence that is independent of the beliefs that compose it.

Thinking about institutions in this way allows us to disaggregate these beliefs, following the arguments of Sperber (1996). Sperber is an anthropologist, who is interested in disaggregating notions such as culture. He pointed out that cultural beliefs—such as a belief in witches—are not shared in the unproblematic way that anthropologists sometimes argue they are. Even if everyone in a community believes in witches, each person's individual belief is slightly different from every other person's belief. While there may be enough rough congruence for social coordination, a culture is not a monolithic entity, but instead (at most) a congregation of roughly similar beliefs.

Similarly, institutions can be thought of as congregations of roughly similar beliefs about the specific rules that apply in particular circumstances. One might go further—under a materialist understanding, the rules have no existence whatsoever independent of the specific beliefs held by particular individuals about how they ought to apply. Individual beliefs about the rules will inevitably vary from person to person. Sometimes, there will be authoritative actors who can partly resolve these disparities. Judges can resolve disagreements over how formal institutions (laws) should be interpreted. Kadi-justice (in Weber's 1922/1978 account) can resolve some, but not all, disputes about less formal rules. Yet even so, under the best possible circumstances, there will be significant dissimilarities between different people's beliefs over the relevant institutions covering a particular situation.

What is valuable about this conceptualization of institutions? First, that it provides an understanding of institutions that is affected by external factors, which has consequences for human behavior, but that is not reducible to either. If institutions are congregations of roughly similar beliefs, it may be easy to see how external circumstances can affect them. Power disparities, the visibility of better solutions, or new ideas about how to organize society may each have powerful consequences for actors' beliefs about how a specific rule ought be interpreted, and, indeed, for what the appropriate rule ought to be. Furthermore, the beliefs that people have about the appropriate rules in a relevant situation have obvious consequences for their actions, both because of their perceptions of how one ought to act in a given circumstance and because of their (possibly correct, possibly erroneous) assessments of how others will respond should they deviate from the rule.

Second, it identifies ways in which institutions can change that are not reducible to external circumstances, although they surely may be heavily influenced by them. Actors' beliefs about the appropriate rule will differ from actor to actor, leading to social friction (where actors find themselves in awkward situations thanks to different interpretations), social learning (when actors with different understandings of a rule can learn from each other), and social opportunism (when actors seek to push for interpretations of the relevant rules that advantage them, potentially disadvantaging others). These interactions are partly endogenous because they are part and parcel of the workings of the institution itself—that is, they are in large part the result of the admixture of individuals' varying beliefs about what the institution in fact consists of. Institutions are rules that are made up of individual beliefs, and a very important aspect of institutional change is shaped by contact between the different beliefs that make up the institution, as individuals come into contact with each other in concrete social settings. Yet such processes of admixing are, obviously, potential sources of institutional change. Thus, one cannot treat institutions as being a simple condensate of other forces (power relations, efficiency considerations, social structure, or ritual requirements), since they may be impelled to change by forces (interactions among those in the community interpreting and applying the institution) that cannot readily be reduced to these external factors.

Finally, as well as providing an account of partially endogenous change, it points to a different set of external influences than those emphasized in the major accounts described above. If institutions are instantiated in beliefs, then the social structures through which beliefs are transmitted (changing in the process of transmission) are likely to play a very important role in shaping institutional outcomes. As Clemens and Cook (1999) have suggested, network theory provides one obvious source of insight into how these processes of social transmission might work and be shaped by social relations. Clemens and Cook also point to the role of heterogeneity of institutions—thinking about institutions as heterogeneous congregations of beliefs allows scholars to build heterogeneity into the foundations of our arguments about beliefs, exploring the ways in which variation in heterogeneity may lead to differences in the likelihood that new beliefs may spread across a given community.

This is certainly not the only way in which one might look to remedy some of the difficulties of social science institutionalism. However, it is one that may plausibly fit well with many of the concerns of scholars interested in spatial development. It points towards an account of institutions that does not waver between theories of institutional stability and theories of institutional change, but rather builds the possibility of innovation (a topic of great concern to economic geography) into the theory, by showing how it is likely to be influenced by the degree of heterogeneity and the relevant network structures of propagation and diffusion in a given society.

For example, one obvious implication of this approach is that we should see more rapid institutional change in circumstances where individuals with significantly differing beliefs about the institution come into frequent contact with each other (Allen et al., 2017). This provides some theoretical basis for understanding why some societies, such as Classical Athens, have seen rapid adaptation and learning, while others with similar power and resources have stagnated in relative terms (Allen et al., 2017; Ober, 2008). A second implication is that rough democracy—here conceived of as a general equality in the ability of actors with varying beliefs to affect institutional change—will plausibly result in more rapid and (over the long term) more socially beneficial institutional change than in situations where there are greater power disparities, with the interpretations of a narrow elite of actors with relatively similar understandings prevailing (Allen et al., 2017; Hong & Page, 2004).

These and other hypotheses may open the path to a new way of thinking about differing patterns of spatial development and how they relate to institutions. For example, they provide a practical linkage to Glückler, Lazega, and Hammer's (2017) argument for networks as an organizing metaphor, because it is through networks that beliefs diffuse and change, making it possible for different patterns of power relations and different patterns of exchange between actors with different understandings to be modeled using network percolation models and similar. If studies of economic development in specific regions and localities, and their relationship to international networks of knowledge diffusion began in discussions of *thickness* and the like, they may end up returning there, but with a very different and more specific set of intellectual tools for investigating how beliefs in fact spread and what consequences this has for institutional change.

References

Acemoğlu, D., Johnson, S., & Robinson, J. A. (2001). The colonial origins of comparative development: An empirical investigation. *The American Economic Review, 91,* 1369–1401. doi:https://doi.org/10.1257/aer.91.5.1369

Acemoğlu, D., & Robinson, J. A. (2006). *Economic origins of dictatorship and democracy.* Cambridge, UK: Cambridge University Press.

Acemoğlu, D., & Robinson, J. A. (2012). *Why nations fail: The origins of power, prosperity, and poverty.* New York: Crown Publishers.

Allen, D., Farrell, H., & Shalizi, C. (2017). *Evolution and institutional change.* Unpublished paper.

Amin, A. (1999). An institutionalist perspective on regional economic development. *International Journal of Urban and Regional Research, 23,* 365–378. doi:https://doi.org/10.1111/1468-2427.00201

Amin, A., & Thrift, N. (Eds.) (1995). *Globalization, institutions, and regional development in Europe.* Oxford, UK: Oxford University Press.

Arrow, K. J. (2012). *Social choice and individual values* (3rd ed.). New Haven: Yale University Press. (Original work published 1951)

Arthur, W. B. (1994). Increasing returns and path dependence in the economy. Economics, Cognition, and Society. Ann Arbor: University of Michigan Press.

Bathelt, H., & Glückler, J. (2014). Institutional change in economic geography. *Progress in Human Geography, 38,* 340–363. doi:https://doi.org/10.1177/0309132513507823

Becattini, G. (1990). The Marshallian industrial district as a socio-economic notion. In F. Pyke, G. Becattini, & W. Sengenberger (Eds.), *Industrial districts and interfirm cooperation in Italy* (pp. 37–51). Geneva: International Institute for Labor Studies

Black, D. (1948). On the Rationale of Group Decision-Making. *Journal of Political Economy, 56,* 23–34. doi:https://doi.org/10.1086/256633

Callaghan, H. (2010). Beyond methodological nationalism: How multilevel governance affects the clash of capitalisms. *Journal of European Public Policy, 17,* 564–580. doi:https://doi.org/10.1080/13501761003673351

Calvert, R. L. (1995). Rational actors, equilibrium, and social institutions. In J. Knight & I. Sened (Eds.), *Explaining social institutions* (pp. 57–94). Ann Arbor: University of Michigan Press.

Clemens, E. S., & Cook, J. M. (1999). Politics and institutionalism: Explaining durability and change. *Annual Review of Sociology, 25,* 441–466. doi:https://doi.org/10.1146/annurev.soc.25.1.441

DiMaggio, P. J., & Powell, W. W. (1983). The iron cage revisited: Institutional isomorphism and collective rationality in organizational fields. *American Sociological Review, 48,* 147–160. Retrieved from http://www.jstor.org/stable/2095101

Dobbin, F. (1994). *Forging industrial policy: The United States, Britain, and France in the railway age.* Cambridge, UK: Cambridge University Press.

Downs, A. (1957). An economic theory of political action in a democracy. *Journal of Political Economy, 65,* 135–150. doi:https://doi.org/10.1086/257897

Farole, T., Rodriguez-Pose, A., & Storper, M. (2011). Human geography and the institutions that underlie economic growth. *Progress in Human Geography, 35,* 58–80. doi:https://doi.org/10.1177/0309132510372005

Farrell, H., & Newman, A. L. (2014). Domestic institutions, beyond the nation-state: Charting the new interdependence approach. *World Politics, 66,* 331–363. doi:https://doi.org/10.1017/S0043887114000057

Fligstein, N., & McAdam, D. (2012). *A theory of fields.* Oxford, UK: Oxford University Press.

Flora, P., Kuhnle, S., & Urwin, D. (Eds.) (1999). *State formation, nation-building, and mass politics in Europe: The theory of Stein Rokkan.* Oxford, UK: Oxford University Press.

Gerth, H. H., & Mills, C. W. (Eds.). (2009*). From Max Weber: Essays in sociology* (H. H. Gerth & C. W. Mills, Trans.). London: Routledge. (Original work published in 1946)

Glückler, J., & Bathelt, H. (2017). Institutional context and innovation. In H. Bathelt, P. Cohendet, S. Henn, & L. Simon (Eds.), *The Elgar companion to innovation and knowledge creation: A multi-disciplinary approach.* Cheltenham: Edward Elgar.

Glückler, J., Lazega, E., & Hammer, I. (2017). Exploring the interaction of space and networks in the creation of knowledge: An introduction. *Knowledge and Networks* (pp. 1–21). Knowledge and Space: Vol. 11. Dodrecht: Springer.

Glückler, J., & Lenz, R. (2016). How institutions moderate the effectiveness of regional policy: A framework and research agenda. *Investigaciones Regionales, 36,* 255–277. Retrieved from https://www.researchgate.net/publication/311652886

Gould, S. J., & Eldredge, N. (1977). Punctuated equilibria: The tempo and mode of evolution reconsidered. *Paleobiology, 3,* 115–151. doi:https://doi.org/10.1017/S0094837300005224

Grabher, G. (1993). The weakness of strong ties: The lock-in of regional development in the Ruhr area. In G. Grabher (Ed.), *The embedded girm: On the socioeconomics of industrial networks* (pp. 255–277). London: Routledge.

Greif, A. (1994). Cultural beliefs and the organization of society: A historical and theoretical reflection on collectivist and individualist societies. *Journal of Political Economy, 102,* 912–950. doi:https://doi.org/10.1086/261959

Greif, A. (2006). *Institutions and the path to the modern economy: Lessons from medieval trade.* Cambridge, UK: Cambridge University Press.

Greif, A., & Laitin, D. D. (2004). A theory of endogenous institutional change. *American Political Science Review, 98,* 633–652. doi:https://doi.org/10.1017/S0003055404041395

Hacker, J. S. (2004). Privatizing risk without privatizing the welfare state: The hidden politics of social policy retrenchment in the United States. *American Political Science Review, 98,* 243–260. doi:https://doi.org/10.1017/S0003055404001121

Hacker, J. S., Thelen, K., & Pierson, P. (2013). *Drift and conversion: Hidden faces of institutional change.* [APSA 2013 Annual Meeting Paper]. Chicago: American Political Science Association.

Hall, P. A., & Thelen, K. (2009). Institutional change in varieties of capitalism. [Special issue] *Socio-Economic Review, 7,* 7–34. doi:https://doi.org/10.1093/ser/mwn020

Hong, L., & Page, S. E. (2004). Groups of diverse problem solvers can outperform groups of high-ability problem solvers. *Proceedings of the National Academy of Science, 101,* 16385–16389. doi: https://doi.org/10.1073/pnas.0403723101

Jepperson, R. L. (2002). The development and application of sociological neoinstitutionalism. In J. Berger & M. Zelditch (Eds.), *New directions in contemporary sociological theory* (pp. 229–266). Lanham: Rowman & Littlefield.

Knight, J. (1992). *Institutions and social conflict. The political economy of institutions and decisions.* Cambridge, UK: Cambridge University Press.

Krasner, S. D. (1982). Regimes and the limits of realism: Regimes as autonomous variables. *International Organization, 36,* 497–510. doi:https://doi.org/10.1017/S0020818300019032

Levi, M. (2013). Can nations succeed? *Perspectives on Politics, 11,* 187–192. doi:https://doi.org/10.1017/S1537592712003374

Mahoney, J. (2000). Path dependence in historical sociology. *Theory and Society, 29,* 507–548. doi:https://doi.org/10.1023/A:1007113830879

Mahoney, J., & Thelen, K. (Eds.). (2010). *Explaining institutional change: Ambiguity, agency, and power.* Cambridge, UK: Cambridge University Press.

McKelvey, R. D. (1976). Intransitivities in multidimensional voting models and some implications for agenda control. *Journal of Economic Theory, 12,* 472–482. doi:https://doi.org/10.1016/0022-0531(76)90040-5

McKelvey, R. D. (1979). General conditions for global intransitivities in formal voting models. *Econometrica: Journal of the Econometric Society, 47,* 1085–1112. doi:https://doi.org/10.2307/1911951

Meyer, J. W., Boli, J., Thomas, G. M., & Ramirez, F. O. (1997). World society and the nation-state. *American Journal of Sociology, 103,* 144–181. doi:https://doi.org/10.1086/231174

Meyer, J. W., & Rowan, B. (1977). Institutionalized organizations: Formal structure as myth and ceremony. *American Journal of Sociology, 83,* 340–363. doi:https://doi.org/10.1086/226550

Milgrom, P. R., North, D. C., & Weingast, B. R. (1990). The role of institutions in the revival of trade: The law merchant, private judges, and the champagne fairs. *Economics & Politics, 2,* 1–23. doi:https://doi.org/10.1111/j.1468-0343.1990.tb00020.x

North, D. C. (1990). *Institutions, institutional change and economic performance.* The Political Economy of Institutions and Decisions. Cambridge, UK: Cambridge University Press. doi:https://doi.org/10.1017/CBO9780511808678

North, D. C., Wallis, J. J., & Weingast, B. R. (2009). *Violence and social orders: A conceptual framework for interpreting recorded human history.* Cambridge, UK: Cambridge University Press.

Ober, J. (2008). *Democracy and knowledge: Innovation and learning in classical Athens.* Princeton: Princeton University Press.

Pierson, P. (2000). Increasing returns, path dependence, and the study of politics. *American Political Science Review, 94,* 251–267. doi:https://doi.org/10.2307/2586011

Piore, M., & Sabel, C. (1984). *The second industrial divide: Possibilities for prosperity.* New York: Basic Books.

Przeworski, A. (2004). Institutions matter? *Government and Opposition, 39,* 527–540. doi:https://doi.org/10.1111/j.1477-7053.2004.00134.x

Riker, W. H. (1980). Implications from the disequilibrium of majority rule for the study of institutions. *American Political Science Review, 74,* 432–446. doi:https://doi.org/10.2307/1960638

Schmidt, V. A. (2012). A curious constructivism: A response to Professor Bell. *British Journal of Political Science, 42,* 705–713. doi:https://doi.org/10.1017/S0007123411000470

Schneiberg, M., & Clemens, E. S. (2006). The typical tools for the job: Research strategies in institutional analysis. *Sociological Theory, 24,* 195–227. doi:https://doi.org/10.1111/j.1467-9558.2006.00288.x

Schofield, N. (1978). Instability of simple dynamic games. *The Review of Economic Studies, 45,* 575–594. doi:https://doi.org/10.2307/2297259

Sen, A. (1997). *Choice, welfare and measurement.* Cambridge, MA: Harvard University Press.

Shepsle, K. A. (1979). Institutional arrangements and equilibrium in multidimensional voting models. *American Journal of Political Science, 23,* 27–59. doi:https://doi.org/10.2307/2110770

Shepsle, K. A. (1986). Institutional equilibrium and equilibrium institutions. In H. F. Weisberg (Ed.), *Political science: The science of politics* (pp. 51–81). New York: Agathon Press.

Skocpol, T. (1979). *States and social revolutions: A comparative analysis of France, Russia and China.* Cambridge, UK: Cambridge University Press.

Sperber, D. (1996). *Explaining culture: A naturalistic approach.* Oxford, UK: Blackwell.

Steinmo, S., Thelen, K., & Longstreth, F. (Eds.) (1992). *Structuring politics: Historical institutionalism in comparative analysis. Cambridge studies in comparative politics.* Cambridge, UK: Cambridge University Press.

Stinchcombe, A. L. (1997). On the virtues of the old institutionalism. *Annual Review of Sociology, 23*, 1–18. doi:https://doi.org/10.1146/annurev.soc.23.1.1

Streeck, W., & Thelen, K. (Eds.) (2005). *Beyond continuity: Institutional change in advanced political economies.* New York: Oxford University Press.

Thelen, K. (1999). Historical institutionalism in comparative politics. *Annual Review of Political Science, 2*, 369–404. doi:https://doi.org/10.1146/annurev.polisci.2.1.369

Thelen, K. (2004). *How institutions evolve. The political economy of skills in Germany, Britain, the United States and Japan.* Cambridge, UK: Cambridge University Press.

Tilly, C., & Ardant, G. (1975). *The formation of national states in western Europe.* Princeton: Princeton University Press.

Weber, M. (1978). *Economy and society: An outline of interpretive sociology* (G. Roth & C. Wittich, Trans.). Berkeley: University of California Press. (Original work published in 1922)

Williamson, O. E. (1975). *Markets and hierarchies: Analysis and antitrust implications.* New York: Free Press.

Williamson, O. E. (1985). *The economic institutions of capitalism: Firms, markets, relational contracting.* New York: Free Press.

Chapter 3
Organizational Fields as Mnemonic Communities

Diego Coraiola, Roy Suddaby, and William M. Foster

Network Structure and Collective Cognition

The concept of the organizational field is central to organization theory. Despite its influence, the construct suffers from a lack of precise definition. Most theorists accept structuration as the core dynamic through which fields emerge (Scott, 1994) and, as a result, most definitions of organizational fields contain an element of *structure* or *place*, on one hand, and an element of collective *meaning* or *cognition* on the other. These two components of organizational fields—place and meaning—have an uncomfortable relationship with each other. Although most definitions of fields acknowledge that organizational fields are simultaneously spatial patterns of interaction of participants and their common meaning systems, there is no clear understanding of how a shared network structure can lead to collective cognition. As a result, most empirical applications of organizational fields tend to emphasize one element (structure or cognition) over the other.

We seek to address this issue by introducing time, history and, most importantly, memory as the bridging mechanism that connects the structural and cognitive elements of organizational fields. We observe that institutional theorists have traditionally adopted the metaphor of fields as either geographical or symbolic structures, but largely neglected the understanding that fields are also temporal structures. As Barley and Tolbert (1997, p. 99) have argued, institutions are "*historical accretions of past practices* and understandings that set conditions on actions" as they "gradually acquire the moral and ontological status of taken-for-granted facts" (emphasis added). We apply this insight to the construct of fields, arguing that fields are

D. Coraiola · W. M. Foster
Augustana Campus, University of Alberta, Camrose, Alberta, Canada
e-mail: coraiola@ualberta.ca; wfoster@ualberta.ca

R. Suddaby (✉)
Peter B. Gustavson School of Business, University of Victoria, Victoria, BC, Canada
e-mail: rsuddaby@uvic.ca

© The Author(s) 2018
J. Glückler et al. (eds.), *Knowledge and Institutions*, Knowledge and Space 13,
https://doi.org/10.1007/978-3-319-75328-7_3

historically embedded processes that are, in equal part, the product of collective action, collective meaning, and collective remembering.

The core of our argument is that the spatial metaphor of organizational fields pays insufficient attention to temporality, and thus lacks the ability of theorizing important issues involved in processes of field creation and reproduction. We propose a new way of understanding organizational fields—as imagined communities that are bounded by collective practices of remembering. These *mnemonic fields* are founded in a collective act of remembering that binds actors together in a common fate. Once created, mnemonic fields provide individual actors with the contents and frameworks of remembering. They define the practices and categories actors use to remember the past, make sense of the present, and imagine the future. Field mnemonics are thus the link between the structure and the cognitive system of meanings in place in an organizational field.

Three main dimensions can be distinguished in every mnemonic field. The genealogical, or non-narrative, dimension accounts for the material practices and artifacts transmitted from the past to the present. The narrative, or symbolic, dimension comprises the narrative practices attached to forms of cultural and communicative memory. The moral, or normative, dimension of the field encompasses the remembrance and forgetting of the good and the bad, as well as the moral appropriateness of the practices and frameworks of remembering. This redefinition of organizational fields as communities of remembrance offers an enriched view of organizational fields and provides an innovative path to the development of research on the reproduction and change of organizational fields and institutions over time.

Our paper proceeds in three parts. First, we review the literature on organizational fields. Then, we introduce collective remembering as a critically important but overlooked element of organizational fields. We review the literature on organizational and collective mnemonics and demonstrate how adopting a tempo-historical consciousness can deepen our understanding of how collective assumptions of place can create collective meaning. We conclude with a discussion of how the implications of viewing the organizational field as a mnemonic structure can generate future research.

Organizational Fields

The field is a central element of institutional theory. Organizational fields are most typically defined as "those organizations that, in the aggregate, constitute a recognized area of institutional life" (DiMaggio & Powell, 1983, p. 148). The construct emerged out of a recognition of the limitations of the concept of environment in traditional contingency theory, which assumed an ontological separation between an organization and its external environment. Institutional theory challenged this assumption with the observation that organizations largely exist in environments comprised of other organizations. As a result, organizations often respond, not to the technical demands of their economic environment, but rather to the social pressures of the environment described by the other organizations that surround them (Evan, 1965; Scott & Meyer, 1991; Suddaby, 2013).

The many attempts to classify and define the factors that characterize organizational fields have produced multiple, sometimes contradictory definitions. Most of these, however, do acknowledge that organizations in a common field share both patterns of structural interaction—in other words, a collective geography or place— and patterns of shared meanings or symbolic systems—in other words, a collective cognition. This assumed binary nature of the construct is perhaps best captured by Scott's (1994, pp. 207–208) definition of organizational fields as "a community of organizations that partakes of a common meaning system and whose participants interact more frequently and fatefully with one another than with actors outside the field."

Despite this clear understanding that organizational fields are constituted by shared structural interactions and common cognitions, most empirical applications of the construct seem to privilege one component of fields over the other. Below we describe four common empirical applications of the construct.

The first two adopt the metaphor of the field as place—that is, as a structured pattern of interactions between organizations. The first, which we term a *functional* approach, narrowly focuses on economic interactions as the primary determinant of the network structure. The second, which we term a *relational* approach, offers a somewhat broader analytic focus on both economic and social interactions between organizations as the defining unit of analysis for the field.

The second two types of applications tend to view the field as defined largely by shared cognitions and focus on the shared meaning systems that generate common rules or governance structures for communities of organizations. The first type, which we term *ideational*, views fields as forming around singly contested issues or ideas. The second type, which we call *cultural*, adopts a somewhat broader lens of multiple shared values, norms, and beliefs that define a common cultural community. We elaborate each of these views below.

Functional Organizational Fields

The most common criterion researchers have used to define an organizational field is its function within a broader social or economic structure (Scott & Meyer, 1991). This has been translated into a focus on the products and services offered by different sets of organizations as well as the inflows and outflows of goods and information. This approach has more generally crystallized with regard to industries (Porter, 1980). An industry involves a group of organizations or sectors that are subject to similar legal, political, social, cultural, and environmental forces and whose existence and activity are linked due to rivalry dynamics within the market for a given product or service. The boundaries in this case are premised on the social structures separating these segments from others within large economic sectors. They make

broader societal influences dismissible and account for most of the internal variation and resilience of relationships over time (McGahan & Porter, 1997).

Relational Organizational Fields

Another common criterion used by researchers to distinguish the boundaries of an
organizational field focuses on the network of relationships established among organizations. The field is based on the level of interconnectedness among different
groups of companies in what Kenis and Knoke (2002) have relabeled as "organizational field-nets." Due to the networked configuration of organizational fields, they
are assumed to exhibit the same properties and share similar features with other
kinds of networks. Among the most important issues dealt with by the literature on
organizational networks are the assumptions about organizational embeddedness
(Dacin, Ventresca, & Beal, 1999; Granovetter, 1985) and the structural composition
of fields (DiMaggio, 1986). The embeddedness thesis argues that organizational
economic activity depends on and is developed within social frameworks of patterned relations among actors within bounded social contexts. The networked nature
of organizational fields makes them amenable to the kind of analysis developed in
other social networks. Measures of density and dispersion, centralization and decentralization, and cohesiveness and "betweeness" are some of the tests this sort of
analysis is able to provide to inform the theorizing about the dynamics of the field
in relation to innovation (Gibbons, 2004; Powell, Koput, & Doerr, 1996), economic
performance (Uzzi, 1996), and corporate philanthropy (Galaskiewicz & Wasserman,
1989).

Ideational Organizational Fields

More recently, a distinct approach to the study of organizational fields has emerged
around the notion of issue-based fields (Hoffman, 1999). This approach minimizes
the importance of previous relationships among actors and a common reference
structure of norms and meanings to focus on the grouping effects of actors' collective attention around a common issue (Anand & Peterson, 2000). Also identified as
a first step in a longer process of field emergence and sedimentation (Zietsma,
Groenewegen, Logue, & Hinings, 2017), this view of organizational fields highlights the temporally based and nonguaranteed aspects of field formation usually
assumed by the other approaches. In this case, the field might or might not evolve
into a full-fledged field with a well-defined set of norms and meanings, based in
repetitive and standardized relationships among the actors. Here, the field is depicted
more as a temporary collective arrangement of actors dragged together by an attention vortex created by environmental jolts and field-configuring events, such as conferences (Garud, 2008; Hardy & Maguire, 2010), ceremonies (Anand & Jones,

2008; Anand & Watson, 2004), crises (Desai, 2011; Sine & David, 2003), and other kinds of social and natural events (Glynn, 2008; Tilcsik & Marquis, 2013) that bring actors together in space and time and reinvigorate existing structures and relationships (Panitz & Glückler, 2017).

Cultural Organizational Fields

A fourth criterion is based on the cultural-cognitive dimension of institutions (Scott, 2008). This approach states that organizations are bound together by a *common meaning system* that actors use to make sense of their realities and in which they ground their actions. The focus on shared meanings refers, first, to a particular language, which includes a vocabulary of motives (Mills, 1940), as well as specific sets of categories and typifications of actions (Berger & Luckmann, 1967). Second, the shared meanings among actors in a field encompass scripted behavior in the form of mental schemes and associated rules and routines that define the standards of microritualized behavior. Third, the cognitive-cultural view of organizational fields emphasizes the prominence of discursive activity within the field, as well as the shared frames and narratives that lie at the base of collective action. The importance of this symbolic dimension of organizational fields can be seen in Zilber's (2006) analysis of the Israeli field of high-technology and in the translation processes that connect field-level meanings and institutions with broader sociocultural frameworks at the social level and provide meaningful practices and structures to guide actions within the field.

This brief explanation of the way organizational fields have been and continue to be conceptualized demonstrates that traditional views have emphasized the role of place (i.e., structure) and meaning (i.e., cognition), but fail to offer any coherent explanation for how these two critical elements of fields mutually constitute each other. We note that social geographers have made significant progress toward bridging place and cognition by demonstrating how a shared set of geographical constraints correlates with shared cognitions (e.g., Glückler, 2013; Glückler, Lazega, & Hammer, 2017). However, most prior conceptualizations of fields have an implicit teleological understanding of time. That is, traditional approaches have privileged a synchronic view of fields as either an unfolding evolution of actors in a process of gradually increasing complexity of structured interaction or as a revolutionary field-configuring event that crystallizes shared meanings and cognitions.

However, even though these approaches each recognize that fields evolve over time, there is little sophistication in how time, history, and collective memories of actors contribute to the structuration of fields. Theories of organizational fields lack a "historical consciousness" (Suddaby, 2016). Past and current research on organizational fields offers little recognition of the role that temporality or history play in the emergence, maintenance, and decay of organizational fields (Suddaby, Foster, & Mills, 2014).

In the balance of this paper we present the theoretical foundation of a conception of organizational fields as the recurrent reconstruction of social structures and meanings through mnemonic practices—that is, practices of remembering, forgetting, and using the past. We argue that although meaning and structure are important components of organizational fields, both are not essentialist or universal elements of fields, but are instead each inseparable from their mutual reproduction over time. Nor is time a universal or essentialist phenomenon, but rather, itself, created through processes of social reproduction and construction—by processes of collective remembering (Halbwachs, 1992). Our core thesis, thus, is that organizational fields are largely mnemonic communities—in other words, historically contingent structures that reflect the collective memory of their participants. We elaborate this argument in the next section.

Mnemonic Fields: Reconceptualizing Organizational Fields as Mnemonic Communities

There is a growing awareness that much of our memory is collective (Halbwachs, 1992), cultural (Sturken, 1997), or constituted at social levels beyond individual recollection (Olick & Robbins, 1998). To capture this notion, Zerubavel (1996) coined the term "mnemonic communities," with which he meant to capture the idea that broader social structures, such as the family, organization, ethnic group, and nation, all engage in practices of commemoration (cooperative remembering) that serve to define a common identity and delineate the boundaries of a specific social institution. Mnemonic communities, thus, are aggregates of social actors bound together by common frameworks of remembering and shared memories of past practices, identities, and collective meanings (Connerton, 1989; Zerubavel, 2003).

We contend that organizational fields are also mnemonic communities. Fields are constituted through acts of remembering by participating actors that engage in a collective process of institutional reflexivity (Suddaby, Viale, & Gendron, 2016) about the past that resignifies and recontextualizes the present in the light of a reconstructed past and a reimagined future. In so doing, actors redeploy historical artifacts, reenact material practices, and recreate cultural narratives that bring together a new social order and a new spatiotemporal nexus connecting the past-present-future of the community, redrawing its boundaries, and reshaping the collective identity of the field. In order to better understand how processes of collective mnemonics occur, however, we must first revisit research on organizational memory.

Organizational Mnemonics

Early studies of organizational memory (OMS) were based in the context of organizational learning and knowledge management. Here organizational memory is conceived of as a property or capacity—that is, a type of "storage bin," filled with the information needed for future strategic use in organizational planning and decision making (Walsh & Ungson, 1991). More recent views of organizational memory based on social or cultural approaches have been proposed (e.g., Feldman & Feldman, 2006; Rowlinson, Booth, Clark, Delahaye, & Procter, 2010). These recent efforts eschew the functional models of memory as a capacity for storing and retrieving information and, instead, view organizational memory as a dynamic process occurring within a specific social context.

Despite the shift in recent OMS research away from functionalist models of memory, most current OMS research is limited by its focus on a rational systems approach to the study of organizations (Scott & Davis, 2007). Most OMS researchers approach organizations as "a highly special type of collective, which is deliberately at the service of a clearly specified cause, e.g. profit maximization or problem solving" (Aksu, 2009, p. 322). As a result, this research falls victim to some of the same criticisms that plagued previous discussions of memory in knowledge management and organizational learning: That organizations are composed of relationships and activities that produce diverse social groups and individuals embedded in broader sociocultural and historical environments (Scott & Davis, 2007). To develop an alternative and more encompassing framework for the study of social mnemonics and organizations we need to address three main limitations of current OMS research.

The first is the methodological, individualist approach to the problem of organizational memory. Most OMS research conceives organizational memory as an aggregate of organizational members' memories. This "collected memory" approach (Olick, 1999) reduces organizational memory to the sum of individual memories. Instead, some authors (Rowlinson et al., 2010) argue that a more convincing and accurate conception of organizational memory is as a collective phenomenon that is qualitatively different from the individual, psychological remembrance of the world. Following this observation, some scholars recognize distinct mechanisms influencing the social processes of remembering in and around organizations (Mena, Rintamäki, Fleming, & Spicer, 2016; Ocasio, Mauskapf, & Steele, 2016), and recent research has focused on material practices of remembering (Decker, 2014), the narrative dimension of memory (Adorisio, 2014), and the re-presentation of the past as collective claims (Lamertz, Foster, Coraiola, & Kroezen, 2016).

A second limitation is the emphasis on the strategic motivation and use of organizational memory. Many studies on organizational memory have focused on organizational mnemonics as a direct product of instrumental, organizational efforts

(Suddaby, Foster, & Trank, 2010; Zundel, Holt, & Popp, 2016). Organizations invent traditions (Rowlinson & Hassard, 1993), construct narratives about the past (Maclean, Harvey, Sillince, & Golant, 2014), appropriate social memory (Foster, Suddaby, Minkus, & Wiebe, 2011), and use historical artifacts to reinforce their values for their audiences (Schultz, Maguire, Langley, & Tsoukas, 2012). Organizational mnemonics, however, are more than the purposeful product of an organization's intentions to store information. Organizational memory can be used to create identity both with internal and external stakeholders (Foster et al., 2011; Suddaby & Foster, 2017; Ybema, 2010) as well as to strategically to manage change (e.g., Anteby & Molnár, 2012; Maclean et al., 2014; Schultz & Hernes, 2013). It can also facilitate or hamper processes of negotiation and renegotiation of the past (Booth, Clark, Delahaye, Procter, & Rowlinson, 2007; Janssen, 2012a; Ybema, 2014) and dynamics of (re)appropriation and (re)interpretation (Schwartz, 1997).

Third, previous research remains stubbornly attached to an organization-centric view of organizational mnemonics. This individualist conception of organizational memory lies at the core of some criticisms about conventional OMS. The solution some authors suggest is the same that is proposed to overcome the problem of methodological individualism. Organizational mnemonics should rely on a "collective memory" approach (Olick, 1999) to "take account of the specific social and historical contexts of organizational memory" (Rowlinson et al., 2010, p. 69). The study of organizational mnemonics remains focused on a single organization, and the collective memory of organizations continues to be seen as an exclusive organizational level phenomenon, tied to organizations or, at best, conceived as a result of some inner organizational culture dynamics (Mai, 2015). This approach to OMS has yet to recognize how organizational remembering is nested within broader cultural frameworks (Ocasio et al., 2016; Weber & Dacin, 2011).

Our alternative definition of organizational mnemonics, is predicated upon Halbwachs's (1992) insight that individual remembrance is determined by frameworks of memory drawn from the different social groups to which they belong. In particular, we assert that the frameworks of memory used by organizations to remember are affected by various social institutions (Ocasio et al., 2016) and by the relations actors establish with other field-level actors. In other words, organizational mnemonics take place within organizational fields and, as such, they are subject to many of the forces and influences operating at the level of the field. For instance, we should expect differences between the way central and peripheral actors remember a common event—just as we would expect a general and a soldier to have different memories of the same battle. In addition, boundary-spanning organizations should engage in different kinds of memory work than other peer organizations within the field. And organizations located at the interstices of multiple fields should exhibit behavior regarding their mnemonic practices that is more like that of other organizations in a similar position than that of organizations located within a particular organizational field.

Thus our argument departs from an organization-centered view of social memory. Instead we focus on organizational fields as sites for collective remembering. Akin to individuals within mnemonic communities, organizations do not remember alone. The dynamics of organizational remembering and forgetting are intermingled and integrated within complex networks of relationships with other actors across time and space. The collective practices of organizational remembering are influenced by existing institutions and organizational fields. These institutions are historically created, mnemonically sedimented, and mythically moralized taken-for-granted practices and meanings that guide social action. Organizational mnemonics are thus institutionally shaped, culturally defined frameworks, practices, and contents of remembrance whose dynamics take place in various fields due to the influence of multiple social actors, such as the state, professions, and social movements.

Mnemonic Fields

Mnemonic communities or communities of remembrance are those in which field membership is attached to a belief in a collectively shared fate. Mnemonic communities emerge around memories that define the field's boundaries and create belonging among members. The creation and reproduction of the community is attached to a central self-definition, which is usually grounded in mythical foundations. Most communities have at the foundation of their collective remembering a shared traumatic experience. In other circumstances, communities of memory are triggered by other kinds of events, all of which exhibit the characteristic of a formative drama, an act that grounds the creation of a collective self-definition and puts into motion processes of identification towards the group (Irwin-Zarecka, 1994).

A mnemonic community requires an act or event that grounds the creation of a collective identity. However, mnemonic communities are usually founded on very ambiguous grounds. This is clearly the case of communities created after traumatic events, in which the grief for the trauma overlaps with the joy of belonging and the realization that the birth of the community was made possible after a tragic loss. The community struggles to remember and wishes to forget that very moment in which it was created. In other words, social processes of remembering establish the foundation and transformation of the community by drawing and redrawing the boundaries of different periods or eras in its historical trajectory. This also holds true for communities founded on other similarly extraordinary events, or whose extraordinariness was built over time in the form of watershed events though communal reflection and remembering. As the research on technology demonstrates (Tushman & Anderson, 1986), technological breakthroughs are intrinsically attached to processes of industry reconfiguration. But new technologies do not act as mere products of a changing environment. Instead, they take an active role in shaping and reshaping those environments as well as the people and the practices that constitute them. A similar process takes place when new cultural tools (Swidler, 1986) become available within a community. The emergence of new meanings and interpretations colonizes the collective experience with anxieties and uncertainties that might promote the divide between different orders of meaning (Zilber, 2007).

The rise of new myths and ideologies also can provide the grounds for the creation of new institutions and fields (Douglas, 1986). In fact, it is usually the case that technological innovation is grounded in new and revolutionary paradigms founded on institutional analogies (Leblebici, Salancik, Copay, & King, 1991). And the belief in the foundation of collectivities of organizations on self-sufficing, integrated chains of rationalized myths is a cornerstone of institutional theory (Meyer & Rowan, 1977). But, as the research on cultural trauma shows (Alexander, Eyerman, Giesen, Smelser, & Sztompka, 2004), communities of memory constituted around trauma hardly ever emerge with the trauma itself. Membership always comes together after reflection over the traumatic experience has taken place and those affected have woven together their remembrances into a new myth of origin. Thus, it is through the very act of remembering that the collective identity of the field is generated, together with a new narrative about the group and its collective fate.

Dimensions of Mnemonic Fields

Organizational fields change over time (Fligstein, 1990). Yet, why is it we still talk about fields as though they were static entities? The literature on field-level change has analyzed many different domains of economic activity, including accounting (Greenwood & Suddaby, 2006), gastronomy (Rao, Monin, & Durand, 2003), forestry (Zietsma & Lawrence, 2010), toxic chemicals (Hardy & Maguire, 2010), county cricket (Wright & Zammuto, 2013), radio broadcasting (Leblebici et al., 1991), and music (Anand & Peterson, 2000). However, the temporal nature of the field itself is rarely problematized.

The permanence of organizational fields over time has been usually taken for granted. Consequently, the field as a metaphor needs to incorporate an enriched view of time and temporality. To better understand fields it is necessary to reflect more deeply on issues of sameness and difference in the collective identity of organizational fields across time and space. To define the field as "the same" is to be able to identify some essential features lying at its core (Albert & Whetten, 1985) that have remained immutable, as well as some minor aspects that might have changed.

We propose three main dimensions of mnemonic fields that interact to produce this core or essence. The genealogical dimension can be uncovered through the longitudinal examination of organizational fields. This sort of analysis makes it possible to unpack how some traces and characteristics from past arrangements, decisions, and practices are maintained and reproduced over time and to envision how these dimensions have a direct influence in the present state of field affairs. The narrative dimension is based on an interpretive understanding of the transmission of varied past modes of life (e.g., rationales, practices, meanings) and implies that continuity with the past might be crafted through communication leading to institutional reemergence and reenactment. The third is a moral dimension. Every act of remembering and every representation of the past embodies in itself a moral and normative component. Past actions imply consequences in the future, as well as deeds, rights, and obligations among actors within the community and from the community in relation to other social actors. Remembrance of the past thus implies a responsibility toward the future and an accountability of actions past.

The Genealogical Dimension

The genealogical dimension of mnemonic fields comprises a legacy of achievements and past experiences. The past provides a foundation for the future and lays the context in which the present takes shape. This influence of the past on the present occurs in two ways (Stinchcombe, 1965). First, the past is imprinted on the structures and organizing frameworks within organizations (i.e., environmental imprinting). Second, the consequences of actions and decisions made in the past are brought to bear on the present state of affairs (i.e., path-dependence effects). Although both approaches might be seen as two sides of the same coin, the distinction is important because it helps to differentiate between models and frameworks of action, which are the focus of research on imprinting, and the consequences of the actions themselves, which are the interest of path-dependence scholars.

The literature on path dependence has been quite successful in arguing for the importance of the past in defining the behavior of organizations in the present. Empirical research in the field has been providing support for some hypotheses. In different levels of analysis scholars have shown the role of self-reinforcing mechanisms in carving the tracks of organizational inertia (Sydow & Schreyögg, 2013). And in the last couple of years they have honed their main assumptions into a clear research framework (Sydow, Schreyögg, & Koch, 2009). However, one major criticism remains about this approach, querying how change is possible in a world of increasing returns and funneling options. Traditional answers to these questions consider external shocks and internal mistakes as the major forces behind changes in organizational paths (Garud, Kumaraswamy, & Karnøe, 2010; Vergne & Durand, 2010). In this sense, once an organization enters a track, self-reinforcing mechanisms are activated and remain so until disrupted by chance. Two alternative answers developed in the literature empower the actors subject to the self-compelling forces from within.

The first answer was provided by Schneiberg (2007) and relied on non-synchronic modes of mnemonic transmission. In his analysis of the institutional change in the American economy in the first half of the twentieth century, he showed that any institutional development leaves behind records of paths not taken in institutional reservoirs that might be used as legacies for the development of new paths in the future. He argued that even when institutional experiments fail they are not completely in vain, because they might be used as resources to feed new developments in the future. In addition, he identified three main mechanisms of transformation operating across time and space. The mechanism of combination works through the bricolage and assembly of existing organizational forms and traces into new compound structures. There is also the mechanism of theorization, through which actors draw analogies and establish connections between the practices they engage within their field in the present and what used to be done in the past. The third mechanism is isomorphism with the past, which argues that actors might copy or transpose past accepted modes of action and structures through processes of revival, translation, and conversion.

The second solution is provided by Garud and Karnøe (2001) and Garud et al. (2010) and consists of embracing a narrative turn in path dependence theory. They started laying out a different ontology for the study of path dependence based on a social constructivist view of reality. They recognized that the paths created in the past will be used by people in the future to act in the world; however, instead of trying to explain how these paths form and how they limit action, the authors focused on how action is possible in the first place. They changed the main theoretical focus of the approach to one of path creation rather than path dependence, based on the assumption that every path is, in fact, a reenactment of or a move away from a path existing in the past. They grounded their approach in Giddens's (1984) theory of structuration and assumed that there is no automatic reproduction of path dependence through reinforcing mechanisms. Path maintenance and reproduction is thus a collective realization by social actors engaged in relational processes that entangle action and artifacts intertwined with perceptions of past, present, and future. Actors engage with the world through narratives. Path creation is thus the process through which opportunities for action are created in the present through narratives that connect initial conditions from the past with expectations for the future.

Scholars of path dependence as well as those studying imprinting have realized the importance of social memory in processes of structuration. Social mnemonics mediates the links between agency and structure, action and institutions. The solutions they provided were both grounded in sociocognitive mnemonic processes. Research has demonstrated that in addition to the influence of present time variables there are also imprinted features and reinforcing mechanisms that come into play in the structuration of organizational fields. Organizational remembering is a collective process. By this we mean that organizational memory is both a collective accomplishment by the members of the organization and a process that takes place through the ties and relationships organizations establish with other actors within an organizational field. The field is not limited to the ties and relationships organizations establish in the present. In fact, most of what constitutes the field depends on past institutional arrangements and past actions that have shaped the field. Organizational fields have an intrinsic genealogical component that is not reducible to the collective consciousness of field actors and which must be uncovered by organizational research.

The analysis here is similar to what Hannan and Freeman (1989) theorized about the evolution of organizational forms within a population of organizations. They argued that "the current diversity of organizational forms reflects the cumulative effect of a long history of variation and selection, including the consequences of founding processes, mortality processes, and merger processes" (p. 20). In spite of their exclusively synchronic view of process of inheritance and transmission, they recognized the differences between genetic and cultural transmission, and conceded that "social and cultural information passes in many different directions among generations" (p. 21). Using their biological metaphor for the sake of clarity, we can look at genealogy as the traces previous generations have passed on to their descendants. At the same time, from a historical point of view, genealogy is the cultural practice of drawing lines of descent between generations of people. The advances in genetic analysis try to bring these two realities together, even if, in fact, they can only provide a narrative competing with the one created by genealogists. What this analysis implies is that there might not be a direct and truthful correspondence between the knowledge the actors use to act in the world and the collective results and consequences of their actions (Giddens, 1984). To look at what of the past is handed over to actors in the future is not the same as to understand how they receive that material and cultural heritage and how they make sense of it. Nevertheless, the limits of the biological analogy need to be noticed, because genes—different from cultural practices and artifacts—do not incorporate the transmission of infused meanings.

Part of what is transmitted from the past to present is embedded in artifacts, routines, and cognitive frames that are not easily available to conscious choice and reflection. In this sense, the genealogical dimension is associated with non-narrative modes of remembering. It makes reference to the memory preserved in bodies and places—for example, images, objects, emotions, sentiments—and acquired by doing through habit and tradition (Dacin, Munir, & Tracey, 2010; Shils, 1981). This is not to say this memory is not embedded in networks of meaning and cannot have their existence properly enunciated and justified within the cosmology of a given community. In fact, it is usually because meanings and things are intrinsically connected and laden with value and emotion that they survive the passage of time. As Zilber's (2002) case study of an Israeli rape crisis center shows, the reproduction of organizational practices might be supported by different sets of meanings. Systems of meanings and systems of practice couple and uncouple over time, opening spaces for new practices to emerge within the same cultures or to the maintenance of symbolic systems within different sets of practices.

This understanding is equivalent to the attempts to look at path dependence and imprinting through a social constructivist lens. An interpretive approach transfers the power originally attributed to an objective foundational event to a representation of that event constructed over time as a watershed moment in the history of the community. Two things are important in this sense. First, it does not matter whether an event is "real" or not. What matters is the extent to which the community orients its actions based on its existence (Weber, 1922/1978). If the event has really happened (whatever the meaning somebody wants to attribute to "reality" in this case), its effects would have been incorporated in society and handed over to the future— were they important enough to be inscribed in the social structure of the community. If the event has not happened, there should be little difficulty in analyzing the representations the community has created and how the remembrance of the event intersects with the whole institutional system that guides specific behaviors within the community. Second, accepting a social constructed view of the event shifts the attention from the importance of a single event to the analysis of its place within the collective narratives of a community. The focus of the research thus moves from the material implications of the event to the way it is symbolically constructed, remembered, and deployed within the mnemonic community.

The Narrative Dimension

In addition to the genealogical dimension, the collective memory of a community also exists in the form of shared narratives about the past. Mnemonic narratives are a fundamental part of collective memory because they provide the context against which the present and the future are assessed and understood. This dimension can be thought of as the symbolic layer that recovers the genealogical traces inherited from the past and infuses past, present, and future reality with meaning. More specifically, although the meaningfulness of social reality is produced through the interaction of mnemonic narratives with other forms of remembering and forgetting, the organization of the past of a community is strongly influenced by the narratives members use to remember their past (Wertsch, 2002; Zerubavel, 2003).

Mnemonic narratives thus embody what is remembered from the past, while also reflecting how a community remembers its collective past. It is by telling stories that the events and the "hard facts" of the past are established, organized, and shared within and between mnemonic communities. In addition to the information about the reality of the historical facts, these narratives convey meaning and significance, as well as emotional and ideological contents associated with each mnemonic episode. In this sense, a community remembers and reconstructs the past through the narratives it (re)tells.

In organization studies, one of the first examples of such mnemonic work is Clark's (1972) analysis of the organizational saga. His study shows how narratives about the past are created and shared over time through successive generations of students. These narratives have the power to infuse the experience of the students with meaning and significance. The benefits of an organizational saga lie in its ability to provide unity and cohesiveness as well as pride and loyalty for the members of the group. Clark's (1972) analysis is a clear instance of the uniqueness paradox (Martin, Feldman, Hatch, & Sitkin, 1983). On the one hand, it reflects a similar set of practices and approaches organizational field members engage in to reinforce their distinctive identity from other organizations in the field. On the other, it allows field members to downplay some of their similarities in order to emphasize their legitimacy and categorical fit.

Mnemonic narratives also work as cultural artifacts. They are specific kinds of cultural tools used by members of a community to make sense of and recreate their social realities. They exist in two major forms. First, these narratives are transmitted from the past as preexisting accounts of the past that became inscribed in the memory of the community. Second, they reflect present interests and understandings that actualize and appropriate the past to accomplish things in the present and to construct projected futures. The stock of knowledge (Berger & Luckmann, 1967) of any mnemonic community is constituted by a narrative infrastructure. An infinite number of stories can be stored in the collective memory of the community, even though they are not all stored in a common repository or are evenly distributed among members of the community (Wertsch, 2008). Moreover, there is a hierarchical relation established among the stories themselves with some stories occupying a more central and important role in the field than others. Because the complexity of mnemonic narratives tends to be linked to the complexity of a society (Brockmeier, 2002), the organization of the mnemonic narratives of a community has much to say about the organization of the community itself.

The growing interest of management and organizational scholars in the study of rhetorical history is significant in this respect. Suddaby et al. (2010) defined rhetorical history as the intentional attempt of organizations and other social actors in using the past strategically to deal with environmental pressures and achieve particular goals. While much in social mnemonics can be attributed to emerging dynamics, there is an increasing recognition of the purposive attempts of specific social actors in controlling processes of social remembering (Mena et al., 2016) and using history strategically (Foster, Coraiola, Suddaby, Kroezen, & Chandler, 2016). Beyond the frontiers of the organizations, where the past can be mobilized to generate continuity or change (Brunninge, 2009; Maclean et al., 2014; Ybema, 2014), managers and entrepreneurs also engage in the production of historical narratives with the purpose of signaling compliance with existing categories and institutions (Hills, Voronov, & Hinings, 2013), challenging or defending the status quo (McGaughey, 2013), and creating new markets and collective identities (Lamertz et al., 2016).

Another way of approaching the stock of stories of a mnemonic field can be seen in the distinction between specific and schematic narratives about the past (Wertsch, 2002). Specific narratives are accounts of specific events situated in time and space. They evidence how people make sense of and describe historical facts and events in their day-to-day realities. Schematic narratives, on the other hand, encompass the idea of deeper narrative structures in the form of discursive templates that are shared among people from the same cultural tradition. These two notions bring together the narrative and genealogical dimensions of collective memory. Mnemonic practices not only reflect but also constitute communities of memory. Among these, the narrative practices of memory are the most powerful forms of enacting reality (Brockmeier, 2002). Narratives bring together a linguistic, semiotic, and performative order that integrates past, present, and future into a single structure of meaning. It is through the recurrent retelling of mnemonic narratives that people learn how to think about the world. It is through the stories inherited from the past and stories representing the past that people acquire the cognitive schemes they need to make sense of their collective realities (Brockmeier, 2002; Wertsch, 2002). These narratives provide cognitive schemes and points of collective convergence and agreement around which people structure their thoughts about the world (DiMaggio, 1997; Douglas, 1986).

The notion of schemata (DiMaggio, 1997; Douglas, 1986) brings together the collective and individual, the cultural and cognitive dimensions of memory. Schemata are social representations, sets of labels, and categorization schemes interlinked in broader systems of categories that simplify and organize cognition. In this sense, they have the dual function of representing reality and providing the tools for actors to act upon it. As products of inherited narratives, they provide individuals with cognitive frames of remembering as well as categorical representations of the past. They organize the mnemonic reality of the world as much as they provide the frameworks within which the world should be remembered. As such, together with the informational and factual portrayal of the past they also transmit a system of values and beliefs. Every act of remembering is, in itself, a political act. People remember within groups based on available collective structures of remembering (Halbwachs, 1992). To remember is, in essence, to become once again a member of the group, to reconnect with other members and their way of remembering, to deploy specific categories and schemes of remembering to make sense of one's own reality. To remember is to embrace a particular way of looking at the world from the standpoint of a group's memories. The content of remembering and the schemes of remembering are both infused with, and supportive of, the system of norms and values of the community. As such, the performance of remembering appropriates aspects of a collective past to reflect upon the present and define an agenda for the future while reinforcing existing categories and worldviews. Used as political instruments, these mnemonic narratives are powerful tools that can generate continuity and discontinuity with the collective past, support boundary work and identity work, and legitimate new connections among present, past, and future.

The Moral Dimension

Last, but not least, is the moral component of mnemonic fields. Every representation of the past within the field is a version among many possible others. Even though the past is a singular construct, it cannot be remembered as is (Lowenthal, 1985). Every act of remembering—which also includes historical attempts at remembering—is always biased towards the present (Halbwachs, 1992). At the core of the nexus between remembering and belonging lies the morality of memory. Mnemonic narratives are also normative statements about the past that go beyond questions of what the past is and how people remember. These narratives define the ground rules for past remembrance by specifying who, what, and how things must be remembered. By implication, each narrative determines what from the present should be remembered in the future and how the remembering process should take place in order to preserve the desired memories from the present to future generations. In so doing, these narratives define a moral order that links the present and the future of the community with the actions and decisions that were made in the past.

The idea of a moral dimension within the field can be understood in two different but interrelated senses. The first makes reference to what from the past is remembered, while the second comprises ways of remembering the past. The first deals with the morality of remembered acts. The second evaluates the morality of acts of remembering and forgetting. These two understandings overlap, to the extent that what a community remembers depends on its frameworks of remembrance. The distinction is, nevertheless, important and bears a connection with the other dimensions of the field. We defined the genealogical dimension as a dimension of material practices that have direct consequences for the ways things are done within the field.

This implies the existence of rules, norms, and acceptable, patterned modes of behavior. Whenever a transgression of existing norms happens within the field, this becomes an instance to be remembered and maybe used to prevent violations of that sort from happening again. In contrast are instances when what is ethically sanctioned is remembered. In both cases the normative and narrative aspects of remembering (Assmann, 2011) are present. In the first normative remembering applies to the transgression being narrated. In the second the norms of remembering define how the past should be narrated and how this should be done.

Organization scholars have just recently started paying more attention to the moral dimension of remembering. Organizational historical accountability and the remembering of corporate irresponsibility are examples of the two major issues attached to moral mnemonics. The notion of historical responsibility asks if collective actors should be accountable for actions that were committed in the past (Schrempf-Stirling, Palazzo, & Phillips, 2016). The example of forced labor at Volkswagen during World War II is illustrative (Janssen, 2012b).

Beyond the implications and the responsibility of what was done in the past, mnemonic communities must also be accountable for their mnemonic practices. For instance, Mena et al. (2016) argued that organizations purposefully engage in practices of forgetting in relation to corporate irresponsibility. In addition to their efforts to publicly identify previous misbehaviors and account for immoral or unethical conceptions held in the past, social actors are also responsible for the records and the views they hold about the past. Purposeful forgetting, or even unreflective oblivion, is being commonly questioned and challenged by a growing number of actors. The ability to recover the past, record the present, and provide evidence of the mnemonic efforts engaged in by communities and organizations has become a valuable asset in many different contexts. The ability to revise, update, and resignify the past through narrative accounts provides a context and a rationale for better understanding previously held notions about the past. Moreover, uncovering historical, purposive actions of organizations can help to demonstrate how the strategic intent of some organizations has negatively affected different actors, thus adding to the growing awareness of the historical responsibility of collective actors.

What both Mena and colleagues (2016) and Schrempf-Stirling and colleagues (2016) demonstrate is that the accountability of organizations towards their pasts is a moral responsibility that does not disappear over time (Irwin-Zarecka, 1994). Additionally, organizations also bear a responsibility towards the memory of the field in which they are embedded. To the extent that the field provides the actors with a common identity, it also works as a governance structure that regulates their behavior and organizes collective action. As Douglas (1986) argues, it is the instituted mnemonic system that provides balance and stability within the community, rather than a transcendental entity that controls its members. Together the genealogical, narrative, and moral dimensions provide a spatiotemporal context that integrates the actors within a field. Each dimension provides basic action standards, blocks of meaning, and normative guidelines that organize interaction and orient the practices within the field. These dimensions also create a sense of belonging that connects multiple actors within the community and provides them with a common identity. Consequently, actors are provided with temporal and spatial references that locate the field and the actions they develop within broader contexts of collective action.

Conclusion

In this paper we introduce the idea that organizational fields should be understood as historically contingent processes. We show how dominant empirical approaches tend to adopt the metaphor of organizational fields as either networks of interaction—in other words, fields-as-place—or shared meaning systems—in other words, fields-as-cognition. Both approaches ignore the temporal elements of field structuration and, as a result, fail to demonstrate how systems of meaning emerge from common interactions over time. Our core contribution is to identify temporality, as constituted through time, history, and memory, as the key mechanism through which fields emerge, are maintained, and erode.

We identify three key dimensions through which temporality connects place with cognition: genealogical, narrative and moral. The genealogical dimension focuses analytic attention on the inexorable flow of time—the passage of events, recurrent activities, or material practices and the accumulation of artifacts—as a critical first step in field structuration. Put simply, the genealogical dimension refers to the past as an uninterrupted flow of events and action—often referred to as the "brute facts" of the past—the accretion of which in repeated patterns contributes to early processes of typification and reification as described by Berger & Luckmann (1967).

The narrative dimension refers to the interpretive practices through which certain brute facts of the past are interpreted as significant and elevated to the status of history. The narrative stage is one of signification, through which events form part of the collective memory of a social unit and which—as a consequence of repeating the story of these events—helps to identify the social unit as ontologically distinct. In this stage, memory is an act of social reproduction that is inseparable from the social unit itself. Collective acts of (re)interpreting the past are invariably focused on a project of structuration of the field and its members as a distinct institutional entity. Each narrative of the past is an act of re-membering or co-memoration, in which actors are positioned in a meaningful and significant role in the uninterrupted flow of the past. It is in this stage of structuration that memory is used to bind actors to place.

The moral dimension of the field refers to a final temporal stage of field structuration in which collective memory is used not only to identify actors, practices, and events as members of a common place, but also acquires a normative status of being legitimate. The moral or normative dimension of field structuration encompasses the institutionalized remembrance or forgetting of the good and the bad. It also refers to the moral appropriateness of certain types of remembering or forgetting.

In sequence, these three dimensions describe the important analytic role offered by viewing fields as mnemonic structures. As we observe, events in time shift ontological status from brute facts of the past, to interpretive significance as history, and then to moral value as myth. We also theorize how memory is used to create first a sense of place and then a sense of meaning over time. Indeed, the three dimensions also describe a schematic process of three stages through which fields produce collective meaning over time—first, how the past is experienced in real time; second, how these experiences are narrated and shared with the next generation; and finally, how these stories are interpreted and reinterpreted through the lens of the shared present and a prospective common future. By acknowledging fields as historically contingent processes and identifying collective remembering as the key interpretive mechanism through which processes of typification and signification occur, time, history, and memory are seen as a vast and unexplored landscape for achieving a better understanding of organizational fields and processes of institutionalization.

References

Adorisio, A. L. M. (2014). Organizational remembering as narrative: 'Storying' the past in banking. *Organization, 21*, 463–476. doi:https://doi.org/10.1177/1350508414527248

Aksu, E. (2009). Global collective memory: Conceptual difficulties of an appealing idea. *Global Society, 23*, 317–332. doi:https://doi.org/10.1080/13600820902958584

Albert, S., & Whetten, D. A. (1985). Organizational identity. In L. L. Cummings & B. M. Staw (Eds.), Research in organizational behavior (pp. 263–295). *Research in Organizational Behavior*: Vol. 7. Oxford, UK: Elsevier Science & Technology.

Alexander, J. C., Eyerman, R., Giesen, B., Smelser, N. J., & Sztompka, P. (2004). *Cultural trauma and collective identity*. Berkley: University of California Press.

Anand, N., & Jones, B. C. (2008). Tournament rituals, category dynamics, and field configuration: The case of the Booker Prize. *Journal of Management Studies, 45*, 1036–1060. doi:https://doi.org/10.1111/j.1467-6486.2008.00782.x

Anand, N., & Peterson, R. A. (2000). When market information constitutes fields: Sensemaking of markets in the commercial music industry. *Organization Science, 11*, 270–284. doi:https://doi.org/10.1287/orsc.11.3.270.12502

Anand, N., & Watson, M. R. (2004). Tournament rituals in the evolution of fields: The case of the Grammy Awards. *Academy of Management Journal, 47*, 59–80. doi:https://doi.org/10.2307/20159560

Anteby, M., & Molnár, V. (2012). Collective memory meets organizational identity: Remembering to forget in a firm's rhetorical history. *Academy of Management Journal, 55*, 515–540. doi:https://doi.org/10.5465/amj.2010.0245

Assmann, J. (2011). *Cultural memory and early civilization: Writing, remembrance, and political imagination*. Cambridge, UK: Cambridge University Press.

Barley, S. R., & Tolbert, P. S. (1997). Institutionalization and structuration: Studying the links between action and institution. *Organization Studies, 18*, 93–117. doi:https://doi.org/10.1177/017084069701800106

Berger, P. L., & Luckmann, T. (1967). *The social construction of reality: A treatise in the sociology of knowledge*. London: Penguin Books.

Booth, C., Clark, P., Delahaye, A., Procter, S., & Rowlinson, M. (2007). Accounting for the dark side of corporate history: Organizational culture perspectives and the Bertelsmann case. *Critical Perspectives on Accounting, 18*, 625–644. doi:https://doi.org/10.1016/j.cpa.2007.03.012

Brockmeier, J. (2002). Remembering and forgetting: Narrative as cultural memory. *Culture & Psychology, 8*, 15–43. doi:https://doi.org/10.1177/1354067X0281002

Brunninge, O. (2009). Using history in organizations: How managers make purposeful reference to history in strategy processes. *Journal of Organizational Change Management, 22*, 8–26. doi:https://doi.org/10.1108/09534810910933889

Clark, B. R. (1972). The organizational saga in higher education. *Administrative Science Quarterly, 17*, 178–184. doi:https://doi.org/10.2307/2393952

Connerton, P. (1989). *How societies remember*. Cambridge, UK: Cambridge University Press.

Dacin, M. T., Munir, K., & Tracey, P. (2010). Formal dining at Cambridge colleges: Linking ritual performance and institutional maintenance. *Academy of Management Journal, 53*, 1393–1418. doi:https://doi.org/10.5465/AMJ.2010.57318388

Dacin, M. T., Ventresca, M. J., & Beal, B. D. (1999). The embeddedness of organizations: Dialogue & directions. *Journal of Management, 25*, 317–356. doi:https://doi.org/10.1177/014920639902500304

Decker, S. (2014). Solid intentions: An archival ethnography of corporate architecture and organizational remembering. *Organization, 21*, 514–542. doi:https://doi.org/10.1177/1350508414527252

Desai, V. M. (2011). Mass media and massive failures: Determining organizational efforts to defend field legitimacy following crises. *Academy of Management Journal, 54*, 263–278. doi:https://doi.org/10.5465/AMJ.2011.60263082

DiMaggio, P. J. (1986). Structural analysis of organizational fields: A blockmodel approach. In B. Staw (Ed.), *Research in organizational behavior* (pp. 335–370). Research in Organizational Behavior: Vol. 8. Oxford, UK: Elsevier Science & Technology.

DiMaggio, P. J. (1997). Culture and cognition. *Annual Review of Sociology, 23*, 263–287. doi:https://doi.org/10.1146/annurev.soc.23.1.263

DiMaggio, P. J., & Powell, W. W. (1983). The iron cage revisited: Institutional isomorphism and collective rationality in organizational fields. *American Sociological Review, 48*, 147–160. Retrieved from www.jstor.org/stable/2095101.

Douglas, M. (1986). *How institutions think*. Syracuse: Syracuse University Press.

Evan, W. M. (1965). Toward a theory of inter-organizational relations. *Management Science, 11*, B-217-B-230. doi:https://doi.org/10.1287/mnsc.11.10.B217

Feldman, R. M., & Feldman, S. P. (2006). What links the chain: An essay on organizational remembering as practice. *Organization, 13*, 861–887. doi:https://doi.org/10.1177/1350508406068500

Fligstein, N. (1990). *The transformation of corporate control*. Cambridge: Harvard University Press.

Foster, W. M., Coraiola, D. M., Suddaby, R., Kroezen, J., & Chandler, D. (2016). The strategic use of historical narratives: A theoretical framework. *Business History*. doi:https://doi.org/10.1080/00076791.2016.1224234

Foster, W. M., Suddaby, R., Minkus, A., & Wiebe, E. (2011). History as social memory assets: The example of Tim Hortons. *Management & Organizational History, 6*, 101–120. doi:https://doi.org/10.1177/1744935910387027

Galaskiewicz, J., & Wasserman, S. (1989). Mimetic processes within an interorganizational field: An empirical test. *Administrative Science Quarterly, 34*, 454–479. doi:https://doi.org/10.2307/2393153

Garud, R. (2008). Conferences as venues for the configuration of emerging organizational fields: The case of cochlear implants. *Journal of Management Studies, 45*, 1061–1088. doi:https://doi.org/10.1111/j.1467-6486.2008.00783.x

Garud, R., & Karnøe, P. (Eds.) (2001). *Path dependence and creation*. Mahwah: Lawrence Erlbaum Associates.

Garud, R., Kumaraswamy, A., & Karnøe, P. (2010). Path dependence or path creation? *Journal of Management Studies, 47*, 760–774. doi:https://doi.org/10.1111/j.1467-6486.2009.00914.x

Gibbons, D. E. (2004). Network structure and innovation ambiguity effects on diffusion in dynamic organizational fields. *Academy of Management Journal, 47*, 938–951. doi:https://doi.org/10.2307/20159633

Giddens, A. (1984). The constitution of society: *Outline of the theory of structuration*. Cambridge, UK: Polity Press.

Glückler, J. (2013). Knowledge, networks and space: Connectivity and the problem of non-interactive learning. *Regional Studies, 47,* 880–894. doi:https://doi.org/10.1080/00343404.2013.7 79659

Glückler, J., Lazega, E., & Hammer, I. (2017c). Exploring the interaction of space and networks in the creation of knowledge: An introduction. In J. Glückler, E. Lazega, & I. Hammer (Eds.), *Knowledge and networks* (pp. 1–21). Knowledge and Space: Vol. 11. Dordrecht: Springer.

Glynn, M. A. (2008). Configuring the field of play: How hosting the Olympic Games impacts civic community. *Journal of Management Studies, 45,* 1117–1146. doi:https://doi.org/10.1111/j.1467-6486.2008.00785.x

Granovetter, M. (1985). Economic action and social structure: The problem of embeddedness. *American Journal of Sociology, 91,* 481–510. doi:https://doi.org/10.1086/228311

Greenwood, R., & Suddaby, R. (2006). Institutional entrepreneurship in mature fields: The big five accounting firms. *Academy of Management Journal, 49,* 27–48. doi:https://doi.org/10.5465/AMJ.2006.20785498

Halbwachs, M. (1992). *On collective memory* (L. A. Coser, Trans.). Chicago: University of Chicago Press.

Hannan, M. T., & Freeman, J. (1989). *Organizational ecology.* New York: Harvard University Press.

Hardy, C., & Maguire, S. (2010). Discourse, field-configuring events, and change in organizations and institutional fields: Narratives of DDT and the Stockholm Convention. *Academy of Management Journal, 53,* 1365–1392. doi:https://doi.org/10.5465/AMJ.2010.57318384

Hills, S., Voronov, M., & Hinings, C. R. B. (2013). Putting new wine in old bottles: Utilizing rhetorical history to overcome stigma associated with a previously dominant logic. In M. Lounsbury & E. Boxenbaum (Eds.), *Institutional logics in action, Part B* (pp. 99–137). Research in the Sociology of Organizations: Vol. 39B. Bingley: Emerald Group.

Hoffman, A. J. (1999). Institutional evolution and change: Environmentalism and the U.S. chemical industry. *Academy of Management Journal, 42,* 351–371. doi:https://doi.org/10.2307/257008

Irwin-Zarecka, I. (1994). *Frames of remembrance: The dynamics of collective memory.* New Brunswick: Transaction.

Janssen, C. I. (2012a). Addressing corporate ties to slavery: Corporate apologia in a discourse of reconciliation. *Communication Studies, 63,* 18–35. doi:https://doi.org/10.1080/10510974.2011.627974

Janssen, C. I. (2012b). Corporate historical responsibility (CHR): Addressing a corporate past of forced labor at Volkswagen. *Journal of Applied Communication Research, 41,* 64–83. doi:https://doi.org/10.1080/00909882.2012.731698

Kenis, P., & Knoke, D. (2002). How organizational field networks shape interorganizational tie-formation rates. *Academy of Management Review, 27,* 275–293. doi:https://doi.org/10.5465/AMR.2002.6588029

Lamertz, K., Foster, W. M., Coraiola, D. M., & Kroezen, J. (2016). New identities from remnants of the past: An examination of the history of beer brewing in Ontario and the recent emergence of craft breweries. *Business History, 58,* 796–828. doi:https://doi.org/10.1080/00076791.2015.1065819

Leblebici, H., Salancik, G. R., Copay, A., & King, T. (1991). Institutional change and the transformation of interorganizational fields: An organizational history of the U.S. radio broadcasting industry. *Administrative Science Quarterly, 36,* 333–363. doi:https://doi.org/10.2307/2393200

Lowenthal, D. (1985). *The past is a foreign country.* Cambridge, UK: Cambridge University Press.

Maclean, M., Harvey, C., Sillince, J. A. A., & Golant, B. D. (2014). Living up to the past? Ideological sensemaking in organizational transition. *Organization, 21,* 543–567. doi:https://doi.org/10.1177/1350508414527247

Mai, D. (2015). *Organizational cultures of remembrance: Exploring the relationships between memory, identity, and image in an automobile company.* Media and Cultural Memory: Vol. 21. Berlin: Walter de Gruyter.

Martin, J., Feldman, M. S., Hatch, M. J., & Sitkin, S. B. (1983). The uniqueness paradox in organizational stories. *Administrative Science Quarterly, 28,* 438–453. doi:https://doi.org/10.2307/2392251

McGahan, A. M., & Porter, M. E. (1997). How much does industry matter, really? *Strategic Management Journal, 18,* 15–30. Retrieved from www.jstor.org/stable/3088208.

McGaughey, S. L. (2013). Institutional entrepreneurship in North American lightning protection standards: Rhetorical history and unintended consequences of failure. *Business History, 55,* 73–97. doi:https://doi.org/10.1080/00076791.2012.687537

Mena, S., Rintamäki, J., Fleming, P., & Spicer, A. (2016). On the forgetting of corporate irresponsibility. *Academy of Management Review, 41,* 720–738. doi:https://doi.org/10.5465/amr.2014.0208

Meyer, J. W., & Rowan, B. (1977). Institutionalized organizations: Formal structure as myth and ceremony. *American Journal of Sociology, 83,* 340–363. doi:https://doi.org/10.1086/226550

Mills, C. W. (1940). Situated actions and vocabularies of motive. *American Sociological Review, 5,* 904–913. Retrieved from www.jstor.org/stable/2084524

Ocasio, W., Mauskapf, M., & Steele, C. W. J. (2016). History, society, and institutions: The role of collective memory in the emergence and evolution of societal logics. *Academy of Management Review, 41,* 676–699. doi:https://doi.org/10.5465/amr.2014.0183

Olick, J. K. (1999). Collective memory: The two cultures. *Sociological Theory, 17,* 333–348. https://doi.org/10.1111/0735-2751.00083

Olick, J. K., & Robbins, J. (1998). Social memory studies: From "collective memory" to the historical sociology of mnemonic practices. *Annual Review of Sociology, 24,* 105–140. doi:https://doi.org/10.1146/annurev.soc.24.1.105

Panitz, R., & Glückler, J. (2017). Rewiring global networks at local events: Congresses in the stock photo trade. *Global Networks, 17,* 147–168. doi:https://doi.org/10.1111/glob.12134

Porter, M. E. (1980). *Competitive strategy: Techniques for analyzing industries and competitors.* New York: Free Press.

Powell, W., Koput, K., & Doerr, L. (1996). Interorganizational collaboration and the locus of innovation: Networks of learning in biotechnology. *Administrative Science Quarterly, 41,* 116–145. doi:https://doi.org/10.2307/2393988

Rao, H., Monin, P., & Durand, R. (2003). Institutional change in Toque Ville: Nouvelle Cuisine as an identity movement in french gastronomy. *American Journal of Sociology, 108,* 795–843. doi:https://doi.org/10.1086/367917

Rowlinson, M., Booth, C., Clark, P., Delahaye, A., & Procter, S. (2010). Social remembering and organizational memory. *Organization Studies, 31,* 69–87. doi:https://doi.org/10.1177/0170840609347056

Rowlinson, M., & Hassard, J. (1993). The invention of corporate culture: A history of the histories of Cadbury. *Human Relations, 46,* 299–326. doi:https://doi.org/10.1177/001872679304600301

Schneiberg, M. (2007). What's on the path? Path dependence, organizational diversity and the problem of institutional change in the US economy, 1900–1950. *Socio-Economic Review, 5,* 47–80. doi:https://doi.org/10.1093/ser/mw1006

Schrempf-Stirling, J., Palazzo, G., & Phillips, R. (2016). Historic corporate social responsibility. *Academy of Management Review, 41,* 700–719. doi:https://doi.org/10.5465/amr.2014.0137

Schultz, M., & Hernes, T. (2013). A temporal perspective on organizational identity. *Organization Science, 24,* 1–21. doi:https://doi.org/10.2307/23362097

Schultz, M., Maguire, S., Langley, A., & Tsoukas, H. (Eds.). (2012). Constructing identity in and around organizations. Oxford, UK: Oxford University Press.

Schwartz, B. (1997). Collective memory and history: How Abraham Lincoln became a symbol of racial equality. *The Sociological Quarterly, 38,* 469–496. doi:https://doi.org/10.1111/j.1533-8525.1997.tb00488.x

Scott, W. R. (1994). Conceptualizing organizational fields: Linking organizations and societal systems. In H.-U. Derlien, U. Gerhardt, & F. W. Scharpf (Eds.), *Systemrationalität und Partialinteresse: Festschrift für Renate Mayntz* [Systems rationality and partial interest: Festschrift for Renate Mayntz] (pp. 203–219). Baden-Baden: Nomos.

Scott, W. R. (2008). *Institutions and organizations: Ideas and interests* (3rd ed.). Los Angeles: Sage.

Scott, W. R., & Davis, G. F. (2007). *Organizations and organizing: Rational, natural, and open system perspectives*. Upper Saddle River: Pearson Prentice Hall.

Scott, W. R., & Meyer, J. W. (1991). The organization of societal sectors: Propositions and early evidence. In W. W. Powell & P. J. DiMaggio (Eds.), *The new institutionalism in organizational analysis* (pp. 108–140). Chicago: University of Chicago Press.

Shils, E. (1981). *Tradition*. Chicago: University of Chicago Press.

Sine, W. D., & David, R. J. (2003). Environmental jolts, institutional change, and the creation of entrepreneurial opportunity in the US electric power industry. *Research Policy, 32*, 185–207. doi:https://doi.org/10.1016/S0048-7333(02)00096-3

Stinchcombe, A. L. (1965). Social structure and organizations. In J. G. March (Ed.), *Handbook of organizations* (pp. 142–193). Chicago: Rand McNally.

Sturken, M. (1997). *Tangled memories: The Vietnam War, the AIDS epidemic, and the politics of remembering*. Berkeley: University of California Press.

Suddaby, R. (2013). Institutional theory. In E. H. Kessler (Ed.), *Encyclopedia of management theory*: Vol. 2 (pp. 380–384). Los Angeles: Sage.

Suddaby, R. (2016). Toward a historical consciousness: Following the historic turn in management thought. *M@n@gement, 19*, 46–60. doi:https://doi.org/10.3917/mana.191.0046

Suddaby, R., & Foster, W. M. (2017). History and organizational change. *Journal of Management, 43*, 19–38. doi:https://doi.org/10.1177/0149206316675031

Suddaby, R., Foster, W. M., & Mills, A. J. (2014). Historical institutionalism. In M. Bucheli, & R. D. Wadhwani (Eds.), *Organizations in time: History, theory, methods* (pp. 100–123). Oxford, UK: Oxford University Press.

Suddaby, R., Foster, W. M., & Trank, C. Q. (2010). Rhetorical history as a source of competitive advantage. In J. A. C. Baum & J. Lampel (Eds.), *The globalization of strategy research* (pp. 147–173). Advances in Strategic Management: Vol. 27. Bingley: Emerald Group.

Suddaby, R., Viale, T., & Gendron, Y. (2016). Reflexivity: The role of embedded social position and entrepreneurial social skill in processes of field level change. *Research in Organizational Behavior, 36*, 225–245. doi:https://doi.org/10.1016/j.riob.2016.02.001

Swidler, A. (1986). Culture in action: Symbols and strategies. *American Sociological Review, 51*, 273–286. Retrieved from www.jstor.org/stable/2095521

Sydow, J., & Schreyögg, G. (2013). *Self-reinforcing processes in and among organizations*. Hampshire: Palgrave Macmillan.

Sydow, J., Schreyögg, G., & Koch, J. (2009). Organizational path dependence: Opening the black box. *Academy of Management Review, 34*, 689–709. doi:https://doi.org/10.5465/AMR.2009.44885978

Tilcsik, A., & Marquis, C. (2013). Punctuated generosity: How mega-events and natural disasters affect corporate philanthropy in U.S. communities. *Administrative Science Quarterly, 58*, 111–148. doi:https://doi.org/10.1177/0001839213475800

Tushman, M. L., & Anderson, P. (1986). Technological discontinuities and organizational environments. *Administrative Science Quarterly, 31*, 439–465. doi:https://doi.org/10.2307/2392832

Uzzi, B. (1996). The sources and consequences of embeddedness for the economic performance of organizations: The network effect. *American Sociological Review, 61*, 674–698. Retrieved from www.jstor.org/stable/2096399

Vergne, J.-P., & Durand, R. (2010). The missing link between the theory and empirics of path dependence: Conceptual clarification, testability issue, and methodological implications. *Journal of Management Studies, 47*, 736–759. doi:https://doi.org/10.1111/j.1467-6486.2009.00913.x

Walsh, J. P., & Ungson, G. R. (1991). Organizational memory. *The Academy of Management Review, 16*, 57–91. doi:https://doi.org/10.5465/AMR.1991.4278992

Weber, K., & Dacin, M. T. (2011). The cultural construction of organizational life: Introduction to the special issue. *Organization Science, 22*, 287–298. doi:https://doi.org/10.1287/orsc.1100.0632

Weber, M. (1978). *Economy and society: An outline of interpretive sociology* (G. Roth & C. Wittich, Trans.). Berkeley: University of California Press. (Original work published 1922)

Wertsch, J. V. (2002). *Voices of collective remembering.* Cambridge, UK: Cambridge University Press.

Wertsch, J. V. (2008). The narrative organization of collective memory. *Ethos, 36,* 120–135. doi:https://doi.org/10.1111/j.1548-1352.2008.00007.x

Wright, A. L., & Zammuto, R. F. (2013). Wielding the willow: Processes of institutional change in English county cricket. *Academy of Management Journal, 56,* 308–330. doi:https://doi.org/10.5465/amj.2010.0656

Ybema, S. (2010). Talk of change: Temporal contrasts and collective identities. *Organization Studies, 31,* 481–503. doi:https://doi.org/10.1177/0170840610372205

Ybema, S. (2014). The invention of transitions: History as a symbolic site for discursive struggles over organizational change. *Organization, 21,* 495–513. doi:https://doi.org/10.1177/1350508414527255

Zerubavel, E. (1996). Social memories: Steps to a sociology of the past. *Qualitative Sociology, 19,* 283–299. doi:https://doi.org/10.1007/BF02393273

Zerubavel, E. (2003). *Time maps: Collective memory and the social shape of the past.* Chicago: University of Chicago Press.

Zietsma, C., Groenewegen, P., Logue, D., & Hinings, C. R. (2017). Field or fields? Building the scaffolding for cumulation of research on institutional fields. *The Academy of Management Annals, 11,* 391–450. doi:https://doi.org/10.5465/annals.2014.0052

Zietsma, C., & Lawrence, T. B. (2010). Institutional work in the transformation of an organizational field: The interplay of boundary work and practice work. *Administrative Science Quarterly, 55,* 189–221. doi:https://doi.org/10.2189/asqu.2010.55.2.189

Zilber, T. B. (2002). Institutionalization as an interplay between actions, meanings, and actors: The case of a rape crisis center in Israel. *Academy of Management Journal, 45,* 234–254. doi:https://doi.org/10.2307/3069294

Zilber, T. B. (2006). The work of the symbolic in institutional processes: Translations of rational myths in Israeli high tech. *Academy of Management Journal, 49,* 281–303. doi:https://doi.org/10.5465/AMJ.2006.20786073

Zilber, T. B. (2007). Stories and the discursive dynamics of institutional entrepreneurship: The case of Israeli high-tech after the bubble. *Organization Studies, 28,* 1035–1054. doi:https://doi.org/10.1177/0170840607078113

Zundel, M., Holt, R., & Popp, A. (2016). Using history in the creation of organizational identity. *Management & Organizational History, 11,* 1–25. doi:https://doi.org/10.1080/17449359.2015.1124042

Chapter 4
Economics of Convention and its Perspective on Knowledge and Institutions

Rainer Diaz-Bone

Knowledge and institutions can be conceptually related in different ways, and different institutional approaches offer different perspectives on this relation. This chapter draws attention to the French pragmatist institutionalism of the so-called economics of convention. I present the core concepts and methodological position of this approach and explore its perspective on knowledge, conventions, and institutions. Thereby, the economic institutionalism of transaction-cost economics (Ronald Coase and Oliver Williamson) has been influential in the field of economics, and Williamson's (1985) theory in particular has been important for the economics of convention as a counterpart.

Considering the relation between institutions and knowledge from the standpoint of acting and coordinating actors, one may question the idea of institutions as external constraints on action and coordination. One may also challenge the idea of pregiven meanings that institutions have for actors as it is thought in Williamson's (1985) transaction-cost approach and the economic institutionalism of North (1990). For economics of convention, the situational handling and meaning of institutions for coordinating actors is regarded as incomplete. This view points to the competence of actors to tap into deeper culturally established knowledge frames—called *conventions*—to interpret and deal with institutions in pragmatic situations. This position is the pragmatic process of "transferring" the institution into the process of action and coordination. It can be referred to as an internal conception of action and coordination.

The approach of economics of convention has been developed since the early 1980s in Paris. Although referring to economics, it is both general socioeconomic and sociological in character (Batifoulier, Bessis, Ghirardello, de Larquier, & Rémillon, 2016; Boltanski & Chiapello, 1999/2005; Boltanski & Thévenot,

R. Diaz-Bone (✉)
Department of Sociology, University of Lucerne, Lucerne, Switzerland
e-mail: rainer.diazbone@unilu.ch

J. Glückler et al. (eds.), *Knowledge and Institutions*, Knowledge and Space 13,
https://doi.org/10.1007/978-3-319-75328-7_4

1991/2006; Diaz-Bone, 2018; Favereau & Lazega, 2002; Knoll, 2015; Orléan, 2014; Storper & Salais, 1997).

Economics of convention is not a paradigm. It started as a scientific movement of French scholars working on a constellation of related problems and topics. From the outset, it has been transdisciplinary. This chapter begins by introducing the core theoretical concepts of the economics of convention, focusing on quality conventions as a key concept (first section) and emphasizing some of the approach's special features (second section). I then turn to the perspective that the economics of convention takes on institutions and knowledge (third section) and delineate the consequences of readjusting the notions of institution and knowledge (fourth and fifth sections). Economics of convention has generated many studies on regional economies, including Storper and Salais's *Worlds of Production* (1997), which compared logics of economic coordination in different regions. This model and some newer developments, such as the concept of global value chains, are then related to regional economic coordination (the sixth section). Because the economics of convention has proven capable of coping with global economic coordination as well, attention thereafter turns to development of the concept of global value chains to perform this task (seventh section). The chapter concludes with a summary of the main arguments and principles relevant for reflection on knowledge and institutions.

Theoretical Architecture of Economics of Convention and its Core Concepts

The best way to approach the economics of convention is to regard it as a scientific movement embedded in both French structuralism and sociological pragmatism (Diaz-Bone, 2018; Dosse, 1995/1999), the two megaparadigms of the social sciences.[1] The analytical focus of economics of convention is on actors coordinating in situations where they have to achieve a common good, have a common goal, and need to resolve uncertainty about involved qualities and meanings.

Coordination is centered on the problem of manufacturing products, providing services, or generating other kinds of outcomes that can be valued and evaluated. Actors have to agree on the criteria and principles governing this valuation and evaluation and the qualities that characterize outcomes of their coordination. One core concept in this regard is the notion of convention. Conventions are not simply traditions, customs, or standards—as in Max Weber's sociology, for example (Weber, 1922/1978). The notion of convention in the economics of convention is complex, and it excludes most of the meanings the word has in other social theory. Conventions are not merely external constraints on or given facts for individual decision-making. As Storper (1997) observed:

---

[1] On structuralism see Dosse (1991/1998a, 1992/1998b, 1995/1999); on pragmatism, Kuklick (2001).

[T]he social science of conventions rejects the distinction, common to modern economics, between decision-making rationality—as the ways in which individuals react to information—and action rooted in the pragmatic and cognitive acts of comprehension, understanding, or interpretation. It is not simply that different versions of comprehension, understanding or interpretation generate different "parameters" for decision-making in the form of different preference schedules or different things to be maximized, but that action leading to coordination is often necessarily a process of mutual comprehension, understanding, and commonality of interpretation between actors under conditions of uncertainty. . . . Conventions are much more than mere cognitive, cultural, or psychological skills that permit actors to survive in markets. When actors undertake an activity, they do so with the expectation that they have a framework of action in common with other actors engaged in that activity. (p. 45)

Conventions can be defined as culturally established frames for the interpretation and evaluation of "what is going on" in situations. They are part of the implicit collective knowledge present in situations, and the skills of how to apply them are part of the competencies that actors have. Actors can thus draw on conventions as ways to engage and coordinate in situations to achieve a common goal. These goals can be conceived of as the collective production of qualities (e.g., goods and processes) and the realization of common goods. It is important to complete this definition by adding four aspects. The first is the view, as taken in economics of convention, that there is a plurality of existing conventions. The second is the approach's view of situations equipped with objects (e.g., instruments, machines, media) and "cognitive forms" for information on which actors rely for their action and coordination. The third important complementary aspect is that actors are regarded as being competent to mobilize conventions in situations and to evaluate conventions critically as appropriate or inappropriate (Storper & Salais, 1997). The fourth is the emphasis that conventions are practical normative orders of worth that function as deeper logics for interpretation and evaluation but also for critique and justification of qualities and, hence, as logics of coordination intended to achieve a common good (Boltanski & Thévenot, 1991/2006).

From the standpoint of economics of convention, conventions are necessary because the meaning of and interpretive approach to the relevance, working, legitimacy, adequacy, and, ultimately, use of institutions is not determined. This meaning of institutions is situationally incomplete. Institutions such as rules, contracts, laws, money, and language are regarded as incomplete because they (and their uses) are pragmatically embedded in situations in which the meaning of the institution for the precise application in a given setting cannot be specified ex ante. Actors must therefore decide on the adequacy of rules, contracts, laws, formal structures, or formal procedures—completing the situational meaning. To be clear, the notion of institution in the economics of convention is rather restricted to a formal and denotated (i.e., written down and formally representable) concept of institution. One may speak of a constrained concept. Institutions are thought of as the manifest dispositives for coordination. In this sense economics of convention shares a somewhat narrow conception of institution with economic institutionalisms, such as Williamson's (1985). However, in many other institutionalist approaches (which are represented in several of the contributions to this book), the concept of institution is understood more broadly to include informal structures as well, or what is called *convention* in economics of convention. Both approaches to defining institutions have their advantages and disadvantages. I show later in this chapter that both the narrower definition of institution in economics of convention and that definition's relation to the concept of convention bring in methodological strategies.

Researchers in the tradition of economics of convention try to adopt the standpoint of actors in situations of coordination in order to reconstruct actors' interpretations and the constellation of conventions that actors rely on when coordinating. Their notion of institution therefore cannot be regarded as a meso- or macroinstitutionalism, such as the notion of sociological neoinstitutionalism (see Meyer & Rowan, 1977, and the contributions in Powell & DiMaggio, 1991).

In economics of convention, it is important to see situations as equipped with objects and collective cognitive forms. Examples of these cognitive dispositives are numerical displays in factories or stories in small family enterprises. The numerical form is characteristic for the industrial world; the narrative form, for the domestic. As Eymard-Duvernay and Thévenot (1983) have demonstrated, collectivities, organizations, and enterprises need to invest not only in tools, machines, and other forms of material equipment but also in cognitive forms so that collectivities can recognize relevant information. In addition, the scope of coordination in time and space is extended by forms. This kind of investment is called *form investment*, or investment in forms.

Coordination in real situations is structured by a *plurality* of conventions (Boltanski & Thévenot, 1991/2006; Diaz-Bone, 2018). The economics of convention is thus really a pragmatist approach, for pragmatism claimed for the recognition of ontological and political pluralism early on (James, 1909). The economics of convention rejects the idea that there is one best way to coordinate in situations of economic production, distribution, and consumption. Actors are considered competent to judge the appropriateness of conventions, to switch conventions, and to forge stable compromises out of different conventions or to criticize other actors grounding their critique on different conventions. Table 4.1 presents a set of eight important quality conventions as orders of worth and as logics of interpretation, evaluation, and coordination. The set is not arbitrary; these quality conventions are an established part of the sociocultural knowledge in western societies. Boltanski and Thévenot (1991/2006) presented a list of criteria ("axioms") to decide which "logic" may be regarded as a quality convention (p. 74).[2]

---

[2] There are six axioms that specify a logic of coordination as a convention that can be mobilized or enacted by a community (see Boltanski & Thévenot, 1991/2006, pp. 74–78). The first axiom ("the principle of common humanity") holds that it is possible to identify members of the community who can apply the convention to establish equivalencies (not to be confused with equality) between these members. The second axiom ("the principle of differentiation") postulates that the different states (of value or worth) are possible for the members, based on the convention. The third axiom ("common dignity") states that all members of the community have the same power to access the different states in it. The fourth axiom ("the order of worth") claims that the different possible states are ordered (in terms of value or worth). The fifth axiom ("the investment formula") postu-

Table 4.1 Eight conventions

Convention	Worth/Quality	Evaluation criteria	Information format	Persons' qualification	Interpersonal relation
Domestic	Tradition, handcraft	Esteem, reputation	Oral, exemplary	Authority and flexibility	Trust
Market	Demand orientation, free exchange	Price	Money units	Desire, purchasing power	Exchange
Industrial	Planning and standardization	Efficiency, productivity	Measurable criteria, statistics	Professional, expertise	Functional link
Inspired	Grace, nonconformity, creativity	Originality, innovative capacity	Newness, emotionality	Creativity, ingenuity	Passion
Opinion	Renown	Amount of recognition	Semiotics	Celebrity	Recognition
Civic	Collective interest	Relevance for collectivity	Formal, official	Equality	Solidarity
Green	Ecology (its integrity)	Environmental compatibility	Narrative	Ecological knowledge	Responsibility
Network	Activity, self-management	Successful projects	Meetings	Capacity for teamwork	Project orientation

Source: Adapted from Diaz-Bone (2018, chap. 5). Copyright 2018 by author and Springer Fachmedien Wiesbaden

Critique for economics of convention is an everyday practice. Qualities are not only constructed and recognized but also questioned and tested. Critique thereby refers to quality conventions and objects. Critique and tests bring tensions into situations (Boltanski & Thévenot, 1991/2006). Both also discover the empirical normativity of coordination. When it comes to pragmatism, normativity is not an issue left up to philosophers. Actors apply convention-based evaluations to persons, things, and actions, so these evaluations refer to the norms and values that conventions represent. Ordinary actors are thus competent in the business of everyday moralities. The daily quarrels and disputes about rights and wrongs center on questions of "appropriateness and justice" (*justesse et justice*) (Boltanski & Thévenot, 1989). All in all, economics of convention has a clear antipositivistic claim: Norms and values are enacted and materialized in situations by the convention-based co-constructions of qualities, objects, and forms. Norms and values are empirical facts in situations; they are *not* metaphysical or philosophical "add-ons". Figure 4.1 presents the concepts of economics of convention and their relations to each other.

---

lates that the benefit of higher states are linked to costs and sacrifices, so self-centered pleasures have to be abandoned. According to the sixth axiom ("the common good"), higher states are related to a higher degree of happiness and goods and, hence, are closer to a common good.

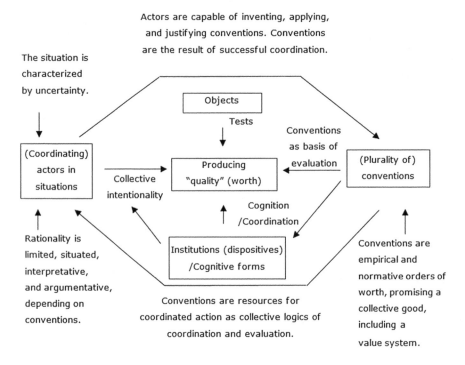

Fig. 4.1 Core concepts of economics of convention. Source: Design by author

Why Convention Theory?

Because economics of convention is influenced by structuralism and pragmatism, it is able to deal with theoretical aspects of action and practices as well as with aspects of cultural frames and institutions. It is not a single-issue approach. It cannot be reduced to the analysis of conventions alone (as shown in the previous section). To answer the question of why it has to offer innovative elements in the interdisciplinary field of institutionalism, consider the following four aspects.

Reintegrating Empirical and Normative Analysis

To understand the relevance of economics of convention, one has to recognize its interest: to grasp coordinating practices in situations wherein actors mobilize realities with qualities relying on normative orders. These qualities are closely linked to common goods and applied moralities. Economics of convention is therefore about social ontologies and social values—both are constructed and related to each other by competent actors in situations. The claim made by economics of convention vis-à-vis its counterpart, Williamson's (1985) economic institutionalism, is that economics of convention is an institutional approach, which reintegrates empirical and normative concepts in the analysis of the empirical coordination of actors who rely on everyday normativities for the purposes of production, distribution, and consumption. Its character is therefore general. It combines pragmatist and structuralist perspectives but also includes ordinary normativities as empirical realities (Boltanski & Thévenot, 1991/2006; Storper & Salais, 1997).

Realizing a Transdisciplinary Practice in Institutional Analysis

As mentioned in the introduction, the character of the economics of convention is transdisciplinarity. It integrates heterodox economics with pragmatic sociology,[3] economic sociology, economic geography, and historical institutionalism without reducing the phenomena under study to only one principle. Today, many highly specialized and single-principle disciplines stand to lose their scientific objects of study. It is important to see that these specializations often coincide with the separation of methodological cultures, that is, the division of quantitative and qualitative methods. The economics of convention is different in these regards because it integrates the experience of many scientific fields and combines a full range of quantitative and qualitative methods that are divorced in other approaches (Diaz-Bone & Salais, 2011, 2012). Moreover, it integrates the analysis of law into its institutionalism. It does not so through economic institutionalism and the law-and-economics approach (Posner, 2007), because in this approach, law is studied almost only as an external constraint on economic coordination. With economics of convention, by contrast, law is internal to action and coordination and must be enacted by convention-based processes of interpretation.

In most (national) sociologies, the subdisciplines of economic sociology, institutionalism, and sociology of law are separated by the way the discipline is organized and its research is published and taught. In that sense economics of convention is different because it combines the analysis of law, labor and economic institutions, economic valuation, quantification and classification, and economic coordination as related phenomena whose analysis has to include the transdisciplinary competence of social scientists (Bessy, 2012; Diaz-Bone, Didry, & Salais, 2015; Diaz-Bone & Salais, 2011).

Using a Pragmatist and Structuralist Methodology

Economics of convention was not developed from theoretical considerations only but rather in processes of empirical research in fields as industrial relations, markets, and a variety of economic sectors. The result is its open, theoretical character,

---

[3] On pragmatic sociology see Nachi (2006) and Corcuff (2011).

which can be described as a network of concepts acknowledging a pluralism of conventions and competent actors in real and (with objects) equipped situations of coordination. Economics of convention also offers a corresponding methodological culture that brings in structuralist and pragmatist methodologies and combines them (Diaz-Bone, 2018). The special methodological view of economics of convention is its interpretation of emerging sociohistorical co-constructions of institutions, conventions, categories, practices, and problems (Salais, Baverez, & Reynaud, 1999).[4] Unlike transaction-cost economics and the law-and-economics approach, economics of convention rejects the idea that there is only one explanatory principle. The two former approaches apply an externalist methodology of explanation, explaining economic performance by the fit of institutional designs. For economics of convention, both the sociohistorical constellation and the agency that issues from it are a focus. They are related to actors' internal perspectives. The analyst adopts the standpoint of actors and studies the way actors interpret institutions and their meaning in situations of coordination (Diaz-Bone et al., 2015; Diaz-Bone & Salais, 2011; Salais et al., 1999). The analysis of structures and actors' practices from an internal point of view enters through the proposal to integrate the methodologies of pragmatism and structuralism (Storper & Salais, 1997).

Addressing Contemporary Core Problems

A fourth point calls attention to the contributions that the economics of convention makes to dealing with contemporary core problems of institutionalism, economic sociology, cultural sociology, and theory development. Key contemporary topics include the social construction of qualities or processes of valuation; the connection between norms, values, and practical action; the awareness of a plurality of institutional settings; and the inclusion of objects and cognition into sociological analysis. Economics of convention is one of the leading approaches in all these areas, and it continues to combine and develop pragmatism and structuralism.

The Relation Between Knowledge and Institutions

In economics of convention, not everything that exerts influence on human action is regarded as an institution (as in the Durkheimian tradition). Institutions are the tools (dispositives) of coordination, and actors marshal them to realize a common good. Economics of convention offers a special perspective on the relationship between institutions and knowledge. As mentioned in the second section, institutions are considered to be incomplete in terms of their meaning. This position has consequences.

---

[4] See also Latsis (2006), who analyzed the methodology of the economics of convention.

1. Institutions are not regarded as external constraints but rather as dispositives that need to be *embedded* by competent actors in situational processes of shared interpretation, evaluation, and coordination. Institutions are enacted and therefore internal to actions.

2. Actors have to evaluate in situations the usefulness and adequacy of institutions as dispositives for the purpose of collective coordination. Institutions can be handled in different ways because they can be evaluated and their meaning can be completed through the use of different conventions.

3. Knowledge about conventions can be regarded as distributed and materialized in processes of coordination, which are stabilized by cognitive forms and convention-based procedures for interpretation, evaluation, and coordination. Knowledge, therefore, is not located in individuals, media, or institutions as such but rather in structured processes that rely on actors' competencies, conventions, and dispositives. The model for this concept of distributed knowledge is the concept of distributed cognition developed by Hutchins (1995). He studied the navigation processes on a U.S. naval vessel and demonstrated the existence of calculative processes that were not restricted to individual human brains but distributed to positions, practices, objects, and actors all over the ship. No one person was able to perform the navigation, nor did any one person control or know all the necessary information about the navigation process on board. The economics of convention has adopted this perspective on cognition and transferred it to knowledge conceived of as a pragmatic reality residing in processes.

4. Learning and training for economics of convention are related primarily to processes and situations, not to individuals. To learn is to implement elements, which change these processes of interpretation, evaluation, and coordination. Training persons is related to trying to enhance environments and situations in which human beings are involved practically.

Favereau (1997) argued that organizational learning is possible just because the meaning of institutions is incomplete, as is the case with organizational rules. Learning articulates itself in the way organizational procedures handle and complement rules practically. Learning is possible by changing established rules and implementing new ones—which are likewise incomplete and need to be embedded in situational procedures of convention-based coordination.

Institution: A Constrained Concept

It should be clear by now that the notion of institution has less scope in the economics of convention than in other institutionalist approaches. In some varieties of institutionalism, the notion of institution denotes almost everything outside the human body, such as rules, organizations and technical infrastructures, culture and cultural patterns, language, law, and money. In the economics of convention, it is important to make a conceptual difference between what an institution is and what it is not. Otherwise, the nearly all-embracing notion of institution loses its analytical power.

Table 4.2 Four perceived situations

Relation between an institution and convention(s) is . . .	Functioning of an institution is judged as . . .	
	"not critical"	"critical"
coherent	(1) normality/reliability	(2) blockage/hegemony
incoherent	(3) a dynamic/a change	(4) a crisis/a failure

Source: Design by author

Economics of convention thus enables one to use the difference between institutions (e.g., tools, or dispositives, of coordination) and conventions (as culturally established resources for evaluation and interpretation of how institutions should be run, brought to bear, and judged) to study four different situations illustrating possible ways to relate institutions and their embedding in convention-based interpretations, evaluations, and coordination. The situations can be differentiated as shown in Table 4.2.

The first situation can be characterized as an uncontested "normality." Institutions perform work (for the purposes actors pursue), and there is no reason to change them. The interrelation between convention(s) and institutions is perceived as mutually stabilizing. An example of this situation is the Parisian traffic system and traffic policy. The traffic system and the political (and contractual) control of the private enterprise RATP, which offers bus and subway stations not more than 400 m (a quarter of a mile) from almost any residence, with frequent connections for everybody at low cost, is perceived by the citizens (not as customers) as stable, reliable, and coherent with the civic and industrial conventions that actors use to interpret, handle, and evaluate the traffic system.

The first situation immediately changes into the second when actors judge the functioning of institutions to be critical. Criticism will mount because actors perceive the coherent relation of conventions and institutions as a problem. In this situation it is not easy to criticize institutions, for they are backed up by at least one convention and therefore experienced as blocked. An example is the control exercised over the French labor market (labor law and labor institutions), which is known to be highly regulated and protective of employees. It is coherent with the way French employees and labor law experts think about job security and actors' legal rights. The labor law is coherent with the related civic and industrial conventions. But many French employees experience this coherence as blockage because they are either not employed (unemployment in France has been high for decades) or have only temporary employment contracts. Employers are reluctant to engage employees on unlimited contracts because of the high amount of regulation and the major difficulties that dismissals entail. Many employees and employers alike are penalized by existing labor regulation and would prefer a more flexible and open labor regulation. The call to decrease the unemployment rate is prevalent in France, but no alternative regulation seems acceptable, so most employees, employers, unionists, politicians, and even many unemployed stick to the existing and coherent way of regulating the labor market.

The third situation is different from the first and the second in that conventions and institutions are not coherently related. However, this situation can be the consequence of new strategies pursued by actors, changing conventions in relation to institutions so that new opportunities, outcomes, and values may be produced or may emerge. This situation will continue to cause change until it converges again with a more coherent one (see for example, Salais et al., 1999). An example is the rise of French industrialization in the Paris region in the early twentieth century (see, Didry, 2002). In keeping with market convention at that time, labor law did not allow collective labor contracts, for it was based on a liberal conception of contracts between individual (and noncollective) actors. But as industrial labor organization intensified, French law was perceived as no longer coherent with new conventions of labor coordination (the industrial and the civic convention). Judges (in law courts) gradually accepted new interpretations of existing labor law and even the deviation from existing law to reconcile it with the new need for collective contracts.

The fourth situation comes across as a problem, increasing the impact of the critique of institutional malfunctioning because of the incoherence between convention(s) and institutions. From the actors' point of view, institutions have failed; cognition turns into the recognition of a real institutional crisis (see Boltanski & Thévenot, 1991/2006; Orléan, 2014, among others). For example, the 2017 presidential election in France made evident that the classical political elite, which for many decades had been divided into a left wing (socialist party) and a right wing (conservative party), would not be able to carry large parts of the electorate. The Gaullist voting system works well in a society with such a cleavage into two big political factions. In 2017 the new candidate, Manuel Macron, belonging to no traditional party, won the first round of the election with only 24% of the vote. No candidate from an established party managed to advance into the second round of the presidential election. In France the traditional socialist party and the conservative party are mired in a fundamental crisis—as is the electoral system itself. Current political movements (including Macron's *en marche*) are supplanting political parties. Many new candidates for political office at the local, cantonal, or departmental level no longer belong to a political party. The incoherence between existing political institutions and conventions is recognized and discussed as failure, but new forms of political mobilization and engagements are rising inexorably, heralding opportunity for political change.

In economics of convention, stability and dynamics are conceived of as stable or unstable constellations of conventions (and compromises between a plurality of them) and institutions. Socioeconomic dynamics, therefore, cannot be reduced to institutional change only, for institutions do not change themselves. In economics of convention, socioeconomic dynamic emerges from the relational processes and constellations between conventions, institutions, and coordinating actors in situations. Insisting on the difference between conventions and institutions protects economics of convention from reducing institutional analysis to the comparison between different institutional arrangements—as the transaction-cost approach does by incessantly comparing organizations and markets (Williamson, 1985). That approach thereby assumes that these institutional arrangements are opposed ideal types. Instead, Favereau (1989a, 1989b) has argued that markets are organized and that organizations cannot be reduced to systems of contracts. All quality conventions can be influential in markets as well as in organizations. Organizations and markets are not limited entities, and they cannot be defined in terms of simple categories. Both are embedded in overarching chains of situations, which are structured by conventions that actors apply as resources for wide-ranging coordination (Favereau, 2014).

Knowledge: Conventions as Deeper Discursive Structures

Although conventions can be regarded as logics of interpretation, evaluation, and coordination, they do not necessarily appear in the form of words and language. Many acts of interpretation, evaluation, and coordination are routine, and many of these processes do not need language use. Normally, conventions are used unconsciously, implicitly, and are not apparent as such. Boltanski and Thévenot (1983, 1991/2006) argued that actors are capable of bringing conventions to the surface when the quality of persons, actions, or objects is questioned. Actors then refer to conventions as practical metaphysics for the justification of qualities and worth, hence the reason why conventions can work as orders of justification. The economics of convention relates conventions to products as foundations for their quality. Exponents of the approach therefore speak of quality conventions.

The strategy of exploring quality conventions as foundations for quality arguments is to analyze discourses as knowledge structures that are internally organized by conventions understood as latent or deeper discursive patterns (Gomez & Jones, 2000).[5] Seen in this light, quality conventions are the discursive structures for economic institutions such as markets, for markets would collapse if there were uncertainty about product quality. In economics of convention, product quality is not an ontologically given property but rather a social construction based on quality conventions. An example is the quality of wine. One can study the German wine market by identifying the quality conventions that pattern the quality categories of wine produced in Germany.

Figure 4.2 sketches the wine market relating wine-quality conventions to organizational forms and resources (as different forms of capital) as a function of the market segment. Similar studies can explain that markets cannot be characterized by single and homogeneous product categories and product qualities (such as simple material properties). Evidently, market models like this one (based on convention theory) contradict the neoclassical conception of markets, which posits standardized and comparable product properties. For competent market participants this relational order of a plurality of quality conventions is the implicit knowledge of a market as an institution.

---

[5] For a similar interpretation of conventions as deeper structures, see Bessy and Chateauraynaud (2014).

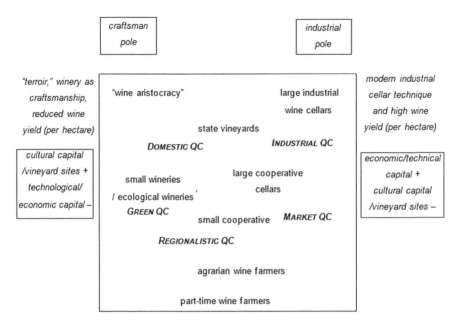

Fig. 4.2 Quality Conventions (QC) in the German wine market. Source: Diaz-Bone (2013, p. 53). Copyright by author

Conventions and Regional Economies

Economics of convention has opposed against two master narratives that are in fact linked to each other. The first one is the view of industrial mass production as the dominant way of organizing economic coordination and a way that would prevail over traditional forms of production such as craftsmanship. The second master narrative is the view of globalization as the second principle of how economic organization was distributed. Piore and Sabel (1984) criticized both views and identified regional economies that exhibited different forms of coordination as highly specialized small firms, which were embedded in regional and flexible networks. Instead of hiring unqualified workers, they engaged highly qualified craftsmen and technicians. They delivered specialized and high-quality products worldwide as well (not only to meet regional demand).

Salais and Storper (1997) elaborated a model—inspired by Piore and Sabel (1984)—presenting different logics of coordination, which they used in the comparative analysis of economic sectors located in regions where companies cooperated to manufacture products. Salais and Storper (1997) introduced the notion of "worlds of production" to describe these forms of regional cooperation. This concept of

Table 4.3 Four Possible Worlds

	Specialized products (economies of variety)	Standardized products (economies of scale)
Dedicated products	The interpersonal world	The market world
	Evaluation of quality: Price	*Evaluation of quality*: Industrial standards by demanders
	Forms of uncertainty: Personal qualities of other producers and consumers	*Forms of uncertainty*: Shifting prices and quantities
	Response to uncertainty: Comprehension among a community of persons	Response to uncertainty: Immediate availability
	Basis of competition: Quality	*Basis of competition*: Prices and rapidity
Generic products	The world of intellectual resources	The industrial world
	Evaluation of quality: Scientific methods	*Evaluation of quality*: General industrial standards
	Forms of uncertainty: The path of knowledge development	*Forms of uncertainty*: Business cycle, demand fluctuations
	Response to uncertainty: Confidence in others	*Response to uncertainty*: Short and medium term forecast of events and behavior
	Basis of competition: Learning	*Basis of competition*: Price

Adopted from Storper & Salais (1997, p. 33). Copyright 1997 by the President and Fellows of Harvard College. Reprinted with permission from the authors and the President and Fellows of Harvard College

worlds of production is as important as that of quality conventions. Both concepts share their character in the economics of convention as logics of coordination. And both are part of systems of such logics of coordination. Table 4.3 presents the four different forms of worlds of production. Their character as ideal types explains why Storper and Salais also speak of "possible worlds" of production (pp. 19, 26), relating them to two general polarities: "specialized versus standardized products" and "dedicated versus generic products" (p. 33).[6]

The model by Storper and Salais (1997) contradicts the master narrative of industrial mass production and globalization in two regards. First, Storper and Salais claim that there are many possible ways to produce, distribute, and consume products (and services). Second, they insist on the importance of the local and regional anchoring of coordination processes. The competencies and qualifications that are relevant ingredients for production are built up in situated and repeated processes, which require a regional center and identity. Moreover, they are related to economic coordination in other regions (and other sectors), so the regional and relational character of economic coordination has to be recognized (see, Bathelt & Glückler, 2011; Storper, 1997).

---

[6] This categorization, or model of worlds of production, has its own grammar, just as the model of quality conventions has had *its* axioms.

Economics of convention has focused on these regionally anchored processes of production. Processes of globalization and the unification of the European Union have strengthened regional identities, as indicated by the emergence of certifications and the establishment of labels such as the French AOC certificate (*appellation d'origine contrôlée*). From the perspective of economics of convention, labels and certification are necessary strategies and signals of form investment, which are dispositives for the ascription of qualities to products. The analysis of agrarian food production, therefore, has been an important application of economics of convention (see the contributions in Allaire & Boyer, 1995; Nicolas & Valceschini, 1995; Ponte, 2016; Sánchez-Hernández, Aparicio-Amador & Alonso-Santos, 2010).

Economics of convention has an explicit link to the regional perspective— namely, the methodology of situationalism, which consists of focusing on situations of coordination and adopting the actor's perspective (Storper & Salais, 1997). Thévenot (2001) has argued for rejection of multilevel models and for their replacement by the notion of the scope of situational coordination: "[O]ur framework . . . challenges the classical macro-micro distinction since judgements of worth are precisely ways of enlarging the scope of an evaluation from a local context and of crafting generalized statements" (p. 418).

Inspired by Storper (1997), one may consider introducing the regionalistic convention (Diaz-Bone, 2018). It would not be a convention established in a specific region but rather a specific way to coordinate and evaluate qualities of products. This capability would be valuable. Not only are products generated in a region (as almost every product is), their quality is attributed to it. As in the example of the German wine market (Figure 4.2), there are regional styles of production, regional taste cultures, regional traditions, and regional identities, all of which are perceived by coordination actors as being linked to the product. This regionalistic convention should be thought of as different from seemingly similar conventions, such as the domestic convention or the green convention, because it is not based on the principle of craftsmanship (as the domestic convention is) or ecological production (as the green convention is). By enlarging the scope of coordination, actors are able to extend collaboration from the local to the global level. The economics of convention questions the use of multilevel models, including micro-, macro-, and sometimes mesolevels of coordination, because those levels imply their own ontologies of entities residing at these levels.[7] But to call this regional convention a convention, one must adopt the idea that these conventions have deeper grammars and criteria—a process still to be undertaken in economics of convention.

---

[7] And every multilevel model should be scrutinized for how it theorizes the ontologies related to the different levels and how it models the process that takes place between them.

Global Value Chains

The global value-chain concept is an excellent example of how one can model wide-ranging global chains of coordination by adopting the theoretical perspective of economics of convention (Daviron & Ponte, 2005; Ponte, 2016).[8] This concept also aptly demonstrates how to model an institutionalist perspective (in this case, how to govern coordination across different stages of production) by focusing on the construction of quality. In a comparative study of coffee production and the social construction of quality, Daviron and Ponte (2005) surveyed the different stages in the production chain of coffee, studying how quality conventions were introduced and applied in different links of the chain. The same coffee beans figuring as raw material at the beginning of the global value chain can wind up as completely different coffee products at the end of the global value chain (as coffee blend) related to different quality perceptions. Daviron and Ponte (2005) compared three different kinds of coffee, one Robusta and two Arabicas, following them from the farm gate to the retailer where consumers can buy the final product. At the farm gate the two kinds of Arabica coffee had identical prices (and not much more than the price of the Robusta type of coffee). In the end, however, one of these two kinds of Arabica coffee had a consumer price more than two and half times higher than that of the other, with the Robusta coffee drawing only about 10% of the sales price attached to the Arabica coffees (Daviron & Ponte, 2005, pp. 210, 212).

How can these differences in price be explained? The explanation for the huge variance at the end of the chain is that the global value chains diverged in the dominant quality conventions in the middle of the chain (the process of roasting and retailing in Europe). It was at that intermediate point of the chain that different logics of quality convention-related coordination exerted their influence. As a result, the "quality" of the produced coffee was transformed into a different "ontology," and this new product ontology became related to a different style how the final product should be consumed: coffee as a mass-produced commodity sold at supermarkets for private consumption at home; or high-quality espresso coffee consumed in a coffee bar. It is not the raw material (at the beginning of the global value chain) that justifies the differences in price. Instead, it is the downstream difference in ways of coordinating production that creates a completely different perception of quality. The emerging question is how these global value chains are governed. It is obvious to refer to quality conventions as principles for the governance of the whole quality chain itself.

---

[8] The concept of the global value chain was developed from the commodity-chain concept (Gereffi & Korzeniewicz, 1994) and the global-value-chain concept (Gereffi, Humphrey, & Sturgeon, 2005).

Summary

Economics of convention is a transdisciplinary and complex pragmatist form of institutionalism. It should be thought of not as a stringent body of theory but rather as a scientific movement that has developed concepts in the course of empirical institutional research. Its core arguments and principles relevant to the study of institutions and knowledge can briefly be summarized.

1. This institutionalism has conceptualized approached knowledge by positing conventions as implicit, collective frames of knowledge that coordinating actors must draw on in situations in order to deal with institutions. In addition, economics of convention offers a perspective from which to understand knowledge as deeper structures of discourses.

2. From an institutionalist perspective, economics of convention can be characterized also as an approach that differentiates institutions from conventions. This distinction is achieved through a constrained concept of institutions: institutions are the manifest (or formal) dispositives for coordination, but the manner of their interpretation, relevance, and handling is open to and combinable with different conventions in situations—four of which were identified in this chapter. Institutions, seen this way, need to be embedded in convention-based and convention-structured forms of knowledge. Economics of convention frames institutions not as external to action and coordination but rather as internal to them.

3. Two main models of how conventions can be theorized and systematized were introduced: the set of quality conventions and the set of worlds of productions. They are closely interrelated, and both sets have been used in many studies based on the economics of convention. The worlds-of-production model has been applied especially in regional and geographical economic research. The model of quality conventions has figured in the analysis of market structures and global value chains.

4. Two empirical applications of economics of convention were presented. They demonstrate how the plurality of quality conventions structures different market segments and the different forms of segmental market knowledge (the wine example). They also show how quality chains (the coffee example) combine quality conventions in various ways and thereby result in different perceptions of quality among consumers)—even when the raw material is similar.

5. Unlike its institutionalist counterpart—transaction cost analysis (Williamson, 1985)—economics of convention regards product ontology not as a given property but rather as the result of convention-based coordination and perception. Discourses and conventions as deeper knowledge structures are essential to generate qualities collectively. In economics of convention, there is no one best way to design economic institutions. Instead, there is a coexisting plurality of quality conventions or worlds of production as principles how to produce, distribute, and consume goods.

References

Allaire, G., & Boyer, R. (Eds.). (1995). *La grande transformation de l'agriculture* [The great transformation of agriculture]. Paris: INRA.

Bathelt, H., & Glückler, J. (2011). *The relational economy: Geographies of knowing and learning.* Oxford, UK: Oxford University Press. doi:https://doi.org/10.1111/jors.12024_4

Batifoulier, P., Bessis, F., Ghirardello, A., de Larquier, G., & Rémillon, D. (Eds.). (2016). *Dictionnaire des conventions: Autour des travaux d'Olivier Favereau* [Dictionary of conventions: On the work of Olivier Favereau]. Capitalismes—éthique—institutions: Vol. 10. Villeneuve-d'Ascq: Presses Universitaires du Septentrion.

Bessy, C. (2012). Law, forms of organization and the market for legal services. *Economic Sociology: The European Electronic Newsletter, 14*(1), 20–30. Retrieved from http://econsoc.mpifg.de/archive/econ_soc_14-1.pdf

Bessy, C. & Chateauraynaud, F. (2014). *Experts et faussaires.* 2nd ed. Paris: Edition Petra.

Boltanski, L., & Chiapello, E. (2005). *The new spirit of capitalism* (G. Elliott, Trans.). London: Verso Books. (Original work published 1999)

Boltanski, L., & Thévenot, L. (1983). Finding one's way in social space: A study based on games. *Social Science Information, 22,* 631–680. doi:https://doi.org/10.1177/053901883022004003

Boltanski, L., & Thévenot, L. (2006). *On justification: Economies of worth* (C. Porter, Trans.). Princeton: Princeton University Press. (Original work published 1991)

Boltanski, L., & Thévenot, L. (Eds.). (1989). *Justesse et justice dans le travail* [Appropriateness and justice at work]. Cahiers du Centre d'études de l'emploi: Vol. 33. Paris: Presses Universitaires de France.

Corcuff, P. (2011). *Les nouvelles sociologies: Entre le collectif et l'individuel* [The new sociologies: Between the collective and the individual] (3rd ed.). Paris: Armand Colin.

Daviron, B., & Ponte, S. (2005). *The coffee paradox: Global markets, commodity trade and the elusive promise of development.* London: Zed Books.

Diaz-Bone, R. (2013). Discourse conventions in the construction of wine qualities in the wine market. *Economic Sociology: The European Electronic Newsletter, 14*(2), 46–53. Retrieved from http://econsoc.mpifg.de/archive/econ_soc_14-2.pdf

Diaz-Bone, R. (2018). *Die "Economie des conventions": Grundlagen und Entwicklung der neuen französischen Wirtschaftssoziologie* [The economy of convention: Foundations and developments of new French economic sociology] (2nd ed.). Wiesbaden: Springer VS.

Diaz-Bone, R., Didry, C., & Salais, R. (Eds.). (2015). Law and conventions from a historical perspective [Special issue]. *Historical Social Research, 40*(1). Retrieved from http://www.gesis.org/en/hsr/archive/2015/401-law-and-conventions/

Diaz-Bone, R., & Salais, R. (Eds.). (2011). Conventions and institutions from a historical perspective [Special issue]. *Historical Social Research, 36*(4). Retrieved from http://www.gesis.org/hsr/archiv/2011/364-conventions-institutions/

Diaz-Bone, R., & Salais, R. (Eds.). (2012). The Économie des Conventions: Transdisciplinary discussions and perspectives [Special issue]. *Historical Social Research, 37*(4). Retrieved from http://www.gesis.org/en/hsr/archive/2012/374-the-economie-des-conventions/

Didry, C. (2002). *Naissance de la convention collective: Débats juridiques et luttes sociales en France au début du XXe siècle* [Birth of the collective convention: Legal debate and social conflict in France in the early twentieth century]. Paris: Editions de l'EHESS.

Dosse, F. (1998a). *The rising sign, 1945–1966* (D. Glassman, Trans.). History of Structuralism: Vol. 1. Minneapolis: University of Minnesota Press. (Original work published 1991)

Dosse, F. (1998b). *The sign sets, 1967–present* (D. Glassman, Trans.). History of Structuralism: Vol. 2. Minneapolis: University of Minnesota Press. (Original work published 1992)

Dosse, F. (1999). *Empire of meaning: The humanization of the social sciences* (H. Melehy, Trans.). Minneapolis: University of Minnesota Press. (Original work published 1995)

Eymard-Duvernay, F., & Thévenot, L. (1983). *Les investissements de forme: Leur usage pour la main d'œuvre* [Form investments: Their use for the craft trades]. Paris: INSEE.

Favereau, O. (1989a). Marchés internes, marchés externes [Internal markets, external markets]. *Revue économique, 40,* 273–328. doi:https://doi.org/10.2307/3502116

Favereau, O. (1989b). Organisation et marché [Organization and market]. *Revue française d'économie, 4,* 65–96. doi:https://doi.org/10.3406/rfeco.1989.1203

Favereau, O. (1997). L'incomplétude n'est pas le problème, c'est la solution [The incompleteness is not the problem—it is the solution]. In B. Reynaud (Ed.), *Les figures de collectif* (pp. 219–233). Les limites de la rationalité: Vol. 2. Paris: La Découverte.

Favereau, O. (2014). "Société" par nécessité, "entreprise" par convention ["Society" by necessity, "enterprise" by convention]. In B. Segrestin, B. Roger, & S. Vernac (Eds.), *L'entreprise: Point aveugle du savoir* (pp. 48–64). Paris: Sciences Humains.

Favereau, O., & Lazega, E. (Eds.). (2002). *Conventions and structures in economic organization: Markets, networks, hierarchies.* Cheltenham: Edward Elgar.

Gereffi, G., J. Humphrey, & Sturgeon, T. (2005). The governance of global value chains. *Review of International Political Economy, 12,* 78–104. doi:https://doi.org/10.1080/09692290500049805

Gereffi, G., & Korzeniewicz, M. (Eds.). (1994). *Commodity chains and global capitalism.* Westport: Greenwood.

Gomez, P-Y., & Jones, B. C. (2000). Crossroads—Conventions: An interpretation of deep structure in organizations. *Organization Science, 11,* 696–708. doi:https://doi.org/10.1287/orsc.11.6.696.12530

Hutchins, E. (1995). *Cognition in the wild.* Cambridge, MA: MIT Press.

James, W. (1909). *A pluralistic universe: Hibbert lectures at Manchester College on the present situation in philosophy.* London: Longmans, Green & Company.

Knoll, L. (Ed.). (2015). *Organisationen und Konventionen: Die Soziologie der Konventionen in der Organisationsforschung* [Organizations and conventions: The sociology of conventions in organization studies]. Wiesbaden: Springer VS.

Kuklick, B. (2001). *A history of philosophy in America: 1720–2000.* Oxford, UK: Oxford University Press.

Latsis, J. (2006). Convention and intersubjectivity: New developments in French economics. *Journal for the Theory of Social Behaviour, 36,* 255–277. doi:https://doi.org/10.1111/j.1468-5914.2006.00307.x

Meyer, J. W., & Rowan, B. (1977). Institutionalized organizations: Formal structure as myth and ceremony. *American Journal of Sociology, 83,* 340–363. doi:https://doi.org/10.1086/226550

Nachi, M. (2006). *Introduction à la sociologie pragmatique* [Introduction to pragmatic sociology]. Paris: Armand Colin.

Nicolas, F., & Valceschini, E. (Eds.). (1995). *Agro-alimentaire: Une économie de la qualité* [Agro-food industry: An economy of qualities]. Paris: INRA/Economica.

North, D. C. (1990). *Institutions, institutional change and economic performance.* Cambridge, UK: Cambridge University Press.

Orléan, A. (2014). *The empire of value: A new foundation for economics* (M. B. DeBevoise, Trans.). Cambridge, MA: MIT Press.

Piore, M. J., & Sabel, C. F. (1984). *The second industrial divide: Possibilities for prosperity.* New York: Basic Books.

Ponte, S. (2016). Convention theory in the Anglophone agro-food literature: Past, present and future. *Journal of Rural Studies, 44*(4), 12–23. doi:https://doi.org/10.1016/j.jrurstud.2015.12.019

Posner, R. A. (2007). *Economic analysis of law* (7th ed.). New York: Aspen.

Powell, W. W., & DiMaggio, P. J. (Eds.). (1991). *The new institutionalism in organizational analysis.* Chicago: University of Chicago Press.

Salais, R., Baverez, N., & Reynaud, B. (1999). *L'invention du chômage: Histoire et transformations d'une catégorie en France des années 1890 aux années 1980* [The invention of unemployment: History and transformations of a category in France between the 1890s and the 1980s]. Quadrige: Vol. 286. Paris: Presses Universitaires de France.

Sánchez-Hernández, J. S., Aparicio-Amador, J. & Alonso-Santos, J. (2010). The shift between worlds of production as an innovative process in the wine industry in Castile and Leon (Spain). *Geoforum, 41,* 469–478. doi:https://doi.org/10.1016/j.geoforum.2009.12.004

Storper, M. (1997). *The regional world: Territorial development in a global economy.* New York: Guilford Press.

Storper, M., & Salais, R. (1997). *Worlds of production: The action frameworks of the economy.* Cambridge, MA: Harvard University Press.

Thévenot, L. (2001). Organized complexity: Conventions of coordination and the composition of economic arrangements. *European Journal of Social Theory, 4,* 405–425. doi:https://doi.org/10.1177/13684310122225235

Weber, M. (1978). *Economy and society: An outline of interpretive sociology.* 2 Vols. (G. Roth & C. Wittich, Eds.; E. Fischoff, H. Gerth, A. M. Henderson, F. Kolegar, C. Wright Mills, T. Parsons, M. Rheinstein, G. Roth, E. Shils, & C. Wittich, Trans.). Berkeley: University of California Press. (Original work published 1922)

Williamson, O. E. (1985). *The economic institutions of capitalism: Firms, markets, relational contracting.* New York: Free Press.

Part II
Institutional Dynamics Between Continuity and Change

Chapter 5
Gastronomic Societies in the Basque Country

Andreas Hess

The French statesman, thinker, and celebrated author of *Democracy in America*, Alexis de Tocqueville (1835–1840/2000), thought that the art of association was crucial to any analysis of modern society. Since time immemorial, eating and drinking together and the socializing, cultural, and even educational effects surrounding such activities have been promoted and praised by its practitioners, ranging from Plato's symposium to beer and sausage consumption in Bavarian beerhalls (the latter with detrimental political consequences, at least under the Nazis). In modern times some of these eating and drinking activities have become differentiated and have come to perform a number of functions. Some have taken on an institutionalized public form (as in restaurants); others have remained rather private in character (e.g., gatherings with friends and families at home). In this chapter I examine the history, development, and societal function of a unique Basque invention, the gastronomic society (Spanish, *sociedad gastronómica*; Basque, *txoko*, a diminutive of *zoco*, "corner"). It has both formal and informal aspects and combines private and public functions to great effect and to the pleasure of those who make use of it.

My investigation proceeds in three steps. I first trace the historical origins of the *txoko* and its development by the end of the twentieth century. I then delve into the formal and informal dimensions of the *txoko* that give life to the institution. I also note homogenization and differentiation processes that explain some cultural peculiarities of the Basque Country and its culinary geography and history. The chapter concludes with an attempt to contextualize the phenomenon of the gastronomic society, particularly in relation to the unique position that the *txoko* occupies as an institution between the public and the private spheres.[1]

---

[1] This chapter is an edited and slightly amended version of Hess (2007) and Hess (2009, above all Chapter 3). As becomes apparent from my argument, the *txoko* is an institution that is more developed in the Spanish part of the Basque Country (Hegoalde) than in the northern, French part (Iparralde).

A. Hess (✉)
School of Sociology, University College Dublin, Belfield, Dublin 4, Ireland
e-mail: a.hess@ucd.ie

© The Author(s) 2018
J. Glückler et al. (eds.), *Knowledge and Institutions*, Knowledge and Space 13,
https://doi.org/10.1007/978-3-319-75328-7_5

History of the *Txoko*

The origins of the gastronomic society lie in San Sebastián, a medium-sized city located on the Cantabrian coastline of a *bahia* (bay), only a few miles from the Spanish-French border (see Fig. 5.1). Thanks to this prime location, the city had developed into the administrative center of the Basque province of Gipuzkoa and had become its capital. San Sebastián's geographical advantage and the ensuing improved communications (trains, electricity, the telegraph, and eventually the telephone had all arrived in a short period) attracted an influx of visitors during the nineteenth century and soon gave rise to early signs of a flourishing tourist industry. This process coincided with a change in the composition of San Sebastián's working population. Rural migration from the countryside into town continued throughout the nineteenth and early twentieth century, and by the late nineteenth century the migrants had already become an integral part of the city's working population. The specific history I describe—the rise of the popular societies and especially the development of the gastronomic society—must be understood as the result of an accelerated process in which both the "plebeian" element of its working population and the portents of the tourist trade helped turn San Sebastián into a modern city with a cosmopolitan character (Aguirre Franco, 1983; Luengo, 1999).

Toward the mid-nineteenth century the city's administration had already recorded the existence of a few dozen establishments in which sociability featured prominently. Some were cafés that tended to appeal to an upper-class clientele, offering billiards and facilities for *tertulias* (gatherings of a small group of like-minded people discussing culture as encountered in literature, the performing arts, or the press). However, most of these businesses were *tabernas* (taverns) and *cidrerias* (Basque, *sagardotegis*, "cider houses"), places where one could have a drink, customarily cider, with friends (Luengo, 1999, p. 45). This situation did not last. Increasingly, the café came to replace the tavern, notably in the city center. The cafés lost their elite and aristocratic character, and the urban space that used to be exclusively owned by a few became subject to "massification" (p. 47). The first popular society, La Fraternal, was founded in 1843, and its creation arguably symbolized that change. Its chief purpose was to bring its members together for the sole purpose of *comer y cantar*, "to eat and sing." Soon, there were other societies, too, mainly of artisan background.

San Sebastián's foremost chronicler, Felix Luengo (1999), recalled the social change that had occurred and that soon became evident culturally as well. That shift lay in the artisan sector, which had become an important sector of San Sebastián's working population and which would emerge before long as the main protagonist in the organization of popular activities and events such as the drum parade, the *tamborrada* (p. 50). In the nineteenth century San Sebastián's class and occupational divisions were manifested in spatially vertical and horizontal segregation, with the aristocratic elite occupying the city center's high-rises and parts of the old town, and

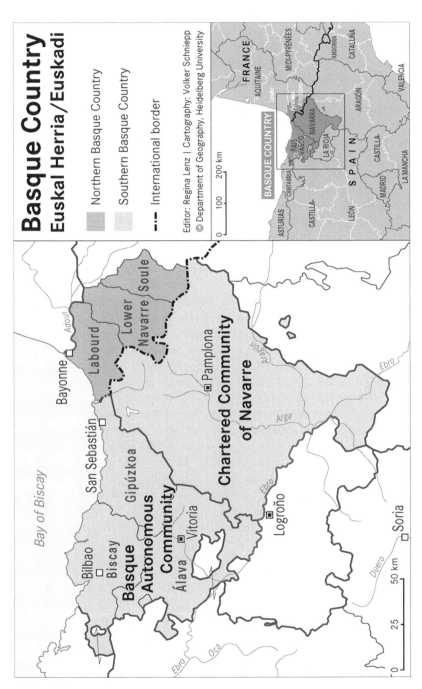

Fig. 5.1 Basque Country: Euskal Herria/Euskadi. Editor: Regina Lenz. Cartography: Volker Schniepp © Department of Geography, Heidelberg University

the rich seasonal visitors and tourists owning the beach chalets along the curve of the *bahia* (pp. 57–86). The not-so-well-off segments of the population lived in much smaller buildings in the surroundings and further from the center.

By the 1920s changing class structure had led to a new arrangement of urban space. Artisans and fishermen, who constituted the meanwhile plebeian majority of the working population, had moved into the old town, close to the harbor.[2] With a significant tourist industry having sprouted in San Sebastián in the latter half of the nineteenth century, the city's development subsequently went beyond a few rich chalets. It increasingly encompassed the construction of tourist infrastructure, including casinos like the Gran Casino Kursaal (completed in 1887). San Sebastián witnessed a true boom in cafés and major hotels. Hotel de Londres, Hotel de Francia, and Hotel Continental all came on line in the 1880s, and more than a dozen new cafés opened their doors. The burgeoning tourist industry, together with the change in San Sebastián's class structure, compelled a cultural change, too. San Sebastián's leading festival and spectacular event was soon introduced: the *Semana Grande* (literally, the big week), which later also boasted a professionally organized *tamborrada*. The institutionalization of the *Semana Grande* was quickly followed by the construction of a new *plaza de torros*, "bull-fighting arena," in Atocha (1876).

Both the tourist industry and the changing plebeian class structure eventuated in further differentiation of popular space. By 1868 the city council recorded the existence of 58 popular establishments, and the number grew to 106 in 1882 (Luengo, 1999, p. 74). The majority of these establishments, the aforementioned *tabernas* and *cidrerias*, were located in the old part of town, which by then was firmly in the hands of artisans and fishermen. One of the problems with the taverns and cider places, though, was their early statutory closing hours: no later than 10:30 p.m. A temporary solution consisted of turning taverns and cider houses into cafés, which were allowed to stay open until 1 a.m. A better, long-term solution was to have one's own new mixed-purpose establishment that combined aspects of the tavern, the café, and eating places. For this purpose one had to invent a separate organizational form, the *sociedad popular*, or "popular society." An early forerunner was the previously mentioned La Fraternal. Others rapidly opened thereafter. In the last three decades of the nineteenth century, a number of newly founded societies opened: Pescadores de San Sebastián (1869), Union Artesana (1870), La Armonia (1872), Neptuno (1878), Primero de Abril (1879), Union Obrera (1880), La Humanitaria (1892), and Euskalduna (1893). Membership ranged from 50 to 80 people, but the recruitment had a clear social profile in that all popular society members came from

---

[2]According to Luengo (1999), San Sebastián's class structure in 1911 was made up of artisans (28.27%); members of the new working class (18.95%); employees and administrators (10.32%); proprietors, industrialists, and members of the independent professions (7.01%); and fishermen, rural employees, clerics, and military personnel (19.43%). The unique constellation, in which the classic industrial working class is underrepresented but various subaltern classes together constitute something like a working plebe, justifies reference to the term *plebeian class structure* (Thompson, 1980). For a detailed discussion of such class relations, see the final part of this chapter.

the environment of artisans and fishermen, and all the new establishments were intended to have inclusive democratic membership.[3]

The new societies provided an infrastructure where people could drink, eat, sing, rehearse, and prepare cultural events, including plays, parades, and festivities such as the *tamborrada*. Some of the older societies also have had a small library or other facilities in which to read.[4] Another social function of the societies was to integrate migrants not only from the rural environment of San Sebastián but also from other parts of Spain. Later came the founding of entire societies whose names hinted at the regional origin of their members.

In the early twentieth century new political movements and parties arrived on the scene and changed the political landscape of the Basque Country. Both the social and the national question became more important and found expression in their own public infrastructure. In San Sebastián, socialists, nationalists, anarchists, republicans, but also various unions and social Catholic groups all established their own societies. As Luengo (1999) has explained, the growing industrialization, commercialization, and tourist infrastructure brought with it an increasing "democratization of recreation" (p. 102). Sports of all kinds reflected such democratization. Football, mountaineering, cars and car racing, *pelota* (the Basque ball game), and Atlantic rowing regattas were no longer restricted to an elite; they were henceforth open to the masses.

The activities described above led to a further democratization and popularization of the *sociedades*, including the participation of immigrants from other parts of Spain, and women. Most of the newly founded societies responded to the altered constituencies and the needs and demands of the increasing spectrum of the new leisure activities. The new wave of societies included prominent names that still exist: Union Artesana, Canyoyetan (1900), La Plata, Gaztelupe (1916), Umore-Ona (1906), Soka-Mutura, Euskal Billera (1901), Amaikak-bat (1907), Sporti Clai, and Ollagorra (1906). Whereas membership in the older societies had been dominated by artisans and fishermen, the societies that developed in the first two decades of the new century symbolized the rise of the new middle class in San Sebastián. These new societies were subject to increased regulation and had to communicate and collaborate with the city's administration. On the whole these changes made perfect sense, largely because the *Semana Grande*, including the *tamborrada*, had developed into full-time activities and demanded long-term planning, official sponsoring, and maximum participation.

---

[3] Both Luengo (1999) and Aguirre Franco (1983) have stressed that the popular societies usually restricted only the overall size of their membership and that any class discrimination therein was unheard of. Gender- and sex-related exclusionary practices prevailed in the early history of the popular societies but became less restrictive over time (see this chapter's discussion of the general function of the *sociedades*). Nonetheless, Unión Artesana, one of the oldest societies, remains exclusively and explicitly male.

[4] In one famous, well-documented anecdote, the famous Basque writer Pio Baroja had been invited to Gaztelupe, one of the best-known *sociedades*, but had found the experience wanting after he had been shown the library—the name that members had given to the society's bodega.

Between 1925 and 1936 San Sebastián witnessed a further major boom, the founding of 55 new societies dealing with a wide range of activities in the realms of music, sports, religious activities, and culture. But the most interesting aspect of the differentiation process was the development of gastronomic, or so-called cooking, societies—organizations whose primary purpose was to cook and consume food. To be sure, a few societies devoted solely to cooking had already been founded at the beginning of the twentieth century, most prominently Cañoyetan (1900) and Euskal Billera (1901). They were joined by societies that were initially more interested in sports but that then turned into cooking societies: Gimnastica de Ulia (1917), Sociedad de Caza y Pesca (1919), and Ur-Kirolak (1922). In the 1920s new cooking societies developed that had their origins first in republican and nationalist circles: Aizepe (1921), Gure Txokoa (1925), Sociedad Illumpe and Donosti Berri (both 1927), and C. D. Vasconia and Zubi Gain (both 1928). The advent of the republic was greeted by another wave of new establishments: Istingarra, Itzalpe, Aitzaki, Gizarta, and Ardatza (all founded in 1932), and Lagun Artea (1934).

The Spanish Civil War and Franco's new regime slowed things down. By 1945 not a single new society had opened. The postwar development and new openings of popular and cooking societies have been described by Aguirre Franco (1983, p. 23) as less utilitarian and more aesthetic than their predecessors. But whatever happens in the future, it is now an acknowledged fact that San Sebastián's cooking societies have not only had a remarkably successful history but have become the city's distinctive modern trade mark. At the beginning of the new millennium, there were 120 cooking societies in San Sebastián, and the estimate is that one out of every 3.5 adults is a member of a *sociedad* (van Wijck, 2000). The popular society, especially the cooking society, has truly become the intersection of San Sebastián's civic culture. Representing a form of being that includes many activities, it has even become a model for export.[5]

The history of popular and gastronomic societies is somewhat different in Bilbao and its environs, located in the Basque province of Biscay (Basque, *Bizkaia*). Resulting from the long history of trade and commerce with England and the enormous affluence of Bilbao, popular establishments in this capital city first aspired to the ideal of the English Gentlemen's club.[6]

The difference between Bilbao and San Sebastián was indisputably one of both real and perceived wealth and class distinctions. A useful illustration is the history of Bilbao's first popular society. Members of the Kurdin Club (established in 1899) tried to imitate the colonial lifestyle of the British (Aguirre Franco, 1983, pp. 60–61; Alonso Céspedes, 1996; Egin Monografias, 1996, pp. 2–3). Not only did they introduce sofas, boot stools, and marble tables to the society, but the drinks were also

---

[5] Historically, the phenomenon first spread to other Gipuzkoan towns, notably those just a short ride away from San Sebastián. The 1920s and early 1930s saw the opening of cooking societies in Tolosa (Gure Kaiola in 1927 and Gure Txokoa in 1931), Zumarraga (Beloqui in 1929), and Zarautz (Gure Kabiya in 1931).

[6] That the English represented an ideal is evident from the history of the city's soccer club, Athletic Bilbao—not Atletico Bilbao.

different, with cocktails and whiskies replacing cider and wine. That the whole enterprise was meant to be somewhat self-ironic and humorous becomes plain from the rituals of the members of the Kurdin Club. They had to wear caftans, imitate religious practices, and worship a certain holiness such as Martell, Hennessy, and Jimenez Lammothe (obviously, all brand names of hard liquor). The irony went even further, with clubs forming within the club: the Club de Hatchis, Club de Opio, and Club del Kiff. As the first rules of the Club stated, "Everyone does what he likes," and the motto seems to be that one has to alienate oneself in order not to be alienated.

It would be wrong to assume from this example that class or wealth alone determined membership. True, the first wave of popular societies in Bilbao bore a greater mark of class distinction than the later waves have, but the subsequent development and history of the *sociedades gastronómicas* in the city and its environs still demonstrates that equal status within the society has remained the rule not the exception and that even the choice of a specific society has not been completely defined or determined by a particular class background. The difference between Bilbao and San Sebastián lies in a certain elevator effect. Class orientation in Bilbao has always been more pronounced than in San Sebastián. Places such as the Kurdin Club have been distinct and appealed, at least originally, to the rich bourgeoisie, a public very much apart.

The history of popular societies—above all, the cooking societies—in Biscay begins outside its capital, Bilbao. Their origins hark back to Biscayan seaside towns and harbors such as Ondarroa, Lekeitio, and Bermeo. As San Sebastián had done earlier, these settlements spread westward along the Cantabrian coastline (Alonso Céspedes, 1996, p. 28). Yet the first officially registered cooking society, Kili-Kolo, is further inland, in Durango. The oldest society in Bilbao, Gure Txoko, with 85 members, was founded fairly late in 1954. Shortly thereafter a second society was created, Txoko Bilboko Umore Ona. In the second half of the 1960s and early 1970s, a true boom ensued, the most prominent of these organizations being Achuritarra (founded 1965) with 200 members, Sociedad Recreativa Deusto (1967) with 150 members, and Abando (1970) with 100 members. At the turn of the previous century, Bilbao had 45 societies in total with an average of 30 to 60 members[7] (Alonso Céspedes, 1996, p. 121). As in San Sebastián, most cooking societies in Bilbao can be found in the *casco viejo* (old part, old town) and in Uribarri and Santutxu. Elsewhere in the city, *txokos* seem to be evenly distributed, confirming again that popular space and related activities are not monopolized by a given urban elite. Outside Bilbao, cooking societies seem to be even more frequented than inside

---

[7] Contravening the overall tendency to include women, *txokos* in Bilbao seem to remain almost exclusively male. Meritxell Alonso Céspedes (1996) reported that only two of the 45 *txokos* that she visited officially welcomed women as members. This statement appears to be confirmed by a report filed by the Diputación Foral de Vizcaya, which researched how many women participated in voluntary associations. The group found that only 0.7% of all respondents stated they participated in a gastronomic society (as cited in Alonso Céspedes 1996, p. 121).

the Biscayan capital. Lekeitio, a small seaside resort, has 17 societies, whereas Bermeo, a slightly larger town than Lekeitio, has 33 ("Las 700 sociedades," 1981).[8] Like Biscay, the province of Álava (Basque, *Araba*) and, most prominently, its capital, Vitoria-Gasteiz (hereafter referred to as Vitoria), took their lead and inspiration from Gipuzkoa and San Sebastián (Idroquilis, 1994). In contrast to cooking societies in Biscay, those in Vitoria developed as early as the 1930s. La Globa (founded in 1934 and having 100 members) was the first and largest cooking society, followed by El Rincon Amado with 30 members. Zaldibartxo was founded in 1941 in Sarria by Vitoria citizens; and Olarizu, founded in 1948, is known for a rather religious and aristocratic membership. In the 1950s there came Zaldiaran and San Juan-La Globa (both founded in 1953). Since 1988, Álava's capital has been home to a federation of popular societies, Gasteizko Elkarteak, which started with eight societies and had grown to 27 societies as members by the end of the twentieth century. The overriding aim of the organization is to help organize the *Fiesta de San Prudencia*, including a *tamborrada*. Other activities include cooking competitions, wine competitions and tastings, and the *Campeonato de Mus* (Mus championship), the famous Basque card game. At the beginning of the twenty-first century there were 126 popular societies in Araba (including cooking and other recreational societies). Half of them are in Vitoria alone, mainly in the old part of this Basque capital (Idroquilis, 1994, p. 41).

In the province of Navarre (Basque, *Nafarroako*), the development of the *sociedades* conformed to the well-established cultural patterns of Basque settlements: more developed in the north and northeast and fizzling out or nonexistent in the south of the region (Aguirre Franco, 1983, p. 64). Navarre's capital city, Pamplona has the highest number of these societies (15), the most prominent being Napardi and Txoko Pelotazale. Tafalla has 14; Tudela, 7; Elizondo, 5; and Alsasua, 4. Referring in Navarre almost entirely to cooking societies, the term *sociedades* is understood more narrowly there than in the provinces of Gipuzkoa and Biscay. In addition, the absence of women in the kitchens of Navarre's cooking societies is conspicuous (Aguirre Franco, 1983).

In the late twentieth century the Basque Autonomous Community (Gipuzkoa, Biscay, and Álava) had 1,300 societies (Idroquilis, 1994, p. 17), but there are many more in Navarre and other Spanish cities and regions, especially in those locations where a significant number of Basques gather. In 1981 the Basque newspaper *Deia* reported that 50,000 Basques were members of cooking societies ("Las 700 sociedades," 1981). The same newspaper reported that in one Biscayan seaside town, Lekeitio, around 80% of the male population attends a cooking society regularly. Today the cooking society has become a symbol of the Basque diaspora worldwide,

---

[8] In his ethnographic work on Bermeo, Homobono Martínez (1987; 1997) dated the first *txoko* back to the mid-1960s. *Txokos* spread with astonishing rapidity in the 1970s. In Bermeo alone, 36 of them were founded. According to the 1981 newspaper account in *Deia*, Bermeo had the second highest number of *txokos* in Biscay (after Bilbao). Homobono Martínez (1987) pointed out that most members came from the fishing sector (p. 350).

and *txokos* can be found in almost any major capital or city that has a significant .
number of Basques, from Buenos Aires to New York City and London.

Formal and Informal Requirements: How the *Txoko* Comes to Life

For a common gastronomic society to function properly, basic institutional arrangements are necessary and a set of established rules have to be observed (Alonso
Céspedes, 1996; Idroqilis, 1994; Luengo, 1999). In 1964 the Franco regime relaxed
its attitude toward civil associations and organizations, introducing a new law of
associations (*ley de asociaciones*). A 1965 by-law then specified possible applications and interpretations. Under the new rules each association or society had to
state its place or location, the reasons or purposes for which the association or society existed, the social environment to which it appealed, the organization's administrative structure, the rules of membership and access, and the rights and
responsibilities of the members. The society or association also had to declare its
nonprofit aims and specify the rules for its possible dissolution. The society or association also had to register officially as such with the Basque government, prove
upon demand that it was adhering to the rules on such matters as official bookkeep-
ing and documentation, and show, if necessary, that it was obeying the outlined
regulations. The law of associations also used to require that the associations or
societies abstain from politics, but today the democratic nature of societies and
associations as a contribution to civil society is universally acknowledged.

The legal framework addresses only minimal formalities and structural requirements of a given society. What is absolutely essential for a society to function is a
proper infrastructure. A gastronomic society affords an infrastructure like that of a
restaurant, but it is not open to the public, only to the society's members or their
guests. Another difference is the arrangement between the kitchen and the dining
area. The kitchen is usually open or semiopen, not completely separate or out of
sight as in restaurants. The kitchen includes everything necessary to prepare food
for sizable groups: two or three ovens, including open fireplaces or grills; cooking
utensils; freezers; and refrigerators. Some societies have more than one kitchen and
more than one room for the preparation and consumption of food.

Seating for relatively big groups is available at one long, square, or round table,
though tables appropriate for smaller gatherings exist as well. A society also has
cleaning equipment, bathrooms, and, most important, space to store the wherewithal
regularly needed for preparing and consuming food (including the basics, such as
salt, pepper, oil, and a well-stocked bodega, or wine cellar). Most societies also have
full bar facilities, along with coffee and espresso machines.

The cooking itself is ordinarily done voluntarily and almost always rests on
experience. In other words, the members with a history of excellence do the cooking. The cook's experience often stems from performance in other circumstances,

such as having cooked on a ship or other vessel, for ceremonies or fiestas, or at the *baserri* (Basque, "farmstead"). The cook's only reward may be a common toast or word of acknowledgement from other members or guests.

After the preparation and the meal, the *digestivo* is served and a bill is written. The people who have partaken in the meal have to pay pro rata. Because the society has supplied the basic infrastructure for consumption and because all the work (buying, preparing, cooking) was voluntary and based on an honor system, the bill is far below the price of an average restaurant meal, probably even less than that of a home-cooked meal. Most of the purchases for the meal are handled through well-established contacts, for members of the society know their local providers and buy directly from them, avoiding the market. Members of the society often happen to be fishermen, happen to work in a *baserri*, or know somebody who does and who can thus sometimes offer the basic ingredients (the fish, the meat) for free or at cut-rate prices. Depending on individual expenses and purchase practices, the bill is sometimes split so that buyer-members can be reimbursed. Yet as a rule one pays pro-rata, and the money thereby collected is placed with an itemized bill into an envelope and is then sent to the treasurer of the society through the internal mail system or put into a cashbox, the *cajetin* (to be collected later by that person).

A society's life needs a legal framework and a location. However, the *txoko* comes to life only because it is an institutional expression of a much more widespread social phenomenon: the *cuadrilla* (clique, circle of friends) (Arpal Poblador, 1985; Ramirez Goikoetxea, 1985). The *cuadrilla* is the result of a complex shift or transfer from a rural environment to complex urban structures. The interaction between the *txoko* and the *cuadrilla* deserves a detailed explanation.

To understand the phenomenon of the *cuadrilla*, it is first necessary to comprehend the part that the *kale* (street) plays in Basque culture (see Arpal Poblador, 1985, pp. 131–145). To do so, one must distinguish between a rural and an urban form of social life in the Basque Country (p. 132). In the countryside one finds the *etxe* (rural house, farmstead), which is agricultural and private in character. Its social type is the *baserritarra*, the man or woman who lives the rural life. Rural life generally denotes being somehow closer to nature or living in a natural environment that remains healthy and unspoiled. By contrast, life in the city or town is symbolized by the *kale*, which is by definition open to the public. This urban life is embodied mainly by the *kaletarra*, the man or woman who lives in the street. Life in an urban environment, be it the town or the city, denotes culture or civilization. It is regarded as artificial, not natural, and therefore associated with values that refer to less-than-wholesome aspects of life. Until the nineteenth century the people of the Basque Country were familiar with only very limited urban development typified by towns having but three streets: *la de arriba*, *la de enmedio*, and *la de abajo* (upper, middle, and lower street) and the houses along those streets (Arpal Poblador 1985, p. 132). Only three sizeable urban centers, developed (Bilbao, Vitoria, and San Sebastian), but even there the old quarters had no more than half a dozen streets, with the *plaza* (square) often being outside the *casco viejo*. Beyond the old center other urban settlements, the *ensanches*, did not form until later. Apart from the *casa solar* (isolated, free-standing rural home), many rather wealthy farmsteads had *la casa en la calle*, a house in the town, so the countryside often extended into town (Arpal Poblador, 1985, p. 134). This image of the street in front of the *caserio* (small farm) can be considered an indication of a continuous conflict that blurred some of the boundaries between countryside, village, town, and city. Only with the turn of the twentieth century did the situation change. But in an age when urban centers and urban life have come to dominate modern Basque society, one can still encounter symbolic representations of rural life in most Basque towns and cities. Analysts have referred to a complex situation in which "symbolic transfers" (Arpal Poblador, 1985, p. 135) from a rural to an urban environment are still common. Its symbol is the "urban villager," who has emerged as a new social type and who combines elements of both *baserritarra* and *kaletarra*.

The urban villager's key social reference point is the *cuadrilla*, a social formation defined by certain characteristics common to the individuals constituting the group: the same generational cohort, the same gender, or the memory of playing together in the same street or *barrio* (neighborhood, quarter) where they grew up. Crucial are those shared experiences or rites of passage that usually mark an individual for life but also foster the entire group's collective memory, such as the *ikastola* (the Basque language school), military service, and important political events. However, the function of the *cuadrilla* has evolved and changed over time. During the Franco years and even during and after the post-Franco political transition, the *cuadrilla* constituted a social infrastructure, a civil-society response that functioned as a stable factor in an unstable political environment. The *cuadrilla* established a kind of parallel world engendering the trust, friendship, responsiveness, and equality in communication, a stability in everyday life that the Franco regime and the exceptionally turbulent post-Franco transition in the Basque Country could not grant (Perez-Agote, 1984, pp. 105–123). Since the late 1990s, however, the *cuadrilla* phenomenon has changed. Whereas the privatization of social life (Perez-Agote 1984, pp. 105–123) opened an escape route during the Franco era and the transition from it, functions other than sheer resistance to the political system have meanwhile become important.

According to sociologist Jesus Arpal Poblador (1985, pp. 136–154) in his brief phenomenology of a typical *cuadrilla*'s life today, the group, usually 5 to 10 people, gathers to spend time and go places as the collective ritual demands. The group meets regularly for drinks, the *txikiteo* or *poteo*, usually either before lunch or before dinner or on other occasions as determined by the festivity calendar or specific occasions such as birthdays or anniversaries. The *txikiteo* consists of making a round through the different bars of a specific zone or barrio, which in most cities is located in the *casco viejo*. Taking place almost daily, the *poteo* may seem almost compulsive to an outsider. The movement and appearances of some *cuadrillas* have sometimes become such an established pattern that the bartender no longer needs to hear the order.

Just as the *cuadrilla* leaves its mark on the vicinity, the vicinity, or a given spatial environment, marks facets of the group's habit. One of the most interesting aspects of the *cuadrilla* phenomenon, though, is that it does not impose unanimity. It is a collective phenomenon that allows time and space for individual expression and creativity. As with any group, various roles evolve within the group; leaders arise who are more popular and acknowledged than others. In some cities and towns these persons have even acquired nicknames that have become so popular that the individual is known only by that name. To gain the respect of one's friends, it is crucial to remain genuine and true to oneself. Some members are known only by their unique appearance, character, or other authentic attitude or history.

Txokos are manifestations of well-established social contacts, principally of the *cuadrilla* type. The *txoko* and the social relations that it represents are a means of reconstituting the reciprocity relations that have their origins in more traditional forms of life, yet they are essentially new in that they represent a modern form of social relations in a growing and increasingly influential urban environment. Originally a peculiar invention of San Sebastián's bourgeoisie, the popular societies, notably the gastronomic societies (Arpal Poblador, 1985; Luengo, 1999), have, over roughly a century, become less class representative or class bound and are now a more inclusive and interclass phenomenon than ever before. The *txoko* in its ubiquity now fulfills a variety of positive societal functions. As argued by Arpal Poblador (1985, p. 138), mechanical solidarity and space that are created for the individual together with a communitarian dimension contribute to a social equilibrium. *Txokos* are thus an institutionalized measure and increasingly an "interclass phenomenon" (Arpal Poblador, 1985, pp. 140–141; Luengo, 1999) against the divisions of modern society, an attempt to introduce a form of integration based on what Habermas and others have called *Lebenswelt* (life world). Ranging somewhere between tradition and modernity, the life world is an attempt to respond to purely instrumental and systemic rationalization and integration. But the *txoko* not only has liberating functions; it also reproduces existing age and sex or gender constellations and often presents society as if it were a community (Arpal Poblador, 1985, pp. 140–141). Some commentators have interpreted the *txoko* as an institutional compensation device that exercises a cooling effect on an overheated society and lessens tensions through a collective group therapy almost resembling a psychodramatic setting. This interpretation suggests that the *txoko* offers an escape route from the necessities of daily life, implying not only a shift toward communality and commensality (the act of eating together) but almost an exit strategy (Aguirre Franco, 1983; van Wijck, 2000).

Yet it would be wrong to perceive the function of the *txoko* solely in extreme terms or in the light of total exit conditions. As an institution, it is as good (or bad) as the society and the members who support it. The fact remains that eating at the *txoko*, particularly during the fiestas, interrupts daily life and routine and definitely conveys what Simmel (1971) termed *conviviality* (pp. 127–129). But the *txoko* as an institution is more than that. As a symbolic reproduction of Basque society and identity, the *txoko* accommodates the transition from rural to urban life, exemplifying a historic reformulation of the community–society divide (Arpal Poblador, 1985; Ramirez Goikoetxea, 1985). As potential cells for reproducing nationalism, the *cuadrilla* and the *txoko* together can also be seen as models of sociability and commensality not bound by rigid class structures, as elements that link classes instead (Luengo, 1999; Perez-Agote, 1984). Lastly, if Luengo (1999) is correct that investigating the levels of sociability is almost like using a thermostat to analyze change in society, then the *txoko* phenomenon, particularly its recent enormous expansion, may indicate that Basque society is becoming more inclusive and thus more democratic than it has been. Enriching the public sphere, yet not in an anonymous, impersonal, or entirely privatized way, the *txoko* has helped reconstruct the social fabric of a community that is otherwise deeply politically divided. In the eyes of at least one commentator, it has also afforded a real alternative to the homogenization process of modern capitalist society (Ramirez Goikoetxea, 1985).

Between Homogenization and Differentiation

Having examined the history and microlevel operations of the cooking societies, I now look at broader issues, namely, the ways in which cooking, eating, and drinking together in the *txoko* are linked to some of the region's physical, cultural, and historical features. It is impossible to discuss social aspects of the *txoko* such as conviviality and commensality unless the question of what the members actually eat and drink when they are together is combined with the historiogeographical question of why they do so particularly in the Basque Country. There is no human activity in which function and content are as interdependent as eating and drinking. Form is indeed condensed substance, and full appreciation of the formal aspects of eating together in the cooking society requires at least a brief historical account of alimentation, nutrition, and cooking, the content that is often linked to unique historiogeographical patterns in the Basque Country.

Overall, Basque cooking has always reflected the old division between the Atlantic North and the Mediterranean South (Iturbe & Letamendia, 2000, p. 48). Developed forms of agriculture have always been limited in the Atlantic zone, primarily because of its rugged terrain and humid climate. Fishing is omnipresent, and the supply of meat and fat generally comes from farm animals such as chickens, goats, lambs, and cows. Standard beverages are alcoholic drinks, apple cider, and some white wine (*txakoli* from microclimates and terroirs such as those in Getaria, Gipuzkoa). By contrast, the southern zone has a rather dry climate and a less rugged, more extensive and farmable terrain that allows for the development of sophisticated crops, such as asparagus, spinach, artichokes, and cereals. Inland, large-scale farming and a cattle industry emerged in the course of the nineteenth century. In terms of nutritional models and cuisine, the fat comes chiefly from olives, not animals. And unlike the Atlantic zone, the south has sophisticated wine-making, above all in parts of Álava and Navarre. The different geographical patterns explain the availability and the peculiar choice of food in the *txokos* of each zone or region. Fish and seafood are found everywhere in the Atlantic zone, whereas meat and vegetables are more likely to make it onto the menu in the southern zone (e.g., Álava and Navarre). By the same token, the choice of wine is distinct to each zone or region, white wine from Getaria or Galicia is more likely to be consumed in *txokos* located in coastal communities, whereas the top-rank red Riojas or the best Navarrese wines are more likely to be consumed where they have been produced.

Over time three main influences have changed food-consumption patterns in the Basque Country. First, alimentation changed radically through the discovery of the New World and the introduction of New World produce such as corn, potatoes, pepper, tomatoes, beans, sugar, and chocolate to the northern and southern zones. Corn, beans, and potatoes were exceptionally influential on nutritional patterns (Busca Isusi, 1987, pp. 13–17; Haranburu Altuna, 2000, pp. 161–162; Iturbe & Letamendia, 2000, pp. 50–52).

The second most important influence was the Catholic Church. It established a religious calendar, which prescribed what foods to avoid and what to eat at which times (Haranburu Altuna, 2000, pp. 118–165, pp. 201–202; Iturbe & Letamendia, 2000, pp. 52–57). Religious abstinence demanded the exclusion of meat, meat soup, eggs, milk products, and animal fat. Abstention was practiced on Wednesdays and Fridays, along with other selected days of the year. On the remaining days, fish was the alternative. Basque society and culture today are much more secularized than they used to be. But secularization does not mean that old consumption habits stemming from a Catholic background have completely disappeared. It is still the tradition in many household kitchens and *txokos* to have fish or seafood around Christmas and the New Year, whereas meat and related dishes are standard on some days of the fiesta. The calendar of festivals is full of days celebrating saints, occasions that call for a certain form of cooking. Additionally, there are birthdays, weddings, retirement, stag nights, and funerals, events that ordinarily determine the choice of what to eat and drink. However, the Catholic church emphasized and actively promoted communitarian habits of eating not only to mark such special events but also to ward off the threat of Protestant individualism. Eventually, eating together, religious belief, and social life developed into a custom, as illustrated by that institutional microcosm, the *txoko*.

The third impact on eating habits and food consumption in the Basque Country came with the modernization of the region's society at the turn of the twentieth century. Especially important was the development of a modern infrastructure (installation and improvement of rail and road networks) and the means of communication (the telegraph, the telephone, and, later, radio and film). Such advances nurtured a modern tourist industry. Combined with industrialization, they resulted in the creation of an urban, industrialized environment and culture. Such changes immediately yielded a new landscape of political cultures. The liberals favored the nascent rationalized form of urban culture, notably in Bilbao and San Sebastián, whereas the traditional rural way of life was besieged by modernization and rationalization processes (Iturbe & Letamendia, 2000, pp. 59–63). The conflict between the two opposing forces eventually gave way to a new, third force, Basque nationalism. Blending aspects of both conservatism and modernization, it had a particular impact on the cuisine and food patterns. Basque nationalism aimed to reconstruct what it means to be Basque, so symbolic capital such as food and the act of eating together became a major focus (p. 62).

The traditional style of rural food preparation and consumption, the urban standardization of cooking in such places as hotels and restaurants, and the nationalist attempt at reconstructing culinary symbolic capital all played a part in producing a new common cuisine to which the new label *cocina vasca* truly applied and for which *txoko* cooking has become an institutional expression. What makes this new constellation so remarkable is the convergence of two processes: homogenization and differentiation (Haranburu Altuna, 2000, pp. 299–305). The homogenization process is unmistakable in the Mediterraneanization of food in the Basque Country, with the olive-based alimentation of the Ebro valley reaching the Cantabrian coast and now prevalent in the Atlantic provinces of Gipuzkoa and Biscay. At the same time, modern transportation and food preservation have made it possible for the fresh fruit and fish of the Atlantic to spread to Navarre and Álava—to such an extent that they are now thought of as staples. Such homogenization has not led to total monotony or dominance, though. Variety and diversity has always existed in the regions. In fact, some people have called for changing the label *cocina vasca* to its plural, *cocinas vascas*, to reflect regional differentiation (Haranburu Altuna 2000, p. 30).

With respect to the development of alimentation and cooking over the last twenty years, modernization and rationalization processes have culminated in what has been referred to as the new Basque cuisine, *la nueva cocina vasca*. The development of the new Basque cuisine is arguably a critique of the rationalization process as it has developed so far. For lack of anything new, adventurous, or surprising on the standard menu or ways of preparing and presenting it, this new movement has pressed for a return to culinary basics and an end to the process of saturation and stagnation. The demand has also been for fresh produce. The avant-garde of this culinary revolution has consisted largely of innovative restaurant chefs and cooking-society experts. (These roles often overlap in the Basque Country.) The history of the new Basque cuisine has been truly revolutionary and so successful that most of the more sophisticated Basque restaurants and *txokos* have incorporated its demands. Throughout the year (mainly during the fiestas but by no means limited to them), the Basque Country now has numerous competitions in which *txoko* cooks continue the innovation and refinement of Basque cooking. They are aided by thousands of *txoko* members and guests who all think they would not enjoy the *cocina vasca* if cooking and eating were isolated or solitary affairs.

Between *Gemeinschaft* and *Gesellschaft*: Plebeian Culture, Moral Economy, and Commensality

In his writings on late eighteenth-century England, E. P. Thompson (1980, 1991) suggested that plebeian culture and moral economy are intrinsically linked. *Plebeian culture* was an auxiliary term that Thompson used to describe a situation in which class was not what classic Marxist theorists assumed it to be. Rather than forming nascent prototypes of the industrial working class, Thompson preferred to see classes as fields of gravity, as heterogeneous constellations of many dimensions and layers in which traditional popular customs played a major part. These common customs also facilitated the survival of a moral economy, one that could assume various meanings to the plebeian crowds, including shared rights, norms or obligations, day-to-day habits, and practices. Taken together, these meanings in many ways constituted a force alien and opposed to elite classes.

A closer look into the stratification of the Basque Country reveals few, if any, clear-cut class structures, except in the metropolitan region of Bilbao, its industrial environs, and a few industrial towns and industrial development zones such as Durango, Eibar, Elgoibar, Ermua, and Hernani. In many ways the Basque Country seems a prime illustration of Thompson's (1980) main notion of plebeian culture. The work of social historians and historical anthropologists repeatedly cited in this chapter, such as Luengo (1999), Homobono Martínez (1987, 1990, 1997), and Arpal Poblador (1985), confirms the existence of such a plebeian cultural macroconstellation and the place that cooking societies play in its moral economy.

Whereas historians and social scientists have hinted at these kinds of macroconstellation and the moral economy that goes with them, the political economist Albert O. Hirschman has looked at microconstellations, by which he mainly meant institutional dimensions. In *The Passions and the Interests* (1977) he first hinted that passions and interests might be much more intrinsically linked in modern times than has often been assumed. Concepts derived from his approach to moral economy, above all the idea of commensality (Hirschman, 1998, pp. 11–32), allow the researcher to take a closer look at the microlevel and the peculiar links that exist between the public and the private sphere and between customs and morals (Hess, 1999).

In his seminal book *Shifting Involvements: Private Interest and Public Action* (1982), Hirschman addressed the problem of periodic shifts that have occurred in modern civil society. In this work he analyzed both the retreat into privacy and the inclination toward public action in wave-like appearances. He found that a sense of disappointment was the main motive behind both private retreat and public action. At that time Hirschman did not discuss social practices in which public concern mingles with private activities and thereby fosters an equilibrium in civil society. Going a step further, Hirschman maintained that merging the private and public spheres was seen as a potential threat to civil society. In his much later essay about commensality, Hirschman (1998) revisited some of his previous arguments. He asked the reader to think about occasions where the merging of the two spheres can actually have positive results and pointed out that "economists [and other social scientists] have often looked at the consumption of food as a purely private and self-centered activity" (p. 28).

Hirschman (1998, p. 29) continued his argument by stressing that social scientists usually forget about other dimensions: While people are consuming food and drink, they gather for the meal, engage in conversation and discussion, exchange information and points of view, tell stories, perform religious services, and so on. From the purely biological stance, there is no doubt that eating has a straightforward relationship to individual welfare. But once eating and drinking are done in common, they normally go hand in hand with a remarkably diverse set of public or collective activities.

Hirschman (1998) further stressed that the function of the common meal can, and really does, vary. He brought to mind Heinrich Mann's novel *Der Untertan* (The Subject), in which the main character, Diederich Hessling, is drawn into a form of beer-drinking and pretzel-eating commensality that can be described only as reactionary in terms of its later outcome, National Socialism. In contrast to such negative examples and experiences, Hirschman then revealed the great potential of commensality: noninstrumental, ends-oriented interaction. It is exactly at this juncture that the Basque cooking society comes in. It seems to me that the *txoko* is a positive example of how commensality, at least when collectively organized and sensibly institutionalized, can cultivate loyalty and help maintain a civic equilibrium. In other words, when such commensality emerges, human beings are not treated merely as means to certain ends but rather as ends in themselves.

Constituting the microinstitutional framework for such ends-centered interaction, the *txoko* promotes the social equilibrium. *Txokos* are an institutionalized measure and increasingly an interclass phenomenon working against the divisions of modern society. In other words, they are an attempt at life-world integration (Arpal Poblador, 1985; Habermas, 1962; Luengo, 1999). Located somewhere between tradition and modernity, *txokos* are attempts to provide answers to purely instrumental and systemic rationalization or system integration. However, unlike public institutions and the public sphere in the roles that Habermas emphasizes and endorses, *txokos* are neither purely public nor purely private institutions. Instead, they occupy a unique space somewhere in the middle of that continuum. It is this intermediate position that enhances the success and popularity of the *txokos*.

Yet not all the *txoko*'s social functions are "progressive." Ultimately, it is as an institution as good (or as bad) as the society and the members who constitute it. The *txoko* is clearly an expression of conviviality as meant by Simmel (Homobono Martínez, 1987). In that sense the *txoko* as an institution is also a symbolic reproduction of Basque society and identity and is especially accommodating of the transition from rural to urban life. It thus exemplifies a historic reformulation of the community–society divide (Arpal Poblador, 1985).

Whatever the details and the individual and collective enjoyment in the *sociedades* are, this institution has obviously become a backbone of modern Basque society. Unlike the disastrous experiences with certain forms of collectivity in the former Soviet Union and Nazi Germany (as totalitarian social and political regimes that tried to eliminate the distinction between private and public), Basque cooking societies exemplify interaction through which the public and the private actually enrich each other. It seems wrong to me to degrade these organizations as being part of an invented tradition or to consider them terrorist recruitment cells or nationalist inventions, as is sometimes implicitly suggested by commentators like Juaristi (1987) and Hobsbawm and Ranger (1983). The opposite is true. The *sociedades gastronómicas* are relatively modern institutions that allow the Basque Country to overcome some of the tensions that arise when an old civilization meets the modern conditions of the twenty-first century. The relationship between the private and the public is a delicate one, and has not always worked out well in modern times. The *txoko*, which uniquely connects both spheres, does appear to be the Basques' most genuine and beneficial reply to the question of how a plebeian culture with a long history can survive under modern conditions.

As I have tried to show, the gastronomic society is unique to Basque society and its historical, cultural, political, and social conditions and its geographic environment. Although the Basque diaspora has partly transported such gastronomic practices to other parts of the world, it remains largely a Basque affair (visitors are always welcome). I therefore remain skeptical about the possibility of transplanting or copying such habits and practices. Emulation is always a possibility, of course. Yet with all the media hype about cooking in recent years, it remains to be seen whether the appropriate cultural and social forms and conditions can be found outside the Basque Country. After all, the purpose is not only that of consuming all that good food and drink but also of doing so for the beneficial and mutual effect on those who regard eating and drinking not just as solitary, entirely private affairs but as social and cultural acts.

References

Aguirre Franco, R. (1983). *Las sociedades populares* [Popular societies]. Colección Guipúzcoa: Vol. 19. San Sebastián: Caja de Guipúzcoa.

Alonso Céspedes, M. (1996). *El caso de los txokos vascos: Sociología de la fratría informal* [Basque *txokos*: A sociological case study on informal fraternities] (Unpublished master's thesis). Universidad de Deusto, Bilbao, Spain.

Arpal Poblador, J. (1985). Solidaridades elementales y organizaciones colectivas en el país Vasco (Cuadrillas, txokos, asociaciones) [Primal solidarities and collective organizations in the Basque Country (Cliques, gastronomic societies, associations)]. In P. Bidart (Ed.), *Processus sociaux: Idéologies et practiques culturelles dans la société basque* (pp. 129–154). Pau: Université de Pau et des pays de l'Adour.

Busca Isusi, J. M. (1987). *Traditional Basque cooking*. Reno: University of Nevada Press.

Habermas, J. (1962). *Strukturwandel der Öffentlichkeit* [The structural transformation of the public sphere]. Darmstadt: Luchterhand.

Haranburu Altuna, L. (2000). *Historia de la alimentación y de la cocina en el País Vasco* [History of food and cooking in the Basque Country]. San Sebastián: Hiria Liburuak.

Hess, A. (1999). 'The economy of morals and its applications'—An attempt to understand some central concepts in the work of Albert O. Hirschman. *Review of International Political Economy, 6,* 338–359. doi:https://doi.org/10.1080/096922999347218

Hess, A. (2007). The social bonds of cooking: Gastronomic societies in the Basque Country. *Cultural Sociology, 1,* 383–407. doi:https://doi.org/10.1177/1749975507082056

Hess, A. (2009). *Reluctant modernization: Plebeian culture and moral economy in the Basque Country.* Oxford, UK: Peter Lang.

Hirschman, A. O. (1977). *The passions and the interests: Political arguments for capitalism before its triumph.* Princeton: Princeton University Press.

Hirschman, A. O. (1982). *Shifting involvements: Private interests and public action.* Princeton: Princeton University Press.

Hirschman, A. O. (1998). *Crossing boundaries—Selected writings.* New York: Zone Books.

Hobsbawm, E. J., & Ranger, T. (Eds.). (1983). *The invention of tradition.* Cambridge, UK: Cambridge University Press.

Homobono Martínez, J. I. (1987). Comensabilidad y fiesta en el ambito arrantzale: San Martin de Bermeo. [Socializing and celebrating in the company of fishermen]. *Bermeo, 6,* 301–392.

Homobono Martínez, J. I. (1990). Fiesta, tradición e identidad local [Celebration, tradition, and local identity]. *Cuadernos de etnología y etnografía de Navarra, 55,* 43–58. Retrieved from http://www.vianayborgia.es/bibliotecaPDFs/CUET-0055-0000-0043-0058.pdf

Homobono Martínez, J. I. (1997). Fiestas en el ámbito arrantzale. Expresiones de sociabilidad e identidades colectivas [Celebrating in the fishing sector: Manifestations of commensality and collective identities]. *Zainak, 15,* 61–100. Retrieved from http://www.eusko-ikaskuntza.org/en/publications/fiestas-en-el-ambito-arrantzale-expresiones-de-sociabilidad-e-identidades-colectivas/art-9041/#small-dialog

Idroquilis, A. P. (1994). *Comer en sociedad* [Eating together]. Vitoria-Gasteiz: Diputación Foral de Álava.

Iturbe, J. A., & Letamendia, F. (2000). Cultura, politica y gastronomia en el País Vasco [Culture, politics, and gastronomy in the Basque Country]. In F. Letamendia & C. Coulon (Eds.), *Cocinas del mundo—La política en la mesa* (pp. 45–78). Madrid: Editorial Fundamentos.

Juaristi, J. (1987). *El linaje de Aitor. La invención de la tradición vasca* [The lineage of Aitor: Inventing the Basque tradition]. Madrid: Taurus.

Las 700 sociedades gastronomicas en Euzkadi siguen siendo un coto privado para hombres [The 700 gastronomic societies in the Basque Country remain a private preserve for men]. (1981, October 30). *Deia* (Bilbao).

Luengo [Teixidor], F. (1999). *San Sebastián—La vida cotidiana de una ciudad* [San Sebastián— The daily life of a city]. San Sebastián: Editorial Txertoa.

Perez-Agote, A. (1984). *La reproducción del nacionalismo. El caso Vasco* [The social roots of Basque nationalism]. Madrid: Centro de Investigaciones Sociológicas.

Ramirez Goikoetxea, E. (1985). Associations collectives et relations interpersonelles au Pays Basque [Communal associations and interpersonal relations in the Basque Country]. In P. Bidart (Ed.), *Processus sociaux: Idééologies et practiques culturelles dans la société basque* (pp. 119–128). Pau: Université de Pau et des pays de l'Adour.

Simmel, G. (1971). *On individuality and social Forms* (D. N. Levine, Trans.). Chicago: University of Chicago Press.

Thompson, E. P. (1980). *Plebeische Kultur und moralische Ökonomie* [Plebeian culture and moral economy]. Frankfurt: Ullstein.

Thompson, E. P. (1991). *Customs in common: Studies in traditional popular culture.* London: Merlin Press.

Tocqueville, A. de (2000). *Democracy in America* (H. C. Mansfield & D. Winthrop, Trans). 2 vols. Chicago: University of Chicago Press. (Original work published 1835–1840)

van Wijck, A. (2000). *Basque male cooking societies* (Unpublished master's thesis). Boston University, Massachusetts.

Chapter 6
Drift and Morphosis in Institutional Change: Evidence from the 'Walz' and Public Tendering in Germany

Johannes Glückler and Regina Lenz

How do institutions change? This question is central to institutional theorists across disciplines. Guided by teleological interest, economists and political scientists, for instance, aim to understand the national differences in institutions and their role in hindering or facilitating innovation and development in order to turn "bad" institutions into more beneficial ones (Ménard & Shirley, 2005; Peters, 2012). By contrast, scholars in organizational institutionalism have focused on understanding how institutions evolve and work and on analyzing the mechanisms of how institutional change proceeds (Greenwood, Oliver, Sahlin, & Suddaby, 2008). In this respect incremental institutional changes can be distinguished from more radical ones. The latter kind is usually associated with external shocks that disrupt the established institutional structure, such as environmental and demographic changes, or the introduction of new technologies (Acemoğlu & Robinson, 2012; Rodríguez-Pose & Storper, 2006). But change can also be triggered endogenously by contradictions and tensions within an institutional structure, which then has to be reinterpreted and renegotiated (Seo & Creed, 2002; Zilber, 2002). It is this endogenous institutional change that needs further study (Powell & Colyvas, 2008; Suddaby, 2010).

In an appraisal of the diversity of empirical studies on institutional change, Streeck and Thelen (2005) identified several mechanisms of gradual institutional transformation. Each of these mechanisms characterizes a particular process, which either transforms existing institutions in response to a new context (e.g., layering, conversion) or leads to their gradual erosion (e.g., drift, exhaustion) and ultimate breakdown (displacement). It is important in that regard to distinguish between different understandings of the term *institution*. In economics and political science, studies focus especially on formal institutions, which are "formalized rules that are in principle obligatory and subject to third-party enforcement" (Hacker, Thelen, & Pierson, 2013, p. 5). Such a concept includes codified formal rules, public policies,

J. Glückler (✉) · R. Lenz
Department of Geography, Heidelberg University, Heidelberg, Germany
e-mail: glueckler@uni-heidelberg.de; lenz@uni-heidelberg.de

© The Author(s) 2018 111
J. Glückler et al. (eds.), *Knowledge and Institutions*, Knowledge and Space 13,
https://doi.org/10.1007/978-3-319-75328-7_6

and the state-backed organizations established to set and enforce them. This definition implies that institutional change is subject to the power struggle between multiple interest groups all seeking to change the rules according to their own benefit. A new policy or a new law thus represents an institutional change, the types of which, such as layering, conversion, and drift, describe the relation between regulation and its outcomes. Layering, for example, refers to introducing "new arrangements on top of preexisting structures intended to serve different purposes" (Schickler, 2001, p. 15). Similarly, the mechanism of conversion is a process in which new actors redirect and transform existing policies and regulations to achieve new objectives (Thelen, 2004). Evidently, these concepts stem from an interest in analyzing the dynamics and effects of policies and respond to the experience that significant policy changes sometimes occur without any change in political outcomes (Levitsky & Slater, 2011). Conversely, there are frequently overlooked, but very significant, changes in political outcomes despite a stability in the structure of policies (Hacker et al., 2013).

We argue in this chapter that limiting the perspective on institutions to regulation and rule-making is likely to obscure the underlying institutional reality that structures actors' practices (Bathelt & Glückler, 2014). Observed institutional practices—institutional form—might therefore follow their own logic and serve different functions that rest on mutual expectations of what is considered legitimate. Drawing on analyses of the ways in which institutional mechanisms work against or in favor of regulation (Glückler & Lenz, 2016; Helmke & Levitsky, 2004), we aim to continue unraveling the processes through which institutions respond to regulatory changes and the social outcomes of such institutional responses. Differentiating between two institutional components, form and function, improves our ability to see which parts of an institution change or remain stable and to discern their corresponding influence on the effect of regulation.

We diverge in two important ways from the framing of the concepts specified above. First, we go beyond a broad understanding of institutions that looks at "durable systems of established and embedded social rules that structure social interactions, rather than rules as such" (Hodgson, 2006, p. 13). We argue instead for a narrower conception. In keeping with the common distinction between formal and informal institutions (Hacker et al., 2013; Helmke & Levitsky, 2004; North, 1990; Williams & Vorley, 2014), we distinguish, albeit more sharply, between regulation and institutions (Bathelt & Glückler, 2014). Policies and regulations are no longer seen as the institutions themselves but rather as part of the institutional context, along with the actors that induce them, such as individuals, governments, and firms (Glückler & Bathelt, 2017). We ask whether newly introduced actions and rules really transform the stable patterns of social life. Instead of solely analyzing the effects of policy changes on social outcomes, we conceive of the relation between institutional change, institutional context (including regulation), and social outcomes. We adopt a relational perspective to define institutions as the stable patterns of interaction that owe their meaning to mutually shared expectations for legitimate action (Bathelt & Glückler, 2014). In other words, an institution is the compound of meaningful, mutually shared expectations and the pattern of interactions that those expectations legitimize in recurrent situations. Institutions refer to the beliefs that actors have about what the rules really are (Farrell, 2018) and to the stable patterns of interactions that those beliefs sustain. Consequently, institutions are observed in actual practice, not in codified rules. This concept is similar to that of decoupling, which is used in organizational institutionalism (Hallett & Ventresca, 2006; Meyer & Rowan, 1977) to convey that organizations sometimes build "gaps between their formal structures and actual work activities" (Meyer & Rowan, 1977, p. 341) in an attempt to be legitimate by conforming to institutionalized rules while actually behaving differently to meet efficiency criteria.

In shifting the focus away from making the rules (regulation) to living the rules in mutually legitimate ways (institutions), we offer an alternative analytical perspective on institutional change. This new angle promises an answer to the question of why purposeful regulation sometimes fails to yield its intended outcomes. More important, it offers an additional level of analysis that allows us to study the forces and mechanisms that work against or in favor of regulation and that should be understood in order to raise the efficacy of what we have called institutional policy-making (Glückler & Lenz, 2016).

Second, we conceptualize modes of change in a framework that has us look explicitly at the differential dynamics of institutional form and function. We explore Campbell's (2010) question of whether an institution's function can change without alteration of its form or vice versa and whether "these two possibilities [are] equivalent or somehow significantly different" (p. 108). Institutional form specifies the meaningful pattern of interactions in recurrent situations, whereas institutional function characterizes the intended or unintended outcome of an institution in compliance with actors' mutual understanding of legitimacy. We argue that each of these two characteristics of an institution may either remain stable or change through its interdependent relation with the institutional context.

Combining the characteristics of these two dimensions into a matrix, we propose four modes of institutional change (Fig. 6.1). This typology goes beyond the simple dichotomy of institutional stasis (same pattern to perform the same function) versus institutional transformation (different pattern to perform a different function), such as layering and conversion. In addition, it allows us to examine how an abiding institutional form gradually performs new functions. This situation partly corresponds to what Hacker (2004), when referring to policies, defines as drift: "changes in the operation or effect of policies that occur without significant changes in those policies' structure" (Hacker, 2004, p. 246). Because the notion of drift refers to alternative uses or effects—be they deliberate or unconscious—of an otherwise unchanged form (Béland, 2007), we endorse this term as a label for an analogous change of institutions. In this chapter institutional drift means a situation in which an institutional form—a stable pattern of practices—is sustained while performing alternative functions or leading to alternative social outcomes. Unlike its original connotation, drift need not only have a negative value only; it can also lead to appreciation, as we show. A fourth and original type of institutional change occurs in the

Institutional function

	Stable function	Shifting function
Stable form	STASIS	DRIFT
Shifting form	MORPHOSIS	TRANSFORMATION (e.g., layering, conversion)

Institutional form

Fig. 6.1 Types of change of an existing institution. Source: Design by authors

reverse case, that is, when an institution gradually adapts its form to yield the same social outcomes under shifting institutional contexts. Borrowing from biology, we refer to this mechanism as morphosis, the nonessential adjustment of a form to shifting environmental conditions in order to retain its original function.

For each of the two more subtle types of institutional change, drift and morphosis, we reconstruct an empirical example of local crafts in Germany. Both have been discussed as instruments for promoting local commerce either through stimulation of local demand or through knowledge creation and learning across distant places. Empirically, we draw on qualitative evidence that we collected during two stages of fieldwork in Baden-Württemberg in 2015.[1] The first case is the centuries-old German institution of the *Walz,* also called *Wanderzeit,* the years during which trained apprentices in the crafts traveled to different towns across a wide region to work as a *Geselle,* or journeyman. This case confirms the logic of institutional drift (Schickler, 2001), albeit for a socially appreciated rather than deprived institution. We demonstrate how a relatively unchanged and persistent morphology has gradually fulfilled alternating social purposes over the last two centuries. The second empirical study, which focuses on local public procurement in the contemporary construction sector, illustrates what we call institutional morphosis, a process by which institutions change their form in order to retain their original function. This second example of institutional change shows how the shift from national to supranational, European regulation has clearly changed the normative requirements of public procurement. However, we present circumstantial evidence that even though the institution's actual form has changed, it has retained one of its original functions of promoting local commerce.

[1] Two groups of graduate and postgraduate students assisted us in related research seminars on economic geography at Heidelberg University. Both case studies were based on 18 semistructured interviews each. We are especially grateful for the excellent work by Hanna Wilbrand, Lukas Bieringer, and Christian Berberich as interviewers and for their remarkably empathetic access to and communication with the journeyman community (Wilbrand, Berberich, & Bieringer, 2015).

Drift of the *Walz*: The German Journeyman's Years on the Road

The Institutional Form of the Walz

Although a key element in the European history of the crafts, the wandering years of craft journeymen did not attract major scholarly interest until the late eighteenth and early nineteenth century (Bade, 1982; Schanz, 1877; Werner, 1981). Today, academic research and popular publications alike refer to the wandering years, the *Walz*, as "amongst the most important institutions in German craftsmanship" (Back, 1985, p. 12). The transition from a medieval feudal order to a modern industrialized society entailed deep societal ruptures, such as the fall of the guilds, the liberalization of industry and trade, and the displacement of traditional crafts by the emergent industrial factories. We demonstrate that the German *Walz* meets all the elementary criteria of an institution: a set of legitimate mutual expectations, a commonly shared understanding of a pattern of interactions in recurrent situations, and devices and practices of sanctions. This institution was a widespread phenomenon in medieval Europe, being known as the *compagnonnage* in France (Truant, 1979) and the wandering journeymen in the British Isles, for instance, but was common in the United States as well (Cooper, 1983; Salinger, 1983). Except in Germany, it had disappeared in most countries by the early twentieth century. Although the *Walz* has ceased as a legal or professional requirement, it continues to exist and has even experienced recent revival, reflecting a general trend toward a resurgence of craft modes of production (Suddaby, Ganzin, & Minkus, 2017). Although the *Walz* has lost its legal and professional status, UNESCO has protected the practice since 2014 within the framework of intangible cultural heritage, paying tribute to the significance of this institution in the history and evolution of the crafts in Europe.

We identify three stages in the institutional morphology of the *Walz*: aspiration, wandering, and homecoming (Table 6.1). In the first stage the person seeking to become eligible as journeyman has to have successfully completed an apprenticeship and must be unmarried, debt-free, without criminal record, and younger than 30 years. To start the wandering phase, which usually lasts two or three years and one day, a journeyman affiliates with one of the journeyman associations or fraternities (*Schächte*), which provide for assistance at home and on travel. The journeyman begins as a novice (*Aspirant*) to be socialized with the values, customs, and responsibilities of being a virtuous member of his fraternity. When the person is prepared for travel, the association arranges for a ceremonial release party (*Losbringen*). Peer journeymen typically use a nail and hammer to pierce one of the novice's ears for an earring (*Nageln*)—traditionally his last cash if he becomes indigent. The novice puts on the traditional garb (*Einkluften*) and a number of obligatory accessories such as a hat, a walking stick (*Stenz*), and a square cloth (*Charlottenburger*) in which to carry his personal belongings (Fig. 6.2). The release from home includes further rituals, such as climbing over the sign marking the town limits (*Spinnermarsch*) and burying some liquor until the new journeyman's return, which all help create a sense

Table 6.1 The German wandering years as an institution

Aspiration (*Aspiranz*)	Wandering (*Walz*)	Homecoming (*Einheimischmelden*)
• Meeting between the novice (*Aspirant*) and a senior journeyman (*Altgeselle*) to learn about the journeyman years • Familiarization between novice and senior journeymen, introduction to a journeyman association • Affiliation with and initiation into the fraternity (*Schacht*): nailing (*Nageln*) and other rituals such as embedding (*Einbinden*) • Release party (*Losbringen*), donning of the traditional garb of the craftsman (*Einkluften*), burying of a bottle of liquor, symbolic climbing over the sign marking the town limits (*Spinnermarsch*), etc.	• Beginning of travel together with a senior journeyman (*Exportgeselle*) who teaches principles, codes, and rules of virtuous behavior • Mobility and lodging: cost-free or very inexpensive (e.g., hitchhiking, "hotel of a thousand stars," lodging with the master) • Self-presentation (*Vorsprechen*) to a master craftsman, with recitation of a secret greeting formula (*Schnack*) being an unmistakable identifier of the fraternity • Either paid employment by the master or his payment of travel money (*Zehrgeld*) for the journeyman to continue walking	• End of the *Walz* after two or three years and one day • Reentry into the off-limits zone (*Bannmeile*) in which the journeyman had been forbidden to ply his trade, recovery of the buried bottle of liquor • Welcoming party organized by the senior journeyman, including family, peer journeyman, and fraternity members, shedding of the garb (*Auskluften*) • Long-term commitment to and compliance with the conventions of the journeyman fraternity, participation in fraternity events (*Aufklopfen*) • Social responsibility for the local home community

Source: Design by authors

of identity and a visible commitment to the shared meanings and expectations embodied in the association.

The second stage is the actual period of wandering. While traveling, the journeyman is obliged to wear the fraternity garb, carry with him only his personal belongings, move cost-free, and avoid coming closer to home than the traditional radius of about 50 km (*Bannmeile*). Since journeymen travel only with their private belongings, there has always been a general understanding about the need to support them with travel money (*Zehrgeld*). To find employment in a foreign city, the journeyman must present himself (*Vorsprechen*) as a legitimate traveling journeyman (to distinguishhimself from local beggars). To do so, he recites a lengthy greeting formula (*Schnack*), typically in rhymes that each apprentice has to learn by heart and keep secret as a unique identifier of the journeyman association. The master, in turn, is expected to employ a journeyman, even if only for a short period, to cover the expenses of traveling and to share his knowledge and experience without keeping secrets (Werner, 1981). When a master has no work to offer, the journeyman receives some money to pay for the day and continue his travel. If a master refuses to pay the token, journeymen may put a mark on the master's workshop and spread the news

Fig. 6.2 Baptist and Josef Treu, two journeymen from Haselbach, Bavaria, in 1908. Source: Alfred Merl. Reprinted with permission

by word of mouth through the journeyman association that every journeyman should shun this master in the future. Given the strong sense of belonging, peer journeymen will usually enforce such sanctions. Part of the institutional form of wandering is that foreign journeymen receive a gift of food, shelter, or money upon their arrival in a town (Werner, 1981). During their stay there, local and foreign journeymen regularly meet at the *Herberge*. Similar to the Basque *txoko* (Hess, 2018), the *Herberge* combines two functions. First, it is a physical place at which to lodge for a few days, seek employment, and socialize with each other. Second, it also serves as a meeting point for the regular gatherings (*Aufklopfen*) of members of the journeyman association. At these assemblies the journeymen elect their representatives, test and promote apprentices, welcome foreign journeymen, settle disputes and sanction misbehavior, collect fees for the fraternity, manage its treasury, assist journeymen in need, and support them on their travels (Werner, 1981).

After two or three years and one day of traveling, the wandering journeyman enters upon the final stage of his professional preparation, homecoming (*Einheimischmelden*). He finally crosses into his hometown's *Bannmeile*, the zone in which he had been forbidden to practice his trade while on the road. Upon the journeyman's return, the responsible senior journeyman (*Exportgeselle*) organizes a welcome party that includes fraternity members, family, and friends. Ceremonial acts such as digging up the liquor and taking off the garb (*Auskluften*) symbolize the end of the journeyman's wandering years. Because journeymen often travel together, the *Walz* creates close friendships among artisans, the social bonds that are the seedbed for nurturing community commitment and reproducing the values and conventions of the local journeyman association back home. Only if senior journeymen cultivate the traditional heritage, teach the values and mutual expectations of a virtuous craftsman, and monitor and sanction compliance with the institutional legacy can the *Walz* survive over time. Hence, Cooper (1983) concluded that the wandering serves as a self-reinforcing system of interdependencies between apprentices, journeymen, and senior craftsmen tied together under the roof of a journeyman association. Senior journeymen are expected to attend the regular meetings to initiate novices; to teach, monitor, and sanction the often unwritten fraternity rules; but also to cultivate friendship, learn about new business opportunities in town, and arrange for community services and social responsibility.

Changes in the Institutional Context: Authorities, Regulation, and Control

The wandering years underwent dramatic changes in regulation over the centuries and across the territories of Germany (Table 6.2). None of these transformations has put an end to this institution, however. Lack of space in this chapter prevents us from reviewing the many regulatory oscillations between mandatory, voluntary, prohibited, and finally liberated wandering until its ultimate legal abolishment. We highlight only two major changes in the institutional context: the transition from the self-governance of a guild-run craft economy (*Zunftzwang*) to state-governed liberalization of trade and industry (*Gewerbefreiheit*) and the subsequent emergence of trade schools and the modern vocational training system in the nineteenth and early twentieth century.

The first shift occurred as a power struggle between the guilds (*Zünfte*), the journeyman associations, and the modern state of the nineteenth century. Artisans in the Middle Ages organized themselves into guilds for each particular craft or trade. Guilds were local and mostly urban associations and became the principle authorities for training, social care, and local market regulation. Initially, the wandering years were voluntary, but by the sixteenth century the guilds formally required journeymen to travel for a few years while practicing their craft (*Wanderzwang*) before they could become eligible master craftsmen in their hometown (Wissell, 1971). By the eighteenth century the guilds had become true power monopolies that used the wandering years as an instrument to regulate the local labor market and protect their city's labor supply from the effects of crowding (Werner, 1981). With that era's rising number of journeymen and aggravated social conditions, journeymen began to represent their own interests through separate organizations, the journeyman associations, which helped journeymen meet their needs and obligations and connected across towns to build a powerful network (Werner, 1981).

Table 6.2 Historical stages in the regulation of the *Walz*

Elements of regulation and control	Medieval to modern times (13th to 18th century)	Industrialization (19th century)	Contemporary times (21st century)
Principal authority	Guilds (*Zunftzwang*)	German states	Journeyman associations (*Schacht*)
Regulation	Voluntary wandering until 15th century Compulsory wandering by the 16th century	Oscillation between compulsory and voluntary wandering Voluntary wandering by 1871 through state liberalization of trade and industry (*Gewerbefreiheit*)	Voluntary, open to women and nonmembers (*Freireisende*)
Control agents	Guild masters Journeyman association	State (mayor, police) Guild masters Journeyman association	Journeyman association
Control devices	Greeting (*Schnack*) Guild certificate (*Kundschaft*) by 18th century Fraternity conventions	Greeting (*Schnack*) State certificates: indenture and the Journeyman's diary (*Wanderbuch*) Fraternity conventions	Greeting (*Schnack*) Fraternity certificate Journeyman's diary (*Wanderbuch*) Fraternity conventions
Meanings andfunctions	Personal maturity Craft proficiency Surplus labor regulation	Personal maturity Economic competitiveness of the state	Personal maturity Understanding between cultures and nations

Source: Design by authors

The end of the eighteenth century heralded a fundamental shift of power from the traditional authorities of the crafts to the emerging territorial states, which sought to liberalize industry and trade and free them from the powerful self-governance of the guilds. State legislation varied widely over time and from one German region to the next. On the one hand, states were motivated to encourage the *Walz* for economic reasons, especially to gain knowledge for the local crafts, and for social reasons, to balance periods of labor surplus in the cities (Puschner, 1988). On the other hand, state authorities were interested in recruiting journeymen for military service and were anxious about traveling journeymen being susceptible to revolutionary conspiracy after the Napoleonic reforms. Territorial rulers therefore aimed to suppress the journeyman traditions (Neufeld, 1986). As a consequence, legal regulation such as that in Bavaria oscillated between liberating journeymen from wandering and obliging them to travel (Werner, 1981). Similarly, Prussia swung between supporting and prohibiting the *Walz* at least in its major cities such as Berlin (Reith, 2005). After a period of such regulatory vacillation, the state successfully deprived both guilds and journeyman associations of their traditional power of self-governance and jurisdiction, eventually abolishing the journeyman's mandatory itinerancy in the nineteenth century. Prussia pioneered the liberalization of the crafts (*Gewerbefreiheit*) in 1810 (Deissinger, 1994), and by 1871 the Industrial Code

(*Gewerbeordnung*) was enforced across all territories of the newly formed German Empire (Bade, 1982; Wissell, 1971).

A second important change in the institutional context of the *Walz* was the establishment of continuation schools (*Fortbildungsschulen*) to bridge the gap between elementary schools and military service in the early nineteenth century. The diffusion of these schools helped harmonize knowledge across craft workshops, cities, and territories, and supported the skill base within the local economies. In Bavaria, for example, those cities that had established such trade schools since 1829 economically outperformed comparable cities that had no such schools in the years thereafter (Semrad, 2015). By the early twentieth century, Georg Kerschensteiner (1854–1932) had reformed the first generation of continuation schools into what became the *Berufsschule*, the modern German vocational school system (Deissinger, 1994). Unlike earlier trade schools, the *Berufsschule* was made obligatory, and masters were henceforth held responsible for sending apprentices to school and monitoring their attendance. Trade schools spread rapidly, heralding the basic structure of modern vocational training (Herrigel, 1996; Thelen, 2004). Both of these shifts rendered the traditional functions of the wandering years obsolete. The vocational system created other means of knowledge acquisition, and the freedom to practice a craft made it possible for artisans to stay in their hometown and seek employment or start their own business as a master after successful apprenticeship. However, all these shifts in state regulation and self-governance of the guilds had little effect on the institutional practice of the wandering years.

Today, the wandering years are no longer required by state law or by statute of craft organizations. Journeymen are allowed to seek qualified employment, set up their own business, and, in some crafts, even become a training workplace. Yet about one thousand journeymen still take to the road in Germany every year.

The Institutional Drift of the Walz

The previous section's characterization of the basic script of how the *Walz* proceeded hundreds of years ago closely resembles contemporary practice among journeymen. Our analysis of the German *Walz* today is based on over a dozen interviews with current and senior journeymen in southern Germany. It confirms the general persistence of the institutional form despite the turmoil in the institutional context. Some inherited practices have indeed lost their original utility. For instance, the recitation of a secret greeting as the journeyman's way of initially presenting himself to work for the master dates back to preliterate times when people could not read written credentials (Werner, 1981). However, our interviews showed that these practices are still based on mutual expectations and are enforced by journeyman fraternities, which sanction journeymen who violate them. The continued existence of a form that has no particular alternative function has become known as *skeuomorphism* in design (Hargadon & Douglas, 2001). Not only have most of the fundamental elements of the institutional form been retained, the expectations underlying them have also become imprinted on contemporary patterns of behavior. Just as the ban on a journeyman's practice of his craft within the prohibited zone surrounding his home town ensured physical separation of the journeyman from his home and family, the use of mobile phones and laptops is forbidden today in order to ensure his communicational isolation from home. Although the fundamental institutional form has remained the same, our own interviews with journeymen as well as a recent survey on contemporary journeymen (Kemlein, 2016) indicate that the institutional function of wandering has drifted from the pursuit of personal maturity and character-building to a search for a livelihood; then to labor market regulation, knowledge transfer, and promotion of local industry and trade; and, currently, to the promotion of cultural understanding and personal experience through travel (Kemlein, 2016; Schanz, 1877; Wadauer, 2005; Werner, 1981; Wissell, 1971).

When wandering was voluntary (i.e., until the sixteenth century), the individual's major motive to embark on travel was to develop personal maturity and professional skills. Historical analysis of the wandering years in the Middle Ages suggests that traveling played a crucial role in gaining access to highly specialized expertise over relatively great geographical distances (Schanz, 1877). A personal longing for travel and foreign places was another motive for young journeymen after they had completed their apprenticeship. Journeyman diaries (*Wanderbücher*) contain manifold descriptions of museums, churches, landscapes, and the memories of new acquaintances (Wadauer, 2005; Werner, 1981).

A first drift occurred in the late eighteenth century, when the guilds had made wandering compulsory for journeymen in order to regulate the local labor surplus by deterring new craftsmen from becoming masters and from entering the local markets. The labor surplus, however, was merely diverted to other cities, and the rise in the number of wandering journeymen made it ever more difficult for them to find appropriate work. Because a certain amount of work experience was obligatory to complete the journeyman phase, the *Walz* became longer and longer, extending up to six or more years. Moreover, the strong protection of local craft markets made it increasingly common among masters to keep trade secrets (Elkar, 1999). In short, the *Walz* turned into a way to make an often miserable living.

By the nineteenth century the intervention of the German states in the self-regulation of the guilds and journeyman associations brought about another institutional drift. The states were interested in liberalizing commerce and trade and in promoting policies designed to increase their economic power. Although formal assessments such as those commissioned by the Habsburg monarchy in 1769 and the Göttingen Academy of Science in 1798 initially bore out the *Walz*'s utility for knowledge acquisition (Reith, 2005), the waves of alternating state regulations on the journeyman years as briefly reviewed earlier in this chapter indicate the intended instrumentalization of the wandering years to promote the economic policy of knowledge transfer. The *Walz* ultimately lost this function with the establishment and rapid spread of continuation schools in the nineteenth century and compulsory trade schools in the early twentieth century. Today, the absence of an obligation to take to the road, the possibility of immediate access to masterhood through a master's examination, and the presence of a diversified vocational training system have

Fig. 6.3 Journeyman
Florian Piper,
photographed in
Surendorf/Schwedeneck,
Schleswig-Holstein, in
2012. Source: Burkhard
Peter Photography.
Reprinted with permission

robbed the *Walz* of its former functions. Wandering is still practiced, however, even with similar artefacts and physical appearances today (compare Fig. 6.2 and Fig. 6.3). The fact that the wandering is protected under the intangible cultural heritage framework mirrors the renewed value of this institution for the crafts and its new function of promoting cultural understanding.

At a theoretical level this example demonstrates the implications of distinguishing between institutions as meaningful patterned behavior from institutions as formal regulation. As formal regulation, the *Walz* with its changing regulation over the years would exemplify exhaustion. In this case, form refers to regulation, so the form changes (regulation is abolished), leaving the function to turn as it may. By contrast, as stable patterns of behavior, the form remains unchanged, whereas regulation is found to have had an effect only on the altered functions of the *Walz* (drift).

Morphosis of Public Procurement in Germany

The Institutional Function of Promoting Local Commerce

Having analyzed the institutional drift of the *Walz*, in which the institution has changed functionally while keeping its form, we now examine the opposite example: change in the institutional form to sustain an institutional function. To illustrate such institutional morphosis, we focus on the dynamics of public procurement in Germany's federal state of Baden-Württemberg. We argue that practices in public procurement have been actively adapted to retain one of its fundamental functions—the promotion of local commerce—even though regulation has explicitly been modified to preclude it. Public procurement also serves other functions, of course, the most important one being that of putting public money to good use. But in this section we focus on public procurement's function as a tool for stimulating the (local) economy, for so it has remained despite deliberate regulatory aims to diminish it.

Every year more than 250,000 public sector bodies in the European Union (EU), such as government departments and local authorities, purchase goods and services from private business worth a total of 14% of EU gross domestic product (European Commission, 2017). Germany, France, and Poland combined account for half of all EU award notices in public procurement (Strand, Ramada, & Canton, 2011). Whenever a school is to be built or a hospital refurbished, local government uses formal procedures to choose the provider that can deliver this service best by meeting a set of regulated criteria based on the principles of nondiscrimination, equal treatment, and competition. Official regulations require public authorities to follow an accountable tendering process and to publicize the criteria for selection and contract awarding to all eligible EU enterprises. Every competent, efficient, and reliable bidder must be given the same chance to apply for the tender (Dreher, 2008).

Apart from the economical use of public money, the promotion of local commerce has always been an actively pursued, or at least consciously welcome, benefit of public expenditures. In line with Keynesian demand-side management policy, public procurement helps stimulate production and thereby secure or even create income and jobs in the region, especially when the economy is weak (Dreher, 2008; Kunert, 1977; Walthelm, 1979). Orders are often large, especially in the construction sector, so public procurement indisputably plays a role in countercyclical economic policy that enhances the individual municipality's local labor market and potential tax revenues (Dreher, 2008; Elverfeld, 1992; Walthelm, 1979). This function of public procurement was deliberately activated in 2009 when procurement law was temporarily changed in the wake of the European economic crisis. Accelerated procedures were allowed and EU thresholds lifted to boost the domestic economy by awarding contracts more locally than usual (Dirnbacher, 2009). In general, Elverfeld (1992) found public demand for construction services in Germany to be organized around regional markets, with protectionism against foreign firms at the national level and discrimination against enterprises from other municipalities at the local level. An empirical assessment of the geography of German public procurement (Söffner, 1979, 1984) showed that construction firms tended to operate mostly in their own vicinity and that 62% of the total contract volume from 1972 until 1982 had gone to bidders located within the same administrative district as the procurement entity (Söffner, 1979). In 1978 less than 1% of tenders were awarded to foreign firms. Between 1979 and 1981 the figure rose to 15% but remained low (Söffner, 1984). In the following section, we argue that this function of local business promotion has persisted despite the regulatory change through which the EU has been trying to prevent any undue preference of local bidders. Although the complexity and formality of the public procurement process has increased, contracting authorities and bidders alike have found ways to institutionalize a gray zone between formal regulation and practical interest in local procurement. The actors have thus adapted the institutional form of public procurement to sustain a traditional function of public procurement, leaving the geography of contract awards virtually unchanged.

Changes in the Institutional Context: The Imperative of Nondiscrimination

The institutional context of public procurement in Germany has undergone three major regulatory changes: (a) a shift from oral to written procurement forms, (b) the formalization of procurement into national procurement guidelines, and (c) reregulation under EU public procurement law moving toward the principle of nondiscrimination.

The original practice of public procurement lasted until the mid-nineteenth century. All providers interested in bidding for a public contract had to attend a convocation, in which the contract was awarded through an "inverse auction" (*Lizitation*). All bidders attended physically and tried to undercut each other's tenders until the lowest one won the contract. This arrangement often led to the financial ruin of the contracted firms or to substandard quality of the delivered results (Dageförde, 2008). With the erosion of the guild system and the introduction of freedom of trade, the demand for a transition to a practice of written submission succeeded. Bidders were subsequently permitted to submit only one offer, without the possibility of adapting it in response to other offers. After an official deadline had expired, the public authority evaluated all offers in secret competition. Bavaria and Prussia were the first states to introduce this form of procurement (in 1833 and 1834, respectively). It was established throughout Germany during the 1850s (Dageförde, 2008). Because the bidders no longer had to be physically present for an auction, the competition opened to a greater number of bidders across larger geographical distances than under the previous procedures. However, contracts were still assigned to the lowest bidder, so the risks of price-dumping and poor quality remained unsolved. As of the 1880s, authorities attempted to reform this process by including quality criteria, requiring public entities to award the contract to the most economical offer (Dageförde, 2008). Dissatisfaction remained, however, because of the fragmentation of differential procurement practices across Germany.

The second shift in the institutional context led to the formalization of procurement into national guidelines. The first attempts to unify the variety of practices throughout Germany came in 1912, but it took until 1926 to supplement national budgetary law with the Procurement Regulation for Public Works (*Vergabe- und Vertragsordnung für Bauleistungen*, VOB) (Dageförde, 2008; Dreher, 2008). During this second shift in German public procurement law, a third change was already underway, the harmonization of procurement law across Europe through

Table 6.3 Changes in public procurement in Germany through EU harmonization

Regulation and control	Before 1999	After 1999
Regulation	National budgetary law (VOB, VOL, VOF)[a]	EU procurement law (VOB, VOL, VOF, GWB, VgV)[a]
Procurement criteria	Economy Efficiency, secured financial coverage	Nondiscrimination Transparency, equal treatment, and competition
Status	Guidelines without legislated norm (*Vergabewesen*)	Legislated norm (*Vergaberecht*)
Bidders' rights	No subjective, enforceable rights	Protection of tenders

Source: Design by authors
[a]VOB/VOL/VOF: specifications of the Procurement Regulation for Public Works/Public Supplies and Services/Professional Services. GWB: *Gesetz gegen Wettbewerbsbeschränkungen* (German Act Against Restraint of Competition). VgV: *Vergabeverordnung* (Regulation on the Assignment of Public Contracts)

encouragement of cross-border bidding (Table 6.3). As a consequence of treaties pushing for the abolishment of barriers to free trade within the EU and prohibiting discrimination due to national origin, the EU issued procurement guidelines that coalesced into specific directives for its member states in the 1990s. These rules then had to be transposed into national legislation by the individual member states and had to be applied to all tenders exceeding a certain threshold in contract value and assumed to be of cross-border interest. In Germany, this transposition into national law became effective in 1999 through procurement-related antitrust legislation (*Kartellvergaberecht*) (Dageförde, 2008).

This third regulatory change has had several effects. First, German public procurement law now provides for four different tendering procedures, depending on the contract volume as defined by EU thresholds: open procedure, restricted procedure, negotiated procedure, and competitive dialogue (Strand et al., 2011). To meet the new principles of transparency and competition, all tenders exceeding the EU thresholds must be published via the EU's online database, Tenders Electronic Daily (TED).[2] The Commission maintains this web portal as a supplement to the official journal of the EU to display all tenders and contract awards within EU member countries (Strand et al., 2011). Second, whereas the guidelines for procurement (*Vergabewesen*) offered no enforceable rights to bidders until 1999 (Dreher, 2008; Rittner, 1988), the new procurement law (*Vergaberecht*) is based on enforceable legislated norms (Table 6.3). They stipulate several aspects of the process: the time and place of the tender's publication, the time by which all bidders need to be informed about the results, the reasons for these results, and a moratorium during which declined bidders may raise objections before a contract can finally be assigned to the selected firm (Brakalova, 2016; Dageförde, 2008). The tendering documents

---

[2]TED (http://ted.europa.eu) publishes about 460,000 calls for tenders annually, representing a worth of €420 billion.

must be itemized in as much detail as possible to enable a valid comparison between the bids. Tenders are now fully transparent to bidders, who are therefore able to monitor and object to the procedure and outcome. Consequently, public procurement tribunals (*Vergabekammern*) and higher regional courts (*Oberlandesgerichte*) have about 1,000 cases to review in Germany every year (Dreher, 2008). Third, and of focal interest in our analysis, the new procurement law has adopted the principle of nondiscrimination, which explicitly bans any geographical preference for regional bidders (Lübeck et al., 2017). The regulatory change outlined in the previous section is thus designed to achieve maximal transparency and accountability and to offer legal privilege for all bidders to enforce a claim against questionable contract award notices. Current regulation thus challenges one of the important traditional functions of public procurement, the promotion of local business and labor.

The Institutional Morphosis of Public Procurement

We argue that the new regulation, quite unlike the regulatory imperative of nondiscrimination, has not overridden the function of local preference. To support this claim empirically, we draw on a TED analysis of all contract award notices issued in Baden-Württemberg's construction sector over two one-year periods: from April 11, 2012, to April 11, 2013, and from April 11, 2016, to April 11, 2017 (Table 6.4). In both the first and the final year of that five-year period, most contracts were awarded to firms located within a radius of 100 km (62 miles) from the construction sites, that is, to firms whose workers were able to reach the sites in about one hour. These awards also constituted the highest percentage of the overall contract volume, which amounted to over €730 million from 2012 to 2013 and €1.2 billion from 2016 to 2017. Although this 100 km radius constitutes only one quarter of the size of the ring from 100 to 200 km, the number of contract awards declined within this second range but rebounded for firms further away than 200 km. The number of contracts awarded to firms in other countries remained below 10 for both years.

A study of EU tendering from 2006 through 2010 (Strand et al., 2011) substantiated the localized pattern of contract awards at a national level as well. It found that cross-border wins accounted for only 3.4% of all tenders. In our interviews in a metropolitan region in Baden-Württemberg, contracting authorities pointed out that they simply did not receive any offers by bidders from other countries, or even from

Table 6.4 Public procurement in the construction sector in Baden-Württemberg

Distance of firm from site	2012–2013		2016–2017	
	No. of contracts	% of volume	No. of contracts	% of volume
0–100 km	271 (49%)	48	625 (55%)	48
101–200 km	90 (16%)	20	173 (15%)	17
> 200 km	190 (35%)	32	335 (30%)	35

Source: Design by authors

other parts of Germany: "We tender a lot on a European scale, with high volumes of orders. But in the last 25 years—nothing." Representatives of the construction industry confirmed this apparent disinterest in tenders from other countries or regions, explaining that they are usually not inclined to bid for tenders in rather distant regions because of little chance of success when bidding against local competitors. We argue that this perception stems from bidders' awareness that the practice of local preference endures.

Because regulation is clear about nondiscrimination and is enforced, bidders and contracting authorities alike must adhere to strict formalities. If they do not, offers must be excluded or the tender is declared void and must be started anew. Both sides have therefore changed their procurement practices, yet their function remains the same as before. This phenomenon illustrates institutional morphosis, for both sides must have found a way to adhere to the new regulation in their practices while continuing to comply with previous mutual expectations on how to behave legitimately. We argue that both parties—contracting authorities and bidders—still believe that tenders should be awarded locally and that experience gained by repeatedly participating in tendering processes under the new regulation has led to the institutionalization of what our interviewees called a gray zone. This leeway allows both sides to institutionalize legitimate expectations and new procurement practices to sustain the function of promoting local business yet still comply with the law. Retaining this gray zone calls for discreet signals that can be understood only by those who know the underlying code. In our case these would be local bidders and procurement entities.

Our interviews helped us identify three specific mechanisms of morphosis: fake positions in the tender, explicit invitation of particular bidders, and the targeted use of discretion for a biased selection.

The contracting authority, for example, can formulate the announcement of the tender in a specific way to signal local preference. Rather obvious ways of doing so exist. One of them is to list several prerequisites that rule out businesses from other regions from the start, such as the necessity of being able to reach the construction site within one hour if problems arise. Another is to state the need to know German and the German construction code. A third is to require submission of specific references as proof of having done similar projects in Germany. Bidders are assigned points on a scale rating the degree to which they comply with a particular requirement, and it is clear that local enterprises score higher on these measures. More subtly, the specifications of the tender may list services or products as necessary that will not actually be needed, thereby encrypting information to insiders. As one interviewee explained,

> For those who are in regular contact with the contracting authority, a code within the tendering specifications exists. For instance, any kind of service with a very high cost and a high quantity . . . makes your offer as a whole very expensive. The specifications state the necessity of a high number of these services, but everybody knows that they won't be needed or, if so, only in a small amount. These are the little tricks for how those involved get information on how to get the contract more easily.

The contracting authority confirmed the existence of such codes:

If an experienced bidder knows that one item won't come whereas another one will be doubled, he can use that [knowledge when calculating] amounts, and he can significantly change his odds. . . . I tell him to put a lower price there, and I have already entered the one I want.

These examples show the need to have the appropriate knowledge and tools to decipher a code that remains invisible to nonlocal bidders. Because the tendering process has become increasingly complex, lengthy, and costly for bidding firms, some of them are willing to participate only if they feel they have reasonable chances of being awarded the contract. That outcome, however, is hard to predict—except when contracting entities hint at their special interest in particular firms with which they have worked successfully before. The contractors can send these signals either by informing favored bidders ahead of time or by specifically inviting them by telephone or mail to participate in the tendering process. In other instances a certain amount of discretion can be used to select the preferred bidder.

Sometimes one realizes what should actually not be happening—that a local procurer has established a relationship of trust with a bidder and would like him to be awarded the contract. Then the procurer tries to help that bidder within what is legally possible. . . . When filling out the form in one case, for example, I entered a cash discount that would have to be subtracted from the total sum of my offer. With this discount I was ranked first, but I was not awarded the contract, and they told me that they couldn't take the discount into account. The nerve of it! The contract was given to the one who had worked with them on earlier projects, who ranked second for this tender. They wanted to have him.

These codes and mechanisms function only when participants know each other and have worked together before. Only then can bidders make use of local knowledge, such as regional specificities like soil composition or how things are done in a particular region. This knowledge can also lead firms to expect similar behavior in other regions—by bidders, contracting authorities, and other firms. For instance, suppliers to firms competing in a tender can play an important role, too, because they are bound to their long-term, local clients and therefore discriminate against external competitors. As one of our interviewees explained,

We once were asked by an investor to submit an offer in southern France, but we didn't even try to submit an offer because . . . coming from here, you cannot obtain concrete or steel at a price in line with that of their local market price. It's the same for Swiss or French firms coming here. They don't get the same conditions as we do from our suppliers. . . . It's a very regional thing. You won't find "Europe" in the construction sector.

These mechanisms illustrate how institutional morphosis develops. In this case, the involved actors changed the known patterns of practices (form) in response to changes in the institutional context in order to sustain the institution's traditional social function, that of promoting local commerce by awarding contracts to local bidders. The mutual expectations of what constitutes legitimate behavior, the institutional function, thus persisted. If the concept of institution were equated with regulation, this case would likely be interpreted as inefficient conversion, for it did not prove possible to change the function.

Conclusion

We have explored the dynamic nature of institutions and contend that these dynamics can unfold in rather subtle ways that make it difficult to assess whether an institution changes or not. There is more to institutional change than the polarity of stability and change. To sharpen the understanding of which elements of institutions change, we have deconstructed the institutions of the wandering years of craft journeymen and the preference for local firms when it comes to offering public procurement contracts in southern Germany. Distinguishing between institutional form and institutional function, we have proposed a simple taxonomic model that helps us comprehend how institutions keep their form although their function responds to changes in the institutional context (drift) and, conversely, how institutions retain a certain function by gradually realigning their form with a shifting context (morphosis). Our cases of drift and morphosis can thus be read either way: as expressions of relative continuity or of change. Our analysis supports finer-grained concepts of institutional change that incorporate an endogenous perspective of institutional change. Our simple model enables us to look at the individual institution in relation to its institutional context. Future research of this kind may go further by taking into account the complexity and interconnectedness of institutions. Because institutions are often nested one in another and thereby afford mutual stability, and because each institution may have more than one function, detailed analysis of interinstitutional interdependencies and their effects on partial changes in form and function is necessary if the possibilities of institutional changes are to be fully perceived (Campbell, 2010). Such work might help deepen insight into the workings of policies that run counter or parallel to the underlying institutional reality and enable us to hone our conceptualization of what we call institutional policy-making (Glückler & Lenz, 2016).

A second important conclusion is that institutions are by no means identical to formal codified rules and enforceable legislation. We have used the German *Walz* and the institutionalization of public procurement to demonstrate that institutional form and function are responses to prescriptive regulations and that these responses may or may not support those rules. Conversely, a dynamic analysis of policy-making may view regulation as a normative response to institutions and institutional changes (see Glückler & Lenz, 2016). If an institution were only the formal, codified rules, then the wandering years could no longer be considered as an institution today. In reality, although the *Walz* had been legislated out of existence by the mid-twentieth century, the institutional form of the German wandering years is still alive today. This institutional drift can be explained only by persistent mutual expectations held by the relevant groups of actors (e.g., apprentices, journeymen, and masters of a craft). These expectations stem from the conviction that a *Walz* should still be undertaken as well as from an agreement on the applicable rules and concurrence on the sanctions to be applied for noncompliance. The case of public procurement also shows that an institution can endure even though regulation changes as part of the institutional context. In response to rather rigorous regulatory attempts to prevent discrimination against nonlocal organizations, the form of public procurement adapted in a way that ensured the previous behavior. Public entities and local bidders have developed a gray zone that allows them to comply with the formalities of the new regulation while abiding by their unchanged mutual expectations of local preference. If institutions are seen as formal rules, then both the *Walz* and public procurement are instances of a transformation in institutional form. In the former case, this change would be an example of exhaustion; in the latter, an illustration of conversion, inefficient though it may be. This analysis shows that the interplay between regulation and its outcomes can be improved by institutional policymaking, which takes into account the underlying institutional reality that either supports or undermines regulations imposed on it.

References

Acemoğlu, D., & Robinson, J. (2012). *Why nations fail: The origins of power, prosperity, and poverty.* New York: Crown Publishers.

Back, K.-H. (1985). *Freie Vogtländer Deutschlands: Reisende und einheimische Bauhandwerker* [Germany's Freie Vogtländer brotherhood: Traveling and local journeymen in the construction trades]. Nienburg: Gesellschaft freier Vogtländer Deutschlands.

Bade, K. J. (1982). Altes Handwerk, Wanderzwang und gute Policey: Gesellenwanderung zwischen Zunftökonomie und Gewerbereform [Traditional crafts, the compulsory years of travel, and good policy: Wandering journeymen between guild economy and reform in trade and industry]. *Vierteljahrschrift für Sozial- und Wirtschaftsgeschichte, 69,* 1–37. Retrieved from http://www.digizeitschriften.de/dms/img/?PID=GDZPPN001395823

Bathelt, H., & Glückler, J. (2014). Institutional change in economic geography. *Progress in Human Geography, 38,* 340–363. doi:https://doi.org/10.1177/0309132513507823

Béland, D. (2007). Ideas and institutional change in social security: Conversion, layering, and policy drift. *Social Science Quarterly,* 88, 20–38. doi:https://doi.org/10.1111/j.1540-6237.2007.00444.x

Brakalova, M. (2016). Germany. In E. Burrows & E. McNeill (Eds.), *The international comparative legal guide to public procurement, 2016: A practical cross-border insight into public procurement* (8th ed., pp. 104–112). London: Global Legal Group.

Campbell, J. L. (2010). Institutional reproduction and change. In G. Morgan, J. L. Campbell, C. Crouch, O. K. Pedersen, & R. Whitley (Eds.), *The Oxford handbook of comparative institutional analysis* (pp. 87–114). Oxford, UK: Oxford University Press.

Cooper, P. A. (1983). The 'traveling fraternity': Union cigar makers and geographic mobility, 1900–1919. *Journal of Social History, 17,* 127–138. Retrieved from https://www.jstor.org/stable/3787243?seq=1#page_scan_tab_contents

Dageförde, A. (2008). *Einführung in das Vergaberecht* [Introduction to public procurement law]. Berlin: Lexxion Verlagsgesellschaft.

Deissinger, T. (1994). The evolution of the modern vocational training systems in England and Germany: A comparative view. *Compare: A Journal of Comparative and International Education,* 24, 17–36. doi:https://doi.org/10.1080/0305792940240103

Dirnbacher, S. (2009, September 12). Deutschland lockert das Vergabeverfahren: Durch eine Beschleunigung sollen Investitionen angekurbelt werden [Germany relaxes the approach to public procurement: Accelerated processes are to stimulate investements], *Wiener Zeitung.* Retrieved July 14, 2017, from http://www.wienerzeitung.at/themen_channel/wirtschaftsservice/geschaeft/244613_Deutschland-lockert-das-Vergabeverfahren.html?em_cnt=244613

Dreher, M. (2008). Entwicklung und Grundfragen des Vergaberechts in Deutschland [Development and fundamental questions of public procurement law in Germany]. In U. Blaurock (Ed.), *Der*

Staat als Nachfrager: Öffentliches Auftragswesen in Deutschland und Frankreich (pp. 1–14). Rechtsvergleichung und Rechtsvereinigung: Vol. 13. Tübingen: Mohr Siebeck.

Elkar, R. S. (1999). Lernen durch Wandern? Einige kritische Anmerkungen zum Thema 'Wissenstransfer durch Migration' [Learning by wandering? Critical remarks on knowledge transfer through migration]. In K. Schulz (Ed.), *Handwerk in Europa vom Spätmittelalter bis zur frühen Neuzeit* (pp. 213–232). Schriften des Historischen Kollegs: Vol. 41. Munich: Oldenbourg.

Elverfeld, D. J. (1992). *Europäisches Recht und kommunales öffentliches Auftragswesen* [European law and local public procurement]. Studien zum öffentlichen Wirtschaftsrecht: Vol. 23. Cologne: Carl Heymanns.

European Commission. (2017). *Public procurement*. Retrieved March 21, 2017, from https://ec.europa.eu/growth/single-market/public-procurement_de

Farrell, H. (2018). The shared challenges of institutional theories: Rational choice, historical institutionalism and sociological institutionalism. In J. Glückler, R. Suddaby & R. Lenz (Eds.), *Knowledge and institutions. Knowledge and Space:* Vol. 13. Cham: Springer.

Glückler, J., & Bathelt, H. (2017). Institutional context and innovation. In H. Bathelt, P. Cohendet, S. Henn, & L. Simon (Eds.), *The Elgar companion to innovation and knowledge creation: A multi-disciplinary approach* (pp. 121–137). Cheltenham: Edward Elgar.

Glückler, J., & Lenz, R. (2016). How institutions moderate the effectiveness of regional policy: A framework and research agenda. *Investigaciones Regionales—Journal of Regional Research, 36,* 255–277. Retrieved from https://www.researchgate.net/publication/311652886

Greenwood, R., Oliver, C., Sahlin, K., & Suddaby, R. (Eds.). (2008). *The Sage handbook of organizational institutionalism*. Los Angeles: Sage.

Hacker, J. S. (2004). Privatizing risk without privatizing the welfare state: The hidden politics of social policy retrenchment in the United States. *American Political Science Review, 98,* 243–260. doi:https://doi.org/10.1017/S0003055404001121

Hacker, J. S., Thelen, K. A., & Pierson, P. (2013, September 17). *Drift and conversion: Hidden faces of institutional change*. Paper submitted to the 2013 Annual Meeting of the American Political Science Association, Chicago. Retrieved from https://ssrn.com/abstract=2303593

Hallett, T., & Ventresca, M. J. (2006). How institutions form: Loose coupling as mechanism in Gouldner's patterns of industrial bureaucracy. *American Behavioral Scientist, 49,* 908–924. doi:https://doi.org/10.1177/0002764205285171

Hargadon, A. B., & Douglas, Y. (2001). When innovations meet institutions: Edison and the design of electric light. *Administrative Science Quarterly, 46,* 476–501. doi:https://doi.org/10.2307/3094872

Helmke, G., & Levitsky, S. (2004). Informal institutions and comparative politics: A research agenda. *Perspectives on Politics, 2,* 725–740. doi:https://doi.org/10.1017/S1537592704040472

Herrigel, G. (1996). *Industrial constructions: The sources of German industrial power*. Structural Analysis in the Social Sciences: Vol. 9. Cambridge, UK: Cambridge University Press.

Hess, A. (2018). Gastronomic societies in the Basque country. In J. Glückler, R. Suddaby & R. Lenz (Eds.), Knowledge and institutions. Knowledge and Space: Vol. 13. Cham: Springer.

Hodgson, G. M. (2006). What are institutions? *Journal of Economic Issues, 40,* 1–25. doi:https://doi.org/10.1080/00213624.2006.11506879

Kemlein, C. (2016). *Die Funktion der Walz in der beruflichen Bildung* [The journeyman years and their functions for the vocational education and training] (Master's thesis, Technische Universität Berlin). Retrieved from https://depositonce.tu-berlin.de/bitstream/11303/5345/4/kemlein_claudia.pdf

Kunert, F.-J. (1977). *Staatliche Bedarfsdeckungsgeschäfte und öffentliches Recht* [Public law and satisfaction of public needs]. Schriften zum Öffentlichen Recht: Vol. 331. Berlin: Duncker & Humblot.

Levitsky, S. & Slater, D. (2011). *Ruling politics: The formal and informal foundations of institutional reform* (Working Paper, Workshop on Informal Institutions). Harvard University, Cambridge, MA.

Lübeck, D., Oest, T., Kohl, B., Wiesner, M., Hattig, O., & Kalenberg, R. (2017). *Mittelstandsfreundliche Auftragsvergabe* [Public procurement conducive to small business]. Retrieved from http://www.eic-trier.de/app/download/5803106002/Leitfaden_Mittelstandsfre undliche+Auftragsvergabe.pdf

Ménard, C., & Shirley, M. M. (2005). *Handbook of new institutional economics*. Berlin: Springer.

Meyer, J. W., & Rowan, B. (1977). Institutionalized organizations: Formal structure as myth and ceremony. *American Journal of Sociology, 83*, 340–363. doi:https://doi.org/10.1086/226550

Neufeld, M. J. (1986). German artisans and political repression: The fall of the journeymen's associations in Nuremberg, 1806–1868. *Journal of Social History, 19*, 491–502. doi:https://doi.org/10.1353/jsh/19.3.491

North, D. C. (1990). *Institutions, institutional change and economic performance*. Cambridge, UK: Cambridge University Press.

Peters, B. G. (2012). *Institutional theory in political science: The new institutionalism* (3rd ed.). New York: Continuum.

Powell, W. W., & Colyvas, J. A. (2008). Microfoundations of institutional theory. In R. Greenwood, C. Oliver, K. Sahlin, & R. Suddaby (Eds.), *The Sage handbook of organizational institutionalism* (pp. 276–298). London: Sage.

Puschner, U. (1988). *Handwerk zwischen Tradition und Wandel: Das Münchner Handwerk an der Wende vom 18. zum 19. Jahrhundert* [The crafts between tradition and change: The Munich crafts at the turn of the eighteenth to the nineteenth century]. Göttinger Beiträge zur Wirtschafts- und Sozialgeschichte: Vol. 13. Göttingen: Otto Schwartz & Co.

Reith, R. (2005). Know-how, Technologietransfer und die Arcana Artis im Mitteleuropa der frühen Neuzeit [Know-how, technology transfer and the arcana artis in Central Europe in the early modern period]. *Early Science & Medicine, 10*, 349–377. doi:https://doi.org/10.1163/1573382054615451

Rittner, F. (1988). *Rechtsgrundlagen und Rechtsgrundsätze des öffentlichen Auftragswesens: Eine systematische Analyse* [Legal principles of public procurement: A systematic analysis]. Schriften zum öffentlichen Auftragswesen: Vol. 5. Hamburg: Jank & Partner.

Rodríguez-Pose, A., & Storper, M. (2006). Better rules or stronger communities? On the social foundations of institutional change and its economic effects. *Economic Geography, 82*, 1–25. doi:https://doi.org/10.1111/j.1944-8287.2006.tb00286.x

Salinger, V. S. (1983). Artisans, journeymen, and the transformation of labor in late eighteenth-century Philadelphia. *The William and Mary Quarterly, 40*, 62–84. Retrieved from https://www.jstor.org/stable/1919528?seq=1#page_scan_tab_contents

Schanz, G. (1877). Zur Geschichte der Gesellenwanderungen im Mittelalter [On the history of the journeyman's wandering years in the Middle Ages]. *Jahrbücher für Nationalökonomie und Statistik, 28*, 313–343. Retrieved from https://www.digizeitschriften.de/dms/img/?PID=GDZPPN000584134

Schickler, E. (2001). *Disjointed pluralism: Institutional innovation and the development of the U.S. Congress*. Princeton: Princeton University Press.

Semrad, A. (2015). Modern secondary education and economic performance: The introduction of the Gewerbeschule and Realschule in nineteenth-century Bavaria. *Economic History Review, 68*, 1306–1338. doi:https://doi.org/10.1111/ehr.12101

Seo, M.-G., & Creed, W. E. D. (2002). Institutional contradictions, praxis, and institutional change: A dialectical perspective. *The Academy of Management Review, 27*, 222–247. doi:https://doi.org/10.5465/AMR.2002.6588004

Söffner, F. (1979). Kleiner Aktionsradius der Bauunternehmen [Small catchment areas in the construction industry]. *ifo-Schnelldienst, 15*, 3–4.

Söffner, F. (1984). *Die Vergabe öffentlicher Bauaufträge in der EG* [Public construction contract awards in the European Community]. Ifo-Studien zur Bauwirtschaft: Vol. 8. Munich: Ifo.

Strand, I., Ramada, P., & Canton, E. (2011). *Public procurement in Europe: Cost and effectiveness*. Retrieved from http://www.eipa.eu/files/topics/public_procurement/cost_effectiveness_en.pdf

Streeck, W., & Thelen, K. A. (Eds.). (2005). *Beyond continuity: Institutional change in advanced political economies*. Oxford, UK: Oxford University Press.

Suddaby, R. (2010). Challenges for institutional theory. *Journal of Management Inquiry, 19*, 14–20. doi:https://doi.org/10.1177/1056492609347564

Suddaby, R., Ganzin, M., & Minkus, A. (2017). Craft, magic and the re-enchantment of the world. *European Management Journal, 35*, 285–296. doi:https://doi.org/10.1016/j.emj.2017.03.009

Thelen, K. A. (2004). *How institutions evolve: The political economy of skills in Germany, Britain, the United States and Japan*. Cambridge, UK: Cambridge University Press.

Truant, C. M. (1979). Solidarity and symbolism among journeymen artisans: The case of compagnonnage. *Comparative Studies in Society and History, 21*, 214–226. doi:https://doi.org/10.1017/S0010417500012834

Wadauer, S. (2005). *Die Tour der Gesellen: Mobilität und Biographie im Handwerk vom 18. bis zum 20. Jahrhundert* [Journeyman tours: Mobility and biographies in the craft professions from the eighteenth to the twentieth century]. Frankfurt am Main & New York: Campus.

Walthelm, V. J. (1979). *Das öffentliche Auftragswesen: Eine rechtssystematische Untersuchung* [A systematic legal analysis of public procurement]. Rechtswissenschaftliche Forschung und Entwicklung: Vol. 7. Munich: Florentz.

Werner, G. S. (1981). Traveling journeymen in Metternichian south Germany. *Proceedings of the American Philosophical Society, 125*, 190–219. Retrieved from http://www.peterspioneers.com/TRAVELING.pdf

Wilbrand, H., Bieringer, L., & Berberich, C. (2015). *Institutionen im Spannungsfeld zwischen Wandel und Persistenz: Das Fallbeispiel der Walz* [Institutions between the poles of change and persistence: The wandering years of journeymen in Germany]. Unpublished student research paper. Department of Geography, Heidelberg University, Germany.

Williams, N., & Vorley, T. (2014). Institutional asymmetry: How formal and informal institutions affect entrepreneurship in bulgaria. *International Small Business Journal, 33*, 840–861. doi:https://doi.org/10.1177/0266242614534280

Wissell, R. (1971). *Des alten Handwerks Recht und Gewohnheit* [Laws and customs of the traditional crafts] (2nd ed.). Berlin: Colloquium.

Zilber, T. B. (2002). Institutionalization as an interplay between actions, meanings, and actors: The case of a rape crisis center in Israel. *The Academy of Management Journal, 45*, 234–254. doi:https://doi.org/10.2307/3069294

Chapter 7
Innovation Under a Protected Label of Origin: Institutional Change in Cognac

Jerker Moodysson and Lionel Sack

Regionally Defined Institutions and Firm Behavior

Recent contributions in economic geography have paid much attention to understanding the dynamics of cluster evolution (e.g., Audretsch & Feldman, 1996; Boschma & Fornahl, 2011; Iammarino & McCann, 2006). A growing niche within this literature indicates that the institutional frameworks within which clusters are embedded not only result from evolutionary processes on the actor and network levels, but also contribute strongly to shaping the evolution as such. There is, however, still scope for research analyzing the interplay between institutions and development, firm behavior, and more aggregated outcomes in terms of the growth, decline, stability, and renewal of clusters (Menzel & Fornahl, 2010). With this chapter we contribute to this field of research by analyzing how regionally defined institutions influence firm behavior in clusters and how this affects the evolution of the cluster as a whole. In particular, we analyze how emerging inefficiencies in an established institutional framework of a cluster contribute to shaping that cluster and to influencing its future development. Our findings show that institutionally grounded inefficiencies open paths for reinterpretation and redefinition of existing institutions, leading to change processes, which we disentangle by applying the conceptual framework of layering, drift, and conversion (Mahoney & Thelen, 2009).

Empirically, our analysis draws on a cluster in which the regional institutional framework has been explicit and stable for long periods. However, despite this stability there have been times of change and renewal. New entrants have emerged, largely reinterpreting the rules of the game in the cluster, and gradually influencing

J. Moodysson (✉)
Jönköping International Business School, Jönköping University, Jönköping, Sweden
e-mail: Jerker.Moodysson@ju.se

L. Sack
CIRCLE, Lund University, Lund, Sweden
e-mail: lionel.sack@circle.lu.se

© The Author(s) 2018
J. Glückler et al. (eds.), *Knowledge and Institutions*, Knowledge and Space 13,
https://doi.org/10.1007/978-3-319-75328-7_7

the behavior of incumbent actors, which initially resisted such external influences. These observations laid the foundation for the main research question addressed in this chapter—namely, (how) do institutions designed to preserve the current state of affairs in a regional cluster influence change and renewal of the cluster over extended periods of time.

The case we use for illustrating institutional change is the spirits industry around the town of Cognac. Firms in the local setting in and around the town of Cognac have been specializing in one product carrying the same name, with strict regulations applying to production techniques and processes. In this laboratory-like regulatory setting, protective laws pertaining to the local label almost entirely preclude product and process innovation. Local firms have nonetheless succeeded in developing new and related products during several periods in the past. In our analysis, we focus on the most apparent of these waves of product innovation, which began in the 1990s.

The Cognac region is a suitable and particularly interesting case for analyzing the role of institutions and institutional change in cluster evolution because it displays highly distinct and controllable features, both in terms of actors and institutional framework and through the presence of well-documented and traceable processes of change and renewal in the cluster over time. The cluster of Cognac hosts a critical mass of actors representing the entire value chain of the spirits industry, including not only suppliers of raw materials (grapes, oak barrels), but also a range of related industries (e.g., vineyards, bottlers, barrel manufacturers, product design companies, cork manufacturers), all located within well-defined regional boundaries. In this respect, it constitutes a textbook example for assessing the dynamics that according to theory are assumed to take place over time in places with strong specialization and product-specific regulation.

The Theoretical Framework

Most cluster studies focus on the emerging stages of cluster evolution—how and why clusters emerge (Braunerhjelm & Feldman, 2008; Maskell & Kebir, 2006)—and to some extent on how being located in a cluster positively or negatively impacts the performance of firms (e.g., Malmberg & Power, 2005). Few studies have paid attention to how clusters evolve at more mature stages despite the fact that evolutionary processes are inherent to all regional economies (Martin, 2010). Some studies have put more emphasis on lock-in mechanisms in clusters (Coenen, Moodysson, & Martin, 2015; Hassink, 2010; Trippl, 2004), and how they shape clusters over time, often focusing on how they can be unlocked by institutional change (e.g., Martin & Sunley, 2006) or mitigated through regional branching processes (Frenken & Boschma, 2007). What these studies revolve around is a basic assumption that history matters and that past events lay the foundation for self-reinforcing, path-dependent processes, which in turn influence the present and future development of the regional industry.

Although much attention has been paid in recent studies to the dynamics of path dependent processes, less has been paid to how new paths are triggered over time and what causes historical accidents or chance events that spur further development (Martin & Sunley, 2006). Because the theories underlying cluster evolution studies stress that history matters, they also imply that such development is based not on chance, but on previously emerged, sustained, and refined local capabilities and routines and their underlying institutions (Trippl, Grillitsch, Isaksen, & Sinozic, 2015). This argument draws on the basic assumption that new paths may be latent in old ones or spin out from existing ones (Martin, 2010), which also implies that new path creation rarely includes major, or radical, shifts.

The literature on regional cluster evolution concludes that some institutions seem more enabling for such spin-out processes than other ones (MacKinnon, Cumbers, Pike, Birch, & McMaster, 2009; Stam & Garnsey, 2006). In order to explain such differences, there is a need for social theory addressing why some actors are able to renew themselves and thereby also influence others to do the same, while others seem to be constrained by forces of path dependence and do not innovate. Agents embedded in regional economies may collectively contribute to bringing forth new ways of doing business and overcoming barriers by confronting them as the result of historically based constraints, thereby stimulating new path creation (Garud & Karnøe, 2001; Simmie, 2012). The core question is which structural aspects either enable these agents to set such dynamic processes in motion or constrain them from doing so.

This focus on structural aspects enabling and constraining agency-initiated change processes brings institutions and institutional change to the forefront of the explanatory model. Institutions are generally defined as guidelines for social behavior, or "settled habits of thought common to the generality of men" (Veblen, 1919, p. 239). As such they, by definition, influence the way actors behave, as well as the extent to which and how actors are able to identify and adapt to changes in their environment (North, 2005). This understanding of institutions has also had a strong impact on recent and ongoing debates in economic geography, focusing on the behavior of actors embraced by regionally confined institutions. Although Hall and Soskice (2001) provided some convincing groundwork for the role of institutions within nations (with their reference being varieties of capitalism), others have put more emphasis on institutions on different spatial scales, breaking them down from the national (e.g., Freeman, 1995; Lundvall, 1992) to the sectoral (Malerba, 2002) and regional levels (Tödtling & Trippl, 2005). They share the view that there is a need for unveiling the relationships between institutions of different types and scales, arguing that these relationships affect the emergence and development of specific sectors and activities, and allow for their growth by providing adaptive pillars of stability and reliability. Simultaneously, institutions are also among the main causes for lock-in (Grabher, 1993; Hassink, 2010; Tödtling & Trippl, 2005), and most institutional studies on innovation systems actually focus primarily on preservation and continuity rather than on change (Grillitsch, 2015; Streeck & Thelen, 2005; Thelen, 2009).

In recent years, scholars have spent much effort trying to explain incremental institutional change based not only on exogenous shocks, such as economic crises and similar, but also incremental processes caused by new windows of opportunity arising when ambiguity (with regard to interpretation and enforcement of behavioral rules) opens up space for actors to interpret or adopt existing rules in new ways (Mahoney & Thelen, 2009). According to this perspective, change thus takes place when key agents mindfully (or not) deviate from the "settled habits of thought." We argue that incentives for such deviation may arise due to emerging institutional inefficiencies, when the positive and intended aspects of the institutional framework— in this case the protection of quality and authenticity of products—are overshadowed by the negative aspects, in this case constraints to product development and production efficiency. As actors suffering from such inefficiencies become increasingly aware of them (and of alternatives to being conformant), their incentives for deviating by acting as institutional entrepreneurs also increase (Battilana, 2006; Sotarauta & Pulkkinen, 2011). At the same time, we argue, the opportunity to act as institutional entrepreneurs also increases with such inefficiencies. Martin and Sunley (2006) discussed this relationship between the constraining institutions and the reinforcing mechanisms pertinent to them—and the difficulties of breaking away from the stability provided by the two. The linked concept of hysteresis, originally drawn from physics and explored for economic systems by Setterfield (1993), explains that such reinforcing mechanisms build up around stable physical (in our case institutional) configurations, becoming stronger with time and making it increasingly difficult to break away from the status quo. In times of stability, Glückler and Bathelt (2017) argue, such institutional hysteresis can significantly hamper technological development and cause large scale innovation failure. Only external shocks (in the form of economic pressure, technological change, or other stresses) and emergent institutional entrepreneurs (internal or external to the setting) can help outplay the built-up rigidity. Such external shocks are close to what Geels (2002) would refer to as major changes in landscape conditions.

From an organizational perspective, the constraints on growth resulting from protective regulations that persist despite technological progress and capacity development among the actors generate excess capacity on the system level. This is comparable to slack within an organization (Bourgeois, 1981)—in other words, redundant employees, unused production capacity, unused knowledge in the organization (in our case in the regional economy), and unnecessary capital expenditures (Nohria & Gulati, 1996). It differs, however, from what the literature refers to as unabsorbed or high discretion slack (i.e., buffering resources with high flexibility), the kind of slack built up over the long term because of a static institutional context, and is defined as absorbed slack, being in particular processed inventory, redundant specialized labor, and low-flexibility machine capacity (Herold, Jayaraman, & Narayanaswamy, 2006; Nohria & Gulati, 1996; Sharfman, Wolf, Chase, & Tansik, 1988). This slack does not exist due to actors' conscious strategic decisions, but is an effect of regulatory limitations that have remained constant while technological capabilities and organizational structures have not. This mismatch between institutional, technological, and organizational development—which we term *institutional inefficiencies*—is in this study perceived as one of the main triggers for radical institutional change and, in parallel, for product diversification in the Cognac cluster.

Inspired by historical sociology and political science, three (often interrelated) microlevel mechanisms are suggested: layering, drift, and conversion. In some (rare) cases these evolutionary processes may lead to institutional displacement, in other words, a situation in which current institutions are abandoned and replaced by new ones (Mahoney & Thelen, 2009). However, institutional displacement is very rare and was not observed in the case this chapter is based on; therefore, the main focus is on understanding the processes of layering, drift, and conversion, which are continuous in all evolving clusters (and economic systems in general).

Layering basically means attaching new rules to existing ones and establishing new institutional layers within a given structure (Mahoney & Thelen, 2009; van der Heijden, 2010). In general, these layers change the ways the original rules structure behavior (Schickler, 2001; Thelen, 2003). Instead of providing entirely new rules, layering, rather, involves revisions, amendments, and additions to existing rules. Layering processes most commonly occur when challenging actors do not have the capacity to actually modify or change existing rules. It is an often observed process, as it is difficult for protectors of the old rules to prevent others from choosing to create amendments or small (layered) modifications instead of entirely rejecting the existing regulation.

Drift describes situations in which the established rules do not formally change (as in conversion), although their impact changes as external conditions significantly evolves (Beland, 2007; Mahoney & Thelen 2009; van der Heijden 2010). These can be shifts in economic or political systems that make regulation redundant or put it into a new and diverted context. Drift particularly occurs when actors choose not to respond to these external changes (van der Heijden, 2010). This inaction can, in fact, over long time periods lead to significant changes in the meaning of institutions. Drift is an important indicator for inefficiencies that have emerged over time and that have been called into question by changes in the external environment. Conversion is described as the process of reinterpretation of existing institutions (Mahoney & Thelen, 2009; Thelen, 2003). Here, the rules remain formally the same, but are enacted and interpreted in a new way. This is not primarily a result of an external change of setting (as in drift), but is mainly encouraged by actors who react to endogenous ambiguities in their established institutional setting. Those actors actively exploit gaps and discontinuities in the institutional framework to transform existing institutions into tools for their own purpose. Typically, such actors are institutional innovators that are particularly good at working within existing structures to craft unexpected solutions to emerging problems. The evolution of the ice cube industry from the 1800s to the mid-1900s (as described in James, 1984) is a good example of conversion and actors reinterpreting the existing setting. The first wave of development in this industry was dominated by large capital-intensive companies that extracted ice from Canadian lakes and transported it by train to the larger cities to serve restaurants and households, but which were outplayed some decades later by firms that developed facilities right outside the cities to produce ice locally. In a third step, electronic equipment firms developed small-scale refrigerators and freezers, making both prevailing systems redundant.

In a concrete attempt to analytically disentangle these layering, drift, and conversion processes this study draws on Scott's (2008) conceptual model of regulative, normative, and cognitive pillars of institutional frameworks. Regulative institutions (or pillars of institutions) are usually legally sanctioned and most often territorially confined. Instrumentality and conformity to rules are the main coercive mechanisms. Normative institutions are morally governed and sustained through appropriateness and social obligations in ongoing systems of social relations (e.g., families, communities, and business networks). These are not necessarily territorially confined, but maintained through continuous interaction in networks and other forms of social groups, with varying geographical configuration. Cognitive institutions, understood as shared conceptions and frames through which meaning is made, are sustained by the logic of orthodoxy and taken-for-grantedness. Similar to normative institutions, the territorial dimension of these institutions is not easy to pinpoint (Scott, 2008). Some would argue that the cognitive dimension is the "deepest," because it rests on preconscious, taken-for-granted understandings. It is however important to note that the regulative dimension in many respects has strong coercive power and might, thus, shape the normative and cognitive dimensions, at least when, as in the case presented in this study, the regulative dimension remains stable through many generations. Scott himself (2008) and most studies building upon that framework have argued that the institutional layers cannot be understood separately, but rather as affecting each other in nu merous ways. Due to its homogeneity of actors and stable institutional framework (particularly on the regulative layer), our current study allows disentangling and analyzing such change processes on the normative and cultural-cognitive layers emerging from and relating to the given regulative stability.

Based on the operational framework outlined in Table 7.1, our study analyzes the evolution of the Cognac cluster over a period of several decades, with particular focus on the moments in history when large scale changes are identifiable (the 1970s and the 1990s). While the regulative framework of cognac production has remained unchanged since the early 1900s, our main analytical focus is geared toward understanding the processes of layering, drift, and conversion that have taken place and influenced the normative and cognitive dimensions of the institutional framework, as well as firm establishment and industry orientation, with accentuated speed and impact during these transformative periods.

Although institutional reconfiguration is somewhat complicated to observe directly, the analysis is based on interpretations of changed behavior in the empirical case and thus uses these observations as indications of institutional reconfiguration.

The remainder of the chapter applies this framework to the Cognac cluster, with particular focus on the change processes taking place as of the 1990s.

Table 7.1 Operational framework for understanding the processes of institutional layering, drift, conversion, and displacement in cluster evolution. Design by authors

Indication			
Layering	Drift	Conversion	Displacement
Condition			
Challenging actors do not have the capacity to modify or change existing rules.	External conditions change; actors choose not to respond to these external changes.	Inefficiencies emerge in the institutional framework.	The institutional framework is outcompeted by changes in the environment, or internally replaced by a new framework.
Institutional Change Process			
Actors create new institutional layers in addition to the existing ones.	Inaction of institutional actors leads to significant changes in the meaning of institutions.	Actors actively exploit inefficiencies in the institutional framework.	Actors exit the old framework and, if applicable, enter an entirely new one.
Aggregate Outcomes			
Revisions, amendments, and additions are made to existing institutions; multiple layers are generated within the same system.	The changed meaning of institutions creates pressures or new incentives for actors embedded in the framework.	Reinterpretation of existing institutions leads to change among challenging actors.	The old framework disappears, and is replaced by a new one.

Research Design and Methods

We became interested in this case through a previous study examining product innovation in the beverage industry that was conducted by one of this chapter's authors in 2010–2012. What we found particularly interesting in Cognac was the homogeneous (regulative) institutional framework that had dominated the local cluster and impacted its firms ever since local production rules were made explicit in 1909. We were also aware that major change processes had taken place in the cluster at several points in the past, with the most marked ones occurring in conjunction with the oil crisis in 1973 (concentration of firms in the cluster during a period of considerable crisis) and in the mid-1990s (major product diversification among some local firms, again following a significant crisis on one of the strategic export markets for local firms). The homogeneity of the context and the explicit regulation of all firms in the cluster mean that institutional change processes are particularly discernible over time and can be illustrated with examples on different levels of the cluster.

With the product's strong historical embeddedness in the region and many local firms still family run, there is detailed data available on the history of local firms, trade organizations, and established product regulations. For cognac, as well for its close relative champagne, traditional and locally confined rules of production apply, whose entire development from their initial explicit introduction is precisely documented in local trade organization archives. To supplement a comprehensive dataset on local firms' current activities still accessible from the previous study, we gathered historical information on local regulations reaching back to the time of their establishment, gained access to regulatory documents, and collected data on the history of firms from local trade organizations. We reexamined a range of firms that we found had undergone particularly interesting developments over the past decades within the cluster (based on our insights from the previous study of product development over time) and conducted semi-structured interviews with their current and former managers. We distinguished between firms that (1) complied (and still comply) with established local regulation, (2) worked on the fringes of that regulation (or even disrespected it at times) and (3) disregarded local regulation as of the 1990s and used their skills and resources to develop other food and beverage products. We conducted 41 interviews with managers and local professionals, following up 12 with further detailed questions about the companies' historical developments. One of the authors collected this data and returned to the firms on several occasions, obtaining further information in informal conversations with local professionals from different parts of the value chain. This helped us triangulate information and obtain a more in-depth understanding of local developments over time.

In addition to the qualitative insights from the interviews and observations, we accessed a descriptive dataset provided by a local trade organization, including balance sheets of local firms and cornerstone data about their historical development (number of employees, annual turnover, type of products). We also sought information on firms that disappeared in the past, but had more difficulty obtaining comprehensive data. We judged that the sample of existing firms was solid enough to provide internal validity for our analysis, because the essential elements of the local industry had proved fairly stable and homogeneous over time. The compilation of all of Cognac's firms in industry datasets and national tax registers gave us certainty that we had not overlooked essential actors in the cluster.

The Case and Observations

Cognac's principal standardized production techniques emerged in the seventeenth century, when the first larger export firms were established, essentially by foreign traders frequenting the region for its salt reserves. Individual producers using distinct distillation techniques were the source of gradually developing production norms, which local vineyards had to follow in order to fulfill the traders' requirements. In the early nineteenth century, Cognac became a global label and was recognized for its quality in the spirits industry. To protect this label, Cognac firms worked on the formulation of written laws binding on all firms producing and trading cognac in global markets. Non-explicit regulation started in the middle of the nineteenth century. The first written law was passed in 1909, becoming one of the first protected labels of origin regulations worldwide and defining the geographical origin of the grapes. A second one was passed in 1937, with more explicit rules regarding specific production techniques (Coussié, 2011).

The initial intention of these regulative institutions was rather simple: to target those who mislead or tend to mislead the consumer [and to protect the] quality and dignity of local products (from Coussié, 2011, p. 58; decree of 1909). Despite its relatively simple foundation, the consequences of this decision were profound in the long run, as is shown in the analysis. The Appellation d'Origine Contrôlée (AOC) regulations resulted in a shared identity and image among local firms, and solidified the trust of their external customers. In addition, although less deliberate, it created a local system of exchangeable goods, which led to an important increase in confidence among local services (such as banking and insurance) and strongly amplified localization economies. The use of the same raw material and production techniques generated similar needs and challenges among local firms, which in turn led to the creation of numerous specialized service and supply firms (e.g., coopers, cork firms, packaging firms, aroma specialists), as well as, over time, a thick set of local inter-firm organizations and public support structures. In that sense, the protective regulations created a stable "comfort zone" in which firms could focus on other central parts of their activity (such as entering new export markets, refining quality within given regulatory boundaries, building up stocks). But, and importantly, it also created a regulatory setting that was primarily rather hostile to change of a more radical and explorative nature.

The laws from 1909 and 1937 formalized rules that had already long existed locally as norms and habits among vintners, distillers, coopers, and other traditional professions. The regulation made these rules explicit—and prevented insiders and outsiders from infringing the label. A number of distinct normative institutions, nevertheless, have developed over time, and go far beyond the formal regulation. Many unwritten rules have been created and are respected by local firms and among different professions within the local system, with some of them subsequently being included in official AOC regulation.

The institutional framework described above has defined much of local development until today. One of its main features, from an institutional change perspective, is its generation over time of a range of inefficiencies (and, as a consequence, of unexploited capacities among local firms) that have put both the institutional framework and its embedded actors under pressure. These inefficiencies (and the reaction of incumbent firms to them over time) are examined in the analysis section as a condition for different types of institutional change. They range from limitations on when distillation may occur to inefficient aging techniques and complexities of the aging process in general. Their structure and impact are further elaborated in the analysis section later in this chapter.

One must say that despite such inefficiencies (or even because of them, for they keep the label exclusive), cognac sales have grown significantly since the 1950s. Overall, they have gradually increased by an average 5.5% per year, growing a total of 400% between 1950 and 2010 (see Figure 7.1). It is interesting to look at periods

Fig. 7.1 Sales of AOC Cognac, 1945–2012. Source: Data from Bureau National Interprofessionnel du Cognac, 2012. Design by authors

of more radical change during this development, as in the oil crisis after 1973 and the East Asian crisis in the early 1990s.

In these moments of crisis and in the aftermath, the following aggregate developments are observed in the cluster (see Figure 7.2).

The wave of diversification after the 1990 crisis is particularly interesting for this study. Following the crisis, a handful of firms started to break away from the traditional cognac label and used their capabilities for different, but related products (mainly other premium spirits). This change did not occur without resistance from established firms and interfirm organizations. One of the early movers was high-end vodka producer Grey Goose (GG), which applied local knowledge and benefited from the area's image, while not following traditional cognac regulations. Within a few years, GG had become a global market leader in its segment, and was sold after eight years to a global corporation in the industry. A range of other actors in the cluster went through similar developments, diverging from the traditional label (and its regulatory implications) to create a distinct new path of development for local and non-local firms. Resistance by the established players in the local arena against the new development was strong. It ranged from unsuccessful attempts to have non-cognac production in the geographic area officially forbidden by local governing bodies (according to interviewed managers of companies working with GG) to a range of small actions trying to keep the new agents from deviating from established practice. One firm traditionally producing Cognac at its vineyard and distillery lost its delivery contracts with one of the largest local cognac brands after the latter discovered it was attempting to produce other premium spirits (according to an interviewed manager of the firm, 18 years after the event). One of the new firms, with

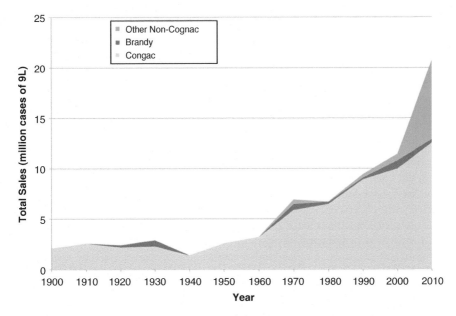

Fig. 7.2 Sales of Cognac, brandy and other non-Cognac products by local firms 1900–2010. Source: Data from Bureau National Interprofessionnel du Cognac, 2012, with additional data from authors' research in 2012 on product innovation among local firms. Design by authors

several years of fast growth in a non-cognac brand, was barred from having a reception area for their invited customers at a local jazz festival, after the four largest established firms threatened to cancel their sponsorship for the entire event (according to an interview with concerned manager of an excluded firm). An entertaining reaction to the rise of nontraditionist firms was a several-year-long ecological enquiry emphasizing that the production site of the most prominent nontraditionist firm was located in the ecosystem of a rare frog variety, with the initiators arguing that the production site permit could therefore not be extended and that the facility should ultimately be relocated.

It took several years for new developments to be tolerated and adopted, first mainly by small and medium-sized firms that saw an opportunity (or were under economic pressure), and then, much later, by the larger and more powerful players in the local setting. It was possible to observe a sequence of institutional changes contributing to the emergence of this new path and influencing its subsequent development as well as its integration into established production structures. The new and nontraditional production is today contributing almost 50% of the cluster's output. Firms did not change the established rules of the games on the regulatory level by adopting new production techniques and breaking away from established institutions. But they did trigger changes on the normative and cultural-cognitive level, with many firms having adopted the new production techniques and added them to their portfolio of activities. As a consequence, this changed mindset also influenced the discourse in the governing board of the formal rules of the game, where traditional rules started to be challenged and new practices established.

Analysis—Periods of Incremental and Radical Change

We were able to identify and isolate many of the features of institutions and institutional change in clusters within the theoretical framework provided by the Cognac case, allowing us to make a detailed analysis of the development of the actors within the system and of how they interacted with established institutions over time and ultimately shaped cluster evolution. We found particularly interesting how actors reacted to the observed and built-up institutional inefficiencies at different times and what aggregate outcomes these generated among actors in the cluster.

In periods of incremental change of the industry and its local environment, the institutional framework remained rather stable and was characterized by features of layering and drift. Examples of layering were firms creating sublabels within the Cognac regulatory framework, (such as *single vineyard*, *single estate*) or soil-related classifications of the final product (i.e., Fine Champagne, Fine de Cognac), which were all in accordance with established rules and created more specific subrules for producers wanting to use those labels. Simultaneously, drift took place because the environment changed and some established rules became redundant. The introduction of cooling equipment, for instance, technically extends the distillation period, which local regulation limited to the winter months (because the wine used for distillation would overferment if not cooled). Yet, the regulations were not adapted. As a result of the stability, continuous rationalization processes within the given rules took place; interfirm organizations managing label-related regulation were founded, and contributed to reinforcing established institutions. Such processes lay the foundation for more thorough processes of change set in motion in periods of external stress, because they accentuate the tension between technological, organizational capacity and institutional constraints, thereby increasing the organizational slack built up within the local production system (Herold et al., 2006; Tan & Peng, 2003).

In periods of more radical transformation more thorough change can be observed, as was seen during both periods of crisis outlined in Figure 7.1, but in particular in the immediate aftermath of the 1990 crisis. A concrete and well-documented example was the change of attitude toward firms that partially broke with tradition and entered new fields of production. These changes also widely impacted the more aggregate development of the industry composition in the cluster, leading to today's situation in which about 50% of total production value is composed of non-cognac products (products breaking away from the traditional institutional configuration). Important to note is that fundamental triggers for change—previously described as inefficiencies—in the periods of both incremental and radical transformation are similar, although their impact differs because the pressure or incentives to adapt differs. When the status quo is radically challenged, as during the crises of the 1970s and the 1990s, new windows of opportunity are uncovered. To take advantage of those windows of opportunity, or to exploit the organizational slack (Bourgeois, 1981; Sharfman et al., 1988), major cognitive change is necessary. Normative and regulatory change, on the other hand, plays a more dominant role in incremental change processes, which largely explains the long periods of stability between the crises.

Our analysis revealed that the incremental changes, as well as the radical ones described above, can be traced back to the basic composition and interpretation of the AOC regulations. In particular, three core aspects of the AOC are worth highlighting. Firstly, the limited distillation period creates inefficiencies and windows of opportunities, which are realized when incentives—due to external pressures—grow strong enough. Cognac can only be distilled between the harvest of the grapes and March 31 of the following year. This regulation has a historical-technological background. The grape juice used for cognac needs to be stored in a cold location after initial fermentation and before distillation (to avoid overfermentation), so it is forbidden to distill in the months after March, when outside temperatures increase significantly. Today this problem has been largely overcome by using cooling containers, but the regulation remains unchanged, with the consequence that distilleries can only use their distilling equipment and knowledge six months per year. This results in significant unexploited resources among cognac producers, although most of these resources are in the form of process inventory, specialized labor, and low flexibility machine capacity, or what the literature refers to as low discretion slack (Sharfman et al., 1988), which is not always easy to transform into increased productivity. From the interviews with distillers, we understood that this is not a major problem when demand is high and distilleries run 24 hours, seven days a week, during the allowed distilling period. Yet, when demand is lower than normal (e.g., at times of diminishing demand) this can cause significant competitive stress for distilleries, putting them under pressure to use their specialized knowledge and production capacity during the other months of the year. Traditionally, a large part of the distillery staff would work in the vineyards or in other related professions during the summer months. However, when the crises—especially that of the 1990s—hit the cognac market, attempts to utilize unexploited capacities for other types of spirits production began, first on a small scale in the face of heavy resistance, but then with gradual acceptance in large parts of the community. This conversion indicates a shift in the perception of this institutionally based slack, from an asset guaranteeing the quality and authenticity of the regional production to an unnecessary cost to be eliminated through new forms of exploitation (Nohria & Gulati, 1996).

Secondly, cognac must be aged in barrels made of certain types of oak. According to local aroma specialists and cellar masters, this is to ensure the consistent quality of cognac, although it also certainly has symbolic value for its customers. The equation of the aging process is relatively simple: The liquid must be exposed to a certain amount of oak surface and in indirect contact with the surrounding air in the cellar. Barrel aging is a fairly inefficient and historical way of ensuring this exposure. Competitors from outside of Cognac can use more modern techniques, for instance aging the liquid in steel tanks and using oak extracts or oak chips that affect the liquid very similarly. This is much more efficient in terms of precision and use of space, but would certainly interfere with the traditional image of cognac. Although the inefficiency of barrel aging does not create a window of opportunity to the same extent as the distillation period, it is still seen as beneficial for new path creation because it contributes to maintaining the exclusivity of cognac and, thus, adds to its luxury and quality image. Producers diverging from the cognac norm cannot, therefore, draw directly on this inefficiency, although their incentive to tap into the local production system is strengthened by a desire to have their products associated with the luxury and authenticity of the Cognac region. And their capacity to do so depends on the availability of highly skilled and specialized employees with reserve capacity—unabsorbed slack—during parts of the year (Tan & Peng, 2003).

Thirdly, the defined aging periods: Cognac has a minimum aging time of two years, with official age categories being VS (at least two years), VSOP (no less than four years) and XO (six years or more). In many cases, the cognac used is older than its minimum specified age. The aging process in general, however, makes planning of production complicated and fairly inefficient, because increases in production will only have an effect on sales in two, four, and six years (or more). For their long-term financial planning cognac firms therefore rely heavily on five-to-ten-year forecasts and struggle with the uncertainties these involve. Also, this limitation creates incentives for alternative and/or unorthodox production, for it is one strategy of spreading risk and balancing investment in order to cope with market fluctuations during the long aging period. The aging imperative is thus an incentive for reducing excess absorbed slack in the form of inflexible investments (Sharfman et al., 1988), while still being able to demand a higher marginal price for the main product on the basis of its reputation for quality and authenticity (Bourgeois, 1981).

All of the above rules have, as indicated, a strong impact on the incentives and opportunities for changed behavior among local firms. However, institutional change regarding the interpretation and observance of the rules is required for these incentives to have a real impact and for the opportunities to be realized. Our study observed that the imposed regulation creates natural tensions within the system and, in addition, particularly exposes it to technological and organizational changes in the industry. Our research also revealed that outsiders (or those locals not using the cognac label) are less constrained by the AOC regulations, and therefore have more possibilities to reconfigure their production, to improve processes, and to act upon or initiate changes in markets. In other words, those actors demonstrate a higher degree of interpretive flexibility and contribute more to the processes of layering, drift, and conversion than the more embedded actors that have built their entire identity and competitiveness on the cognac label (Strambach, 2010). This is an important part of the reason why the change agents (i.e., institutional entrepreneurs) identified in this study were either newcomers to the region or incumbent actors that left the region for a while and subsequently returned with new perceptions and experience.

Table 7.2 specifies the institutional change processes that we identified both as the results of the incentives and opportunities that the regulations bring and as nec-

Table 7.2 Causes and aggregate outcomes of transformation processes in the Cognac cluster

Indication			
Layering	Drift	Conversion	Displacement
Condition			
Regulation is controlled by the most influential actors in the cluster; smaller firms need to comply or exit the label.	Actors decide to stick to existing regulation, while the external context undergoes significant changes.	Regulatory inefficiencies open windows of opportunities for change agents.	Regulation becomes outcompeted due to major changes in the environment (not observed in the Cognac case).
Processes			
Regulative			
Established regulation remains unchanged.	Established regulation remains unchanged.	Established regulation remains unchanged.	Established regulation remains unchanged.
Normative			
Different labels within the cognac category emerge (e.g. single estate, single vintage, French brandy).	Changes in the beverage industry (uprating of traditional low-cost drinks).	New practice slowly becomes a norm among local firms (after cognitive change below).	A new institutional framework becomes a norm and potentially leads to new regulation (not observed).
Cognitive			
Actors become comfortable with new labels, slowly adopting change on the normative and regulatory dimension.	Embedded firms come under pressure and need to react to emerging changes in the environment.	External actors use local production capacity and knowledge in a new way (e.g. Grey Goose).	Adaptive firms reject old rules and generate or integrate an entirely new institutional framework (not observed in study).
Aggregate Outcomes			
A multitude of institutional layers emerges within the cluster over time (some staying within the given framework, others going beyond it).	A multitude of firms looks into incremental change within the given framework; others become ready for more radical change.	New opportunities emerge within the cluster; a need arises for change agents to exploit them.	A major shift occurs in the cluster from one (disappearing) institutional framework to an entirely new one (not observed in study).

Source: Design by authors

essary conditions for the actors' abilities to realize those opportunities. The overview compares changes in the regulative, normative, and cognitive dimensions with the subsequent outcomes in terms of layering, drift, and conversion, as well as displacement, which was not observed. As touched upon above, it is important to note that the regulative dimension in the Cognac case has remained largely unchanged over time because of region's regulatory specificities and AOC status, with only minor incremental changes or legal adaptations to current requirements occurring. Thus, main attention is paid to changes in the normative and cognitive dimension of the institutional framework.

One of our key observations in the study was that incremental institutional change processes (layering and drift) were mainly driven by the regulatory and normative pillars (cf., Mahoney & Thelen, 2009), while more radical change processes (conversion, displacement) are prompted much more by major changes on the cognitive level (e.g., through external entrants, returning locals). Observed processes of institutional layering were the consequence of power relations in the cluster, in which the largest established players control regulation, while smaller, less powerful actors (in institutional terms) can only abide by the imposed structures, or create their own institutional layers within the given framework (Battilana, 2006). In Cognac, this could be observed with small and medium-sized firms creating sublabels of regulation (often with stricter rules than the largest players could commit to), such as single vintage or single estate products—the latter meaning that the cognac produced and sold in bottles only comes from one single vintage, or even just one estate (where the largest cognac firms source their cognac from several hundred vineyards in order to produce enough quantity).

Drift mainly relates to changes occurring in the external environment, while local regulation remains the same, with the result of this being that the meaning (or purpose) of regulation changes, not explicitly, but by being moved into a new and different context. In the cognac case, there have been many examples of firms external to the cluster (and to its regulation) innovating in production techniques or product concepts (such as avoiding the complex ageing process in oak barrels) and entering new market segments or, in particular, developing higher profit margins. These changes put firms subject to cognac regulation under significant pressure (e.g., through their marketing budgets falling far behind those of their external competitors in relative terms), forcing them to engage in incremental change within the given institutional framework or to prepare for more radical change. Many of the firms that engaged in more radical change at later stages (i.e., after the 1990s crisis) had, significantly, undergone processes of layering and drift in preceding years. In general, the different institutional change processes described in this section are not to be seen as separate from each other, but are, rather, occurring simultaneously and provide aggregate among firms that shape the cluster (and its institutional framework) over time (Martin, 2010).

Conversion differs in many ways from layering and drift. Where the main driving forces in the latter two are general (and rather incremental) changes in institutions, conversion found its driving energy in change agents with radically different mindsets (often external entrants or local returners) that perceive the local production system differently and exploit windows of opportunity provided by the local institutional framework (Sotarauta & Pulkkinen, 2011). One can, for instance, name the radically divergent products that emerged after the 1990s crisis, when a wave of foreign entrants started using local skills in a new way, particularly by producing beverage products that can be distilled throughout the year, therefore also after March 31, when cognac distillation, by regulation, must cease. They also recombined local skills in a way that eliminated general institutional inefficiencies in the local system (e.g., the complex aging process or constraints in terms of sourcing raw materials), which allowed them to generate additional value representing close to

50% of the local cluster's current production output. Established actors in the Cognac cluster initially reacted with much skepticism and resistance to new developments. Only with time and some highly successful developments among "new" firms did local actors start adopting the new practices and accepting institutional change of more radical nature. The last ones to adopt the new practices were the largest players in the cluster, those with the most influence (and stake) in the old and established regulatory structure.

Conclusions

We have argued in this chapter that the institutional framework in a given regional cluster is crucially important for the behavior and development of firms there. Consequently, it is also one of the factors decisively shaping the evolution of the cluster in a wider sense. Yet, at the same time the evolution of the cluster requires adaption of the institutional framework, for changed behavior depends by nature on changed perception of and adherence to behavioral rules. In other words, the rules of the game set the limits and define the possibility of change taking place, while change intrinsically also influences the rules of the game. In the case of the Cognac cluster and its recent evolution as presented and analyzed in this study, the institutional framework's regulative dimension has been stable and largely unchanged for a very long period, which made it possible to disentangle particular developments related to actors' responses to emerging institutional inefficiencies and with institutional change in the nonconstrained layers (the normative and cultural-cognitive).

Despite this stability of regulative institutions, there have been major behavioral changes among the cluster's actors during the last two decades, which in turn have led to substantial transformations in the composition and orientation of the local industry. These changes have been imposed—and generated—by incremental as well as more radical changes in the normative and cognitive dimensions of the institutional framework. Incentives and opportunities for such change are always present because of the institutional inefficiencies that result with fixed and inflexible industry regulations and because of the organizational slack this generates, although the actors in the regional setting have differing capabilities to act upon these incentives and realize new opportunities. The most established and powerful incumbents display a low degree of interpretative flexibility and inclination to renew themselves and challenge established behavioral rules because of their high stakes in the current state of affairs, whereas newcomers and returners are more likely to act as change agents or *institutional entrepreneurs*. This is because their incentive for and potential gain from challenging established norms and regulations are greater than their stake in preserving the status quo.

Three interrelated processes of institutional change were identified in Cognac. Layering is the process of adding new layers to an existing institution, thereby incrementally influencing its form and direction. In Cognac, this process was mainly rooted in the normative dimension of the institution, when new attitudes toward and interpretations of the regulations were added, which initially generated subgroups of actors with different modes of behavior that then, however, were gradually diffused to wider parts of the cluster to become normalized. It was usually a matter of small modifications that over time generated cumulative processes. A closely related process of institutional change is defined as drift, a process in which the consequences of existing institutions are adapted to changes in the exogenous environment, such as global crises or altered market conditions, which generate fresh incentives for change within established regulations. In Cognac, these were also incremental, but had an important impact on the cluster because they were cumulative over time. A more radical change process is referred to as conversion. Although its roots are mainly in the cognitive dimension of the institution—through actors being able to identify and exploit new windows of opportunity arising from inefficiencies in the current system—this process also feeds into the normative dimension when new practices are diffused to wider groups in the cluster. In principle, these three inter-related processes also have the potential to generate comprehensive institutional change in the regulative dimension, in the literature referred to as displacement (Mahoney & Thelen, 2009), yet this was not observed in the present study. Despite quite far-reaching transformation of the composition and direction of local industry, the formal regulations defining its rules of the game have remained unaltered.

This study of relatively recent change processes in Cognac provides insights into the general understanding of the relation between institutional and industrial change, in particular in regional economies. One specific observation requiring a concluding comment is the obstinate and sluggish nature of institutional change and the severe challenges thus facing institutional entrepreneurs. The maintained stability of the regulative institution—the protected label of origin—can indeed be interpreted as if no or very minor institutional change has actually occurred in the region and as if the layering, drift, and conversion observed among local actors in this study merely illustrate industrial branching in Cognac, rather than institutional change. We argue, however, that the observed developments imply more thorough institutional change, because the industrial branching, or diversification process, takes place within a dense and historically homogeneous community of local producers, substantially influencing their market strategies and modes of production and, thus, spilling over into the way they handle their traditional business. The actors and companies populating the local cluster are largely the same families that have been there for hundreds of years and acted as gatekeepers protecting the authenticity of their production and the identity of the region. The fact that those same gatekeepers adapt their interpretation of what is actually possible within the regulatory framework; add new layers to their historically based routines and modes of production; and expand their horizons while preserving the authenticity underpinning the cluster's competitive advantage indicates more thorough institutional change.

While the Cognac case is rather specific when it comes to both geographic location and institutions, the findings of this study raise questions of a more general nature that require further investigation. One such question has to do with the role of institutions as either barriers or enablers for transitions within modern industries aimed at addressing what are referred to as the grand societal challenges. The recent change processes in Cognac at the focus of this study were largely triggered by external shocks in the form of economic crises in the 1970s and 1990s. These shocks primarily generating economic pressure on a local production system were quite concrete through their immediate impact on its short and medium-term profits. According to our analysis, this mobilized institutional entrepreneurship in the local community. While the current grand challenges connected to climate change, energy, environment, demographics, security, health, and education will require radical changes in the way we produce, consume, live, and interact, the pressures these challenges generate are less well defined in terms of both urgency and geographic impact zones. Questions that arise are whether such pressures would mobilize the same type of locally embedded institutional entrepreneurship; where these movements are most likely to occur; and what impact any institutional change eventually initiated by those institutional entrepreneurs will have—either regionally, or globally. Addressing such questions would provide fruitful ground for advancing our understanding of the relation between agency, space, and institutions.

References

Audretsch, D. B., & Feldman, M. P. (1996). Innovative clusters and the industry life cycle. *Review of Industrial Organization, 11,* 253–273. doi:https://doi.org/10.1007/BF00157670

Battilana, J. (2006). Agency and institutions: The enabling role of individuals' social position. *Organization, 13,* 653–676. doi:https://doi.org/10.1177/1350508406067008

Béland, D. (2007). Ideas and institutional change in social security: Conversion, layering, and policy drift. *Social Science Quarterly, 88,* 20–38. doi:https://doi.org/10.1111/j.1540-6237.2007.00444.x

Boschma, R., & Fornahl, D. (2011). Cluster evolution and a roadmap for future research. *Regional Studies, 45,* 1295–1298. doi:https://doi.org/10.1080/00343404.2011.633253

Bourgeois, L. J. (1981). On the measurement of organizational slack. *The Academy of Management Review, 6,* 29–39. Retrieved from http://www.jstor.org/stable/257138

Braunerhjelm, P., & Feldman, M. (2008). Cluster genesis: Technology-based industrial development. *Economic Geography, 84,* 245–246 doi:https://doi.org/10.1111/j.1944-8287.2008.tb00409.x.

Coenen, L., Moodysson, J., & Martin, H. (2015). Path renewal in old industrial regions: Possibilities and limitations for regional innovation policy. *Regional Studies, 49,* 850–865. doi:https://doi.org/10.1080/00343404.2014.979321

Coussié, J. V. (2011). *Le Cognac—Un produit régional. Un marché mondial de L'incidence des grands évènements sur ses expéditions et son histoire* [Cognac—a regional product, a global market. The impact of major events on its trade and history]. Cognac: Atelier Graphique Cognaçais.

Freeman, C. (1995). The 'National System of Innovation' in historical perspective. *Cambridge Journal of Economics, 19,* 5–24. doi:https://doi.org/10.1093/oxfordjournals.cje.a035309

Frenken, K. & Boschma, R. A. (2007). A theoretical framework for evolutionary economic geography: Industrial dynamics and urban growth as a branching process. *Economic Geography, 7,* 635–649. doi:https://doi.org/ 10.1093/jeg/lbm018

Garud, R., & Karnøe, P. (2001). *Path dependence and creation.* New York: Psychology Press.

Geels, F. (2002). Technological transitions as evolutionary reconfiguration processes: A multi-level perspective and a case-study. *Research Policy, 31*, 1257–1274. doi:https://doi.org/10.1016/S0048-7333(02)00062-8

Glückler, J., & Bathelt, H. (2017). Institutional context and innovation. In H. Bathelt, P. Cohendet, S. Henn, & L. Simon (Eds.), *The Elgar companion to innovation and knowledge creation: A multi-disciplinary approach*. Cheltenham: Edward Elgar.

Grabher, G. (1993). *The embedded firm: On the socioeconomics of industrial networks*. London: Routledge.

Grillitsch, M. (2015). Institutional layers, connectedness and change: Implications for economic evolution in regions. *European Planning Studies, 23*, 2099–2124. doi:https://doi.org/10.1080/09654313.2014.1003796

Hall, P. A., & Soskice, D. (2001). *Varieties of capitalism: The institutional foundations of comparative advantage*. Oxford, UK: Oxford University Press.

Hassink, R. (2010). Locked in decline? On the role of regional lock-ins in old industrial areas. In R. Boschma & R. Martin (Eds.), *Handbook of evolutionary economic geography* (pp. 450–469). Cheltenham: Edward Elgar.

Herold, D. M., Jayaraman, N., & Narayanaswamy, C. R. (2006). What is the relationship between organizational slack and innovation? *Journal of Management Issues, 18*, 372–392. Retrieved from http://www.jstor.org/stable/40604546

Iammarino, S., & McCann, P. (2006). The structure and evolution of industrial clusters: Transactions, technology and knowledge spillovers. *Research Policy, 35*, 1018–1036. doi:https://doi.org/10.1016/j.respol.2006.05.004

Lundvall, B.-Å. (1992). *National systems of innovation: Towards a theory of innovation and interactive learning*. London: Pinter.

MacKinnon, D., Cumbers, A., Pike, A., Birch, K., & McMaster, R. (2009). Evolution in economic geography: Institutions, political economy, and adaptation. *Economic Geography, 85*, 129–150. doi:https://doi.org/10.1111/j.1944-8287.2009.01017.x

Mahoney, J., & Thelen, K. (2009). Explaining institutional change: Ambiguity, agency, and power. Cambridge, UK: Cambridge University Press.

Malerba, F. (2002). Sectoral systems of innovation and production. *Research Policy, 31*, 247–264. doi:https://doi.org/10.1016/S0048-7333(01)00139-1

Malmberg, A., & Power, D. (2005). (How) do (firms in) clusters create knowledge? *Industry and Innovation, 12*, 409–431. https://doi.org/10.1080/13662710500381583

Martin, R. (2010). Roepke lecture in economic geography—rethinking regional path dependence: Beyond lock-in to evolution. *Economic Geography, 86*, 1–27. doi:https://doi.org/10.1111/j.1944-8287.2009.01056.x

Martin, R., & Sunley, P. (2006). Path dependence and regional economic evolution. *Journal of Economic Geography, 6*, 395–437. doi:https://doi.org/10.1093/jeg/lbl012

Maskell, P., & Kebir, L. (2006). What qualifies as a cluster theory? In B. Asheim, P. Cooke, & R. Martin (Eds.), *Clusters and regional development: Critical reflections and explorations* (pp. 30–49). New York: Routledge.

Menzel, M.-P., & Fornahl, D. (2010). Cluster life cycles—dimensions and rationales of cluster evolution. *Industrial and Corporate Change, 19*, 205–238. doi:https://doi.org/10.1093/icc/dtq014

Nohria, N., & Gulati, R. (1996). Is slack good or bad for innovation? *The Academy of Management Journal, 39*, 1245–1264. doi:https://doi.org/10.2307/256998

North, D. C. (2005). Institutions and the process of economic change. *Management International, 9*(3), 1–7. Retrieved from the ProQuest database.

Schickler, E. (2001). *Disjointed pluralism: Institutional innovation and the development of the U.S. Congress*. Princeton: Princeton University Press.

Scott, W. R. (2008). *Institutions and organizations: Ideas and interests*. Los Angeles: Sage.

Setterfield, M. (1993). Towards a long-run theory of effective demand: Modeling macroeconomic systems with hysteresis. *Journal of Post Keynesian Economics, 15*, 347–364.

Sharfman, M. P., Wolf, G., Chase, R. B., & Tansik, D. A. (1988). Antecedents of organizational slack. *The Academy of Management Review, 13*, 601–614. http://www.jstor.org/stable/258378

Simmie, J. (2012). Path dependence and new technological path creation in the Danish wind power industry. *European Planning Studies, 20*, 753–772. doi:https://doi.org/10.1080/09654313.201 2.667924

Sotarauta, M., & Pulkkinen, R. (2011). Institutional entrepreneurship for knowledge regions: In search of a fresh set of questions for regional innovation studies. *Environment and Planning C: Government And Policy, 29*, 96–112. doi:https://doi.org/10.1068/c1066r

Stam, E., & Garnsey, E. (2006). New firms evolving in the knowledge economy: Problems and solutions around turning points. In W. Dolfsma & L. Soete (Eds.), *Understanding the dynamics of a knowledge economy* (pp. 102–128). Cheltenham: Edward Elgar.

Strambach, S. (2010). Path dependence and path plasticity: The co-evolution of institutions and innovation—the German customized business software industry. In R. Boschma & R. Martin (Eds.), *The handbook of evolutionary economic geography* (pp. 406–431). Cheltenham: Edward Elgar.

Streeck, W., & Thelen, K. (2005). *Beyond continuity: Institutional change in advanced political economies*. Oxford, UK: Oxford University Press.

Tan, J., & Peng, M. W. (2003). Organizational slack and firm performance during economic transitions: Two studies from an emerging economy. *Strategic Management Journal, 24*, 1249–1263. doi:https://doi.org/10.1002/smj.351

Thelen, K. (2003). The paradox of globalization: Labor relations in Germany and beyond. *Comparative Political Studies, 36*, 859–880. doi:https://doi.org/10.1177/0010414003256111

Thelen, K. (2009). Institutional change in advanced political economies. *British Journal of Industrial Relations, 47*, 471–498. doi:https://doi.org/10.1111/j.1467-8543.2009.00746.x

Trippl, M. (2004). *Innovative Cluster in alten Industriegebieten* [Innovative clusters in old industrial areas]. Vienna: LIT.

Trippl, M., Grillitsch, M., Isaksen, A., & Sinozic, T. (2015). Perspectives on cluster evolution: Critical review and future research issues. *European Planning Studies, 23*, 2028–2044. doi:https://doi.org/10.1080/09654313.2014.999450

Tödtling, F., & Trippl, M. (2005). One size fits all?. Towards a differentiated regional innovation policy approach. *Research policy, 34*, 1203–1219. doi:https://doi.org/10.1016/j.respol.2005.01.018

van der Heijden, J. (2010). A short history of studying incremental institutional change: Does explaining institutional change provide any new explanations? *Regulation & Governance, 4*, 230–243.

Veblen, T. (1919). *The place of science in modern civilization and other essays*. New York: B. W. Huebsch.

Chapter 8
The Art of Reconstructing a Shared Responsibility: Institutional Work of a Transnational Commons

Tiina Ritvala

> *I am a victim, perhaps, of trained incompetence in a discipline*
> *that cultivates statistics and words as means to grasp the social.*
> *Sociologists could become more adept with maps, floor plans,*
> *photographic images, bricks and mortar, landscapes and*
> *cityscapes, so that interpreting a street or forest becomes as*
> *routine and as informative as computing a chi-square. That*
> *visualizing (I think) is the next step.*
>
> *(Gieryn, 2000, pp. 483–484)*

Among the greatest and most threatened shared assets and resources for life on earth are its oceans and seas. Over time, they have served not only as a source of food, livelihood, and inspiration but also as dumping grounds for industrial, municipal, and agricultural waste by nation-states, organizations, and individuals who may have been acting rationally from their own point of view, but not collectively. In his seminal work, Hardin (1968) called this collective damage the "tragedy of the commons." As proposed by Hardin (and many others), the solution to this tragedy is either state ownership or privatization. This response rationalized and legitimated governments' control over the commons and disempowered broader agency—suggesting, for instance, that individual citizens have no voice regarding the commons. The studies by political scientist and Nobel laureate Eleanor Ostrom (1990) questioned the existence of purely selfish and norm-free users of the commons and showed that individuals may create cooperative institutions, social norms, and moral sentiments to avoid the tragedy of the commons. The pioneering work by Ostrom established the notion of the commons as including both material-economic and sociosymbolic dimensions. From the perspective of the present book, what is interesting about the commons is that they have material dimensions (shared

T. Ritvala (✉)
Department of Management Studies, Aalto University, Helsinki, Finland
e-mail: tiina.ritvala@aalto.fi

© The Author(s) 2018
J. Glückler et al. (eds.), *Knowledge and Institutions*, Knowledge and Space 13,
https://doi.org/10.1007/978-3-319-75328-7_8

geographies) as well as strong symbolic ones (shared social norms and rules about their use and protection).

The desire to identify mechanisms for symbolically reconstructing a shared space for promoting social change brings the context of the commons to the intellectual terrain of scholars who study institutional work. The notion of institutional work as "the purposive action of individuals and organizations aimed at creating, maintaining and disrupting institutions" (Lawrence & Suddaby, 2006, p. 215) builds on the sociology of practice, which stresses that any human activity is materially mediated by shared practical understandings. Whereas the mutually constitutive entanglement of the material and the social in everyday life, often called sociomaterial practices (Orlikowski, 2007), has a long tradition in the broad framework of organization theory (Leonardi, 2012), this interrelationship is less developed within the institutional-work approach (Monteiro & Nicolini, 2015; Raviola & Norbäck, 2013). Further research on how individuals work with both material and sociosymbolic spaces in their efforts to change institutions is important for enriching the understanding of the ways in which individuals interpret and work to change their contexts (Lawrence & Dover, 2015; Meyer, Höllerer, Jancsary, & van Leeuwen, 2013; Powell & Colyvas, 2008). A context with a particularly strong symbolic, but also material, power is art—a context where artists critically examine and theorize the ills (and joys) of the world.

In this chapter I argue that the production of art is an important form of institutional work and legitimating rhetoric for institutional change (Suddaby & Greenwood, 2005). The theoretical question that guides this study is how art can be used as a form of sociomaterial institutional work. The empirical context for the study is the environmental condition of the Baltic Sea in northern Europe. Empirically, I aim to discover how art can be used to recreate a shared awareness of the tragedy of the commons as represented by pollution in the Baltic Sea. Paradoxically, the Baltic Sea is one of the most studied and protected, but also polluted, seas in the world (HELCOM, 2010). It is an ecologically unique ecosystem with shallow bays and is therefore highly sensitive to the environmental impacts of human activities. The Baltic Sea is a transnational commons, that is, a common resource shared and used by people and organizations residing in the different coastal states of the sea—a sea not controlled by any single nation-state.

Institutional Work in the Context of Transnational Commons

The notion of institutional work invites scholars to focus on the interaction between institutions and the "actors that populate them", as formulated by Lawrence, Suddaby, and Leca (2011, p. 57). They conceived of institutions as "enduring elements of social life" (p. 53), as norms and rules that influence the thinking and behavior of individuals and collective actors by "providing templates for action, cognition, and emotion." With respect to the commons, these norms and rules define "who has access to a resource; what can be harvested from, dumped into, or engineered within a resource; and who participates in key decisions about these issues and about transferring rights and duties to others" (Ostrom, et al., 2002, p. 21).

In recent years a rising number of scholars have embraced the notion of institutional work and have studied the microlevel work in various contexts and aims, ranging from institutional maintenance (e.g., Currie, Lockett, Finn, Martin, & Waring, 2012; Zilber, 2009) to institutional creation (e.g., Hargadon & Douglas, 2001; Lawrence, Hardy, & Phillips, 2002). Studies have also incorporated specific spatial contexts such as a province (Zietsma & Lawrence, 2010), a regional cluster (Ritvala & Kleymann, 2012), and a university campus (Dacin, Munir, & Tracey, 2010; Lok & de Rond, 2013). However, very little scholarly attention has been paid to how institutional workers mobilize and incentivize others to work for transnational commons (Wijen & Ansari, 2007).

Transnational commons are inherited gifts (Barnes, 2006). Ranging from the atmosphere to the deep ocean floor, they do not belong to any single nation, group, or individual. Two defining characteristics of the commons are that exclusion of beneficiaries is costly and that exploitation by one user reduces resource availability for others. These characteristics result in situations in which people, by maximizing their own short-term interests, produce damage for all users in the long term (Ostrom, Burger, Field, Norgaard, & Poucansky, 1999). I subscribe to a social-constructivist perspective on the commons, a standpoint from which the tragedy of the commons is not seen as materializing by itself but rather as having to be socially constructed (Hannigan, 1995). For instance, ocean pollution becomes a problem only after oceans are collectively constructed as shared assets and responsibilities on which to act. This view is aligned with institutional theory, according to which environmental problems are primarily behavioral and cultural in nature rather than technological or economic (Ansari, Wijen, & Gray, 2013; Hoffman & Jennings, 2015). Transnational commons contain geographic location, material form, as well as meaning and value through which they are constructed and remembered (Gieryn, 2000; Lawrence & Dover, 2015). Thus, a transnational commons such as a particular location in a sea is a unique and memorable physical place linked to identities, emotions, values, cultural interpretations, and human experiences—dimensions that are all influenced by material and symbolic means and experiences.

The value of concentrating on institutional work as a way of exploring the construction of meaning in transnational commons stems from its emphasis on the situated practices of reflective actors in relation to the surrounding institutions (Lawrence et al., 2011). As the notion of institutional "work" suggests, it is firmly rooted in the sociology of practice, where practices are seen as embodied, materially mediated arrays of human activity (Lawrence & Suddaby, 2006, p. 218). This conceptualization makes it possible to study how material and sociosymbolic elements may help actors affect institutions. Curiously, and in accordance with the opening quotation, the study of institutional work has centered greatly on text, although discourse encompasses both verbal and visual material representations (Meyer et al., 2013).

Responding to calls to integrate multimodal data more thoroughly than has been the case, institutional scholars have recently begun to increase their attention to the role of visual and material artifacts in institutional processes (e.g., Hardy & Phillips, 1999; Phillips, Lawrence, & Hardy, 2004; Siebert, Wilson, & Hamilton, 2016). For instance, the study by Raviola and Norbäck (2013) showed how the introduction of new technology creates a need for institutional work by human actors. Jones and Massa (2013) and Gawer and Phillips (2013) suggested that the design of material artifacts is a form of institutional work that legitimates intended institutional projects. Another important study, by Monteiro and Nicolini (2015), pointed out the power that "silent" objects such as awards exert in institutional work. Their research showed how artifacts may inform the institutional work of education by, for instance, circulating information and extending human reach in time and space. In a study on creating housing for the hard-to-house, Lawrence and Dover (2015) inquired into how place, understood as a meaningful material and symbolic location, influences institutional work by containing, mediating, and complicating it. They suggested that one strategy to foster institutional change is to construct an issue as a local one that needs to be resolved through the inclusion of previously excluded people such as the homeless—thereby shifting the boundaries that separate actors.

Taken together, these studies suggest that places and artifacts offer material and symbolic resources and act as "interpretive filters" (Lawrence & Dover, 2015, p. 387) that help actors shape institutions. However, more research is needed to explore how the material and the symbolic in constant dialogue promote institutional work. As advocated by Orlikowski (2007), there is a need to go beyond a limiting duality that treats the material and the social as separate entities. In this chapter I also argue that researchers must go beyond the built realm and study how sociomateriality contributes to the construction of meaning where nature is concerned. Indeed, there is "a striking lack of attention to natural resource issues" (George, Schillebeeckx, & Liak, 2015, p. 1597) in the fields of organization and management.

When it comes to environmental issues, the use of powerful visuals is a common tactic in setting agendas and gaining attention. Photographs and other visual artifacts are often used to communicate complex ideas to broad audiences and to appeal to emotions (Meyer et al., 2013). For instance, the picture of a polar bear struggling to find ice in the Arctic Sea is often used as a warning sign for global warming and climate change. Mazur and Lee (1993) discussed how visuals are often simplified, streamlined, and even distorted to create a dramatic vision. For example, NASA satellite images of the Antarctic ozone depletion have occasionally been manipulated to convey the erroneous impression of a discrete hole in the atmosphere over the South Pole (p. 711). By contrast, other types of visual and material artifacts figure in the construction of meaning by feeding positive emotions and actions. The case study presented and discussed in this chapter aims to add to the understanding of how the production of art may serve as a material and symbolic resource in institutional work.

Methods

I adopted an interpretive single-case-study design because it is well-suited to comprehending sociomateriality in the construction of meaning embedded in a specific place and time. This choice is consistent with the body of institutional theory that contains interpretative accounts of institutional processes (e.g., Lawrence & Suddaby, 2006; Zilber, 2006).

Empirical Case

The Baltic Sea is unique and vulnerable and thus highly sensitive to the impacts of human activities. Because of the sea's shallowness and narrow passage to the Atlantic Ocean through the Danish straits, the water residence time is extremely long, around 30 years. Despite legal instruments, intergovernmental cooperation, and efforts by cities and NGOS (e.g., the World Wide Fund for Nature) since the 1960s, the condition of the Baltic Sea remains poor. For years, business organizations and wealthy individuals ignored the scientific, unwanted facts attesting to the degradation of coastal waters. It was only when the toxic algae blooms became widespread and readily observable in the late 1990s that action was taken, not only by government but also by private actors (Lyytimäki & Hildén, 2007). The case study in this chapter deals with the pioneering civil society initiative by the John Nurminen Foundation (hereafter referred to as the foundation).

The foundation has its roots in a family company, which originated as a trading house and shipping company in Rauma, Finland, in 1886. The foundation itself was established in 1992 with the aim of preserving the history of seafaring. In 2004 it inaugurated its environmental work because, according to its founder Mr. Juha Nurminen, "it didn't make sense to preserve the history of the Sea [the original mission of the foundation] when the whole sea was dying in front of our eyes" (*Helsingin Sanomat*, 2013, para 7[1]). In 2005 the foundation commenced its first major project to remove phosphorus from the three biggest wastewater treatment plants in St. Petersburg, the largest city on the Baltic Sea coast.

In 2013 the foundation launched an art campaign called Horizon, the main subject of analysis in this chapter. Through the campaign, private individuals could make a €50 donation to Horizon artwork, which was to be built in Helsinki, the capital of Finland. The campaign is part of the Baltic Sea Challenge, a project by Helsinki and Turku, a city on the country's southwest coast, to improve the condition of the Baltic Sea. The design of the artwork was donated by designer, Professor Hannu Kähönen. Many companies participated in the campaign. For instance, a global provider of stainless steel donated the material for the artwork. The first part of the artwork was installed in the summer of 2013; the last part, in early 2016. The

---

[1] All English renditions of Finnish quotations in this chapter are my own unless noted otherwise.

artwork campaign raised €220,000, with the money going partly to finance a storage and dosing equipment for phosphorus coagulation chemicals at the wastewater treatment plant in the city of Gatchina in southwestern Russia.

Data and Analysis

As is typical of deep case studies, my study draws on several qualitative sources. Data was collected in two stages between 2009 and 2016 and consisted of interview and documentary material. In the first stage (2009 to 2014), I conducted 24 one-on-one semistructured interviews and a one-on-two semistructured interview, all in Finnish, as part of a research project on cross-sector partnerships to protect the Baltic Sea. The interviewees were employees of the foundation (4), managers of public and private organizations that have participated in the work of the foundation (20), and an environmental journalist from the leading local newspaper. The interviews lasted between 60 and 120 minutes and were all recorded and transcribed.

In the second stage (2015 to 2016), I returned to the field to study, partly in situ, how the Horizon artwork was designed and structured. At this point the interview with designer Kähönen and his colleague, together with their set of photographs and sketches, were critical sources of information. Elicitation through pictorial and other types of artifacts (e.g., insertion of a photograph into a research interview) is a widely accepted technique of qualitative inquiry (Banks, 2007). Visual images stir deeper elements of human consciousness than words do, producing a kind of information different from that gathered through strictly word-based interviews. This effect has a physical basis. The parts of the human brain that process visual information are evolutionarily older than those that process verbal information (Harper, 2002). Interviews based solely on words thus engage less of the brain's capacity than do those that use both images and words. Moreover, images help people remember and have primacy over texts in the "memory industry" (Meusburger et al., 2011, p. 4). Instead of the rather typical situation in which a researcher initiates photo elicitation, the respondents in my interviews introduced the photographs in the middle of our exchange. At that point I became more of a listener, and the interview became a source of cocreation and dialogue rather than a "one-way flow of information from subject to researcher" (Harper, 1998, p. 35). The photographs acted as a window onto the world of the respondents who were helping me understand how their life experiences, values, and emotions stimulated the creative process and influenced the shape and materials used in the artwork. The photographs also helped me comprehend how the materiality of the place and the artwork influenced the process and its material and symbolic outcome. In addition, the foundation furnished a set of photographs of the Horizon artwork. A third source of information, published by the foundation between 2013 and 2016, consisted of 14 press releases on the Horizon artwork and 15 web log entitled "Baltic Sea and Me." The goal of using this documentation was to expand the understanding of how the artwork and, more broadly, the value of a clean Baltic Sea was presented to the stakeholders of that water body.

The data analysis was an iterative process that moved from examination of the interview transcripts and visual and textual documentation to a rather analytical level. As it progressed, I linked the emerging insights to the recent literature on institutional work that highlights the role of material and visual dimensions in institutional projects. The analysis enabled me to identify three mechanisms mediating the artistic form of institutional work for positive environmental change: creating emotional response, educating, and empowering.

Findings: The Production of Art as a Form of Institutional Work

In the summer of 1997, Juha Nurminen was to depart from Porvoo in Finland for boating with his 10-year-old son. As the boy prodded the stinking water with a stick and made faces, Juha said to him, "Nothing to worry about. Let's go to the open water, the water is clear there" (*Helsingin Sanomat*, 2013, para 3). But it turned out that the sea was full of porridge-like toxic algae there as well. "It was an enormous shock. I realized the Baltic Sea was severely ill" (p. 3).

Suddenly, along with the news of the problem with visible and massive algae blooms, the issue of eutrophication (enrichment of water with nutrients) reached the local headlines. The extensive algae blooms sparked strong and abiding emotions among people—some interviewees stated how they were even embarrassed that they had not woken up to this environmental issue until they had been starkly confronted by these algae blooms. Hence, material and visual objects functioned as a kind of alarm that led individuals to critical self-reflection, as explained by a journalist during our interview on March 12, 2015:

> In 1997 there was really bad algae in the Baltic Sea during the summer. The eastern Gulf of Finland had no oxygen at all and was full of algae porridge. In my own interest I started to wonder what on earth was going on. Could we just blame Russia and St. Petersburg, or could we do something ourselves?

The national newspaper subsequently introduced a series on the Baltic Sea. Twenty news stories on the algae situation were published within just two weeks during the summer of 1997. These stories cast eutrophication as an important policy issue and dramatized the subject symbolically and visually (Lyytimäki, 2007, Figure 8.1). In addition, the Finnish Environment Institute began to monitor the algal situation as people started to exhibit symptoms of poisoning while swimming. The accompanying photographic material had a central part in this collective awakening: "I believe that the key triggering factor for the action to save the Baltic Sea was blue-green algae during those summers. This photographic material still exists" (Mayor of Helsinki).

The outrageous visual images also caught the attention of designer Kähönen, an enthusiastic sailor himself:

Fig. 8.1 Blue-green algae in the eastern Gulf of Finland, summer 1997. Source: Finnish Environment Institute. Reprinted with permission

During the years, I have become increasingly worried about the dramatic loss of clarity in the water. Now, here and there, visibility is less than one metre [3' 4"], whereas only 20 years ago it was possible to see schools of fish glistening 10 metres [about 33'] deep. Anyone who visits the archipelago will by now be only too familiar with the continuous increase in the volumes of harmful blue-green algae. Around the world, I have seen places that have been irrevocably ruined, leaving me with a desolate impression of the greed and negligence of man. Water pollution changes our attitudes not only towards the sea, but also towards ourselves. We must hope the Baltic Sea will not become such a memorial.

(H. Kähönen, 2014)

Subjective experiences thus worked as triggers for various actors to engage in moral reflections and personal action. The fundamental aim of these subjective accounts, besides improving the environmental condition of the sea, was to change cognitive institutions (beliefs, assumptions, and frames that inform action) and norms that are rooted in collective moral understandings about appropriate behavior (Lawrence & Suddaby, 2006). Rather than seeing the protection of the Baltic Sea as belonging to the highly institutionalized context of interstate cooperation and governmental funding, people came to feel that it was a collective responsibility of corporations, nonprofit organizations, and citizens.

Mechanisms of Institutional Work

In-depth study of the design and construction process of the Horizon artwork identified three vital mechanisms by which the production of the artwork, as both a material and sociosymbolic space, constitutes a form of institutional work. The three mechanisms are called creating emotional response, educating, and empowering. I describe these findings in more detail below.

Creating Emotional Response

Emotions are at the heart of art (Silvia, 2006) and institutions (Voronov & Vince, 2012). Through artwork the designer wanted to convey his strong emotional attachment to the Baltic Sea (see also Figure 8.2).

> For me, the Baltic Sea is an important source of relaxation, wellbeing, and spiritual balance. When you see and feel the waves, the wind, the salty seawater and the horizon gleaming in front of you, your nerves will rest and your mind become[s] cleansed. The sea is unlimited. It has taught me things about my own relationship with nature, and about the humility and care you need when you encounter changes at sea. The sea cannot be controlled: we must adjust to its movements. The sea is a powerful aesthetic experience for me, and one I want to re-experience every summer, sailing in the Archipelago Sea or the Åland archipelago. The clear blue reflection of the sky on the surface of the water and the clean fragrance of the sea are inbuilt allegories of beauty. (H. Kähönen, 2014)

A principal aim of the designer was to evoke positive emotions in the viewer:

> Prompting the individual to act does not necessarily involve painting horror scenarios about the future. It is rather the question of how to breed enthusiasm so that one wants to change their own behavior. In a way, one should offer [clear water] as a sort of luxury, minimalist luxury. (H. Kähönen, 2014)

Fig. 8.2 Designer Professor Hannu Kähönen in the web log "Baltic Sea and Me," September 16, 2014. Source: John Nurminen Foundation. Reprinted with permission

Fig. 8.3 Plate test by Creadesign Oy. Source: Creadesign Oy. Reprinted with permission

One of the major mechanisms for creating such an emotional response and identification with the sea is to breed collective memories, that is, particular memories commonly shared by a particular (mnemonic) community, such as the nation (Zerubavel, 1996). My interview data brims with expressions engendering nostalgia, such as "everybody of my generation remembers the childhood summers when the water was crystal clear [rather than 'home to stinking algae']" (Nonprofit director, personal communication, February 28, 2013), reflecting the fact that most adults identify the most significant places in childhood as being outdoors (Sebba, 1991). Such emotional response is considered important:

> I believe that the message gets through if you can identify with [the story]. This goes for books and movies alike. If you can bring that out at a personal [and emotional] level, it has an impact so that you want to change your behavior [toward the Baltic Sea]. (H. Kähönen, personal communication, February 11, 2016)

The material and visual choices of the artwork were aimed to capture the movement and gleaming of the sea, the reflection of the sky, and the purity of water: "This picture of the horizon is what inspired me—the way [the water] glimmers . . . — optimal weather for sailing" (H. Kähönen, 2014). These visual artifacts, such as the movement and silvery gleaming of the sea, were caught by 4,225 gleams that move along with the wind, as modeled in 3D computer graphics (Figure 8.3).

The gleam of the metal sheet was tested with brushed and brushless stainless steel (Figure 8.4). These material and visual choices were ultimately intended "to resonate with the feeling of having clear water—the time when the water was transparent [down to the bottom]" (H. Kähönen, personal communication, February 11, 2016).

In addition, the physical and symbolic location of the artwork was important in the production of the desired image. Most crucially, the place had to be both windy

Fig. 8.4 Experimenting with the reflective surface by Creadesign Oy. Source: Creadesign Oy. Reprinted with permission

Fig. 8.5 Illustration of the place, by Creadesign Oy. Source: Creadesign Oy. Reprinted with permission

and sunny in order to produce the effect of the sea's gleaming. A site close to the sea was also symbolically important to have. The place that Helsinki designated for the artwork was initially situated along a pedestrian and bicycle route not far from the seaside. Later, in response to the wish of the designer, a place on the pier next to the ferries sailing between Helsinki and Tallinn was made available instead (Figure 8.5).

Yet the goal of these material and visual choices was not just to produce a visual image and emotional identification with the Baltic Sea but to convert them into a thirst for knowledge:

> I tried to bring the vulnerability of the sea into this work so that people would understand this. From this follows the question of . . . the underlying facts explaining the vulnerability of the sea. This was what I was pondering—so that it would not remain just a visual experience but would spark an interest in understanding why the Baltic Sea is unique. (H. Kähönen, personal communication, February 11, 2016)

Educating

Educating means "educating of actors in skills and knowledge necessary to support the new institution." It is thus an important and often necessary form of cognitive work to facilitate behavioral changes (Lawrence & Suddaby, 2006, p. 227). The Horizon artwork performed educational work by creating new cognitive conceptions of the Baltic Sea. The artwork's length of 54 meters [177'] corresponded with the average depth of the Baltic Sea. The designer wanted to highlight the vulnerability of the Baltic Sea concretely:

> The Baltic Sea is a small basin of brackish water with an average depth—54 metres—that is considerably [less] than that of many other seas. The average depth of the Mediterranean, for example, is 1,500 metres [4,921'], and its salinity is of a completely different scale. Because of the low salinity levels and water volumes of our own Baltic Sea, its flora and fauna cannot withstand the increasing strain caused by the phosphorus discharged [in]to the water from agriculture and with wastewaters. (H. Kähönen, 2014)

In our interview he continued:

> To ensure that the information imparted [by an artwork] comes across well in one go, one must avoid communicating too many things. We [carefully] considered the text in terms of what additional information we could add so that people would manage to read it. (H. Kähönen, personal communication, February 11, 2016)

Information plaques were an important part of the artwork. They gave key facts about the Baltic Sea, such as its average depth, its area, and the population of the region. A map of the Baltic Sea region illustrated the catchment area. The meaning and implications of the term *catchment area* were then explained to the reader: "The area from which surface and groundwater flow into the Baltic Sea. All human activity within the catchment area has an impact on the condition of the Baltic Sea" (see Figure 8.6).

This information was presented in five languages: Finnish, Swedish, English, Russian, and Polish. From an institutional perspective the Baltic Sea represents a high degree of institutional complexity (Greenwood, Raynard, Kodeih, Micelotta, & Lounsbury, 2011) involving 11 countries with diverse environmental standards and values. The artwork imbued a kind of boundary object (Star & Griesemer, 1989) with interpretive flexibility that allows people from diverse cultures and social worlds to work together without broad political consensus at the national level:

Fig. 8.6 Environmental information in a nutshell: the Horizon work of art. Photograph from the John Nurminen Foundation. Reprinted with permission

> I believe that in a human mind, a white crest on top of a wave can never become an ugly experience. This symbol of purity is an important part of our collective consciousness, and I believe that regardless of any cultural issues, it is always and all over the world understood in the same way. (H. Kähönen, 2014)

In so doing, it also empowered actors typically considered marginal in environmental politics to act at the grassroots level.

Empowering

Empowering means giving marginalized actors (individual citizens) ability to act and collectively produce an effect (Nilsson, 2015, p. 386). The Horizon artwork invited each person to buy a gleam of the Horizon artwork and thereby make his or her name part of the history of Baltic Sea protection. A visually compelling fundraising video was used to heighten the impact of the campaign. The video first pictured an entirely yellow sea and a text reading "Phosphorous doesn't belong in the sea. Removing phosphorous from the sea is the most efficient way to protect the sea." The viewer was then invited to participate in the rescue efforts: "Through your donation of €50, your name will remain part of the history of Baltic Sea protection." Simultaneously, the yellow sea started to turn blue, gleam by gleam.

The message of the campaign was that everyone's input is needed and that everyone can contribute. "Actions are born of new attitudes" and of "doing deeds that may seem small," as later put in a web log (Lehtinen, 2015). The Horizon artwork thus provided a permanent material object through which distributed agency can come about (Raviola & Norbäck, 2013). The artwork functioned as a symbol for a cleaner Baltic Sea and served as a vehicle for mobilizing individual citizens—particularly the citizens of Helsinki, for whom "the Baltic Sea is the living room and landscape," as expressed by Mayor Jussi Pajunen ("Horisontti," 2013, para 5).

The designer also pursued a moral and normative purpose by creating "a reminder of the fragility of marine nature. . . . If we wish to leave something beautiful to our children, reminding them of ourselves and our culture, that something should be a clean Baltic Sea" (Kähönen, 2014). This message was well received. For instance, a local kindergarten celebrated Father's Day by organizing a benefit walk on which fathers and children enjoyed the outdoors together. The money traditionally used for a breakfast and gifts to mark Father's Day were donated to the Horizon campaign). Such initiatives were much appreciated by the designer: "Luckily, environmental awareness is growing continuously. I am particularly delighted by the earnestness with which the younger generation has embraced these matters" ("Horizon Is Ready," 2016, para 2). Thus, there was a strong aspirational vision (Nilsson, 2015) for an attitudinal change meant to benefit the next generations.

Discussion

My objective in this chapter has been to understand theoretically how art can be used as a form of sociomaterial institutional work. To answer this question, I asked empirically how art can be used to recreate a shared awareness of the tragedy of the commons as represented by pollution in the Baltic Sea. I synthesize my findings in Figure 8.7.

The first element of the model is the institutional worker, the artist, who creates a context between the work of art and the viewer, a framework in which a common meaning system and a common institution are constructed. The institution, the focus of work that is conducted, is the norms pertaining to the commons represented by the Baltic Sea. Essentially, the artist's intent is to convey "the commonality of the commons"[2]—the acceptance of the common responsibility for the Baltic Sea. The commons has both a bounded material component (the geographical space) and a powerful symbolic space (the set of sociomaterial practices in which people engage). The nature of the agency of artists then enables them to use their art to reconstruct the Baltic Sea socially as a common responsibility. In this vast undertaking they employ three broad mechanisms: creating emotional response, educating, and empowering.

Creating emotional response entails generating nostalgia over a lost common experience. The nostalgia relates to meaningful private physical places as well as to collective symbolic spaces that capture cultural memories and shared social histories of whole generations. Harnessing such mnemonic communities (Zerubavel,

---

[2] I thank Roy Suddaby for the notion of the commonality of the commons.

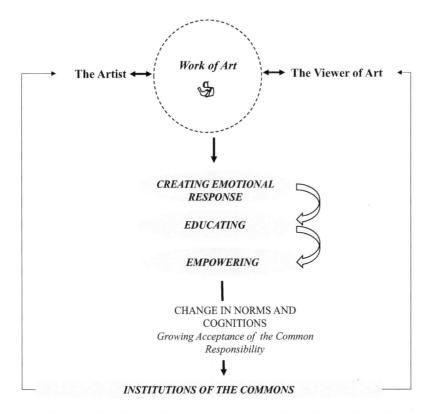

Fig. 8.7   The production of art as a form of institutional work. Source: Designed by author

1996) and imagined communities (Anderson, 1983/2006) to act for a common good instills art with great symbolic power. The belief in the mobilizing power of affirmative emotions such as nostalgia is in keeping with positive psychology, which suggests that positive emotions broaden people's momentary repertoires of thought and action (Fredrickson, 2001). For instance, gratitude motivates moral action because grateful people feel a sense of duty to repay what is owed (Fredrickson, 2000). An integral part of harnessing nostalgia was the act of reproducing nature as closely as possible through visual and aesthetic means and material choices. Both art and the commons are thus as much a symbolic or mnemonic construction as a physical or material one.

The emotional response created by artwork supports cognitive responsiveness, piques curiosity, and triggers viewers' search for knowledge about the issue. This quest leads to the second form of institutional work for which art may be used, educating. Educating is a form of boundary work (Gieryn, 1983) in which the commons become semiotically constructed as a bounded and shared space. By engaging in this boundary work, the artist constructs the commons as a shared category. Although a work of art is outwardly material, its core is highly symbolic and deeply embedded in history and emotions. The operation of art at the unconscious and aesthetic levels also offers interpretive flexibility and opens them to a wide variety of interpretations across language and cultural barriers (Meusburger et al., 2011). This outcome permits artworks to act as a boundary object and to promote the flow of transnational knowledge (Georg, 2015).

The third form of institutional work for which art may be used—empowering—invests marginalized actors with authority through new interpretations of how they affect the commons. In the studied case the work of art offered a means for people at the grassroots level to donate money and engrave their names into the history of Baltic Sea protection. This opportunity helped them "step out of their established roles, adopt a reflexive stance, and engage in the institutional work" (Lawrence et al., 2011, p. 56). In this emancipatory manner marginal actors may play a part—albeit a small one—in institutional work, illustrating the beautifulness of smallness (Schumacher, 1999).

If successful, these forms of sociomaterial institutional work will lead to the growing recognition of the Baltic Sea as a tragedy of the commons—that is, as a shared space (both material and symbolic) for which all of the surrounding actors (including corporations, nation-states, municipalities, and NGOs) share responsibility. Ultimately, agreement that responsibility for the well-being of the sea does not fall only to government but rather to each and every individual as well would signify a profound institutional change.

The identified qualities—the emphasis on subjectively lived experiences, emotions, cognitions, empowerment, and moral dimensions of institutions—are closely aligned with the concept of positive institutional work as recently proposed by Nilsson (2015). By building on the literature treating institutional work and on positive organizational scholarship, he defined positive institutional work as "the creation or maintenance of institutional patterns that express mutually constitutive experiential and social goods" (p. 373). He calls for current theorizing on institutional work to improve the incorporation of actors' subjective experiences into evaluations of legitimacy, to recognize inquiry as a powerful form of institutional agency, and to explore how inclusion figures in the stabilization of positive institutions. My case study suggests that material and symbolic objects such as artworks may have a powerful function in such experiential and emancipatory processes. I now conclude by discussing avenues for future research.

Conclusion

Although it is often stressed that institutions are both material and symbolic, surprisingly few studies by organizational institutionalists primarily investigate the mutually constitutive relationship between material and symbolic elements affecting institutional processes (Lawrence & Dover, 2015; Monteiro & Nicolini, 2015). Indeed, the literature on institutional work is largely confined to the study of cognitions and social relations. Little attention goes to the interplay of the physical places and the emotions that these physical and symbolic spaces elicit (Siebert et al., 2016).

This chapter contributes to the literature on institutional work in that I specifically examine how art may be used as a form of sociomaterial institutional work. This endeavor is important, for adding these dimensions to research by institutional scholars may enhance the understanding of institutional microfoundations—how material and symbolic elements influence the manner in which individuals interpret their context, experience institutions, and exercise agency (Powell & Colyvas, 2008; Suddaby, 2010).

By analyzing the nuanced interplay between human agency and art, I believe this chapter extends scholarship on institutional work in important ways. The findings highlight the interaction between materiality, emotions, and sociosymbolic meanings in supporting institutional change. This study therefore responds to the calls for directing attention to emotional aspects of institutional work (Moisander, Hirsto, & Fahy, 2016; Scott, 2014; Voronov & Vince, 2012) and to subjective ways in which people experience institutionalized meanings, practices, and spaces (Nilsson, 2015; Siebert et al., 2016; Suddaby, 2010; Zilber, 2009). The study also suggests that artifacts with great material and symbolic power may be instrumental in the realization of the emancipatory potential of institutional work (Lawrence et al., 2011; Nilsson, 2015) because they include previously marginalized actors. The emancipatory potential of art may be especially significant because of its deep, almost universal appeal, which may help bridge cultural divides. Art also affords a common reference point (e.g., clean seascape), which may cultivate moral sensibility and encourage viewers to act in the common good. As pointed out by Nilsson (2015), the moral and aspirational orientation reflected in the idea of the common good has, with few exceptions (e.g., Kraatz, 2009, on leadership as institutional work) become increasingly rare in post-Selznick institutional theorizing. I believe there is great potential for future research that digs ever deeper—both conceptually and empirically—into how positive institutional work is facilitated by material and symbolic artifacts. Scandinavian institutionalism, with its focus on artifacts as active carriers of ideas (e.g., Czarniawska & Joerges, 1996), may prove useful in that effort.

Acknowledgment Aalto University and SCANCOR-Weatherhead Partnership, Harvard University. I am grateful to Roy Suddaby for developmental and thoughtful comments. I would also like to acknowledge the valuable insights provided by David Antal, Johannes Glücker, Nina Granqvist, Dennis Jancsary, Regina Lenz, and Tammar Zilber.

References

Anderson, B. R. (2006). *Imagined communities: Reflections on the origin and spread of nationalism*. London: Verso. (Original work published 1983)

Ansari, S., Wijen, F., & Gray, B. (2013). Constructing a climate change logic: An institutional perspective on the "tragedy of the commons." *Organization Science, 24*, 1014–1040. doi:https://doi.org/10.1287/orsc.1120.0799

Banks, M. (2007). *Using visual data in qualitative research*. Thousand Oaks: Sage.

Barnes, B. (2006). *Capitalism 3.0: A guide to reclaiming the commons*. San Francisco: Barret-Koehler.

Currie, G., Lockett, A., Finn, R., Martin, G., & Waring, J. (2012). Institutional work to maintain professional power: Recreating the model of medical professionalism. *Organization Studies, 33*, 937–962. doi:https://doi.org/10.1177/0170840612445116

Czarniawska, B., & Joerges, B. (1996). Travels of ideas. In B. Czarniawska & G. Sevón (Eds.), *Translating organizational change* (pp. 13–48). Berlin: Walter de Gruyter.

Dacin, M. T., Munir, K., & Tracey, P. (2010). Formal dining at Cambridge colleges: Linking ritual performance and institutional maintenance. *Academy of Management Journal, 53,* 1393–1418. doi:https://doi.org/10.5465/AMJ.2010.57318388

Fredrickson, B. L. (2000). Gratitude, like other positive emotions, broadens and builds. In R. A. Emmons (Ed.), *Kindling the science of gratitude* (pp. 145–166). Dallas: John Templeton Foundation.

Fredrickson, B. L. (2001). The role of positive emotions in positive psychology: The broaden-and-build theory of positive emotions. *American Psychologist, 56,* 218–226. doi:https://doi.org/10.1037//0003-066X.56.3.218

Gawer, A., & Phillips, N. (2013). Institutional work as logics shift: The case of Intel's transformation to platform leader. *Organization Studies, 34,* 1035–1071. doi:https://doi.org/10.1177/0170840613492071

Georg, S. (2015). Building sustainable cities: Tools for developing new building practices? *Global Networks, 15*, 325–342. doi:https://doi.org/10.1111/glob.12081

George, G., Schillebeeckx, S. J. D., & Liak, T. L. (2015). The management of natural resources: An overview and research agenda. *Academy of Management Journal, 58*, 1595–1613. doi:https://doi.org/10.5465/amj.2015.4006

Gieryn, T. F. (1983). Boundary-work and the demarcation of science from non-science: Strains and interests in professional ideologies of scientists. *American Sociological Review, 48*, 781–795. doi:https://doi.org/10.2307/2095325

Gieryn, T. F. (2000). A space for place in sociology. *Annual Review of Sociology, 26*, 463–496. doi:https://doi.org/10.1146/annurev.soc.26.1.463

Greenwood, R., Raynard, M., Kodeih, F., Micelotta, E., & Lounsbury, M. (2011). Institutional complexity and organizational responses. *Academy of Management Annals, 5*, 317–371. Retrieved from https://ssrn.com/abstract=2266644

Hannigan, J. A. (1995). *Environmental sociology: A social constructionist perspective*. London: Routledge.

Hardin, G. (1968). The tragedy of the commons. *Science, 162*, 1243–1248. doi:https://doi.org/10.1126/science.162.3859.1243

Hardy, C., & Phillips, N. (1999). No joking matter: Discursive struggle in the Canadian refugee system. *Organization Studies, 20*, 1–24. doi:https://doi.org/10.1177/0170840699201001

Hargadon, A. B., & Douglas, Y. (2001). When innovations meet institutions: Edison and the design of the electric light. *Administrative Science Quarterly, 46*, 476–501. doi:https://doi.org/10.2307/3094872

Harper, D. (1998). An argument for visual sociology. In J. Prosser (Ed.), *Image-based research: A sourcebook for qualitative researchers* (pp. 20–35). London: Falmer Press.

Harper, D. (2002). Talking about pictures: A case for photo elicitation. *Visual Studies, 17*, 13–26. doi:https://doi.org/10.1080/14725860220137345

HELCOM (Helsinki Commission). (2010). *Hazardous substances in the Baltic Sea: An integrated thematic assessment of hazardous substances in the Baltic Sea*. Baltic Sea Environment Proceedings No. 120B. Helsinki: Helsinki Commission. Retrieved from http://www.helcom.fi/Lists/Publications/BSEP120B.pdf

Helsingin Sanomat [Web log post]. (2013, October 17). Retrieved from http://www.hs.fi/elama/art-2000002681572.html

Hoffman, A. J., & Jennings, P. D. (2015). Institutional theory and the natural environment: Research in (and on) the anthropocene. *Organization & Environment, 28*, 8–31. doi:https://doi.org/10.1177/1086026615575331

Horisontti (the horizon), a work of art designed by Hannu Kähönen, reminds us of the uniqueness of the Baltic Sea during The Tall Ships Races Helsinki. (2013, May 16) Retrieved from https://www.johnnurmisensaatio.fi/en/joint-campaign-of-the-john-nurminen-foundation-and-the-city-of-helsinki-acknowledges-the-names-of-donors-who-support-the-baltic-sea-in-an-artwork-located-in-jatkasaari-helsinki/

Horizon is ready! The. The Horizon, a work of art reminding us of the protection of the Baltic Sea, is now gleaming in full length. (2016). Retrieved from https://www.johnnurmisensaatio.fi/en/the-horizon-is-ready-the-horizon-a-work-of-art-reminding-us-of-the-protection-of-the-balticsea-is-now-gleaming-in-full-length/

Jones, C., & Massa, F. G. (2013). From novel practice to consecrated exemplar: Unity temple as a case of institutional evangelizing. *Organization Studies, 34*, 1099–1136. doi:https://doi.org/10.1177/0170840613492073

Kähönen, H. (2014, September 16). Baltic Sea and me [Web log post]. Retrieved from https://www.johnnurmisensaatio.fi/en/hannu-kahonen-and-the-baltic-sea/

Kraatz, M. S. (2009). Leadership as institutional work: A bridge to the other side. In T. B. Lawrence, R. Suddaby, & B. Leca (Eds.), *Institutional work: Actors and agency in institutional studies of organizations* (pp. 59–91). Cambridge, UK: Cambridge University Press.

Lawrence, T. B., & Dover, G. (2015). Place and institutional work: Creating housing for the hard-to-house. *Administrative Science Quarterly, 60,* 371–410.

Lawrence, T. B., Hardy, C., & Phillips, N. (2002). Institutional effects of interorganizational collaboration: The emergence of proto-institutions. *Academy of Management Journal, 45,* 281–290. doi:https://doi.org/10.2307/3069297

Lawrence, T. B., & Suddaby, R. (2006). Institutions and institutional work. In S. R. Clegg, C. Hardy, T. B. Lawrence, & W. Nord (Eds.), *The Sage Handbook of organization studies* (2nd ed., pp. 215–254). London: Sage.

Lawrence, T. B, Suddaby, R., & Leca, B. (2011). Institutional work: Refocusing institutional studies of organization. *Journal of Management Inquiry, 20,* 52–58. doi:https://doi.org/10.1177/1056492610387222

Lehtinen, H. (2015, September 8). Baltic Sea and me [Web log post]. Retrieved from https://www.johnnurmisensaatio.fi/en/eero-lehtinen-and-the-baltic-sea/

Leonardi, P. M. (2012). Materiality, sociomateriality, and socio-technical systems: What do these terms mean? How are they different? Do we need them? In P. M. Leonardi, B. A. Nardi, & J. Kallinikos (Eds.), *Materiality and organizing: Social interaction in a technological world* (pp. 25–48). Oxford, UK: Oxford University Press.

Lok, J., & de Rond, M. (2013). On the plasticity of institutions: Containing and restoring practice breakdowns at the Cambridge University boat club. *Academy of Management Journal, 56,* 185–207. doi:https://doi.org/10.5465/amj.2010.0688

Lyytimäki, J. M. (2007). Temporalities and environmental reporting: Press news on eutrophication in Finland. *Environmental Sciences, 4,* 41–51. doi:https://doi.org/10.1080/15693430701295866

Lyytimäki, J. M., & Hildén, M. (2007). Thresholds of sustainability: Policy challenges of regime shifts in coastal areas. *Sustainability: Science, practice, & policy, 2,* 61–69. doi:https://doi.org/10.1080/15487733.2007.11908007

Mazur, A., & Lee, J. (1993). Sounding the global alarm: Environmental issues in the US national news. *Social Studies of Science, 23,* 681–720. doi:https://doi.org/10.1177/030631293023004003

Meusburger, P., Heffernan, M., & Wunder, E. (2011). Cultural memories: An introduction. In P. Meusburger, M. Heffernan, & E. Wunder (Eds.), *Cultural Memories: The geographical point of view* (pp. 3–14). Knowledge and Space: Vol. 4. Dordrecht: Springer.

Meyer, R. E., Höllerer, M. A., Jancsary, D., & van Leeuwen, T. (2013). The visual dimension in organizing, organization, and organization research: Core ideas, current developments, and promising avenues. *Academy of Management Annals, 7,* 489–555. doi:https://doi.org/10.1080/19416520.2013.781867

Moisander, J. K., Hirsto, H., & Fahy, K. M. (2016). Emotions in institutional work: A discursive perspective. *Organization Studies, 37,* 963–990. doi:https://doi.org/10.1177/0170840615613377

Monteiro, P., & Nicolini, D. (2015). Recovering materiality in institutional work: Prizes as an assemblage of human and material entities. *Journal of Management Inquiry, 24,* 61–81. doi:https://doi.org/10.1177/1056492614546221

Nilsson, W. (2015). Positive institutional work: Exploring institutional work through the lens of positive organizational scholarship. *Academy of Management Review, 40*, 370–398. doi:https://doi.org/10.5465/amr.2013.0188

Orlikowski, W. J. (2007). Sociomaterial practices: Exploring technology at work. *Organization Studies, 28*, 1435–1448. doi:https://doi.org/10.1177/0170840607081138

Ostrom, E. (1990). *Governing the commons: The evolution of institutions for collective action.* New York: Cambridge University Press.

Ostrom, E., Burger, J., Field, C. B., Norgaard, R. B, & Policansky, D. (1999). Revisiting the commons: Local lessons, global challenges. *Science, 284*, 278–282. doi:https://doi.org/10.1126/science.284.5412.278

Ostrom, E., Dietz, T., Dolšak, N., Stern, P. C., Stonich, S., & Weber, E. U. (Eds.). (2002). *The drama of the commons.* Washington, DC: National Academy Press. doi:https://doi.org/10.17226/10287

Phillips, N., Lawrence, T. B., & Hardy, C. (2004). Discourse and institutions. *The Academy of Management Review, 29*, 635–652. doi:https://doi.org/10.5465/AMR.2004.14497617

Powell, W. W., & Colyvas, J. A. (2008). Microfoundations of institutional theory. In R. Greenwood, C. Oliver, K. Sahlin, & R. Suddaby (Eds.), *The Sage handbook of organizational institutionalism* (pp. 276–298). Thousand Oaks: Sage.

Raviola, E., & Norbäck, M. (2013). Bringing technology and meaning into institutional work: Making news at an Italian business newspaper. *Organization Studies, 34*, 1171–1194. doi:https://doi.org/10.1177/0170840613492077

Ritvala, T., & Kleymann, B. (2012). Scientists as midwives to cluster emergence: An institutional work framework. *Industry and Innovation, 19*, 477–497. doi:https://doi.org/10.1080/13662716.2012.718875

Schumacher, E. F. (1999). Small is beautiful: Economics as if people mattered (3rd ed.). Vancouver, BC: Hartley & Marks.

Scott, W. R. (2014). *Institutions and organizations: Ideas, interests, and identities* (4th ed.). Thousand Oaks: Sage.

Sebba, R. (1991). The landscapes of childhood: The reflections of childhood's environment in adult memories and in children's attitudes. *Environment and Behavior, 23*, 395–422. doi:https://doi.org/10.1177/0013916591234001

Siebert, S., Wilson, F., & Hamilton, J. R. A. (2016). "Devils may sit here": The role of enchantment in institutional maintenance. *Academy of Management Journal, 60* (4), 1607–1632. doi:https://doi.org/10.5465/amj.2014.0487

Silvia, P. J. (2006). Artistic training and interest in visual art: Applying the appraisal model of aesthetic emotions. *Empirical Studies of the Arts, 24*, 139–161. doi:https://doi.org/10.2190/DX8K-6WEA-6WPA-FM84

Star, S. L., & Griesemer, J. R. (1989). Institutional ecology, 'translations' and boundary objects: Amateurs and professionals in Berkeley's museum of vertebrate zoology, 1907–39. *Social Studies of Science, 19*, 387–420. doi:https://doi.org/10.1177/030631289019003001

Suddaby, R. (2010). Challenges for institutional theory. *Journal of Management Inquiry, 19*, 14–20.doi:https://doi.org/10.1177/1056492609347564

Suddaby, R., & Greenwood, R. (2005). Rhetorical strategies of legitimacy. *Administrative Science Quarterly, 50*, 35–67. doi:https://doi.org/10.2189/asqu.2005.50.1.35

Voronov, M., & Vince, R. (2012). Integrating emotions into the analysis of institutional work. *Academy of Management Review, 37*, 58–81. doi:https://doi.org/10.5465/amr.2010.0247

Wijen, F., & Ansari, S. (2007). Overcoming inaction through collective institutional entrepreneurship: Insights from regime theory. *Organization Studies, 28*, 1079–1100. doi:https://doi.org/10.1177/0170840607078115

Zerubavel, E. (1996). Social memories: Steps to a sociology of the past. *Qualitative Sociology, 19*, 283–299. doi:https://doi.org/10.1007/BF02393273

Zietsma, C., & Lawrence, T. B. (2010). Institutional work in the transformation of an organizational field: The interplay of boundary work and practice work. *Administrative Science Quarterly, 55*, 189–221. doi:https://doi.org/10.2189/asqu.2010.55.2.189

Zilber, T. B. (2006). The work of the symbolic in institutional processes: Translations of rational myths in Israeli high tech. *Academy of Management Journal, 49,* 281–303. doi:https://doi.org/10.5465/AMJ.2006.20786073

Zilber, T. B. (2009). Institutional maintenance as narrative acts. In T. B. Lawrence, R. Suddaby, & B. Leca (Eds.), *Institutional work: Actors and agency in institutional studies of organizations* (pp. 205–235). Cambridge, UK: Cambridge University Press.

Chapter 9
Know Thy Place: Location and Imagined Communities in Institutional Field Dynamics

Tammar B. Zilber

How do members of an institutional field[1] construct its location? Institutional fields are central to institutional dynamics, for this interorganizational level is where the institutional drama unfolds (Scott, 2014; Zietsma, Groenewegen, Logue, & Hinings, 2017). Nonetheless, the conceptualization of institutional fields has transformed since the early days of neoinstitutionalism. Whereas early understandings of fields rested on the assumption that they are geographically bounded and inhabited by members who are quite close to each other, later conceptualizations seem to underline fields as deterritorialized social processes that form around issues and their negotiation (Wooten & Hoffman, 2008). In particular, by the 2000s, institutional fields had come to be conceived mainly not as geographical or spatial phenomena but rather as shared *discursive* worlds (Phillips, Lawrence, & Hardy, 2004; Wooten & Hoffman, 2008). Accordingly, institutional fields, like other forms of communities (Anderson, 1983; Gherardi & Nicolini, 2002; Said, 1978; Zerubavel, 2003), have been increasingly understood to be constituted through language and a continual "conversation" among various stakeholders (Hoffman, 1999). However, institutional actors are also located in distinct places—actual locations, locales, or senses of place (Agnew, 1987). The question is thus how places are worked out in such conversations within institutional fields. Which discursive practices do actors use to construct the semiotic space of their institutional field?

To explore these questions, my case study focuses on the Israeli high-tech industry. I ask how actors in this field construct the meaning and implications of its

---

[1] Although fields are central to institutional theory, there are many different definitions thereof and some confusion between the terms *organizational fields* and *institutional fields*. Following Zietsma, Groenewegen, Logue and Hinings (2017), I see these designations as interchangeable. In this chapter I use *institutional field* to highlight the concept's importance to the institutional drama.

T. B. Zilber (✉)
The Jerusalem School of Business Administration, The Hebrew University of Jerusalem, Jerusalem, Israel
e-mail: TZilber@huji.ac.il

© The Author(s) 2018
J. Glückler et al. (eds.), *Knowledge and Institutions*, Knowledge and Space 13,
https://doi.org/10.1007/978-3-319-75328-7_9

location. Conceiving conferences as field-level events (Henn & Bathelt, 2015; Lampel & Meyer, 2008), I draw on an ethnographic study of an Israeli high-tech conference held in 2005 in Santa Clara, California. I examine how participants discussed—both directly and indirectly—"location" in configuring Israeli high tech as an institutional field. In short, I demonstrate how, for Israeli high-tech stakeholders, "place" is not a fixed and rigid location. Rather, it is constantly deliberated, invented, imagined, and even flexibly fabricated. Overall, the data suggests that place was constructed in different ways by the various actors in the studied event. As opposed to a quite common, perhaps axiomatic construction of Israeli high-tech as bounded by its peripheral geographical location, it was also constructed by some participants as an integral part of a global field. Specifically, Israeli high-tech was depicted by various members as part of three different imagined communities: one based on imaginative geography, one on practice, and one on memory.

I illuminate discursive practices operating in the constructions of place of, and within, institutional fields and highlight the theoretical implications of such discursive maneuvering for rethinking the meaning of location in institutional fields.

Theoretical Grounding: Institutional Fields, Place, and Knowing

Place, Institutional Dynamics, and Institutional Fields

Issues of location have been central to theorizing institutionalization processes. Whether conceptualizing institutionalization as diffusion or as translation of ideas (structures, practices, and meanings; Czarniawska & Joerges, 1996), institutionalization involves the travel of ideas across spatial and social borders (e.g., organizations, fields, or nation-states). Yet, whereas scholars have pointed out and analyzed broad patterns of such movement, they have paid only scant attention to the detailed dynamics of place involved in them (Lawrence & Dover, 2015). Institutional theorists seem to have taken the very travel of ideas for granted and have missed the spatial turn that affected the social sciences and, more specifically, management and organization theory (Taylor & Spicer, 2007). The common methodological choice to focus on institutional dynamics in one location has contributed much to making the issues of movement in space (and of place) analytically transparent, treating it as a given and objective phenomenon.

The disregard of place in institutional analysis is especially surprising in the study of institutional fields. The original formulation of institutional fields (DiMaggio & Powell, 1983) implied its embeddedness within a bounded geographical location that allowed proximity and interaction between field members (Wooten & Hoffman, 2008). The definition of institutional fields has since evolved and has taken a discursive turn (Phillips et al., 2004). Place is still central within a discursive conception of institutions, yet it is hidden and quite implicit. Institutional fields are defined as *"richly contextualized spaces* where disparate organizations involve themselves with one another in an effort to develop collective understandings regarding matters that are consequential for organizational and field-level activities" (Wooten & Hoffman, 2008, p. 138, emphasis added). Fields, then, are not necessarily constructed through physical proximity but rather through processes of "referencing" between actors, for actors note and pay attention to each other when partaking in the same conversation (Wooten & Hoffman, 2008, p. 139). How are such contextualized spaces constructed?

Adopting a discursive definition of institutional fields, I build on a constructivist understanding of place as a continuing process (Patterson & Williams, 2005). I thus assume that it is not merely a given, objective, and geographical location as such but rather an assignment of meaning, values, and material form to a geographical location. "A place is a unique spot in the universe . . . [that] has physicality [and is] interpreted, narrated, perceived, felt, understood, and imagined" (Gieryn, 2000, pp. 464–465). Given the discursive turn, I ask how the sense of an institutional place—"the subjective and emotional attachment people have to place" (Cresswell, 2004, p. 7; see also Agnew, 1987)—is negotiated among members of an institutional field.

Institutional Fields, Collective Identity, and Field-level Events

Institutional fields materialize, and are negotiated, through various platforms, including field-wide organizations, field-wide agreements (e.g., standards, measurement tools and rankings), and field-level happenings (e.g., committees, contests, rituals, and events; for a review see Zilber, 2014). Whether field-level events configure the field (Lampel & Meyer, 2008) or "just" reproduce it (Henn & Bathelt, 2015; Schüßler & Sydow, 2015), they are important for constructing field-level collective identity. Field-level events serve as an arena for collective sense-making (Garud, 2008; Lampel & Meyer, 2008; Maguire & Hardy, 2006; McInerney, 2008; Oliver & Montgomery, 2008; Zilber, 2007), for they redirect actors' attention (Anand &Watson, 2004) and offer an opportunity for actors to present and discuss issues that they find important (Anand & Jones, 2008; McInerney, 2008). Field-level events also facilitate interactions among field constituencies, distribute prestige, and allow for conflicts to be expressed and worked out (Anand & Watson, 2004) or downplayed (Zilber, 2011). They thus establish and foster the social structure of the field and its identity (Glynn, 2008; Lampel & Meyer, 2008; Moeran, 2010; Moeran, 2011; Oliver & Montgomery, 2008; Rao, 1994; Stam, 2010). Field-level events may therefore be an instructive site to explore how field members come to know—that is, to construct—the location of their field or their sense of place in their institutional field.

Methodology

An Israeli Hi-tech Event as a Case Study

My study is focused on an Israeli high-tech industry conference held in November 2005 in Santa Clara, California. The conference was organized by The Israel Venture Association (IVA) and was entitled, "The Israeli Hi-tech VC Conference: Exploring Growth Opportunities." In the newswire announcing the conference, the organizers underscored that the gathering would include three of the world's largest investors in venture-capital (VC) funds as well as senior executives from leading U.S. technology companies and senior members of the VC community in Israel, "aiming to identify partnership and acquisition opportunities among the start-up ventures taking part in the conference" (IVA newswire, November 2, 2005). The event, so declared the organizers, was "the sixth of a series of conferences IVA has organized throughout the world during the past two years (the latest one was in Tokyo) in an effort to generate new business opportunities for funds and start-ups in Israel" (IVA newswire, November 2, 2005).

To judge from this text, place seemed to be a crucial matter for the organizers and participants. They organized a special event at the heart of U.S. high-tech industry and marked the positions of Israeli high-tech in its quest to be recognized by and cooperate with the leading actors in the field. This concern with place was explicit in a statement added by the organizers:

> According to Avi Zeevi, the conference chairman and founding partner in Carmel Ventures, "[w]e decided to hold the conference this year in the Valley in light of the significant progress in the global standing of the Israeli high-tech industry and venture capital during the past year. The event will constitute an exceptional opportunity for Israeli companies and entrepreneurs to meet leaders of the American technology industry located in this region and will enable venture capital funds to meet with potential investors and partners." (IVA newswire, November 2, 2005)

I use the Israeli high-tech industry for my case study because that sector is an extreme case (Yin, 1984/2014). First, the high-tech industry is a global phenomenon because it not only has centers worldwide but also produces and uses communication technologies that seemingly transcend geographical locations and boundaries. It has created and is interconnected through cyberspaces that allow for instantaneous interaction with people thousands of miles away. Constructing a sense of place in such a globalized, "flat" world (Friedman, 2005) may require more effort and may be more apparent—and thus easier to depict and analyze—than in low-tech settings.

Second, the Israeli high-tech is a thriving industry, part of the global high-tech field. Location is an exceptionally loaded nexus in Israeli identity, constantly negotiating a balance between the global (the Western world) and the local (the conflictual Middle East). The conference under study was not held in Israel but rather in the global hub of high-technology more than 7,500 miles away: Silicon Valley. The dynamics of place may be more evident and easier to capture in that context than in conferences held in Israel.

Data Collection and Analysis

This study is based on participant observations (Atkinson & Hammersley, 1998), notably of the discursive activity as it unfolded during the event. All the deliberations were recorded and later transcribed. The event started with an evening "networking reception." An intensive day of plenary sessions and simultaneous one-on-one meetings at the Santa Clara Marriott Hotel ensued. The conference ended with a Black-Tie Optional Gala dinner for the 2005 International Partnership Award, hosted by the California Israel Chamber of Commerce at the Computer History Museum in Mountain View. All in all, 41 different speakers took part across eight different sessions. Speakers' affiliations varied. They included politicians (e.g., the California State Controller and the former Israeli Minister of Finance), diplomats (e.g., the Ambassador of Israel to the United States), senior VC and high-tech executives (including Israelis such as Shai Agassi, then an executive board member of SA, and Americans such as Dan Rosensweig, then COO of Yahoo!), and service providers (representative of Israeli and American Law and accounting firms).

I read the more than 200 resulting pages of proceedings, presentations, and field notes, using content analysis (Lieblich, 1998) to identify the material's main substantive categories through cyclical refinement from the concrete and specific to the abstract and general. This process was focused especially on issues of location and place. I examined explicit statements about the Israeli hi-tech industry, the differences and similarities between it and the high-tech industry in other locations, and explicit reflections about "the Israeli character" and its similarities or differences from the character of other nations. I also used explicit markers—such as names of locations (e.g., states, cities, and landmarks), organizations (e.g., universities such as Technion, one of Israel's premier institutes of higher education; MIT; and Harvard), and location-bound historical events and institutions (e.g., military operations or service in the Israeli Defense Force)—to identify implicit themes concerning place. Likewise, whenever I noticed the use of Hebrew words in the mainly English proceedings, I strove to understand the context and meaning of such language use. In particular, I tried to understand the possible ways such linguistic usage marks, or at least evokes, the location of the speakers and the audience. I also noticed stories of personal experiences and jokes about cross-cultural experiences of the speakers, trying to figure out their implicit meanings. Drawing on all these markers and segments of text, I then asked generally what significance the location of the Israeli high-tech industry had in those exchanges. How did different participants construct place, and what meaning did they give it?

I mapped the different constructions of place throughout the texts produced, disseminated, and consumed (Phillips et al., 2004) during the event and identified the different voices they reflected. Each speaker spoke from specific and idiosyncratic experiences, understandings, and interests. All speakers had stakes in the industry and its construction. My analysis suggests that all of them—regardless of their nationality or official roles—took part in constructing a rich and varied discourse about place as it pertained to Israeli high-tech. The following sections present my account of this collective, yet heterogeneous, discourse.

Locating the Field of Israeli High-Tech: Imagined Geography, Practice, and Memory

Place was constructed as referring to a very wide range of aspects, including issues of location, context, language, values, history, and culture. At the heart of these different constructions was a continuous effort to bridge a seemingly huge geographical and cultural divide between the Israeli and U.S. high-tech industries. Focusing on place, I found that speakers constructed three kinds of communities: an imagined geographical community (Said, 1978), a practice community (Gherardi & Nicolini, 2002), and a mnemonic community (Zerubavel, 2003).[2] These three constructions of communities were used to blur the boundaries between the Israeli and U.S. industries.

Divided We Stand

To appreciate the explicit and implicit efforts to construct the two industries as part of the same institutional field, it is first necessary to highlight the constructions that differentiate between them. They consisted repeated, direct, and explicit mentions of Israel's geographical location, with speakers referring to the country's small size and its distance from its markets in the United States, the Far East, and even Europe.

Over and beyond the geographical distance, speakers often constructed cultural differences. For example, one speaker referred to—or constructed—the unique characteristics of Israeli "mentality," including the inclination to "team work" (Ron Moritz, Chief Security Strategist, Computer Associates, plenary session, "Israel: A Source of Strategic Partnership Opportunities").[3] Another speaker stressed the ability to transcend cross-cultural differences, for Israelis are "global in our blood," given the diversity in Israeli society and its multilingual population (Dr. Levy Gerzberg, cofounder and Chief Executive Officer of Zoran, plenary session, "Building Israeli Global Category Leaders"). He also called to mind Israelis' "tenacity . . . [and] attitude of winning." Optimism, too, drew attention (as conveyed through a common saying in Hebrew that foreigners quickly learn, *i'h'yeh beseder*, 'all will be O.K.' (Dr. Sass Somekh, President, Novellus Systems, plenary session, "Israel: A Global Source of Innovation"). An additional example of constructed

---

[2] I thank Roy Suddaby, one of the editors of this volume, for pointing me in this direction.

[3] All the citations in this section are from the studied conference—The Israeli Hi-tech Industry VC Conference: Exploring Growth Opportunities—held in November 2005 in Santa Clara, California, and organized by the Israeli Venture Association.

cultural differences between Israelis and other peoples was the Israeli tendency to be creative, to think "out of the box," and to be determined to find unconventional solutions (Amnon Lamdan, founder and Chief Executive Officer, Mercury Interactive, plenary session, "Building Israeli Global Category Leaders").

Alongside such admiring comments, many speakers were critical of Israelis' character. They were even condescending:

> When we first opened there [some 20 years ago], we didn't know what to expect, so we recruited a group of Israeli managers[.] . . . We went over there, and you know, the management team that worked was smart, spoke well, and seemed to know what they were doing. And we put a bunch of stuff over. We thought we had a few problems in some areas. We asked them about it, and we learned a different word from them. It is *no problem*, 'just leave us alone and we'll take care of it'. . . . Maybe they thought it was a sign of weakness to ask for help. And, of course, that turned out to be a terrible, terrible weakness in the company. . . . We taught them a lesson that says, hey, if you don't improve your operation, we are going to shut you down. And they said no kidding, you're going to shut us down? . . . Then we got a different response. They said well, how about we send a few people over to the United States and learn some management techniques there? . . . [O]ver the last 10 years there has been a tremendous amount of international experiences. [Israelis] have drifted into various companies; the knowledge is infusing into Israel. So now when I see new Israeli companies going up, there isn't a lack of management talent, . . . [T]hey have [had] to acknowledge international standards in all of their activities, and I think it is a very helpful situation. (Ken Levy, Chairman of the Board, KLA-Tencor, plenary session, "Israel: A Global Source of Innovation")

Many participants made jokes about Israelis, delivering complex messages of both acclaim and criticism regarding their character and culture. Joseph Vardi, a known Israeli entrepreneur, offered a humorous opening to the panel discussion he chaired:

> We just want to set the rules for the panel discussion. We will try to create an Israeli environment for the next hour, which means that the panelists don't have to wait until they each have a turn with one of the microphones. And if you want to interrupt, prevent, or to object or to ask the other panelists a question, by all means go ahead and do it. The audience is requested to keep their cell phones on so that we can hear the rings. . . . (Dr. Joseph Vardi, Chairman, International Technologies Ventures, plenary session, "Internet vs. Traditional Media")

Another speaker addressed the issue of formality versus casualness:

> The reason I tossed my jacket off, by the way, is since Silicon Valley, since I've spent seven years here, I feel much more comfortable without the jacket on. And the other thing to point out I think was on my first trip to Israel. Somebody said to me, you'd better lose the tie as well because it is only gangsters and politicians that wear ties in Israel today. (W. Robert Genieser, Managing Partner, Vertex Europe)

Yet another brought up the topic of Israeli impatience and the tendency not to listen to others:

> Amnon said earlier that we are not good listeners. . . . So one day I am walking into a presentation like this, and I hear the instructor saying, you know Israelis are not known to be very good listeners. So I told her you are absolutely wrong. Israelis are very good listeners, especially when they are talking. (Dr. Levy Gerzberg, cofounder and Chief Executive Officer of Zoran, plenary session, "Building Israeli Global Category Leaders)

The conference abounded with a discourse, both positive and negative, that highlighted how different and distant the Israeli and U.S. high-tech industries are from each other. At the same time, a unifying discourse was also apparent, one that highlighted the similarities between the two industries. Exactly how did speakers manage to construct them as similar and as part of the same institutional field? In the following sections I demonstrate how place was used linguistically to construct three kinds of united communities.

Constructing an Imagined Geographical Community

Although nobody debated the objective geographical location of Israeli high-tech, its meaning was constructed in a way that created an imagined geographical community. Geographical knowledge, according to Said (1978), is grounded in cultural and symbolic domains. A geographical fact "is far less important than what poetically it is endowed with, which is usually a quality with an imaginative or figurative value we can name and feel" (Said, 1978, p. 55). Through a process of "fabrication and poesis" involving "anxiety, desire and fantasy" (Gregory, 1995, p. 456), "profoundly ideological landscapes" are created (Gregory, 1995, p. 474). Speakers thus interpreted the geographical facts in ways that united Israelis and Americans, presumably in the "same" (imagined) place.

This imagined geographical community was created through a series of discursive steps. To begin with, actors mentioned how far away Israel was and used the California scene to illustrate this distance: "It is easier to drive your car down the 101[4] than it is to fly all the way to Israel," said Ruth Alon, General Partner in Pitango Venture Capital, while chairing a plenary session on life science. A chief executive officer of an Israeli-born firm agreed that, given the distance, "you sit on planes all the time." In the same vein, Ken Levy, Chairman of the Board of KLA-Tencor, claimed that "a great strength of Israel is that it is far away, but they are willing to travel. You see four Americans and ninety-five Israelis on the plane" (plenary session, "Israel as a Source of Innovation").

Acknowledging the distance *between Silicon Valley and Israel*, speakers highlighted various factors that help Israeli high-tech transcend it, including the very willingness of Israelis to travel often and government support to the industry (Yaakov Neeman, Senior Partner in Herzog Fox & Neeman law firm and former Israeli Minister of Finance). Also credited were infrastructure (e.g., a strong legal system); the existence of top research universities (e.g., the Hebrew University of Jerusalem, which manages its intellectual property in the emerging nanotechnology market as Harvard, MIT, and UC Berkeley do); the technological units of the Israeli Defense Forces; and high-quality manpower, partly because of the massive immigration to Israel of former USSR citizens well trained in science and technology.

---

[4] Route 101, a key North-South route on the U.S. west coast, serves as a major road in Silicon Valley.

Speakers proved to be quite creative in bridging the distance. Some claimed that geography is not that important, asserting that "money is global" and "the quality of the people is far more important than the geography" (Allen Hill, President and Chief Executive Officer, VisionCare Ophthalmic Technologies, Inc., plenary session, "Life Science") or that this "handicap" (distance) is losing its meaning as "the world becomes flatter" (Clinton Harris, Managing Partner, Grove Street Advisors LLC, plenary session, "Israel: A Global Source of Innovation").

Not only that the distance may be bridged, some speakers turned it into an advantage. Given the distance, the infrastructure, and government support, doing business in Israel—so the argument went—is less expensive than doing it in North America, especially in the phase of research and development:

> Why is Israel successful? . . . [F]or a long time Israel has been the lowest cost place to do innovation or technology development and certainly from the venture-capital perspective, it is the lowest cost place to do that. You have extremely high-quality people. They are very creative and innovative. In part we pay them less than we pay in Silicon Valley; and in part we have arrangements over there in terms of government subsidies and the like. (Clinton Harris, Managing Partner, Grove Street Advisors LLC, plenary session, "Israel: A Global Source of Innovation")

Speakers also discussed the very concept of the "global," arguing that the U.S. market should not be considered the same as "the global."

> Well, surprisingly enough, the Asian markets for companies are not the emerging markets, they are the established market. The emerging markets are more like markets in the U.S. and Europe that are emerging out of some stagnation, investment in previous technologies, and . . . self-assurance that we have got everything set and we don't need to improve anything . . . . [T]he market today is definitely in Asia, a lot of things are happening there, there is a lot of money. (David Welsh, General Partner, Partch International, plenary session, "Information and Communications Technology")

Actors thus portrayed the markets as changing so that the relevant distance of Israel from "the market" changes as well. This distance may even turn into an advantage, given the skills and capabilities that Israeli companies have had to develop and the experience they have in dealing with markets that are far away (Erez Schar, Managing Partner, Evergreen Venture Partners, plenary session, "Israeli VCs: Bridging Capital and Opportunities").

Constructing a Community of Practice

Another way to construct the similarity between the fields of U.S. and Israeli high-tech was to situate them both as part of one global "community of practice" (Lave & Wenger, 1991). Communities of practice are united in that they share the same professional language, tacit skills, and identities and abide by the same rules and norms (Gherardi & Nicolini, 2002). Because communities of practice transcend borders (organizational and geographical) through "shared expertise and passion for a joint enterprise" (Wenger & Snyder, 2000, p. 139), the construction of Israeli and

U.S. high-tech as belonging to the same practice community allowed actors to symbolically construct a united field.

This imagined community was constructed by using the seemingly universal and neutral discourses of economics and technology. Speakers underscored Israel's economic and high-tech standing, which places the country on a par with U.S. high-tech hubs:

> [T]he last one was Bill Gates, and two weeks ago he visited us in Israel. In order to be accurate, let me quote to you what he said about Israel: "If you are good in certain areas, success leads to success in other areas. Israel is more similar to the U.S. in these areas than any other country I have ever visited." It is no exaggeration of Bill Gates to say that the kind of innovation going on in Israel is critical to the future of the technology business. . . . We had 13 IPOs this year . . . . We have more than 40 M&A transactions over 3 billion dollars. Israeli fundraisers estimate this year 1.4 billion dollars, compared to 800 million dollars last year, and practically zero in the year 2003. We are at the rate of 1.5 billion dollars in investments into a VC-backed company. We are, based on these numbers, number four after California, Massachusetts, [and] Texas, and way ahead of every European country today. (Yoram Oron, Chairman of the Board, Israel Venture Association; Founder and Managing Partner, Vertex Venture Capital, opening plenary session)

Speakers also tended to frame Israeli high-tech challenges in abstract and general terms. For example, panelists in a plenary session entitled "Israel: A Source of Strategic Partnership Opportunities" discussed partnerships between big multinational firms and small Israeli firms, comparing a "friendly hug" with a "bear hug" and suggesting universal principles for managing such relationships in order to ensure that the small firms are "meaningful in that dialogue."

In lieu of such general and abstract language of economic practices, successful Israeli entrepreneurs who were invited to tell their stories drew universal lessons about the trials and tribulations of developing a technological idea into a business.

> So we started as a DSV [Dynamic Signature Verification] company here and in Silicon Valley, in Sunnyvale [California] actually and in Haifa [a city in the north of Israel]. . . . [T]rust me, I didn't know what the market was. We were a bunch of techies. We knew how to design very fast chips, and we said, "Let's design a DSV and see who will bite." . . . Later on I learned that design doesn't mean anything till you see the revenues. . . . I had business plans, powerpoint presentations, but no revenues. . . . Then we said, "O.K., . . . let's try and change the direction," . . . and actually this is what Zoran has being doing since then. . . . [W]e jumped into an existing market, and we made [a] real dent[.] . . . [W]e are looking into these markets that we see the growth coming, and we ride on the growth. . . . Several years ago there was a student at Stanford [who] made an observation . . . which I confirmed again this summer when I watched the Tour de France. Do you know that in the Olympic Games, when you look at long-distance runners, . . . 5 K, 8 K, 10 K, marathon, . . . the guy who is the first more than half of the laps . . . is never the winner. . . . [B]eing the first is not always first to profit. (Dr. Levy Gerzberg, cofounder and Chief Executive Officer of Zoran, plenary session, "Building Israeli Global Category Leaders")

In addition, speakers assumed that high-tech people around the world face similar choices—should we invest in infrastructure or in content? What is the future of online games? And what about the WiMax, the new transmission standard? Is it "going to be [a] huge [or] overhyped phenomenon" (Information and

Communications Technology panel, W. Robert Genieser, Managing Partner, Vertex Europe)? Such sharing created a shared imagined community of practice that was reinforced time and again. It allowed for downplaying the distant and presumed difference. When a U.S.-based business lawyer was asked his opinion about alternative exit routes, he began his answer by stating, "I don't think it is first of all uniquely an Israeli issue. It is a market issue in terms of the IPOs" (VC panel, Robert Grossman, Principal Shareholder, Greenberg Traurig).

In such a presumably unified community of practice, professional identity is stronger than national identity, as reflected in the following joke.

> Three people in the French Revolution . . . were supposed to be executed with the guillotine. So, it's an engineer, a doctor, and a lawyer. The lawyer comes up and they put his head on the deck, whatever, and they pull the string and the machine doesn't work, and they let him go because this is what they do if the first time it doesn't work out. And then the doctor comes up and the same thing happens, so they let him go. And then the engineer comes up and he says, 'If you give me a minute, I think I can fix it, right.' (Tuvia Barlev, Chief Executive Officer and cofounder, Actelis, plenary session, "Information and Communications Technology")

The joke thus made fun of engineers—those tech guys, as many of the audience were. It was this professional identity that rendered the joke funny and united them within a shared community of practice.

Constructing a Mnemonic Community

Another common discursive practice used at the conference was reference to shared "collective memory" (Halbwachs, 1925/1992; Olick, 1999), which serves as the basis for "mnemonic communities" (Zerubavel, 2003). Mnemonic communities (including organizational fields; see chapter by Coraiola, Suddaby, & Foster in this volume) remember—that is, construct—the past in a similar way and share events and artifacts of commemoration. In particular, they tell narratives about their past that offer similar implications for their present and future (Liu & Hilton, 2005).

Some speakers reflected on the similarities between Israeli and U.S. histories:

> I want to share this story with you about my trip to Israel. I was there just last year. . . . I will tell you, nothing in my entire life felt more like Silicon Valley five years ago: the energy, the dynamism, the entrepreneurship, the belief that anything is possible. The only place in the world I have seen anything like Silicon Valley is in Jerusalem today and in Tel Aviv. You are doing something stunning there. . . . California is so similar to Israel—an agriculture economy 50 years ago, now grown up to be . . . technology based, leading the rest of the world in that area. (Steve Westly, California State Controller, opening plenary session)

He then went even further and connected history and character:

> What is more interesting to me, though, is that Israel, like California, . . . is a state of mind. It is a place where people think, and they connect to higher purposes, with innovation, with leadership. It goes far beyond a job industry, and I feel that California shares this inextricably.

The speaker thereby constructed a historical similarity, which serves as a basis for shared cultural values and similar character helping to bridge the more than 12,000 km [over 7,500 miles) that separate the two locations. Similarly, Daniel Ayalon, Ambassador of Israel to the United States, started his talk with claims about the similarity between Israeli and American values and then moved to set them on the same side of the historical clashes between cultures:

> [F]rom my vantage point in Washington [D.C.], I am following very closely the high-tech joint ventures between the United States and Israel. We have never had better relations . . . , as we have a real basis of sharing values [and] building practices. And, of course, we have the same interest of stability and prosperity. Not to mention [that] we also face now the same threats of radicalism and proliferation of weapons of mass destruction, [and], of course, the extreme ideology and international terrorism by these generic Islamic Jihad or Al Qaida, which is a very loose structure and organization but yet very dangerous, as we saw yesterday in Amman. (Daniel Ayalon, Ambassador of Israel to the United States, opening plenary session)

The fact that shared memory and cultural values associated with it serve as resources for community-building is apparent from the following example. The speaker reflects a logic similar to the one linking Israel and the United States— except that he links Israel and China instead.

> [W]hat is the source of this funny name, Zoran. It is pronounced in Hebrew "Tzoran." Many people don't know it, but it is the oldest word for silicon. It is silicon in Hebrew, and that is the reason we chose it some twenty-two years ago. The funny thing is that eight years ago I learned that if you pronounce it almost like in Hebrew, it means "outstanding" in Chinese. When I discovered that, we switched to China. Actually, this is our largest market today. (Dr. Levy Gerzberg, cofounder and Chief Executive Officer of Zoran, plenary session, "Building Israeli Global Category Leaders")

Because language is a central marker of location, it serves in this context to connect the Hebrew word with relevant meaning in Chinese, associating the speaker's firm with this huge and awakening market.

Discussion: Locating the Field

Building on the understanding of place as a cultural and social construction (Cresswell, 2004) and of institutional fields as discursive constructions (Hoffman, 1999), I explored how actors reshuffle presumably self-evident notions of place in an institutional field. The diverse constructions of place during the conference highlight the concept's importance to institutional dynamics. The varied configurations of the location of Israeli high-tech highlights the power of discursive practices, or rhetorical strategies (Suddaby & Greenwood, 2005), to transform place as part of the construction of field-level collective identity (Brown & Humphreys, 2006). Actors assumed Israel's peripheral location to be distant and small in comparison to U.S. or other global markets, yet they simultaneously undermined these seemingly objective geographical facts. Actors used various discursive practices to globalize and Americanize the field of Israeli high-tech. They created similarity between Israeli and U.S. high-tech industries and placed them within a shared institutional field while downplaying the differences.

This remarkable shift was achieved through three discourses of community. In one of them—an imagined geographical community discourse (in the spirit of Said, 1978)—the speaker would acknowledge geographical facts while infusing them with new meanings so that distance was shortened or deemed irrelevant. Second, a practice-community discourse (following Gherardi & Nicolini, 2002) involved the use of the languages of economics and technology to portray Israeli and U.S. high-tech members as professionals who engage in the same practices and thus share the same collective identity. Finally, a third discourse constructed a mnemonic community (after Zerubavel, 2003), depicting Israeli and U.S. high-tech as sharing similar collective memories and related cultural values.

Further theorizing the pragmatics of discursive practices can yield new insight into the construction of place in institutional fields. For example, place was central to all these discourses, but there were some important differences in the ways it was constructed. In the imagined geography discourse place was infused with new and diverse meaning that changed its more common peripheral understandings. By contrast, the shared-practice discourse and the memory discourse constructed place as obsolete by offering new—nonspatial and deterritorialized—ways to understand a common institutional field. Whereas the shared-practice community discourse resorted to the universality (and thus unity) entailed in economics and technology, the collective memory discourse integrated all members into a new, shared institutional field by anchoring them in a common morality and character.

Interestingly, these different discourses of place were produced by all participants at the event, regardless of their nationality or professional background. Unlike previous studies on the construction of place, which portray different actors as offering different constructions (e.g., different constructions of a wall as communicated by residents from its different sides; see McKee, 2013), in this case all actors spoke in a multiplicity of voices. But this portrayal may be an artifact of the data used—varied and rich, yet from only one conference with a relatively small number of speakers. Research based on data from numerous conferences may allow closer examination of how subject positions (Phillips & Hardy, 2002) in an institutional field are related to *specific* uses of this or that discursive practice of place. For instance, political agendas were pursued by some of the conference's actors, including the California State Controller, who was running for the state governorship, and the Israeli ambassador, who was quick to use the shared-memory discourse to underline the closeness of Israel and the U.S. as allies and to legitimate the Israeli government and its policies. Other participants had financial interests. Members of the VC community were looking for investments, and representatives of start-ups were looking for money. Some U.S.-based actors tended to underscore the differences between U.S. and Israeli managers, whereas their Israeli counterparts seemed to stress the common ground of the two professional groups. There is a need to inquire further into and theorize about the interface between actors' subject positions in an institutional field and the multifaceted construction of place.

Nonetheless, the various constructions of place and the U.S. and Israeli high-tech industries reflect actors' agency. The conference under study was indeed a highly public and interest-driven event. All speakers had various agendas they were promoting through their participation. Clearly, the discursive practices used were strategic, deliberate, and designed to be persuasive (Suddaby & Greenwood, 2005). It is the flexibility of place that makes it such a potent discursive resource in identity work (Larson & Pearson, 2012). Because place is a construction, it can be used by institutional actors in different, sometimes contradictory ways in their abiding efforts to articulate their identity as part of institutional work (Lawrence & Suddaby, 2006). Institutions, knowledge, and place are intertwined, for institutional field members draw on place in order to know—to construct—the field of which they are part.

Acknowledgments This research was funded by the Israel Science Foundation (grant No. 1230/05). Many thanks are due Yehuda Goodman for the on-going discussion on this project.

References

Agnew, J. (1987). *The United States in the world economy: A regional geography*. Cambridge, UK: Cambridge University Press.

Anand, N., & Jones, B. C. (2008). Tournament rituals, category dynamics, and field configuration: The case of the Booker Prize. *Journal of Management Studies, 45,* 1036–1060. doi:https://doi.org/10.1111/j.1467-6486.2008.00782.x

Anand, N., & Watson, M. R. (2004). Tournament rituals in the evolution of fields: The case of the Grammy Awards. *Academy of Management Journal, 47,* 59–80. doi:https://doi.org/10.2307/20159560

Anderson, B. (1983). *Imagines communities: Reflections on the origin and spread of nationalism*. London: Verso.

Atkinson, P., & Hammersley, M. (1998). Ethnography and participant observation. In N. K. Denzin & Y. S. Lincoln (Eds.), *Strategies of qualitative inquiry* (pp. 110–136). Thousand Oaks: Sage.

Brown, A. D., & Humphreys, M. (2006). Organizational identity and place: A discursive exploration of hegemony and resistance. *Journal of Management Studies, 43*, 231–257. doi:https://doi.org/10.1111/j.1467-6486.2006.00589.x

Cresswell, T. (2004). *Place: A short introduction*. Malden: Blackwell Publishing.

Czarniawska, B., & Joerges, B. (1996). Travels of ideas. In B. Czarniawska & G. Sevón (Eds.), *Translating organizational change* (pp. 13–48). Berlin: Walter de Gruyter.

DiMaggio, P. J., & Powell, W. W. (1983). The iron cage revisited: Institutional isomorphism and collective rationality in organizational fields. *American Sociological Review, 48,* 147–160. Retrieved from http://www.jstor.org/stable/2095101

Friedman, T. L. (2005). *The world is flat 3.0: A brief history of the twenty-first Century*. New York: Farrar, Starus and Giroux.

Garud, R. (2008). Conferences as venues for the configuration of emerging organizational fields: The case of cochlear implants. *Journal of Management Studies, 45,* 1061–1088. doi:https://doi.org/10.1111/j.1467-6486.2008.00783.x

Gherardi, S., & Nicolini, D. (2002). Learning the trade: A culture of safety in practice. *Organization, 9*, 191–223. doi:https://doi.org/10.1177/1350508402009002264

Gieryn, T. F. (2000). A space for place in sociology. *Annual Review of Sociology, 26,* 463–496. doi:https://doi.org/10.1146/annurev.soc.26.1.463

Glynn, M. A. (2008). Configuring the field of play: How hosting the Olympic Games impacts civic community. *Journal of Management Studies, 45*, 1117–1146. doi:https://doi.org/10.1111/j.1467-6486.2008.00785.x

Gregory, D. (1995). Imaginative geographies. *Progress in Human Geography, 19*, 447–485. doi:https://doi.org/10.1177/030913259501900402

Halbwachs, M. (1992). *On collective memory* (L. A. Coser, Ed. & Trans., with an introduction by L. A. Coser). Chicago: University of Chicago Press. (Original work published 1925)

Henn, S., & Bathelt, H. (2015). Knowledge generation and field reproduction in temporary clusters and the role of business conferences. *Geoforum, 58*, 104–113. doi:https://doi.org/10.1016/j.geoforum.2014.10.015

Hoffman, A. J. (1999). Institutional evolution and change: Environmentalism and the U.S. chemical industry. *Academy of Management Journal, 42*, 351–371. doi:https://doi.org/10.2307/257008

Lampel, J., & Meyer, A. D. (2008). Field-configuring events as structuring mechanisms: How conferences, ceremonies, and trade shows constitute new technologies, industries, and markets. *Journal of Management Studies, 45*, 1025–1035. doi:https://doi.org/10.1111/j.1467-6486.2008.00787.x

Larson, G. S., & Pearson, A. R. (2012). Placing identity: Place as a discursive resource for occupational identity work among high-tech entrepreneurs. *Management Communication Quarterly, 26*, 241–266. doi:https://doi.org/10.1177/0893318911435319

Lave, J., & Wenger, E. C. (1991). *Situated learning: Legitimate peripheral participation.* Cambridge, UK: Cambridge University Press.

Lawrence, T. B., & Dover, G. (2015). Place and institutional work: Creating housing for the hard-to-house. *Administrative Science Quarterly, 60*, 371–410. doi:https://doi.org/10.1177/0001839215589813

Lawrence, T. B., & Suddaby, R. (2006). Institutions and institutional work. In S. R. Clegg, C. Hardy, T. B. Lawrence, & W. R. Nord, (Eds.), *The SAGE handbook of organization studies* (2nd ed., pp. 215–254). London: Sage.

Lieblich, A. (1998). Categorical-content perspective. In A. Lieblich, R. Tuval-Mashiach, & T. Zilber (Eds.), *Narrative research: Reading, analysis, and interpretation* (pp. 112–126). Applied Social Research Methods Series: Vol. 47. Thousand Oaks: Sage.

Liu, J. H., & Hilton, D. J. (2005). How the past weighs on the present: Social representations of history and their role in identity politics. *British Journal of Social Psychology, 44*, 537–556. doi:https://doi.org/10.1348/014466605x27162

Maguire, S., & Hardy, C. (2006). The emergence of new global institutions: A discursive perspective. *Organization Studies, 27*, 7–29. doi:https://doi.org/10.1177/0170840606061807

McInerney, P. B. (2008). Showdown at Kykuit: Field-configuring events as loci for conventionalizing accounts. *Journal of Management Studies, 45*, 1089–1116. doi:https://doi.org/10.1111/j.1467-6486.2008.00784.x

McKee, R. J. (2013). The symbolic meanings of physical boundaries: The F Street Wall. *Space and Culture, 16*, 4–15. doi:https://doi.org/10.1177/1206331212451678

Moeran, B. (2010). The book fair as a tournament of values. *Journal of the Royal Anthropological Institute, 16*, 138–154. doi:https://doi.org/10.1111/j.1467-9655.2009.01601.x

Moeran, B. (2011). Trade fairs, markets and fields: Framing imagined as real communities. *Historical Social Research, 36*, 79–98. Retrieved from http://www.jstor.org/stable/23032428

Olick, J. K. (1999). Collective memory: The two cultures. *Sociological Theory, 17*, 333–348. doi:https://doi.org/10.1111/0735-2751.00083

Oliver, A. L., & Montgomery, K. (2008). Using field-configuring events for sense-making: A cognitive network approach. *Journal of Management Studies, 45*, 1147–1167. doi:https://doi.org/10.1111/j.1467-6486.2008.00786.x

Patterson, M. E., & Williams, D. R. (2005). Maintaining research traditions on place: Diversity of thought and scientific progress. *Journal of Environmental Psychology, 25*, 361–380. doi:https://doi.org/10.1016/j.jenvp.2005.10.001

Phillips, N., & Hardy, C. (2002). *Discourse analysis: Investigating processes of social construction.* London: Sage.

Phillips, N., Lawrence, T. B., & Hardy, C. (2004). Discourse and institutions. *Academy of Management Review, 29*, 635–652. doi:https://doi.org/10.5465/AMR.2004.14497617

Rao, H. (1994). The social construction of reputation: Certification contests, legitimation, and the survival of organizations in the American automobile industry: 1895–1912. *Strategic Management Journal, 15*(S1), 29–44. doi:https://doi.org/10.1002/smj.4250150904

Said, E. W. (1978). *Orientalism.* London: Routledge & Kegan Paul.

Schüßler, E., & Sydow, J. (2015). Organizing events for configuring and maintaining creative fields. In C. Jones, M. Lorenzen, & J. Sapsed (Eds.), *Oxford handbook of creative industries* (pp. 284–300). Oxford, UK: Oxford University Press. doi:https://doi.org/10.1093/oxfordhb/9780199603510.013.029

Scott, W. R. (2014). *Institutions and organizations: Ideas, interests, and identities* (4th ed.). Los Angeles: Sage.

Stam, W. (2010). Industry event participation and network brokerage among entrepreneurial ventures. *Journal of Management Studies, 47*, 625–653. https://doi.org/10.1111/j.1467-6486.2009.00909.x

Suddaby, R., & Greenwood, R. (2005). Rhetorical strategies of legitimacy. *Administrative Science Quarterly, 50*, 35–67. doi:https://doi.org/10.2189/asqu.2005.50.1.35

Taylor, S., & Spicer, A. (2007). Time for space: A narrative review of research on organizational spaces. *International Journal of Management Reviews, 9*, 325–346. doi:https://doi.org/10.1111/j.1468-2370.2007.00214.x

Wenger, E. C., & Snyder, W. M. (2000). Communities of practice: The organizational frontier. *Harvard Business Review, 78*(1), 139–145.

Wooten, M., & Hoffman, A. J. (2008). Organizational fields: Past, present and future. In R. Greenwood, C. Oliver, K. Sahlin-Andersson, & R. Suddaby (Eds.), *The SAGE handbook of organizational institutionalism* (pp. 130–148). London: Sage.

Yin, R. K. (2014). *Case study research: Design and methods* (5th ed.). Thousand Oaks: Sage.

Zerubavel, E. (2003). *Time maps: Collective memory and the social shape of the past.* Chicago: University of Chicago Press.

Zietsma, C., Groenewegen, P., Logue, & Hinings, C. R. (2017). Field or fields? Building the scaffolding for cumulation of research on institutional fields. *Academy of Management Annals, 11*, 391–450. doi:https://doi.org/10.5465/annals.2014.0052

Zilber, T. B. (2007). Stories and the discursive dynamics of institutional entrepreneurship: The case of Israeli high-tech after the bubble. *Organization Studies, 28*, 1035–1054. doi:https://doi.org/10.1177/0170840607078113

Zilber, T. B. (2011). Institutional multiplicity in practice: A tale of two high-tech conferences in Israel. *Organization Science, 22*, 1539–1559. doi:https://doi.org/10.1287/orsc.1100.0611

Zilber, T. B. (2014). Beyond a single organization: Challenges and opportunities in doing field level ethnography. *Journal of Organizational Ethnography, 3*, 96–113. doi:https://doi.org/10.1108/JOE-11-2012-0043

Part III
The Impact of Institutions on Regional Learning and Development

Chapter 10
Regional Innovation Transitions

Michael Storper

The Problem: Innovation and Turbulent Regional Economic Performance

Since the Industrial Revolution, the world economy has enjoyed ongoing productivity increases that have steadily raised global living standards in the context of a growing world population. This represents a change from the reality prior to roughly 1820, which was marked by long-term stagnation in both living standards and population levels, a condition referred to as the Malthusian Trap (Maddison, 1982). The vast historical literature on the Industrial Revolution, complemented by recent advances in growth theory, demonstrates that capitalism has been able to break this historical trap for more than two centuries through a powerful systemic capacity to generate productivity-increasing innovations.

Within this two-century period, however, innovation has not occurred evenly over time nor over geographical territory. The time dynamic is that major innovations occur in waves, and are centered on sets of technologies and their principal industries, such as the textile technology revolution of the late eighteenth and early nineteenth centuries, with its harnessing of water power sources and its mechanical innovations for weaving. In the nineteenth century, technologies around steel, coal, and railroads generated another major wave of productivity increases. In the very late nineteenth century and early twentieth century, the internal combustion engine, electricity, and more mechanical engineering technologies generated another astonishing wave of productivity gains (Gordon, 2016).

M. Storper (✉)
Luskin School of Public Affairs, UCLA, Los Angeles, CA, USA

Department of Geography and Environment, London School of Economics, London, UK

Center for the Sociology of Organizations, Sciences Po Paris, Paris, France
e-mail: storper@ucla.edu

© The Author(s) 2018
J. Glückler et al. (eds.), *Knowledge and Institutions*, Knowledge and Space 13,
https://doi.org/10.1007/978-3-319-75328-7_10

The uneven geography of that greatest wave of innovation, the Industrial Revolution of the late eighteenth century, generated a *great divergence* in world incomes between Europe and some of its overseas outgrowths and the rest of the world (Pomeranz, 2000). This outcome is perhaps only now being reshaped with the possible rise of East Asia as a center of world innovation, but it is too early to tell. Studies of the geography of innovation, stemming largely from the pioneering work of Feldman (1994) and Jaffe (1989), have also established that innovation is geographically concentrated and uneven at the finer geographical scale of subnational regions. The invention of the internal combustion engine in the late nineteenth century sustained the rise of distinct regional centers of the mechanical engineering industries in Europe and the Americas (Storper & Walker, 1989). More recently, the information technology (IT) revolution of the 1970s generated the IT industries and in combination with open capital market policies stimulated the growth of the modern finance sector. Both have contributed to the concentration of skills, capital, entrepreneurship, and leading firms in certain metropolitan regions of the developed economies.

Within the United States, for example, in 2001, the 50 largest regions had per capita incomes 27% greater than the U.S. economy as a whole, with this advantage growing to 34% by 2015. Per capita income in the Brownsville, Texas, metropolitan region is $23,000 per year compared to about $75,000 in the San Francisco Bay Area and Washington, DC, or about one third as much as in the higher-income metropolitan regions. From the 1960s until as recently as the 1980s, population, employment, and incomes grew faster in suburbs and nonmetropolitan areas than in central cities in general and large metropolitan areas in particular, as the dominant industries of the mid-twentieth century matured and de-agglomerated. The income levels of U.S. states converged from 1880 to 1980, during which time the richest state (Connecticut) went from being 4.5 times richer than the poorest (Arkansas) to just 1.76 times. In the new millennium, the coefficients of variation of both gross domestic product (GDP) per capita and total GDP between U.S. states have increased steeply. (Drennan & Lobo, 1999; Ganong & Shoag, 2012; Moretti, 2012; Yamamoto, 2008). Researchers now speak of a new *great inversion* and a *new geography of jobs* within countries, as shown in Figure 10.1 (Moretti, 2012). What will be the geography of this next wave of innovation and its effects on population and incomes? At the present time, the genetics and molecular biology revolutions are generating biotechnology industries, artificial intelligence industries, robotics industries, and many other sectors whose contours are yet to be fully defined, but which surely will create powerful winner regions.

Most urban and regional development theory concentrates on the broad structural determinants of the pattern of economic development, and to some extent, the dynamics of resilience or failure. It identifies the characteristics of broad categories of places, such as *high skill cities, manufacturing cities, high income regions,* and *low income regions,* as well as the overall geographical pattern defined by each major wave of innovation and economic growth, something like the structural clubs of different kinds of places in each phase.

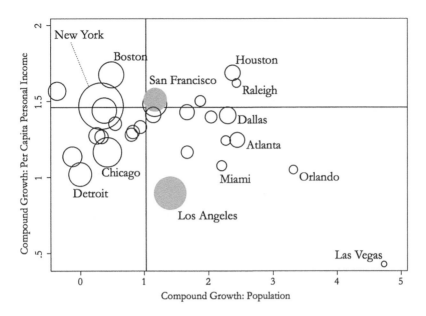

Fig. 10.1 Population and per capita income, compound annual growth rates, 1970–2012, 30 largest Combined Statistical Areas in 2012. Solid horizontal and vertical rules represent average growth rates for population and income among all Combined Statistical Areas. Points are scaled according to population in 2012. From Storper, Kemeny, Makarem, & Osman (2015, p. 11). Reprinted with permission. © 2015 by the Board of Trustees of the Ireland Stanford J University. All rights reserved. By permission of the publisher, sup.org. No reproduction or distribution is permitted without prior publisher's permission

But theory and research say little about why specific places join certain clubs or fall out of them. The overall divergence in development that occurs with major waves of innovation is complemented by individual turbulence in regional performance. In the United States, Detroit was the sixth richest metropolitan region in 1970; it is now 52nd on the list of all U.S. metro regions with more than two million population, and joins Cleveland as a case of declining income rank with population loss, as shown in Table 10.1. Seattle, Minneapolis, Washington, DC, San Francisco, and Houston have combined population growth and improvement in their income rank. Orlando, Miami, and Phoenix have had great population growth without moving up the ranks of per capita incomes. Among older metropolitan regions, Boston is now one of the top five American metropolitan regions in income, but it was not even in the top 10 in 1970. New York is a case of income resurgence with moderate population growth.

The city-regions that have been successful in some combination of maintaining high relative per capita incomes and retaining or growing population have done so through transitions in their economic base. A successful transition is a dynamic of the local economic base that involves keeping, creating, or attracting activities that

Table 10.1 U.S. combined statistical areas with population above two million, ranked according to per capita personal income levels

| | Income rank | | | Population change |
Combined Statistical Area	1970	1990	2010	(%) 1970–2010
San Jose–San Francisco–Oakland, CA	**1**	**2**	**1**	56.5
New York–Newark–Bridgeport, NY–NJ–CT–PA	2	1	2	12.4
Chicago–Naperville–Michigan City, IL–IN–WI	3	6	11	19.7
Los Angeles–Long Beach–Riverside, CA	**4**	**10**	**25**	79.1
Washington–Baltimore–N. Virginia, DC–MD–VA–WV	5	3	3	60.3
Detroit–Warren–Flint, MI	6	12	52	−0.5
Minneapolis–St. Paul–St. Cloud, MN–WI	7	7	9	60.8
Seattle–Tacoma–Olympia, WA	8	9	6	99.1
Cleveland–Akron–Elyria, OH	9	13	36	−7.0
Philadelphia–Camden–Vineland, PA–NJ–DE–MD	10	8	10	13.8

Note. Calculations by Thomas Kemeny from U.S. Bureau of Economic Analysis Regional Economic Accounts data

are innovative and entrepreneurial and have high profit margins, skills, and wages (Feldman, 2014; Feldman & Lowe, 2011). By contrast, the city-regions that fall down the ladder of incomes, sometimes in combination with population stagnation or loss, are those whose economic base has not been successful in capturing the innovative industries of the period.

Turbulence opens up a major puzzle for the geography of innovation. The factors that distinguish the pathways of supposedly structurally similar regions are usually relegated to the sidelines of research, as *effects of history*, *shocks*, or *accidents*. In this paper, I shall address this question by comparing the economic transitions of two regions in detail. In 1970, the Greater Los Angeles and San Francisco Bay Area metropolitan regions—defined here as their respective Combined Statistical Areas (CSA)—had very similar levels of per capita income, ranking fourth and first respectively among large U.S. metropolitan regions. By 2010, they had almost a one-third difference in per capita income and Los Angeles had slipped to 25th place. This contrast in fates is perplexing, because Los Angeles and San Francisco belonged to the same high-income, high-tech club in 1970; they faced the new economy from similar structural starting points. Via a detailed comparative analysis of how these two regions faced the new economy, I advance an explanation of why some regions succeed in major innovation transitions—by which I mean major transformations of the economic base of a region that occur through the shaping or uptake of major waves of innovations—and others largely fail at such transitions.

A Brief Introduction to Los Angeles and San Francisco

By any standard, the Los Angeles and San Francisco metropolitan regions are large, wealthy, and dynamic. Los Angeles, in this context, means the Greater Los Angeles CSA, which had 18.679 million residents in 2015, making it the second most populous metropolitan area in the United States, with a 4.48% population increase from 2010 to 2015. Los Angeles is one of the largest economies in the world, with a nominal gross metropolitan product that would rank it as the world's 16th largest economy, after Mexico (112 million inhabitants) and above Indonesia (220 million). Meanwhile, the San Francisco Bay Area CSA had a 2015 population of 8.713 million, growing 6.87% since 2010. It would be the 22nd largest economy, just after Argentina (35 million) and before Sweden. Depending on the method of calculation employed, the overall size (regional gross output) of the economy of Greater Los Angeles is third or fourth among metropolitan regions in the world, while that of the San Francisco Bay Area is about ninth. In terms of per capita income, San Francisco is consistently in the top five metro areas in the world in per capita income. In that latter group, Los Angeles ranks about 20th. However, from a national perspective, Los Angeles is on the verge of falling out of the highest income group of big metropolitan regions, while San Francisco remains among the leaders. As Figure 10.2

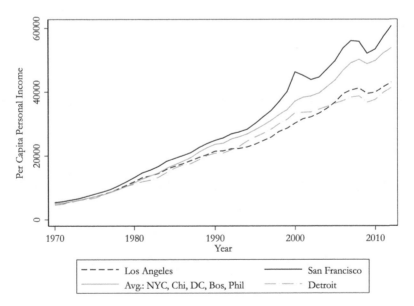

Fig. 10.2 The evolution of per capita personal income in large metropolitan areas, 1970–2012. CSA definitions are used, with boundaries laid out by the U.S. Office of Management and Budget (2013). CSAs represented in this chart comprise the list of regions that had populations over five million people in 1970. From Storper et al. (2015 p. 7). Copyright 2015 by Stanford University Press. Reprinted with permission. © 2015 by the Board of Trustees of the Ireland Stanford J University. All rights reserved. By permission of the publisher, sup.org. No reproduction or distribution is permitted without prior publisher's permission

illustrates, in 1970 per capita personal income in Los Angeles was 6% less than that of San Francisco. By 2012, the gap was almost 30%.

The stakes of this turbulence are very big. For example, though by world standards these are still wealthy regions, their divergent income levels have widened the gap in their public spending capacities. In their Californian context, each region's public agencies have tax receipts that are capped at about 7% of regional GDP.[1] At this identical rate, the Bay Area now collects and spends $25,000 per regional resident, while Greater Los Angeles can only raise $18,500 per resident. Economic divergence thus can give rise to circular and cumulative gaps in regional public investment capacity, with important potential impacts on quality of life and the capacity to invest in measures that may reinforce differential long-term economic performance. This unfavorable comparison is not only due to the Bay Area's excellent economic performance. A number of major American metropolises successfully navigated the transition to the new economy, as shown in Figure 10.2.

This comparison is particularly interesting because Los Angeles would have seemed to be an ideal candidate to lead the innovation transition to the new economy. From 1910 to 1970, metropolitan Southern California multiplied its population 21-fold, climbing the income ranks of American metro regions to become not only very big, but very prosperous as well. It did so through a several-decades-long leadership in innovative entrepreneurship. Southern California became home to many household names in manufacturing, technology and entrepreneurship, coupled with additional innovations in infrastructure, lifestyles, and consumption. From 1900 to the 1970s, Southern California combined quantitative and qualitative growth successfully in a way perhaps not equaled by any other metropolitan area in the western world.

Changes in Specialization: The Key Determinant of Income Levels

The proximate cause of divergence and turbulence is to be found in changes in specialization, reflecting different levels of creating or absorbing innovative activities. The Bay Area became the world center of the IT industry, generating Silicon Valley (which did not exist as such in 1970) (Table 10.2). The Bay Area then enjoyed the growth of IT-related corporate headquarters and has recently become a significant hub of cutting-edge sectors such as biotechnology, mobile device applications, cloud computing, and artificial intelligence. In contrast, Los Angeles experienced dramatic downsizing of its mass manufacturing and high-tech aerospace and defense sectors and replaced them with lower-wage sectors, such as light manufacturing and international trade and logistics. Los Angeles's concentration of corporate headquarters declined and the region currently seems to be losing out in biotechnology. In other words, San Francisco had a successful regional innovation transition in its

---

[1] In other words, prior to their residents' tax contributions to state and federal governments.

Table 10.2 Tradable industry groups in 1970 and 2010

	Employees	Employment Share (%)	Employees	Employment Share (%)
	Los Angeles		San Francisco	
Tradable Industry Group	1970		1970	
Information Technology	81,872	2.6	38,621	2.70
Aerospace and Defense	108,083	3.4	455	0.03
Logistics	39,851	1.3	21,313	1.50
Entertainment	22,978	0.7	2,171	0.15
Apparel	56,965	1.8	7,806	0.06
	2010		2010	
Information Technology	153,524	2.7	255,334	10.20
Aerospace and Defense	47,960	0.9	735	0.02
Logistics	129,651	2.3	23,505	0.90
Entertainment	141,025	2.5	14,686	0.50
Apparel	50,788	0.9	819	0.03

Note. Calculations are based on collections of four-digit Standard Industrial Classification (SIC) codes (1970) and six-digit North American Industry Classification System (NAICS) codes (2010) using County Business Patterns. Adapted from Storper et al. (2015, p. 36)

specialized, tradable-industry activity base, while Los Angeles was much less successful in building the innovative industries of the post-1970 period.

The reason I focus on tradable industries is that they are the motor force in a region's economic development. The size of tradable industries in a region is not limited by local population levels or incomes, because a great deal of their output is traded. Moreover, spatial concentration in these industries, made possible by their tradability, can generate productivity gains and also enhance ongoing innovation, hence affirming and prolonging regional advantage. In contrast, nontradables, even though responsible for the majority of any economy's employment, are largely proportionate to population and local budget constraints and do not serve as a primary motor force in development.

Table 10.3 shows a more detailed breakdown of tradable specializations of the two regions, using subsectoral categories. In San Francisco the IT group of sectors increases its role; whereas in 1970 IT had roughly the same share of employment in the two regions, by 2010 its share is four times greater in the Bay Area than in Greater Los Angeles. The high-wage clusters in Los Angeles account for only 6% of total employment, against nearly 11% for IT in the Bay Area. Notice also that Los Angeles's specialized core accounts for a decreasing share of total employment, whereas San Francisco's increases. This gives a picture of the Southern California economy as becoming fuzzier over time (with a lower level of overall tradable specializations) while the Bay Area economy becomes more sharply focused.

Moreover, the Bay Area becomes relatively better specialized than Los Angeles. To see this requires considerable disaggregation. The more aggregated the categories, the more likely is serious unobserved heterogeneity and error in the comparison. For example, a comparison of three-digit sectors that suggests similarity of two

Table 10.3 Specialization: The ten largest tradable industries by employment, 1970 (SIC) and 2010 (NAICS)

Tradable Industry	Employment Share	Tradable Industry	Employment Share
		1970 (four-digit SIC)	
Los Angeles		San Francisco	
Aircraft	2.7%	Trucking, except local	1.5%
Trucking, except local	1.2%	Semiconductors	0.9%
Electronic components NEC	0.8%	Business consulting services	0.9%
Communication transmitting equipment	0.8%	Wholesalers NEC	0.7%
Business consulting services	0.8%	Electronic components NEC	0.7%
Aircraft equipment	0.8%	Electronic computing equipment	0.6%
Wholesalers NEC	0.7%	Truck equipment	0.6%
Electronic computing equipment	0.7%	Communication transmitting equipment	0.5%
Truck equipment	0.6%	Commercial machines and equipment	0.5%
Motion picture production, except television	0.5%	Electric measuring instruments	0.5%
Total	9.6%		7.3%
		2010 (six-digit NAICS)	
Los Angeles		San Francisco	
Motion picture and video production	1.4%	Software publishers	1.9%
Hotels and motels	1.4%	Custom computer programming services	1.8%
General warehousing and storage	0.6%	Electronic parts & equipment wholesalers	1.7%
Computer systems design services	0.5%	Computer system design services	1.6%
Custom computer programming services	0.4%	Hotels and motels	1.5%
Freight transportation arrangement	0.4%	Research and development in physical, engineering, and life sciences (not biotechnology)	1.5%
Women's clothing wholesalers	0.4%	Computer and peripheral wholesalers	0.9%
Women's, girls', and infants' cut and sew apparel contractors	0.4%	Data processing, hosting, and related services	0.6%
Other aircraft parts and auxiliary equipment	0.3%	Semiconductor and related device manufacturing	0.5%
Electronic parts & equipment wholesalers	0.3%	Wineries	0.4%
Total	6.1%		12.4%

Note. 1970 and 2010 data are imperfectly comparable due to the switch from four-digit SIC codes to six-digit NAICS codes in 1997. NEC = not elsewhere classified. Adapted from Storper et al. (2015, p. 36)

Table 10.4 Average wages in ten tradable sectors with highest employment, 2010

Tradable Sector	Wages ($)	Tradable Sector	Wages ($)
Greater Los Angeles		San Francisco Bay Area	
Motion picture and video production	69,016	Software publishers	169,432
Hotels and motels	*26,217*	*Custom computer programming services*	*111,648*
General warehousing and storage	40,878	*Electronic parts and equipment wholesalers*	*139,661*
Computer systems design services	*90,874*	*Computer systems design services*	*111,312*
Women's clothing wholesalers	50,931	*Hotels and motels*	*30,260*
Custom computer programming services	*89,295*	R&D in physical, engineering, and life sciences (not biotechnology)	133,834
Freight transportation arrangement	50,684	Computer and peripheral wholesalers	155,961
Women's, girls', and infants' cut and sew apparel contractors	18,548	Data processing, hosting, and related services	120,464
Other aircraft parts and auxiliary equipment	65,685	Semiconductor and related device manufacturing	131,059
Electronic parts and equipment wholesalers	*77,947*	Wineries	54,954

Note. Sectors featured in both regions are italicized. Wages are in nominal 2010 dollars. Adapted from Storper et al. (2015, p. 39)

regions—say in information technology—could mask underlying dissimilarity in the four-digit components of those three-digit sectors, with the regions carrying out different kinds of work and, most importantly, with different wage levels, growth prospects, and innovation trajectories. In the above comparisons, I disaggregated as much as possible in order to avoid such unobserved heterogeneity.

Table 10.4 sheds further light on this issue by using wage data, showing that wages differ across the two regions within the same broad industry groups. This suggests that the specializations of the two regions are even more different than implied in Table 10.3. Table 10.5 supports this interpretation by displaying wage heterogeneity within the very detailed six-digit components of the IT sector, thus showing that wage differences are not due to unobserved differences within sectors.

Still another way to examine differences in the quality of economic specializations is to compare the content of work in them, which is a proxy for embodied skill levels. According to Autor, Levy, and Murnane (2003), the higher the level of nonroutine and cognitive work carried out by an economy, the higher its skill levels and innovation content. Table 10.6 shows that the average level of nonroutineness of the work carried out in the two regions was nearly identical in 1970. Subsequently a wide gap opened up, with the Bay Area having much more nonroutine and cognitive work in its economy by 2008 than Los Angeles, with the latter city falling behind the national average and the Bay Area surging above it. Moreover, Los Angeles's level of nonroutineness is lower than one would expect if its economy were to have

Table 10.5 Average wages in information technology sectors, 2010

Sector	Average Wages ($)	
	Greater Los Angeles	San Francisco Bay Area
Overall IT Agglomeration		
Information Technology Agglomeration (43 six-digit sectors)	86,169	128,216
Selected six-Digit Sectors		
Software Publishers (511210)	128,583	169,432
Custom Computer Programming Services (541511)	89,295	111,648
Computer System Design Services (541512)	90,874	111,312
Computer Equipment and Software Merchant Wholesalers (423430)	80,416	155,961

Note. Wages are averages expressed in nominal 2010 dollars. Adapted from Storper et al. (2015, p. 91)

Table 10.6 Aggregate regional nonroutine cognitive task indices

Region	1970	1980	1990	2000	2006−2008
Los Angeles	2.58	2.54	2.78	2.88	2.82
San Francisco	2.61	2.68	3.11	3.57	3.47
United States	2.40	2.41	2.75	2.99	2.95

Note. In each case, person-level sample weights are used to estimate task means. Higher values of non-routineness indicate that the occupational mix in a region is tilted toward jobs that require greater non-routine interaction and analytics, here taken as a proxy for sophistication. Each outcome reported here had an acceptably small linearized standard error. The calculations are based on the Integrated Public Use Microdata Series (IPUMS) 1% 1970 metro sample; the 5% 1980, 1990, and 2000 samples; and the 3% American Community Survey sample for 2006–2008. Adapted from Storper et al. (2015, p. 45)

had the average national level of nonroutineness for each of its sectors, while San Francisco's levels are higher than expected. Further corroborating this point, in 1970 Los Angeles had patents per capita equaling about 90% of those in the Bay Area; by 2010, they were only 16% (Storper et al., 2015, p. 183).

All in all, then, a clear picture emerges of sharply divergent specialization in terms of wages, the drivers of income differences, which are underpinned by differences in tasks and skills in a way that strongly suggests divergent innovative content of the regions' economic bases.

The Causes of Divergent Specialization: Standard Explanations from Urban Economics

Mainstream theories offer a number of ways they attempt to account for regional economic transitions: the education and skills of the workforce; the role of immigration in changing the skills base; the effect of housing costs and cost of living on

Table 10.7 Wages by educational attainment for workers active in the labor market

	Wages ($)				
Educational Attainment	1970	1980	1990	2000	2005–2010
Los Angeles, college graduates	11,705	20,408	40,317	54,115	68,730
San Francisco, college graduates	11,127	19,981	41,397	69,807	90,102
Los Angeles, some college	7,631	14,128	25,690	31,959	37,936
San Francisco, some college	7,432	14,057	26,027	38,354	43,608
Los Angeles, high school graduates	6,789	12,319	20,557	24,601	29,727
San Francisco, high school graduates	7,059	12,886	21,191	28,631	32,830
Los Angeles, some high school	5,762	9,782	14,177	16,050	19,690
San Francisco, some high school	6,041	9,328	14,447	15,402	19,452

Note. Calculations made using IPUMS data. College graduates are defined as workers with at least four years of college. Adapted from Storper et al. (2015, p. 55)

selecting for the skills base (i.e., the composition of the workforce). Most of the emphasis in the mainstream models is hence about labor supply (Glaeser & Maré, 2001). In these models, workers with different skills sort themselves into different regions. Highly skilled workers cluster together because they want to interact with one another. Regions with highly regulated housing markets will exclude low-skill workers and drive them to regions with lower cost housing. Jobs are said to follow people, hence shaping differences in specialization, with selective migration according to skills playing a central role (Glaeser, 2008). Even though innovation per se is backgrounded in this reasoning, there is nonetheless a strong implicit view that it (like all other changes in regional economic specialization) is driven by changes in labor supply.

In this immigration-supply model, average regional wage differences must be accounted for by the proportions of differently skilled groups, not by interregional differences in wages to each group by skill, since the models explicitly assume that migration equalizes the latter (i.e., migration enhances composition differences but equalizes skill-wages). Yet Table 10.7 demonstrates that wage gaps between San Francisco and Los Angeles for people with similar education increased steadily over the period. By 2005–2010, Bay Area workers at every skill level all earned about one-third more than their Los Angeles counterparts. Average regional wage differences are therefore not entirely due to the composition of each labor force in terms of educational endowments, but instead because people at all educational levels appear to have higher quality work on average in San Francisco than in Los Angeles.

The quantity of low-skill immigration to Greater Los Angeles was greater than that going to San Francisco, even though both currently have the same overall proportion of foreign born (38%). For these differences in migrant skills to be considered a cause of gaps in average regional wages (and by extension, to have driven specialization), the wage gaps would have to be—once again—proportional to the roles of different migrant groups rather than due to differences in the rewards each group receives across the two regions. As Table 10.8 shows, every group of immigrants in the Bay Area earns on average more than that group does in Los Angeles. In other words, considerable differences in average regional wages would exist even

Table 10.8 Wages of immigrant workers by education attainment

Educational Attainment	Wages ($)				
	1970	1980	1990	2000	2005–2010
Los Angeles, college graduates	10,153	17,981	33,503	45,561	61,171
San Francisco, college graduates	9,313	17,773	37,081	64,433	87,026
Los Angeles, some college	7,114	12,441	21,695	28,105	35,477
San Francisco, some college	6,913	12,807	23,107	33,890	41,289
Los Angeles, high school graduates	6,233	10,904	16,396	21,649	27,319
San Francisco, high school graduates	6,393	11,351	17,726	24,853	30,238
Los Angeles, some high school	5,908	87,130	12,853	17,650	22,079
San Francisco, some high school	6,029	95,840	14,343	19,198	23,850

Note. Calculations made using IPUMS data. College graduates are defined as workers with at least four years of college. Adapted from Storper et al. (2015, p. 67)

if the regional labor forces were composed of identical proportions of workers from each national origin and skill group.

Both regions have long-term and extensive Asian and Latin American communities with deep social networks that predate the current period and each experienced major upticks in migration by the two groups during this period, although these migrations differed from earlier waves (Myers, Goldberg, Mawhorter, & Min, 2010). In the new migration, Asians with generally higher skills were drawn to the Bay Area in greater proportion because they were better adapted to the demands of growing industries there. Mexicans were probably disproportionately drawn to Southern California instead of the Bay Area because they largely lacked the skills required by the Bay Area's burgeoning new economy sectors, or perhaps because those who did migrate to the Bay Area acquired these skills in the better jobs they found there. Along these lines, other American metropolitan areas with a great deal of Latin American immigration, such as New York and Houston, likely performed much better in income growth than Los Angeles because the structure of demand in those cities offered higher quality jobs, greater on-the-job learning, or better career ladders to Latin Americans.

Mainstream theories also emphasize aggregate changes in labor supply, with higher-wage regions having more housing regulation (supply restriction) than lower-wage regions. But Los Angeles and San Francisco had roughly the same level of residential housing supply expansion and similar levels of housing and land development regulation, allowing them both to have high levels of population growth.[2]

In the period under examination, there was obviously a self-reinforcing cycle of changes in labor supply and labor demand. But the evidence shown in this section demonstrates that differences in labor supply did not independently drive the wage and income changes that are the observable economic effects of divergence in spe-

---

[2] For a detailed analysis of the role of housing regulation and supply expansion, see Storper et al. (2015, pp. 59–65).

cialization. The different labor supply changes observed, in other words, can be considered more as outcomes of Bay Area success in high-end, new economy industries and Los Angeles's weakness, than as causes thereof.

Innovation as a Lottery: Accidents, Size, and Background

The *new economic geography* (NEG) stresses the importance of agglomeration in innovative industries, but it has no single model of why—during major innovative transitions—such agglomerations will locate in specific places. Three such explanations have emerged from the interface between NEG and innovation studies: accidents; size and lock-in; and technological relatedness.

Development as a Lottery: Accidents and Shocks

One possibility is that the geography of breakthrough agglomerations is due to random shocks. In this account, the Bay Area was simply lucky to get Silicon Valley, just as Los Angeles was lucky to get aerospace and Hollywood in the early 20th century. Key versions of the accident or lottery theory center on either unusual individuals or anchor firms. Thus, in some accounts, Silicon Valley is where it is because William Shockley—the inventor of the silicon-based semiconductor—decided in 1956 to relocate from New Jersey to be near his aging mother in Menlo Park, California. Another anecdote concerning Shockley is that after he attracted the best associates to his first-mover firm, his difficult management style and abrasive personality caused them all to quit on the same day (known as *Shockley's massacre*), thus launching the Silicon Valley process of development through spinoff. There are also more hagiographic versions of "great person" stories. One such trope refers to Steve Jobs's unique marriage of functionality and aesthetics when he invented the Macintosh operating system graphic interface. Many other such great person stories can be found in the annals of innovation. But so many prominent names are associated with Silicon Valley—from Shockley and Terman to Hewlett and Packard and Jobs and Gates and Brin and Page and Thiel—that it seems unlikely that all could be there due to coincidence. Moreover, Saxenian (1994) powerfully argued that mere presence of early innovators is not enough. Plenty were located in Boston, but they did not survive. Zuckerberg left Boston for Silicon Valley because Boston was not the right place to transform a breakthrough invention into a full-fledged innovation, just as happened in New Jersey decades earlier, when Shockley left for the Bay Area.

Another idiosyncratic influence on agglomeration might be decisions by key firms at key moments. Motorola located the largest early semiconductor facility in the world in Phoenix in the 1950s, for example, but this did not establish Phoenix as a subsequent center of the IT industry (Scott & Storper, 1987). Motorola made the mistake of believing that it could be a geographically isolated first-mover in a technologically innovative industry. It turned out that only those firms—such as Fairchild and Hewlett-Packard—that were first-movers but did not isolate themselves from the emerging open source networks of Silicon Valley were able to keep up with the rapidly rising technology curve.

Negative random shocks also figure prominently in explanations of sharp turning points in regional fortunes. At the end of the Cold War, the Department of Defense reduced investments in the aerospace sector, which was highly concentrated in Southern California, and congressional pressure led much remaining procurement to be awarded to other regions (Markusen, Hall, Campbell, & Deitrick, 1991). But the direct and indirect employment losses attributable to the "build-down" of aerospace in the 1990s in Southern California account for less than 3% of the approximate 30% difference in regional per capita incomes (Storper et al., 2015). The Bay Area suffered a substantial negative employment and investment shock in 2000 with the crash of the *dot.com* boom but then fully recovered and went on to further expansion. Many other regions have overcome negative shocks by creating and capturing new waves of innovation. Boston had very bad luck from the 1950s onward in its mill-based industries and was as a result not even among the top ten metro regions ranked by income in 1970 (Table 10.1). However, the city bounced back by building up new economy sectors. New York deindustrialized from the 1960s through the 1970s, but recovered by reinvigorating its finance sector, and went on to a strong presence in the design of applications, life-sciences, and new media. Seattle transitioned from an old mechanical engineering and resource-based economy to a center of high technology. Negative shocks are indeed important to regional economies, but research needs to identify more precisely what distinguishes those regions that transition effectively from those that do not.

The theories about the ability to respond to negative shocks or to transition from one positive response to opportunity to another take up the roles of size, diversification of the economy in question, and the preexisting technology base of regions. I now consider them.

The Size of Agglomerations

The NEG models a snowball process of how regions progressively draw in supplier firms, human talent, and knowledge. Formally, regional agglomerations have economies of scale, driving a wedge between the leading region's productivity and innovation levels and those of the other regions that host the industry. Once this happens, the leading industry's position is said to be locked in (Krugman, 1991; Rosenthal & Strange, 2001; Thisse, 2010). If the comparable size of agglomeration in a closely related technology sector were sufficient to lock in positions from one period of development to the next, then Los Angeles was surely in a better position to capture the semiconductor-driven IT industry than the Bay Area (Tables 10.2 and 10.3). Indeed, Los Angeles County firms constituted the biggest cluster of semiconductor producers as late as 1970, and at that time their semiconductors were the most technologically advanced. Greater size alone failed to help the Los Angeles IT sector transition from its high-quality, expensive chips to mass produced, cheaper ones and their commercial applications.

Moreover, advantages from size are always partial and are ultimately challenged by product standardization and declining trade costs (allowing de-agglomeration). Silicon Valley's cluster has had this kind of ongoing job loss since the 1970s (Saxenian, 1994). In the face of this, as each previous innovation wave has matured, the Bay Area has created the next wave—from chips to personal computers, to servers and network-ware, to the Internet, to mobile broadband hardware and applications—so that reference is now made to *Silicon Valley 7.0* (Lécuyer, 2006). Scale in one area does not lead straightforwardly to mastering the next wave of innovation.

Technological Relatedness and Subsequent Specialization

Another common extension of NEG models to regional economic dynamics is the notion that previous technological endowments have a strong role in shaping subsequent capture or creation of innovation. In the comparison at hand, both regions were home to close technological antecedents of the IT industry. Most detailed historical analyses of the rise of Silicon Valley demonstrate that it grew from the preexisting communications equipment sector in the Bay Area (Lécuyer, 2006). As Table 10.3 shows, that sector was just as big in proportional terms in Los Angeles in 1970 as its Bay Area counterpart and thus much bigger in absolute terms. The overall IT sector in the two regions accounted for identical shares of their core employment in 1970. And if aerospace and IT are considered together—two key technology sectors united through the demand for communications technology for guiding missiles and satellites—then a priori, the technological antecedents for the IT revolution were much bigger in Southern than in Northern California.

There are many other examples of regions that capture major new sectors with little *technological* relatedness to their preexisting activities. Los Angeles was not a major mechanical engineering region in the 1920s and 1930s, when it became the aircraft engineering center of the United States and, by the 1940s, the world's biggest aerospace cluster. Los Angeles had no previous background in the entertainment industry when the movie studios were established there around 1915. Detroit had fewer antecedents in mechanical equipment than Illinois in the 1890s, but rapidly became the center of U.S. car technology and manufacture. In these, and many other examples, there were technological *windows of locational opportunity*. These ruptures in technological relatedness largely obviate the advantages of preexisting agglomeration economies and create a relatively flat playing field for a short time in the early days of a technology's existence (Scott & Storper, 1987).

Additional arguments about antecedents can now be considered. One such argument is that more diversified economies have a greater probability of successful transitions than narrowly specialized ones. This idea, often attributed to Jane Jacobs

(1969), holds that evolution is a probabilistic process, so having more irons in the fire will likely enable more recombination into future success. Theoretical models of *nursery cities* draw on that notion (Duranton & Puga, 2001). However, in spite of the existence of this notion for many decades, no significant empirical backing for it has been generated. In the case of Los Angeles and San Francisco, the former city was the bigger and more diversified economy in 1970, yet its innovation transition was less successful. I show that diversity per se is not an inherent advantage in the innovation transition but rather—when it does exist—requires connection through relational infrastructure to make it advantageous.

The literature also abounds with stories of narrowly specialized economies that are locked into their technologies and do not transition after negative demand shocks or technology shifts. Thus, Detroit is held up as a case of overspecialization. And yet there are highly specialized centers of mechanical engineering and automotive technology that have mastered subsequent waves of technology, such as Stuttgart. Boston was once narrowly specialized in mill-based industries, as was Seattle in forest products and mechanical engineering, but both are high-tech centers today.

Benjamin Chinitz (1961) made a more subtle argument about the qualities of antecedents. He reasoned that dominant industries tend to monopolize talent, factor supplies, and attention, potentially crowding out other activities, and are hence able to channel the evolution of regional economies down distinctive pathways. New York's antecedents were said by him to be more favorable than those of Pittsburgh. Evolutionary economic geographers give this notion a specific contour, holding that antecedent technologies matter, such that the capacity for regional economic evolution is governed by possibilities for moving into cognate technologies, which they dub *related variety* (Frenken, van Oort & Verburg, 2007). Based on the evidence at hand, such relatedness would clearly have favored Los Angeles and yet San Francisco got ahead.

A somewhat different version of the evolution argument combines technological and organizational antecedents. Saxenian's (1994) seminal comparison of Route 128 and Silicon Valley can be interpreted as showing that the types of entrepreneurship, production organization, and system coordination that existing firms and actors know in a region will shape what it becomes and what kinds of new activities it can generate and capture. Allen Scott, echoing Markusen et al. (1991) has recently argued that the failure of Los Angeles to move into the new economy occurred because the aerospace model of organization—the *genetic codes* of aerospace— weighed it down too much (Aoyama, Powell, Saxenian, & Scott, 2017). But the Bay Area's principal high-tech firms, such as Hewlett-Packard, had an organization almost identical to the aerospace firms in Los Angeles in the 1950s and 1960s; they were *systems houses* using Pentagon guidelines for concurrent engineering. In a parallel example, Seattle was dominated by the assembly lines of Boeing and by large-scale natural resource companies, but now is considered home to some of the most innovative companies in the new economy, who are revolutionizing many organizational practices.

This discussion leaves us with an unsolved mystery. Standard explanations for major regional innovation transitions, whether they are derived from mainstream urban and regional economics or the extensions of agglomeration economics into innovation studies, cannot account for the great variety of outcomes.

Relational Infrastructure Potentiates Breakthrough Entrepreneurship and New Organizational Practices

If none of the standard accounts fully explains the divergent economic trajectories of the two regions, then a remaining candidate is that there is significant difference in the institutions that shape major transitions of the regional economic base. Institutions are defined here in an expansive way as collective rules, routines, beliefs, or conventions that give regularity to individual behavior in a way that may take precedence over strict individual calculation or self-interest, or that may shape such behavior by generating expectations of payoffs or sanctions from coordination with others. Such institutions can be formal or informal, and can be encapsulated within organizations or in a wider societal environment.

An institutional framework for explaining innovation emerged in the 1990s, when Lundvall and Johnson developed the concept of the National Innovation System, a complex armature of organizations and rules that shapes the *know-how, know-who, and know-what* of an economy (Lundvall, 2007). The notion was subsequently scaled to the region. Iammarino (2005) defines a Regional System of Innovation (RSI) as "the *localised* network of actors and institutions in the public and private sectors whose activities and interactions generate, import, modify and diffuse new technologies *within and outside the region*" (p. 499, emphasis in original). Because institutions are means of providing regularity to behavior, they are always underpinned by networks of persons. Networks can range from small-scale and interpersonal to large-scale and anonymous. Networks are a key observable dimension of institutions, though institutions are not reducible to their networks.

In the comparison at hand, sharp differences in networks and, ultimately, the entire RSI, are indeed in evidence. I examine four such differences, all of which are institutional dimensions of the RSIs of Los Angeles and San Francisco. First, greater cross-network connections in the Bay Area allowed that region's entrepreneurs to invent new organizational practices (Powell & Sandholtz, 2012). Second, early on there were organizational sites for this mixing of networks and for sustaining the mix. Third, the Bay Area developed many informal networks (*invisible colleges*) of technologists, researchers, and entrepreneurs, making it easier to bring them together for new projects. Fourth, elite leadership networks were stronger in the Bay Area and more informed by new economy ideas than in Los Angeles. The joint effects of these four differences—what I call the overall *relational infrastructure* of the regions—is that the RSIs differed in structure, overall strength, and direction.[3]

---

[3] Lazega (2017) also uses the term *relational infrastructure*, with some overlap to my usage, but generally with a narrower meaning having to do with the membership of individuals in organizations or in interorganizational contexts.

Stated another way, there are four observable and measurable dimensions of the differences in the institutionalized RSIs of the two regions, and I use this term to summarize their joint and cumulative effects.

Cross-Network Connections

In the early days of Bay Area IT, there was more than one community that was strongly interested in new information technologies, and there were people who spanned different networks, whose roles as go-betweens enabled the mixing of sensibilities and knowledge (Turner, 2006). From the 1960s onward in the Bay Area there was an *appropriate technology* network of people whose origins lay outside of the Stanford engineering community or the defense-related one. Buckminster Fuller was the utopian alternative technology guru who invented the geodesic dome and proposed alternative technology futures for cities and modern life in general. He embodied the futuristic practicality that would later infuse the developers of personal computers (Foege, 2013). Though he came from the East Coast, his principal breakthroughs occurred while in residence at San Jose State University.

On the other hand, there were traditional engineering networks, organized around the defense-aerospace-communications sector and marquee names such as Hewlett, Packard, and Litton. These networks centered on both Berkeley and Stanford, but Stanford was critical because it contained the Stanford Research Institute, founded by Frederick Terman to link researchers to entrepreneurship (Lécuyer, 2006). Stanford also had the Stanford Artificial Intelligence Laboratory and the Augmented Human Intellect Research Center in the 1960s, both of whose founders—John McCarthy and Douglas Engelbart—and the students working in their labs, were deeply involved in the Bay Area counterculture and political activism (Markoff, 2005).

Critically, Fuller and others did not reject contact with the traditional engineering networks. In the 1960s, they were already creating a bridge between the Bay Area hippies and the tech enthusiasts, as shown by Theodore Roszak in his 1969 book, *The Making of a Counter Culture*. The key published forum for this meeting of counterculture and innovation culture was *The Whole Earth Catalog*. The *Catalog* was published by Stewart Brand, a Stanford-educated biologist, Buckminster Fuller acolyte, and leading Bay Area environmentalist, who also coined the term *personal computer* and the phrase "information wants to be free." As Foege (2013) noted: "Besides its listings touting primitive tools and sustainable farming methods, the compendium included entries on stereo systems, welding equipment, cameras and computers" (para. 6). Brand was a key figure in building the three-way relationship between tech, wealthy Bay Area elites, and the environmental movement, a third powerful network. He was close to David Brower, who had been the executive director of the Sierra Club and founder of Friends of the Earth and the Earth Island Institute. Brand and Ken Kesey (of *Magic Bus* fame) were the co-producers of the Trips Festival, a rock music gathering held in San Francisco with the world's first light show, involving the Bay Area artistic networks in the early technology movement. The proof of this network-spanning is that Steve Jobs cites the *Catalog* in his 2005 commencement address at Stanford as one of the major sources of inspiration for the Apple personal computer and its operating system, and for the overall aesthetic of the company (Jobs, 2005).

A new vision of technology was generated by this cross-network pollination. Bay Area environmentalist movements not only had a traditional elite focus on land conservation, but also had a utopian notion of using capitalism to make a better world through a rationalist and technological approach to better modern living. The difference between alternative technologists and mainstream engineers was not about the virtues of technological solutions to social problems, but more that the former had an innate preference for decentralization and small scale, and the latter for centralization and scale (Turner, 2006). The phenomenon is explicitly emphasized by such early industry leaders as Jaron Lanier, who wrote in 2013 that "it's hard to overstate how influential" (p. 205) the crossover between countercultural spirituality and tech culture was in the early days of Silicon Valley. This crossover took the specific organized form of the Global Business Network, a durable meeting place for environmentalists and technologists founded by, among others, Stewart Brand.

Important members of the San Francisco downtown finance and corporate elite were on the boards of directors of the major environmental organizations—drawn in especially through the leadership of David Brower. The result was a fourth important Bay Area node in the networks that interacted with the technology community. This mixture of straight-laced elite and bohemian experimentalism had boundary-spanners such as Brand and others moving between them.

The cross-network mixing had a geographical dimension. Hewlett and Packard started out in the 1930s, far outside the orbit of downtown San Francisco. In the 1960s, Bay Area elites were still based in San Francisco and focused on the traditional industrial base of the region. Silicon Valley was a *greenfield*, a fringe of the region, with little geographical or network integration with San Francisco. But that city's elites subsequently incorporated the growing Silicon Valley interests and generated strong and multi-layered exchanges between the old and the new industries, but especially between the likes of Hewlett, Packard, Jobs, the environmentalists, the downtown San Francisco corporate leadership, researchers, and the alternative technology movement (Lazarus, personal communication, 2009). This never happened in Southern California, where Los Angeles-based leadership networks actually became more cut off from Orange County's emerging tech networks, as I discuss below, and neither of them mixed with alternative technology communities nor with the super-charged entrepreneurial world of Hollywood.

Organized Sites of Cross-Network Contact

A key organized site of contact between these different networks was established in 1969, when Xerox founded the Palo Alto Research Center (PARC). Three networks came together there: the engineering-based corporate world, with its focus on military procurement; the conventional, academic engineering research community; and the Bay Area alternative technology circle. PARC's first employees were academics with no experience of corporate culture and little interest in it. In 1972, *Rolling Stone* (then headquartered in San Francisco) published an article about PARC, authored by Stewart Brand. In it, Brand described the employees of PARC as knowledge-fueled hippies with computing as a utopian project to create more freedom and creativity. PARC seems to have picked up on the atmosphere in the other aforementioned labs from earlier in the 1960s. In 2013, in an article in *The New Yorker,* Nathan Heller described the current wave of applications developers locating in San Francisco in analogous terms, as technology-fueled youth seeking freedom, creativity, and a non-conformist lifestyle, and cited other articles from the late 1960s that described the makeshift nature of San Francisco culture at that time in much the same terms. Paul Duguid, an early presence at PARC, confirmed the Center's key role as a bridge between networks and different ideas about how to push the commercial application of the new technologies. These commercial applications decisively transformed the vision of the defense-engineering crowd (Duguid, personal communication, 2009). It was crucial that the contacts between these networks, initially informal and casual, had a site where their contact would become sustained when it was fragile and given the imprimatur of legitimacy. PARC deepened relationships among key early actors that came from very different worlds.

None of this occurred in Southern California, where the much larger defense-engineering milieu had no such boundary-spanning networks to pull it out of its comfort zone and provide it with a new technological-commercial imaginary. The University of Southern California, UCLA, and the California Institute of Technology (Caltech) never developed the networks that would put research scientists closely in contact with engineers, much less the intermediate hippie-environmentalist network tissue that often brought them in contact in the Bay Area.

Informal Networks: Invisible Colleges

Invisible college networks of technologists who have worked together in one way or another are many times bigger and denser in the Bay Area than in Los Angeles. To take just one recent example, 55% of Bay Area life science researchers have worked together in a firm or research organization, compared to only 2% in Greater Los Angeles (Casper, 2009). In the Bay Area from the early 1970s to 2005, there were three times the patents of university researchers with a commercial assignee as in Los Angeles, or six times the density per capita (Casper, 2009; Kenney & Mowery, 2014). The percentage of patents issued to Bay Area firms or researchers that cite other Bay Area patent holders is almost four times as high as the percentage of patent holders in Los Angeles that cite patent holders in Los Angeles (Sonn & Storper, 2008).

These numbers are the result of a process in the Bay Area consisting of serial entrepreneurship and serial science-entrepreneurship interactions. The more people who established these networks, the more there were to draw on as new projects and ventures took place. Each round of this incipient system brought exponential increases in the size of the informal networks and ever larger pools of networked people to draw into new ventures. Borrowing the language of Feldman and Zoller (2012), the density of new economy *dealmakers* in the Bay Area—another network—is today many times that of Southern California, and highly disproportional to the differences in size of the two economies or their high-technology employment. As the former director of the Southern California Association of Governments put it:

> the Bay Area got ahead of the curve with respect to the notion of networking systems that allowed for further dissemination of ideas, inventions to innovations . . . the Bay Area began to see the need for networks and networks operating within networks sooner than we did here. (Pisano, personal communication, 2009)

Structure, Strength, and Content of Leadership Networks

Over the period under examination, Bay Area leadership groups became broader and more inclusive, while those in Greater Los Angeles weakened and became more fragmented. Moreover, elite leadership groups in the Bay Area early on endorsed a new economy view of the world and the Bay Area's role in it, while the standpoint favored in Los Angeles looked backward, viewing a previous era of mass production in their region as a desirable future to be relaunched.

Storper et al. (2015) measured the connections among members of boards of directors of the principal corporations in the two regions, and the contrast was striking, as can be seen in Figure 10.3. In the Bay Area, even when a control is carried out for the higher level of industrial specialization of the economy, there are more board interlocks, signifying a more networked elite.

But in addition, the elite in San Francisco gave itself a strong formal organization for sustaining networking, the Bay Area Council. Mark Pisano, longtime director of the Southern California Association of Governments, contrasted the leading business network in Southern California, the Los Angeles Chamber of Commerce, to the leading San Francisco network, the Bay Area Council:

> When I first came here I went to the Los Angeles Chamber, which at that point in time was a five county chamber and said let's have a public and private coordination and the Los Angeles chamber said, "We don't need the public sector and we really don't want to venture with you." You had a different attitude between the Bay Area Council, which existed at that time and their regional organizations . . . And I think to this date we still don't have the [equivalent of the] Bay Area Council down here. (Pisano, personal communication, 2009)

Max Neiman, the Associate Director and Senior Fellow at the Public Policy Institute of California, echoed this view:

> So, there is a cohesiveness up here politically and institutionally that doesn't exist in Southern California. Southern California is much more decentralized politically. You don't have anything really like the Bay Area Council in Southern California. (Neiman, personal communication, 2009).

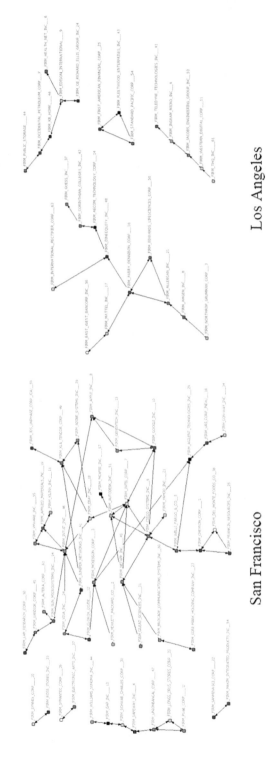

San Francisco

Los Angeles

Fig. 10.3 Board Interlocks in the San Francisco Bay Area and Greater Los Angeles, 2010. From Storper et al. (2015, pp. 173–174). Copyright 2015 by Stanford University Press. Adapted with permission. © 2015 by the Board of Trustees of the Ireland Stanford J University. All rights reserved. By permission of the publisher, sup.org. No reproduction or distribution is permitted without prior publisher's permission

Jim Lazarus of the Bay Area Council saw it this way:

> The Bay Area Council calls us all together, so that we can say, okay, we want these projects in the Bay Area or in Northern California, and now we are going to lobby as one . . . (Lazarus, personal communication, 2009)

To investigate these impressions more systematically, Storper et al. (2015) measured what is known technically as the *nBetweenness centrality* of the Bay Area Council and the Los Angeles Chamber of Commerce in the networks of their respective regions. This statistic represents the degree to which an organization in a network lies on the shortest path between all pairs of firms in that network. If the nBetweeness score of a particular organization in a network is 15%, then this organization lies on 15% of the shortest paths between all pairs of organizations in that network. To make this more concrete, consider two Bay Area firms: Del Monte Foods and Genentech. If David West, the chief executive officer (in 2013) of Del Monte, wants to find a mutual acquaintance at Genentech, the shortest path through the network of board interlocks is as follows: Del Monte Foods ➔ Bay Area Council ➔ San Francisco Chamber of Commerce ➔ The Christensen Fund ➔ Genentech. Hence, the Bay Area Council represents a link on the shortest chain that connects these two firms, suggesting that its members are likely to be involved in connecting these two firms.

The Bay Area Council lies on 18% of all the shortest paths of overlapping board memberships between pairs of firms in the Bay Area network (Table 10.9). Meanwhile, the Los Angeles Chamber of Commerce lies on just 6% of the shortest paths. The Bay Area Council is the most central organization in either region. In addition, both the Silicon Valley Manufacturing Leadership Group and the San Francisco Chamber of Commerce are more central than any business leadership organization in Greater Los Angeles.

Not only were Bay Area networks stronger, broader, and more inclusive, but the content of the visions they articulated was different. Douglass North, in accepting the Nobel Prize in economics, affirmed that beliefs and attitudes matter in economic development, because they serve as a decentralized coordinating force under uncertainty (North, 1993). A content analysis of 30 years of reports of major business leadership groups and public agencies charged with economic development revealed that in the Bay Area, through its Bay Area Council Economic Institute, there had been a perceptible and consistent focus since the late 1970s on the Bay Area as a knowledge economy, whose comparative advantage in the world had shifted to high-skill, knowledge-based activity. In contrast, very little mention of Southern California as a knowledge economy can be found in the reports of its economic development council or chamber of commerce prior to 2010 (Storper et al., 2015). Indeed, Southern California's reports focus on going back to the past by driving costs and taxes lower with the goal of restoring mass manufacturing to the region. In other words, in the Bay Area, a forward-looking vision reigned, while in Greater Los Angeles an atavistic analysis dominated the discussions. And this latter vision corresponded to active support for light manufacturing and logistics in Southern California, both low-wage industries with virtually no technological learning. Thus,

Table 10.9 nBetweenness of regional business leadership organizations and business leaders

Region	Business Leadership Organization	nBetweeness (%)
Greater Los Angeles	Los Angeles Chamber of Commerce	5.9
	Los Angeles Economic Development Corporation	1.7
	Valley Industry & Commerce Association	0.6
	Orange County Business Council	0.0
	CALSTART	0.0
San Francisco Bay Area	Bay Area Council	18.0
	Silicon Valley Manufacturing Leadership Group	6.0
	San Francisco Chamber of Commerce	5.8
	Semiconductor Industry Association	5.0
	Joint Venture Silicon Valley (JVSV)	0.0

Adapted from Storper et al. (2015, p. 180)

the Bay Area and Los Angeles were pushed in different directions by the attitudes and beliefs popularized by their leadership groups, backed up by the different shape and overall strength of leadership networks in the two regions.

The Biotechnology Case: History Repeats Itself

Nothing exemplifies the difference in how the relational infrastructures of Greater Los Angeles and San Francisco documented previously shaped different responses to challenges and opportunities better than the pathways traveled by the two regions in the emerging biotechnology sector. The science of gene splicing emerged contemporaneously in the two regions. In 1976, Arthur Riggs and Keiichi Itakura were the first to demonstrate that strands of DNA could be synthesized; they achieved this at City of Hope medical research center in Southern California. At the same time, Stanley Cohen, at the University of California, San Francisco (UCSF), and Herbert Boyer, at Stanford, were carrying out the research that would lead to the Cohen-Boyer patents for recombinant DNA in 1980, 1984, and 1988. Moreover, each region developed a pioneering flagship firm: Amgen in Los Angeles, Genentech in San Francisco.

Both Genentech and Amgen were initially founded by venture capitalists, in concert with research scientists, respectively at UCSF and the University of California, Los Angeles. Genentech was founded in 1976 by UCSF biochemist Boyer, working with Robert Swanson, a young venture capitalist. The key feature of Genentech was that it encouraged its scientists to publish their findings in academic journals and kept these research scientists in strategic managerial positions and on the board of directors.

Amgen was the brainchild of a Silicon Valley venture capitalist, William Bowes, who wanted to create a biotech firm with an all-star scientific advisory board. Bowes asked a Stanford geneticist to assemble the board, but he declined, turning the task over to Winston Salser, a molecular biologist based at UCLA. The first break with Bay Area tradition occurred: Amgen was located in Thousand Oaks in order to be equidistant from UCLA, the University of California, Santa Barbara, and Caltech, effectively isolating it from all of them. Powell and Sandholtz (2012) note that:

> This geographical isolation is certainly one cause and consequence of Amgen's development as a sort of scientific island, manifest not only in its singular achievement of FIPCO (fully-integrated pharmaceutical company) status, but also in its aggressive (and on the whole, successful) legal battles to protect its core patents. (p. 411)

Within three years, the scientists were eliminated from management, following a successful initial public offering. Powell and Sandholtz (2012) call Amgen a "commerce dominated company" (p. 411) in contrast to the science-dominated major companies of the Bay Area.

> [Amgen's] . . . commerce model builds on an alternate framework, with management in the lead role and science brought on board, though more as a passenger than driver . . . important science was harnessed but an academic ethos was not adopted. Publishing was not encouraged; the scientific advisory boards provided a seal of approval but did not dictate or set business strategy. (Powell & Sandholtz, 2012, p. 420)

Genentech, meanwhile, actively encouraged its scientists to start up other firms and interact with the Bay Area high tech entrepreneurship environment, through revolving doors, feeding into the previously mentioned invisible colleges.

Thus, Amgen's managers took a conception of how to succeed that borrowed from the standard playbook of the old-economy corporate world that dominates in Greater Los Angeles. The paradoxical outcome of this is that although Los Angeles has a world-class biotechnology firm, one that was a first-mover, but that company has not become the seed for a major biotech cluster. The Genentech approach had much more favorable consequences for regional economic development in the Bay Area. From 1976–2005, four times more biotech firms were created in the Bay Area than in Los Angeles, more than twice the patents, more than ten times the venture capital funding, and more than 50 times the revenues from initial public offerings (Casper, 2009).

What is in the Air: Contrasting Regional Zeitgeists

Paul Duguid, one of the participants in Xerox Corporation's PARC in the 1970s, used the term *zeitgeist* to describe the Bay Area's *open source culture.* He stressed that the zeitgeist is not *technology specific,* by which he meant that it is general to the region (Duguid, personal communication, 2009). The juxtaposed examples of IT and biotech demonstrate that there is a broader regional context at work and not just technology- or industry-specific factors that govern regional industrial evolution.

Zeitgeist is a German term that translates as the *spirit of the age,* here meaning the spirit of the age in a certain region. Zeitgeist consists of the shared ideas and practices and ways of organizing things that take hold in economic environments. These shared ideas, beliefs, practices, and ways of doing are often not fully evident to the people who do them. The *Economist* (2015) magazine recently said, along these lines, that "Cambridge's genius is off-balance-sheet." These notions correspond to what the analytical philosopher David Lewis (1969) defined as "conventions,"[4] which are something like rules of thumb, and are similar to the beliefs as used by North (1990, 1993). Conventions shape economies by helping large and decentralized communities of actors to stay on the same page, underpinning the functioning of an organizational ecology.

The entertainment industry in Hollywood was the exception to Southern California's conservative zeitgeist. Beginning in the 1950s, Hollywood responded to the twin challenges of competing technology (television) and a U.S. Department of Justice anti-trust action that broke its monopolistic distribution networks (studio-owned movie theaters). In response, it became a project-based industry and by the 1970s was already pioneering flexible combinations of firms and knowledge and inputs from external networks (Storper & Christopherson, 1987). The giant firms (the studios) transformed themselves from mass production movie factories into investors, product developers, and marketers of films and their branded offshoots. They are very much like venture capital organizations today.

Yet Hollywood's transformation into a new organizational ecology did not transform the wider Los Angeles economy. There are many reasons for this. Part of it is that the language of art, dominant in Hollywood, has few natural connections to the language of engineering. This situation contrasts to Silicon Valley, which is based on engineering, and thus has been able to draw from and contribute to engineering communities in that region. But Los Angeles's problem is not uniquely one of technological unrelatedness between Hollywood and technology. Seattle has transitioned from mechanical engineering and forest products to an Internet-based economy and Boston from mill-based manufacturing to a research-and-development-based economy. Los Angeles's entertainment agglomeration has actually flourished, but there are virtually no networks to allow it to transfer its organizational skills to the region's engineering firms. Even when New Economy opportunities like Amgen came Los Angeles's way, the region's weak or non-overlapping networks and conservative zeitgeist pulled it back to the business practices of an earlier era.

Conclusion

In this detailed paired comparison of the innovation transitions of two major metropolitan regions, I have proceeded first by considering the standard explanations of divergent pathways of economic change and found them wanting. This turned attention to institutions, and especially regional innovation systems. I decomposed the

---

[4] Lewis defines these as: "A regularity R, in the behavior of members of a population P, when they act in a recurrent situation, S, is a convention . . . for the members of P, when: Each conforms to R; Each anticipates that others will conform to R; Each prefers to conform to R on the condition that others do so. Since S is a problem of coordination, the general conformity to R results in coordination." (Lewis, 1969, p. 42)

RSI into four distinctive elements—together comprising the relational infrastructure of a region—and showed that the two regions under examination differ significantly in all four areas. By combining this information with a historical perspective, and by showing the parallels to a more recent example—biotechnology—of their divergent reaction to technological opportunities, I showed that these region-wide institutional structures provide a plausible explanation of their different innovation transitions.

A paired comparison has the advantage of depth and controls for many sources of additional variation, but the disadvantage of small sample size. What remains now is to extend this deep case study approach to a larger sample of cases. To do so, robust but detailed data on the forces documented in this paper are needed, as well as systematic data on a larger number of regional innovation transitions. It seems promising that the type of explanation advanced here could successfully fill in some existing gaps in the current understanding of transitions. At the present time, explanations range from fully historicist and unique (luck), to attempts (not very successful on balance) to reduce such transitions to technological antecedents, factor endowments, size, and diversity. As defined here, the institutional differences documented in this comparison might then emerge as a missing link between these other factors and outcomes, the common element in what is a dizzying set of differences in the starting and ending points of regional transitions.

Acknowledgments This chapter is based on research funded by a grant from the John Randolph Haynes and Dora Haynes Foundation and on wider research project reported in a book, *The Rise and Fall of Urban Economies: Lessons from San Francisco and Los Angeles*, (Storper et al., 2015). I am grateful to the coauthors of that book for their contributions to this research, but the interpretations and modifications in this chapter are my own.

References

Aoyama, Y., Powell, W., Saxenian, A., & Scott, A. (2017, April 5). [Review of the book *The rise and fall of urban economies: Lessons from San Francisco and Los Angeles*, by M. Storper, T. Kemeny, N. Makarem, & T. Osman]. *AAG Review of Books*.

Autor, D. H., Levy, F., & Murnane, R. J. (2003). The skill content of recent technological change: An empirical exploration. *Quarterly Journal of Economics, 118*, 1279–1334. doi:https://doi.org/10.1162/003355303322552801

Casper, S. (2009). *The marketplace for ideas: Can Los Angeles build a successful biotechnology cluster?* Los Angeles: The John Randolph Haynes and Dora Haynes Foundation.

Chinitz, B. (1961). Contrasts in agglomeration: New York and Pittsburgh. *American Economic Review, 51*, 279–289. Retrieved from http://www.jstor.org/stable/1914493

Drennan, M. P., & Lobo, J. (1999). A simple test for convergence of metropolitan income in the United States. *Journal of Urban Economics, 46*, 350–359. doi:https://doi.org/10.1006/juec.1998.2126

Duranton, G., & Puga, D. (2001). Nursery cities: Urban diversity, process innovation, and the life cycle of products. *American Economic Review, 91*, 1454–1477. doi:https://doi.org/10.1257/aer.91.5.1454

Feldman, M. P. (1994). *The geography of innovation*. Boston: Kluwer Academic.

Feldman, M. P. (2014). The character of innovative places: Entrepreneurial strategy, economic development and prosperity. *Small Business Economics, 43*, 9–20. doi:https://doi.org/10.1007/s11187-014-9574-4

Feldman, M. P., & Lowe, N. J. (2011). Restructuring for resilience. *Innovations: Technology, Governance, Globalization, 6*(1), 129–146. doi:https://doi.org/10.1162/INOV_a_00063

Feldman, M. P., & Zoller, T. D. (2012). Dealmakers in place: Social capital connections in regional entrepreneurial economies. *Regional Studies, 46*, 23–37. doi:https://doi.org/10.1080/0034340 4.2011.607808

Foege, A. (2013, February 27). California's successful dilettantes. *Zocalo Public Square*. Retrieved from http://www.zocalopublicsquare.org/2013/02/27/californias-successful-dilettantes/chronicles/who-we-were/

Frenken, K., van Oort, F., & Verburg, T. (2007). Related variety, unrelated variety and regional economic growth. *Regional Studies, 41*, 685–697. doi:https://doi.org/10.1080/00343400601120296

Ganong, P., & Shoag, D. (2012). Why has regional income convergence in the U.S. stopped? Harvard Kennedy School Faculty Research Working Paper Series (RWP12-028). Retrieved from http://scholar.harvard.edu/files/shoag/files/why_has_regional_income_convergence_in_the_us_declined_01.pdf

Getting to Cambridge: The political philosophy of Britain's most successful city. (2015, August 22). *The Economist*, para. 8. Retrieved from http://www.economist.com/news/britain/21661670-political-philosophy-britains-most-successful-city-getting-cambridge

Glaeser, E. L. (2008). *Cities, agglomeration and spatial equilibrium*. Oxford: Oxford University Press.

Glaeser, E. L., & Maré, D. C. (2001). Cities and skills. *Journal of Labor Economics, 19*, 316–342. doi:https://doi.org/10.3386/w4728

Gordon, R. J. (2016). *The rise and fall of American economic growth*. Princeton: Princeton University Press.

Heller, N. (2013, October 14). Bay Watched: How San Francisco's new entrepreneurial culture is changing the country. *The New Yorker*. Retrieved from http://www.newyorker.com/magazine/2013/10/14/bay-watched

Iammarino, S. (2005). An evolutionary integrated view of regional systems of innovation: Concepts, measures, and historical perspectives. *European Planning Studies, 13*, 497–519. doi:https://doi.org/10.1080/09654310500107084

Jacobs, J. (1969). *The economy of cities*. New York: Random House.

Jaffe, A. B. (1989). Real effects of academic research. *American Economic Review, 79*, 957–970. Retrieved from http://www.jstor.org/stable/1831431.

Jobs, S. (2005). Commencement speech, Stanford University. Retrieved from http://www.network.world.com/community/blog/apples-steve-jobs-stanford-commencement-speech-transcript

Kenney, M., & Mowery, D. C. (2014). *Public universities and regional growth: Insights from the University of California*. Redwood City: Stanford University Press.

Krugman, P. R. (1991). Increasing returns and economic geography. *Journal of Political Economy, 99*, 483–499. doi:https://doi.org/10.3386/w3275

Lanier, J. (2013). *Who owns the future?* New York: Simon & Schuster.

Lazega, E. (2017). Organized mobility and relational turnover as context for social mechanisms: A dynamic invariant at the heart of stability from movement. In J Glückler, E Lazega, & I Hammer (Eds.), Knowledge and networks (pp. 119–142). Knowledge and Space: Vol. 11. Cham: Springer.

Lécuyer, C. (2006). *Making Silicon Valley: Innovation and the growth of high tech, 1930–1970*. Cambridge, MA: MIT Press.

Lewis, D. K. (1969). *Convention: A philosophical study*. Cambridge, MA: Harvard University Press.

Lundvall, B.-A. (2007). National innovation systems: Analytical concept and development tool. *Industry and Innovation, 14*, 95–119. doi:https://doi.org/10.1080/13662710601130863

Maddison, A. (1982). *Phases of capitalist development*. Oxford, UK: Oxford University Press.

Markoff, J. (2005). *What the dormouse said: How the 60s counterculture shaped the personal computer industry*. London: Penguin.

Markusen, A., Hall, P., Campbell, S., & Deitrick, S. (1991). *The rise of the gunbelt: The military remapping of industrial America.* New York: Oxford University Press.

Moretti, E. (2012). *The new geography of jobs.* Boston: Houghton Mifflin Harcourt.

Myers, D., Goldberg, S., Mawhorter, S., & Min, S. (2010). Immigrants and the new maturity of Los Angeles. In A. Modarres (Ed.), *State of the City* (pp. 12–27). Los Angeles: Pat Brown Institute, California State University. Retrieved from http://popdynamics.usc.edu/pdf/2010_Myers-etal_Immigrants-New-Maturity-LA.pdf

North, D. C. (1990). *Institutions, institutional change and economic performance.* Cambridge, UK: Cambridge University Press.

North, D. C. (1993). *Economic performance through time* [Nobel prize lecture]. Retrieved from http://www.nobelprize.org/nobel_prizes/economic-sciences/laureates/1993/north-lecture.html

Pomeranz, K. (2000). *The great divergence: China, Europe and the making of the modern world economy.* Princeton: Princeton University Press.

Powell, W. W., & Sandholtz, K. (2012). Chance, nécessité, et naïveté: Ingredients to create a new organizational form. In J. F. Padgett & W. W. Powell (Eds.), *The emergence of organizations and markets* (pp. 379–433). Princeton: Princeton University Press.

Rosenthal, & Strange. (2001). The determinants of agglomeration. *Journal of Urban Economics, 50,* 191–229. doi:https://doi.org/10.1006/juec.2001.2230

Roszak, T. (1969). *The making of a counter culture: Reflections on the technocratic society and its youthful opposition.* Garden City: Doubleday.

Saxenian, A. (1994). *Regional advantage: Culture and competition in Silicon Valley and Route 128.* Cambridge, MA: Harvard University Press.

Scott, A. J., & Storper, M. (1987). High technology industry and regional development: A theoretical critique and reconstruction. *International Social Science Journal, 39,* 215–232.

Sonn, J. W., & Storper, M. (2008). The increasing importance of geographical proximity in knowledge production: An analysis of US patent citations, 1975–1997. *Environment and Planning A, 40,* 1020–1039. doi:https://doi.org/10.1068/a3930

Storper, M., & Christopherson, S. (1987). Flexible specialization and regional industrial agglomerations: The case of the U.S. motion picture industry. *Annals of the Association of American Geographers, 77,* 104–117. doi:https://doi.org/10.1111/j.1467-8306.1987.tb00148.x

Storper, M., Kemeny, T., Makarem, N., & Osman, T. (2015). *The rise and fall of urban economies: Lessons from Los Angeles and San Francisco.* Redwood City: Stanford University Press.

Storper, M., & Walker, R. (1989). *The capitalist imperative: Territory, technology and industrial growth.* New York: Basil Blackwell.

Thisse, J.-F. (2010). Toward a unified theory of economic geography and urban economics. *Journal of Regional Science, 50,* 281–296. doi:https://doi.org/10.1111/j.1467-9787.2009.00651.x

Turner, F. (2006). *From counterculture to cyber-culture: Stewart Brand, the Whole Earth network, and the rise of digital utopianism.* Chicago: University of Chicago Press.

Yamamoto, D. (2008). Scales of regional income disparities in the USA, 1955–2003. *Journal of Economic Geography, 8,* 79–103. doi:https://doi.org/10.1093/jeg/lbm044

Chapter 11
Institutions and the Thirst for 'Prestige' Transport Infrastructure

Andrés Rodríguez-Pose, Riccardo Crescenzi, and Marco Di Cataldo

Decision-makers, people in the construction industry, and most of the rest of the population love transport infrastructure. Roads, railways, ports, and airports are generally popular, highly visible, and tangible, can frequently be built within the span of an electoral cycle, can produce additional votes, and may even generate medium- and long-term economic growth. A ruler's legacy is also often associated with specific infrastructure developments. Infrastructure in general, and transport infrastructure in particular, is thus usually the first option when devising development strategies (Flyvbjerg, 2009). Often, the glitzier the type of transport infrastructure, the better. Motorways (superhighways) tend to be preferred to secondary roads, high-speed rail to freight trains, and international airports to heliports. If transport infrastructure is to appeal to the population and achieve its goals, it needs to shock and awe.

Governments have consequently flocked to make infrastructure the key axis of their development strategies. The European Union (EU), for example, has made the building of transport infrastructure one of the cornerstones of its regional development policy. So intense has been the improvement of transport in the less developed areas of the continent that countries and regions whose endowment of transport infrastructure clearly used to lag have become leaders after more than 25 years of investment. Spain, for instance, now has the largest motorway network among the EU's first 15 members. The country also tops the ranking in kilometers (km) of motorways per capita, with Portugal ahead in km per GDP (Table 11.1). The United Kingdom comes last in the latter two classifications. Spain also has the largest network of high-speed rail lines. New airports have also been built—and, to a lesser extent than in the high years of the economic boom of the 2000s, are still being built—all over the European periphery (Albalate & Bel, 2012).

A. Rodríguez-Pose (✉) · R. Crescenzi · M. Di Cataldo
Department of Geography and Environment, London School of Economics, London, UK
e-mail: A.Rodriguez-Pose@lse.ac.uk; r.crescenzi@lse.ac.uk; m.di-cataldo@lse.ac.uk

© The Author(s) 2018
J. Glückler et al. (eds.), *Knowledge and Institutions*, Knowledge and Space 13,
https://doi.org/10.1007/978-3-319-75328-7_11

Table 11.1 Infrastructure endowment in the EU 15, in 2011

Member states	Km motorways	Km motor-ways per 1,000 km^2	Km motorways per 10,000 inhabitants	Km motorways per €1 billion of GDP
EU 15	61,504	18.98	1.53	5.6
Portugal	2,623 (7)[a]	28.49 (5)	2.49 (3)	15.6 (1)
Spain	13,515 (1)	26.77 (6)	2.93 (1)	12.8 (2)
Sweden	1,855 (8)	4.12 (14)	1.96 (6)	6.3 (3)
Austria	1,696 (10)	20.22 (9)	2.01 (5)	6.2 (4)
France	11,042 (3)	20.08 (10)	1.69 (7)	5.8 (5)
Germany	12,645 (2)	35.43 (4)	1.55 (10)	5.3 (6)
Belgium	1,763 (9)	57.75 (2)	1.59 (8)	5.2 (7)
Denmark	1,128 (11)	26.18 (7)	2.02 (4)	5.1 (8)
Greece	1,103 (12)	8.36 (12)	0.98 (13)	4.7 (9)
Netherlands	2,637 (6)	63.50 (1)	1.58 (9)	4.6 (10)
Italy	6,629 (4)	22.00 (8)	1.09 (12)	4.4 (11)
Finland	739 (13)	2.19 (15)	1.37 (11)	4.3 (12)
Luxembourg	147 (15)	56.84 (3)	2.80 (2)	3.9 (13)
Ireland	423 (14)	6.04 (12)	0.92 (14)	2.6 (14)
United Kingdom	3,559 (5)	14.54 (11)	0.57 (15)	2.3 (15)

[a]Rank is noted in parentheses. Countries ranked by Kms of motorways a relative to GDP.
Source: Adapted from Eurostat data

However, frequent tales of underused motorways, closed high-speed railway lines, and empty airports suggest that the hopes associated with the construction of new transport infrastructure in Europe have not always been met and that new infrastructure investment has sometimes been a complete waste of public resources that could have been used more effectively for other purposes. There are at least two potential explanations as to why new transport infrastructure does not always deliver. One is the famous two-way road argument: Because firms and workers in lagging areas find agglomeration economies attractive, changes in accessibility due to new roads, train links, and airports may benefit the core economic areas at the expense of less advanced ones (Puga, 2002; Puga & Venables, 1997). The net growth effect of reductions in transport costs may therefore be zero or even negative. An alternative explanation is that the returns on investment in infrastructure are mediated by the quality of regional government institutions that share responsibility for ensuring the selection and realization of specific projects. The local institutional environment in which investments are made will affect the relevance and type of new infrastructure investments and, hence, their economic returns. Ineffective institutions abet opportunities for private gain at the expense of a sound provision of public goods (Acemoğlu & Dell, 2010). Hence, in weak government quality conditions, new investment in transport infrastructure may be subject largely to political and individual interests rather than to economic and collective ones (Crain & Oakley, 1995; Henisz, 2002). Institutional failure can therefore be at the heart of a growing propensity to finance glitzy, "flagship," and large-scale transport projects (i.e., motorways, high-speed rail lines), which politicians tend to embrace when seeking reelection (Cantarelli, Flyvbjerg, Molin, & van Wee, 2010; Rodríguez-Pose, 2000), at the expense of less flashy, "ordinary" transport investments (i.e., secondary roads, freight railways). It may also aggrandize the role of political and business pressure groups, bringing about problems such as collusion at the tender stage and misrepresentation of costs, benefits, and the time needed for implementation (Flyvbjerg, 2009; Kenny, 2007; World Bank, 2011). A convergence of partisan politics, business interests, weak accountability, and corruption may thus prevent new infrastructure from generating the expected positive multiplier effect on the local economy and sustained economic development.

In this chapter we reflect on these issues for the case of Europe, looking at how institutional weaknesses—proxied by poor government quality—often result in decisions determining which type of infrastructure to build and whether individual rather than collective interests prevail. Such decisions would be reflected in the construction of "prestige" transport infrastructure (motorways rather than secondary roads), which fosters the interests of decision-makers and large infrastructure firms and may even be popular but which entails highly questionable economic and social returns.

Does Investment in Infrastructure Always Lead to Growth?

Transport infrastructure is essential for the development of economic activity (Button, Leitham, McQuaid, & Nelson, 1995). Enhanced local accessibility is at the root of improvements in the quality of services, reductions in labor costs, and rises in productivity (Biehl, 1986; Moreno, Artís, López-Bazo, & Suriñach, 1997; Vickerman, 2007). Adequate transport infrastructure also provides incentives for the sorting of economic activity and facilitates economic growth (Lewis, 1998). However, once a necessary basic threshold of infrastructure provision has been reached, the impact of additional public investment becomes uncertain. One claim, for example, is that OECD countries have reached a level of transport infrastructure provision at which additional expansions are likely to have only limited effects on economic performance (OECD, 2009).

Hence, the key questions emerging from past research on transport infrastructure and economic performance relate to the potential existence of an optimal level of infrastructure development and to the effects on economic growth of additional investments in transport infrastructure beyond that level. Initial research on this matter did not consider the existence of such a threshold. According to Aschauer (1989) and Munnell (1990), there was a linear positive effect of transport infrastructure investment on aggregate productivity. This thesis, however, has drawn heavy criticism in subsequent economic research (Button, 1998), which for both the United States (Holtz-Eakin & Schwartz, 1995; Kelejian & Robinson, 1997) and Europe (Cappelen, Castellacci, Fagerberg, & Verspagen, 2003; Crescenzi & Rodríguez-Pose, 2012) has cast doubt on the effectiveness of infrastructure investment. In the case of Europe, this skepticism has been highlighted by both single-country (e.g., Bronzini & Piselli, 2009; Cadot, Röller, & Stephan, 1999; Stephan, 2000) and cross-national research (e.g., Cappelen et al., 2003; Crescenzi & Rodríguez-Pose, 2012), which increasingly reports much lower elasticities than those found by Aschauer (1989) or even insignificant coefficients. Similarly, spatial analyses searching for spillovers from different types of infrastructure find that economic growth effects are limited at best to certain categories of public capital (e.g., del Bo & Florio, 2012; del Bo, Florio, & Manzi, 2010; Moreno & López-Bazo, 2007).

The explanations as to why the results of additional investments in infrastructure have not lived up to expectations vary, but they generally point to the diverse conditions across different types of regions. New Economic Geography (NEG) analyses have tended to find an explanation in the asymmetric impact that variations in transport costs have on areas with different geographical and economic characteristics (Fujita, Krugman, & Venables, 1999; Fujita & Thisse, 2002). In particular, the role of different types of roads has attracted considerable scrutiny. Puga and Venables (1997), Puga (2002), and Ottaviano (2008) have distinguished between the economic effect of long-distance roads, which alter overall accessibility and cause further economic concentration, and short-distance or local infrastructure, which generally facilitates the diffusion of public services and the formation of human capital within regions. In their opinion short-distance or local infrastructure has the more positive effect on the development of lagging areas. Studies outside the NEG framework have further emphasized how differences in overall endowments between the core and the periphery have affected the returns on investment in transport infrastructure (Cappelen et al., 2003; Rodríguez-Pose & Fratesi, 2004; Vickerman, 1995).

How Do Institutions Shape Infrastructure Decisions and Economic Growth?

In considerations of the returns on transport infrastructure, one crucial factor that has so far attracted limited attention is the institutional conditions in each territory. The system of incentives and constraints linked to the existing set of institutions and the efficiency of the local political administration may determine the extent to which investment in transport infrastructure can deliver on its economic promises (Acemoğlu & Dell, 2010; Crain & Oakley, 1995; Henisz, 2002; Mauro, 1997). Political and institutional factors can influence both infrastructure spending and its economic returns at every phase of the investment (Esfahani & Ramírez, 2003; Levy & Spiller, 1996). Yet few researchers have empirically explored how local institutional conditions shape the economic impact of transport infrastructure. Except for Crescenzi, Di Cataldo, and Rodríguez-Pose (2016), we know of no analyses of the triple link between government institutions, infrastructure investments, and economic growth for European regions.

However, institutions and government quality matter. From the planning and selection of a transport project to its execution, the characteristics of local institutions, particularly the quality of local government, play an important part in determining that project's future efficiency. The link between transport infrastructure investment and the planning system, the need for large budgets, the high number of actors involved, and the difficulty in applying effective control mechanisms make the transport sector especially vulnerable to political interference (Cantarelli et al., 2010; Flyvbjerg, 2009; Wachs, 1989), corruption (Kenny, 2006; Paterson & Chaudhuri, 2007; Tanzi & Davoodi, 1997, 1998), and collusion (World Bank, 2011). The quality of local government shapes the risk of moral hazard, affecting the capacity of decisions on infrastructure investment to deliver from an economic perspective (Buchanan, 1989).

There are three potential mechanisms mediating the influence that the quality of government has on decisions about the type of infrastructure to build. Poor institutional systems may lead to (a) political economy factors inflating investment in transport, (b) a widespread system of corruption and collusion, and (c) significant cost overruns and delays. In this section we expand on these mechanisms and illustrate how the economic returns on investment in transport infrastructure are deeply affected by the presence of deficient institutions.

On How Transport Investment Projects Spiral out of Control

The planning and financing of transport infrastructure is fundamentally a political topic. In theory, decision-makers should base their decisions on the anticipated long-term economic returns on any individual project. However, medium- to long-term economic returns are not necessarily the immediate goal of the people taking decisions on infrastructure. Electoral returns and, in certain cases, private interests often condition what sort of investment receives priority and what type of infrastructure prevails. Decision-making on new transport investment in European countries is thus "generally politicised, rarely fully transparent, and there is little ex-post analysis on whether projects and policies meet expectations" (Short & Knopp, 2005, p. 363). Even when the investment is preceded by ex-ante impact studies, the secrecy that frequently surrounds forecasting methods does not necessarily preclude deliberate cost-benefit misrepresentations (Cantarelli et al., 2010; Short & Knopp, 2005; Wachs, 1989). Incumbent decision-makers may "purposely spin scenarios of success and gloss over the potential for failure" (Flyvbjerg, 2009, p. 350) of transport projects in order to strengthen their own political positions.

In these contexts, transport infrastructure tends to be the knee-jerk reaction. Infrastructure investment is tangible, highly visible, and generally well received by the population. This very visibility makes transport infrastructure appealing to decision-makers, who may regard new investment as an excellent opportunity for ribbon-cutting before elections, without the disadvantage of a large public backlash. The popularity of infrastructure expenditure is frequently more an outcome of political decisions than of any solid economic valuation (Cadot, Röller, & Stephan, 2006). It often gives rise to an inflation of expenditures on "tangible" infrastructure projects as opposed to less tangible and visible investments in, say, education, training, or innovation (Rodríguez-Pose, 2000). Given the visibility and electoral returns on infrastructure investment, local administrations in weak institutional contexts tend to resort to promoting large new infrastructure projects instead of investing in the maintenance of existing transport networks or the construction of alternative, less glitzy and less visible projects (Kenny, 2007; Tanzi & Davoodi, 1997). However, long planning horizons and elevated risk of cost miscalculations cast uncertainty over many megainfrastructure projects (Flyvbjerg, 2009), especially in territories characterized by feeble levels of governance.

When vested political and economic interests shape the activity of local administrations in poor institutional environments, suboptimal projects may become common. In those contexts Cadot et al. (1999) and Kemmerling and Stephan (2008) demonstrated that special interests and pork-barrel politics can drive infrastructure investment decisions more than concerns for overall social welfare and economic efficiency do. In weak institutional contexts, transport infrastructure projects may then often fall prey to collusion and clientelism (Cadot et al., 2006).

Examples of political interests and/or weak local institutions leading to suboptimal infrastructure are plentiful. Many of them can be found in Spain, a country that went from a significant underendowment of roads relative to its European partners to the largest motorway network in Europe. Substantial investments in motorways in the 1990s enabled Spain to catch up on its transport infrastructure. Investment in that field rose even further in the 2000s, when the road deficit relative to the European core was no longer evident. In the 10 years from 1999 to the outbreak of economic crisis in 2009, more than 5,000 km of motorways were built—thanks in part to cofunding from the European regional development effort (Minder, 2011). In 2009 Spain boasted a motorway network 22.4% larger than France's, despite having a territory 9.3% smaller and a population approximately 73% that of its northern neighbor (Fig. 11.1).

The last wave of investment in motorways came through the adoption of new forms of toll-road concessions that set favorable conditions for private groups (Acerete, Shaoul, & Stafford, 2009). Under these circumstances the Spanish entrepreneurial sector threw its considerable economic weight behind efforts to inflate investments in new roads. These expenditures were seldom, if ever, preceded by accurate cost-benefit analyses and the formulation of financial and long-term economic plans. They paved the way for inefficient projects or "white elephants" of questionable economic and public utility (Robinson & Torvik, 2005).

One of the most glaring examples is the toll motorway connecting Madrid and Toledo (AP-41), inaugurated in 2006. The project was based on the participation of concessionaires—a number of private firms who were forecasting traffic intensities in excess of 25,000 vehicles per day. The actual figures have been nowhere close to the original and loosely justified predictions. According to official data by Spain's Ministerio de Fomento (2017), the number of daily vehicles peaked at 2,800 in 2008. The number of users declined to a paltry 881 in 2016. The new motorway has

Fig. 11.1 Infrastructural white elephants in Spain: extensive motorway network. Source: By Gestion.Inf.And. – Own work. Used under Creative Commons Attribution 3.0 Unported. Retrieved from https://commons.wikimedia.org/w/index.php?curid=6026287

not been able to draw enough travelers away from its competitor, the A-42, a preexisting toll-free motorway that runs almost parallel to the AP-41. By early 2017, the Spanish government was about to take, or had already taken, control not just of the company responsible for the AP-41 but of nine toll motorways that had been constructed since the mid-1990s at an estimated cost of more than €5 billion. The traffic volume that had been so optimistically predicted for all toll roads never materialized. In 2016 toll-road traffic was 23.4% lower than in 2006, despite the expansion of the toll network. All the companies in charge of their management had gone bankrupt, leaving the Spanish state little option in the absence of private suitors.

Other examples of infrastructural white elephants have become common in Spain. Because Spain has the largest high-speed rail network in Europe, that system represents a particular source of pride for Spanish decision-makers and the population in general (Fig. 11.2). But in terms of operating costs alone, the network is far from breaking even. Occupancy levels remain well below those of France and, especially, Japan (Albalate & Bel, 2012). One particularly embarrassing example occurred when the high-speed link between Toledo, Cuenca, and Albacete had to shut down barely one year after it had opened. The cover of the Spanish satirical magazine *El Jueves* famously commented on this closure on July 2, 2011, pointing out that the daily maintenance costs ranged around €18,000 for an average daily traffic volume of just nine passengers.

Fig. 11.2 Infrastructural white elephants in Spain: high-speed rail network. Source: By Jose Hilla Julia—originally posted to Flickr as Los viaductos. Used under Creative Commons Attribution 2.0 Generic. Retrieved from https://commons.wikimedia.org/w/index.php?curid=15010824

Airports in Spain also account for plenty of cathedrals in the desert. Of the 46 publicly managed airports—many of them built with great fanfare during the boom years of the late 1990s and early 2000s—only 8 made a profit in 2013 (Palet, 2014; Rodríguez-Pose & Fratesi, 2004). Airports in Albacete, Son Bonet, Sabadell, Burgos, and Córdoba had fewer than 10,000 passengers in 2016, and seven others did not reach 50,000 (Departamento de Estadisticas, 2016). The grand total for that year in Huesca-Pirineos was 95 passengers. One particular source of public embarrassment is the case of the "ghost" airport of Ciudad Real. This privately funded, but publicly backed, airport caught the attention of the world when, as reported by *The Financial Times* (Buck, 2015), the highest offer it attracted at auction was €10,000 from a Chinese bidder, despite having cost close to €1 billion (Fig. 11.3).

Spain has no monopoly on the proliferation of white elephants, however. Portugal also has a large number of them. One highly controversial project was the Vasco da Gama Bridge in Lisbon, which opened to traffic in 1998 and is the longest bridge in Europe (Fig. 11.4). It is the second bridge in the city over the river Tagus, built in theory to alleviate congestion on the 25 de Abril Bridge. The project was realized by a "joint venture" of private companies and financed with government grants, private resources, and loans from the European Investment Bank and the Cohesion Fund, with the EU being the primary contributor. The project was intensely promoted by the Ministry of Public Works of Portugal, supported by 17 municipal governments

Fig. 11.3 Auction for
Ciudad Real airport.
Financial-Times-heading.
Source: Retrieved from
https://www.ft.com/
content/368d6998-2c81-
11e5-acfb-cbd2e1c81cca

FINANCIAL
TIMES
Spain

Spanish ghost airport costing €1bn attracts offer of just €10,000

Ciudad Real airport was built during construction boom
JULY 17, 2015 by: **Tobias Buck** in Madrid

Fig. 11.4 The Vasco da Gama Bridge in Lisbon. Source: By Paulo Valdivieso, originally from Flickr. Used under Attribution – Share Alike 2.0 Generic. Retrieved from https://commons.wiki-media.org/wiki/File:Lisboa_(3962906626).jpg

of the Lisbon metropolitan area, and quickly approved by the European Commission despite the existence of at least two alternative locations for the installation (Bukowski, 2004; Painvin, 2009). The bridge was built in just three years and opened at the same time as the 1998 Lisbon Expo.

But the Vasco da Gama Bridge failed to alleviate congestion on the 25 de Abril Bridge (de Melo, 2000). The location of the new structure, which connects Lisbon's northern ring to Montijo, a less densely populated area to the southeast of the Lisbon agglomeration, has never attracted the expected volume of 132,000 vehicles a day. Daily traffic across the bridge averaged only some 55,650 vehicles in 2015, and traffic has been declining since it peaked at about 67,500 vehicles in 2004 (for both statistics see INE, 2017). In nearly twenty years of the new bridge's operation, traffic on the 25 de Abril has not seen any major reduction; indeed, it has remained well above intended capacity (Painvin, 2009). In 2015 traffic crossing the 25 de Abril Bridge was 2.5 times that of the Vasco da Gama Bridge (the ratio was 2.2 in 2003) (INE, 2017). Overall, the political desire to have the longest bridge in Europe prevailed over the need to reduce congestion in the city, meaning that a choice of a long bridge that would be internationally noticed took precedence over more sensible alternatives connecting densely populated areas. A choice for political and international visibility resulted in the construction of a bridge connecting Lisbon to a relatively lightly populated area, neglecting alternatives running parallel to the existing 25 de Abril Bridge or between the city and the busy suburb of Barreiro in the south. The consequences are clear: no alleviation of congestion in Lisbon, limited new development, and a white elephant struggling to cover costs.

On Corruption and Collusion in Transport Infrastructure Investment Decisions

Superfluous or wrongly planned infrastructure investment may also be the upshot of inadequate policy-making and scarce economic resources. When the responsibility for investment planning is decentralized, regional and local authorities may lack sufficient financial muscle to implement investments with higher returns. If political decentralization is not accompanied by an adequate devolution of economic powers, financial instability and coordination problems may arise. In Italy, for example, the 2001 constitutional reform transferred a large share of responsibility for programming, planning, and managing road development to regions. However, Italian regional governments have never had enough financial resources to take over this task properly (Casadio & Paccagnella, 2011). The regions have thus been forced either to further decentralize powers to the provinces or to create new ad hoc organizations for the management and realization of road investments (Marangoni & Marinelli, 2011).

Next to a lack of funding capacity, local corruption is also a main factor behind the inefficient planning of public capital spending. In competitive auctions economic efficiency is best ensured when infrastructure projects are contracted to the companies presenting the best bid. This process requires a great degree of transparency. However, the outcome of the auctions is often perverted by corruption and collusion. In weak institutional environments bribery can entice government officials to select suboptimal bids or, when contractors are few, collusion may often set in.

Several studies have documented the existence of cartels controlling construction bids in European countries. A 2002 enquiry unveiled fraud, unjustified subsidies, and bribery on a vast scale from a state–corporate network monopolizing the construction sector in The Netherlands (Van den Heuvel, 2005). In Italy the responsibility for managing auctions[1] on highway and road concessions belongs to the regions, with construction companies often lamenting a supposed lack of neutrality when awarding contracts. In the south of the country, at least one third of projects are contracted to firms with close links to the awarding administration (Bentivogli, Casadio, & Cullino, 2011). Corruption and collusion in the transport sector are severe in many Eastern European countries as well (Kenny, 2006). According to a 2003 investigation, a cartel of firms in Romania regularly raised the price of road construction tenders by up to 30% over their market equilibrium level (Oxford Business Group, 2004). Numerous cases of predefined tender prices have also emerged in Slovakia (OECD, 2006) and Poland (Cienski, 2013).

Sometimes, collusion alone suffices to make sure that medium- and long-term socioeconomic interests are overlooked in favor of the short-term interest of large construction firms. This mechanism has been prevalent, for example, in Spain. In 1989 that country had 5 of the top 50 construction companies in the world, a number commensurate with the economic size of the country at the time. In 2009, after 20 years of heavy investment in transport infrastructure, mainly fueled by European Structural Funds and coinciding with the end of the construction boom in the country, Spain boasted five of the top 15 construction companies in the world. In just two decades Spain had become, together with France, the main global hub of large construction companies. These companies became so powerful that they could shape national, regional, and local infrastructure policies to reflect their own short-term interests. Two mechanisms dominated. Construction companies could directly lobby government, but also they frequently employed or coopted former top government officials (including former ministers) as board members, making sure that corporate influence on government decisions strengthened. Unsurprisingly, Spanish governments hence came to favor large prestige projects that could help boost the balance sheet of construction companies to the detriment of other, frequently smaller projects.

On Cost Overruns and Delays

Cost overruns and delays tend to be the norm in the implementation of transport infrastructure. According to Flyvbjerg, Holm, and Buhl (2005), nine out of ten large-scale infrastructure projects are underestimated in terms of total costs, with overruns averaging 20% for road projects. Political and economic factors are generally regarded as the main explanation for cost overruns (Cantarelli et al., 2010). Especially in areas with weak institutions and governance systems, political and economic interest groups often voluntarily misrepresent the costs and benefits of a project in order to facilitate its approval. Higher transparency and efficient public control are necessary as antidotes to such practices (Flyvbjerg, 2009).

---

[1] The national level is responsible for a few projects of national relevance (e.g., *Grandi opere*), whereas the regional level manages all other auctions.

Increases in the total costs of infrastructure projects may be also related to distortions while the work is taking place. Overlapping government responsibilities, underfunding, and/or lack of coordinating experience tend to be at the root of delays in implementation. Legal disputes—often a consequence of clashes between local authorities and the companies constructing the new infrastructure—can cause severe delays and generate extra costs. Additional time and cost overruns can also stem from the incapacity of legal institutions (either national or local) to enforce the project's procurement contracts and from the lack of appropriate bureaucratic structures for monitoring the execution of work.

Such conditions are more prevalent in areas where rent-seeking, the presence of organized crime, or both abound. These endemic situations may help make white elephants out of what initially appear to be feasible projects. The renovation of the Italian A2 motorway between Salerno and Reggio Calabria illustrates the point. Work on it began in 1962 and was not completed until December 22, 2016, with the opening of the Laria Tunnel. Meddling by organized crime, attested to by the National Anti-Mafia Commission, together with protracted court disputes, made costs skyrocket, with the Italian state paying over 300 million Euros in compensation to the private contractors for *costi aggiuntivi* (added costs) (Turano, 2011, para. 1, 4). A motorway whose construction was expected to last for three years took almost fifty-five years to finish.

In other cases money simply disappears. Greece has received an amount of European funding similar to that allocated to Portugal, but despite the same demonstrated preferences for building new infrastructure, Greece's current endowment of infrastructure, particularly its road network, is a fraction of Portugal's.

What are the Economic Implications for Areas with Weak Institutions?

Political meddling, delays, and unexpected cost overruns tend to be much more serious in areas with weak institutions and poor quality of government. Many lagging European regions regularly exhibit the problems described above. Achieving the full growth potential of lagging regions almost certainly requires modern transport networks that improve interregional communications. But excessive pursuit of prestige transport infrastructure projects in many of Europe's less advanced regions has undermined the desired overall effect of local and regional development strategies and of EU development funding. Poor quality of government in most regions of the EU's periphery has meant that a fair share of them have had only limited experience in the planning, monitoring, and evaluation of projects. Beset by corruption, lack of transparency and accountability, inefficient rule of law, and low government effectiveness, many lagging regions have acquired a distinct taste for large, visible prestige infrastructure projects driven fundamentally by criteria other than economic ones.

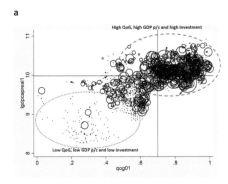

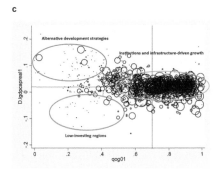

Area of circle proportional to Δ Motorways/1000 inhab; horizontal line= mean of log per capita GDP; vertical line= mean of QoG

Area of circle proportional to Δ Motorways/1000 inhab; horizontal line= mean of Δ log per capita GDP; vertical line= mean of QoG

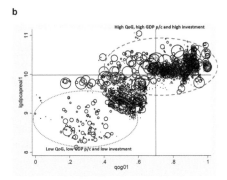

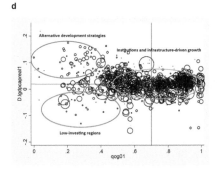

Area of circle proportional to Δ Other Roads/1000 inhab; horizontal line= mean of log per capita GDP; vertical line= mean of QoG

Area of circle proportional to Δ Other Roads/1000 inhab; horizontal line= mean of Δ log per capita GDP; vertical line= mean of QoG

Fig. 11.5 Regional per capita gross domestic product (GDP) and quality of local government in less advanced regions of the European Union, 1995–2009. The area of each circle corresponds to the annual regional variation in the length of roads (in km) from 1995 to 2009. The horizontal axis indicates the mean of the log per capita GDP. The vertical axis indicates the mean of the quality of government

This situation has had important consequences for the returns on transport infrastructure projects across southern Europe. As highlighted by Crescenzi et al. (2016), institutional conditions and the quality of government in the regions of the EU have in recent years heavily influenced decisions on which type of transport infrastructure to build. Choices of transport infrastructure, in turn, have affected the returns on new investment in infrastructure. This relationship is graphically depicted in the four parts of Fig. 11.5. Parts 11.5a and 11.5b correspond to a static relation between income and institutions, showing that a given level of per capita GDP tends to be associated with gains in institutional quality as measured by the Quality of Government Index elaborated by the Quality of Government Institute at the

University of Gothenburg (Charron, Lapuente, & Rothstein, 2010). Parts 11.5c and 11.5d illustrate a dynamic representation of this relation. The annual rise in per capita GDP is plotted against the corresponding level of regional government quality. Observations pertaining to parts 11.5a and 11.5c are weighted according to the regional investment in motorways (as a proxy of rather prestigious and glitzy infrastructure investments). In parts 11.5b and 11.5d they are weighted according to improvements in other roads (proxying rather run-of-the-mill infrastructure investments). Parts 11.5a and 11.5b suggest that the quality of government has risen with the amount of transport investment in the regions of the EU, as indicated by the areas of the corresponding circles. The circles are bigger for observations on the right than for those in the lower-left quadrant. Two macroclusters are identifiable. The first one includes regions with a lower-than-average quality of government institutions and income and with fewer overall investments in infrastructure (dotted oval). The second macrocluster comprises regions with a relatively high score on quality of government, higher GDP, and more investment in transport infrastructure (dashed oval) than other regions.

Overall, the study of the relation between GDP and quality of government depicted in Figs. 11.5, parts c and d yields some interesting insights on the growth strategies adopted by European regions since the mid-1990s. We identify three subgroups of observations based on the peculiarities of their development path. The first group, marked by a blue oval, includes all regions that have experienced rapid growth despite having lower-than-average institutional quality and a low rate of transport investments. These regions have probably benefitted from a convergence effect and have allocated their resources to axes of development other than infrastructure, such as innovation, education, or enterprise development. The second group, marked by a red oval, is composed of slowly growing regions (lower-left quadrant). These territories, characterized by weak institutional structures, have undergone a low rate of infrastructural growth. The third group consists of regions in the green oval: those that have maintained a positive growth rate from 1995 to 2009, characterized by an acceptable or high quality of institutions and capable of successfully expanding their network of motorways and other roads. Overall, Fig. 11.5 suggests a variety of possible combinations between institutions and investments in road infrastructure and of outcomes in terms of regional economic performance. One of these outcomes is the fact that greater investment in the prestigious motorways than in humble secondary roads has brought about virtually no direct economic growth, whereas investment in secondary roads in regions with comparatively high quality of government has intensified economic dynamism (Crescenzi et al., 2016). The implication is that any potential positive rates of returns from infrastructure investment are strongly mediated by the presence of adequate institutions of governance, which influence decisions about what type of infrastructure to build and about the returns of infrastructure investment. In short, basing transport infrastructure strategies primarily on motorway construction has not been very efficient, whereas promoting secondary roads—a choice often preferred by regions with superior government quality—has strengthened economic outcomes.

The reason may be that secondary roads, whose comparatively modest scale and glamor make them less appealing to decision-makers and construction companies than prestige motorways but whose burden on public finances is also less, allow for greater investment in skills and innovation and often enhance intraregional rather than interregional connectivity. The latter distinction is relevant especially for peripheral areas located far from the main urban centers and endowed with fewer economic resources than other regions. In the absence of complementary interventions to improve the regional transport network, it may be that large-scale projects have little chance of stimulating the economic potential of a region. Even worse, they would in all probability generate important opportunity costs by subtracting vital resources from other key infrastructure interventions or axes of development.

What are the Implications for Public Policy?

The quality of institutions in any given territory shapes decisions about different types of investment and, within infrastructure investments, decisions about which type of infrastructure to build. The previous pages have shown that poor institutions, and particularly a low quality of government, have important implications for choices about different types of infrastructure, and that this infrastructure, in turn, affects economic performance. As Esfahani and Ramírez (2003) put it, "achieving better [economic] outcomes requires institutional and organizational reforms that are more fundamental than simply designing infrastructure projects and spending money on them" (p. 471). However, achieving institutional reform is easier said than done. The reshaping of institutional structures is a challenging task for policymakers, because reforms will have to be designed specifically for the environment in which they are to be applied. However, institution-building needs to be a top priority of development planners, given the large flow of resources that government bodies receive but cannot or will not manage appropriately.

It is becoming ever clearer that, without adequate institutions, more investment on prestigious types of transport infrastructure such as fancy airports, high-speed rail lines, or multilane motorways is not a panacea for economic development. Major investment in such projects in peripheral areas of Europe have made those places more accessible than they once were but not necessarily wealthier. Economically backward territories will likely end up better off by embarking on less ambitious transportation projects and striving instead to advance along other key axes of development, such as education, training, innovation, and local institutional conditions. Initiatives of that kind are the ones that will increase returns on efforts to improve transport infrastructure and promote local accessibility. Focusing on integrated, place-sensitive strategies is the way forward. Sharpening the emphasis on prestige infrastructure projects, by contrast, will probably result only in white elephants and cathedrals in the desert.

Acknowledgement This paper closely follows some of the ideas presented in Crescenzi, R., Di Cataldo, M., & Rodríguez-Pose, A. (2016). Government quality and the economic returns of transport infrastructure investment in European regions. *Journal of Regional Science, 56,* 555–582. doi:10.1111/jors.12264

References

Acemoğlu, D., & Dell, M. (2010). Productivity differences between and within countries. *American Economic Journal: Macroeconomics, 2*(1), 169–188. doi:https://doi.org/10.1257/mac.2.1.169

Acerete, B., Shaoul J., & Stafford A. (2009). Taking its toll: The private financing of roads in Spain. *Public Money and Management, 29,* 19–26. doi:https://doi.org/10.1080/09540960802617327

Albalate, D., & Bel, G. (2012). *The economics and politics of high-speed rail: Lessons from experiences abroad.* Lanham: Lexington Books.

Aschauer, D. A. (1989). Is public expenditure productive? *Journal of Monetary Economics, 23,* 177–200. doi:https://doi.org/10.1016/0304-3932(89)90047-0

Bentivogli, C., Casadio, P., & Cullino, R. (2011). I problemi nella realizzazione delle opere pubbliche: le specificità territoriali [Problems in the construction of public works: The territorial specificities]. In F. Balassone & P. Casadio (Eds.), *Le infrastrutture in Italia: Dotazione, programmazione, realizzazione* (pp. 401–437). Seminari e convegni—Workshops and Conferences: Vol. 7. Rome: Bank of Italy.

Biehl, D. (1986). *The contribution of infrastructure to regional development.* Brussels: Publication Office of the European Communities.

Bronzini, R., & Piselli, P. (2009). Determinants of long-run regional productivity with geographical spillovers: The role of R&D, human capital and public infrastructure. *Regional Science and Urban Economics, 39,* 187–199. doi:https://doi.org/10.1016/j.regsciurbeco.2008.07.002

Buchanan, J. M. (1989). The public choice perspective. In J. M. Buchanan, *Essays on the Political Economy* (pp. 13–24). Honolulu: University of Hawaii Press.

Buck, T. (2015, July 17). Spanish ghost airport costing €1 bn attracts offer of just €10,000: Ciudad Real airport was built during construction boom. *Financial Times.* Retrieved from https://www.ft.com/content/368d6998-2c81-11e5-acfb-cbd2e1c81cca

Bukowski, J. (2004). Multi-level networks as a threat to democracy? The case of Portugal's Vasco da Gama Bridge. *Journal of Southern Europe and the Balkans, 6,* 275–297. doi:https://doi.org/10.1080/1461319042000296822

Button, K. J. (1998). Infrastructure investment, endogenous growth and economic convergence. *Annals of Regional Science, 32,* 145–162 doi:https://doi.org/10.1007/s001680050067.

Button, K. J., Leitham, S., McQuaid, R. W., & Nelson, J. D. (1995). Transport and industrial and commercial location. *Annals of Regional Science, 29,* 189–206. doi:https://doi.org/10.1007/BF01581806

Cadot, O., Röller, L.-H., & Stephan, A. (1999). A political economy model of infrastructure allocation: An empirical assessment (FS IV 99-15). Retrieved from https://core.ac.uk/download/pdf/7195763.pdf

Cadot, O., Röller, L.-H., & Stephan, A. (2006). Contribution to productivity or pork barrel? The two faces of infrastructure investment. *Journal of Public Economics, 90,* 1133–1153. doi:https://doi.org/10.1016/j.jpubeco.2005.08.006

Cantarelli, C. C., Flyvbjerg, B., Molin, E. J. E., & van Wee, B. (2010). Cost overruns in large-scale transportation infrastructure projects: Explanations and their theoretical embeddedness. *European Journal of Transport and Infrastructure Research, 10,* 5–18. Retrieved from http://arxiv.org/pdf/1307.2176

Cappelen, A, Castellacci, F., Fagerberg, J., & Verspagen, B. (2003). The impact of EU regional support on growth and convergence in the European Union. *Journal of Common Market Studies, 41,* 621–644. doi:https://doi.org/10.1111/1468-5965.00438

Casadio, P., & Paccagnella, M. (2011). La difficile programmazione delle infrastrutture in Italia [The difficulties of planning infrastructure in Italy]. In F. Balassone & P. Casadio (Eds.), *Le infrastrutture in Italia: Dotazione, programmazione, realizzazione* (pp. 293–313). Seminari e convegni—Workshops and Conferences: Vol. 7. Rome: Bank of Italy.

Charron, N., Lapuente, V. V., & Rothstein, B. (2010). *Measuring the quality of government and subnational variation* (Report for the European Commission, Directorate-General Regional Policy, Directorate Policy Development). Gothenburg: University of Gothenburg. Retrieved from http://ec.europa.eu/regional_policy/sources/docgener/studies/pdf/2010_government_1. pdf

Cienski, J. (2013, January 30). EU halts €5bn for Poland over fraud fears. Financial Times. Retrieved from https://www.ft.com/content/590cb0fa-6afa-11e2-8017-00144feab49a

Crain, W. M., & Oakley, L. K. (1995). The politics of infrastructure. *The Journal of Law and Economics, 38,* 1–17. Retrieved from http://www.jstor.org/stable/725815

Crescenzi, R., Di Cataldo, M., & Rodríguez-Pose, A. (2016). Government quality and the economic returns of transport infrastructure investment in European regions. *Journal of Regional Science, 56,* 555–582. doi:https://doi.org/10.1111/jors.12264

Crescenzi, R., & Rodríguez-Pose, A. (2012). Infrastructure and regional growth in the European Union. *Regional Science, 91,* 487–513. doi:https://doi.org/10.1111/j.1435-5957.2012.00439.x

de Melo, J. J. (2000). The Vasco da Gama bridge on the Tagus Estuary: A paradigm of bad decision making, but good post-evaluation. *World Transport Policy and Practice, 6*(2), 20–31. Retrieved from http://hdl.handle.net/10362/5925

del Bo, C. F., & Florio, M. (2012). Infrastructure and growth in a spatial framework: Evidence from the EU regions. *European Planning Studies, 20,* 1393–1414. doi:https://doi.org/10.1080 /09654313.2012.680587

del Bo, C. F., Florio, M., & Manzi, G. (2010). Regional infrastructure and convergence: Growth implications in a spatial framework. *Transition Studies Review, 17,* 475–493. doi: https://doi. org/10.1007/s11300-010-0160-4

Departamento de Estadisticas. (2016). *Tráfico de pasajeros, operaciones y carga en los aeropuertos españoles: Datos provisionales* [Passangers, operations, and freight traffic in Spanish airports: Provisional data] (Annual 2016). Retrieved from http://www.aena.es/csee/ccurl/825/352/ Estadisticas_2016.pdf

Esfahani, H. S., & Ramírez, M. T. (2003). Institutions, infrastructure, and economic growth. *Journal of Development Economics, 70,* 443–477. doi:https://doi.org/10.1016/S0304-3878(02)00105-0

Flyvbjerg, B. (2009). Survival of the unfittest: Why the worst infrastructure gets built—and what can we do about it. *Oxford Review of Economic Policy, 25,* 344–367. doi:https://doi. org/10.1093/oxrep/grp024

Flyvbjerg, B., Holm, M. K. S., & Buhl, S. L. (2005). How (in) accurate are demand forecasts in public works projects? The case of transportation. *Journal of the American Planning Association, 71,* 131–146. doi:https://doi.org/10.1080/01944360508976688

Fujita, M., Krugman, P., & Venables, A. J. (1999). *The spatial economy: Cities, regions, and international trade.* Cambridge, MA: MIT Press.

Fujita, M., & Thisse, J.-F. (2002). Economics of agglomeration: Cities, industrial location, and regional growth. Cambridge, UK: Cambridge University Press. Retrieved from https://fenix. tecnico.ulisboa.pt/downloadFile/1126518382175106/Economics%20of%20agglomeration. pdf

Henisz, W. J. (2002). The institutional environment for infrastructure investment. *Industrial and Corporate Change, 11,* 355–389. doi:https://doi.org/10.1093/icc/11.2.355

Holtz-Eakin, D., & Schwartz, A. E. (1995). Infrastructure in a structural model of economic growth. *Regional Science and Urban Economics, 25*, 131–151. doi:https://doi.org/10.1016/0166-0462(94)02080-Z

INE (Instituto Nacional de Estatística). (2017). *Tráfego médio diário (N.°) nas pontes* [Average daily traffic by bridge]. Retrieved October 9, 2017, from https://www.ine.pt/xportal/xmain?xpid=INE&xpgid=ine_indicadores&indOcorrCod=0008936&contexto=bd&selTab=tab2

Kelejian, H. H., & Robinson, D. P. (1997). Infrastructure productivity estimation and its underlying econometric specifications: A sensitivity analysis. *Regional Science, 76*, 115–131. doi:https://doi.org/10.1111/j.1435-5597.1997.tb00684.x

Kemmerling, A., & Stephan, A. (2008). The politico-economic determinants and productivity effects of regional transport investment in Europe. *EIB Papers, 13*(2), 36–60. Retrieved from http://hdl.handle.net/10419/44890

Kenny, C. (2006). Measuring and reducing the impact of corruption in infrastructure (Policy Research Working Paper, No. 4099). Retrieved from http://hdl.handle.net/10986/9258

Kenny, C. (2007). Infrastructure, governance and corruption: Where next? (Policy Research Working Paper, No. 4331). Retrieved from http://hdl.handle.net/10986/7314

Levy, B., & Spiller, P. T. (Eds.). (1996). *Regulations, institutions, and commitment: Comparative studies of telecommunications*. New York: Cambridge University Press.

Lewis, B. D. (1998). The impact of public infrastructure on municipal economic development: Empirical results from Kenya. *Review of Urban and Regional Development Studies, 10*, 142–156. doi:https://doi.org/10.1111/j.1467-940X.1998.tb00092.x

Marangoni, D., & Marinelli, G. (2011). Il crescente ruolo delle amministrazioni locali nella programmazione e gestione della viabilità stradale [The growing role of local administrations in the planning and management of roads]. In F. Balassone & P. Casadio (Eds.), *Le infrastrutture in Italia: Dotazione, programmazione, realizzazione* (pp. 619–648). Seminari e convegni—Workshops and Conferences: Vol. 7. Rome: Bank of Italy.

Mauro, P. (1997). The effects of corruption on growth, investment, and government expenditure: A cross-country analysis. In K. A. Elliott (Ed.), *Corruption and the global economy* (pp. 83–108). Washington, DC: Institute for International Economics.

Minder, R. (2011, June 24). Spain's building spree leaves some airports and roads begging to be used. *The New York Times*. Retrieved from http://www.nytimes.com/2011/06/25/business/global/25iht-transport25.html?pagewanted=all&_r=1&

Ministerio de Fomento (Ministry of Public Works and Transport). (2017). *Tráfico en autopistas estatales de peaje* [Traffic on state toll motorways]. Retrieved October 5, 2017, from http://www.fomento.es/BE/?nivel=2&orden=06000000

Moreno, R., Artís, M., López-Bazo, E., & Suriñach, J. (1997). Evidence on the complex link between infrastructure and regional growth. *International Journal of Development Planning Literature, 12*, 81–108.

Moreno, R., & López-Bazo, E. (2007). Returns to local and transport infrastructure under regional spillovers. *International Regional Science Review, 30*, 47–71. doi:https://doi.org/10.1177/0160017606296728

Munnell, A. H. (Ed.). (1990). *Is there a shortfall in public capital investment? Proceedings of a conference held at Harwich Port, Massachusetts, June 1990*. The Federal Reserve Bank of Boston Conference Series: Vol. 34. Retrieved from https://pdfs.semanticscholar.org/0d66/fd9a783a177ddc4428b65860d52e4ce96b95.pdf

OECD (Organisation for economic co-operation and development). (2006). *Annual report on competition policy developments in the Slovak Republic*. Paris: OECD.

OECD (Organisation for economic co-operation and development). (2009). Infrastructure investment: Links to growth and the role of public policy. In OECD (Ed.), *Economic policy reforms: Going for growth* (pp. 163–178). Paris: OECD.

Ottaviano, G. I. P. (2008). Infrastructure and economic geography: An overview of evidence. *EIB Papers, 13*(2), 8–35. Retrieved from http://hdl.handle.net/10419/44891

Oxford Business Group. (2004). *Emerging Romania, 2003*. London: Oxford Business Group.

Painvin, N. (2009). Large projects, giant risks? Lessons learned—Suez Canal to Boston's Big Dig [Transportation global special report]. *Fitch Ratings: Global Infrastructure & Project Finance.* Retrieved from http://www.financequebec.com/Fitch%20Large%20Projects,%20Giant%20 Risks.pdf

Palet, L. S. (2014). Spain's 'ghost airports': A national embarrassment? *Ozymandias* [Ozy, on-line periodical]. Retrieved from http://www.ozy.com/acumen/ spains-ghost-airports-a-national-embarrassment/33041

Paterson, W. D. O., & Chaudhuri, P. (2007). Making inroads on corruption in the transport sector through control and prevention. In J. E. Campos & S. Pradhan (Eds.), *The many faces of corruption: Tracking vulnerabilities at the sector level (pp. 159–190).* Washington, DC: The World Bank. Retrieved from http://citeseerx.ist.psu.edu/viewdoc/download?doi=10.1.1.132.45 31&rep=rep1&type=pdf

Puga, D. (2002). European regional policies in the light of recent location theories. *Journal of Economic Geography, 2,* 373–406. doi:https://doi.org/10.1093/jeg/2.4.373

Puga, D., & Venables, A. J. (1997). Preferential trading arrangements and industrial location. *Journal of International Economics, 43,* 347–368. doi:https://doi.org/10.1016/S0022-1996(96)01480-8

Robinson, J. A., & Torvik, R. (2005). White elephants. *Journal of Public Economics, 89,* 197–210 doi:https://doi.org/10.1016/j.jpubeco.2004.05.004.

Rodríguez-Pose, A. (2000). Economic convergence and regional development strategies in Spain: The case of Galicia and Navarre. *EIB Papers, 5*(1), 88–115. Retrieved from http://hdl.handle. net/10419/44791

Rodríguez-Pose, A., & Fratesi, U. (2004). Between development and social policies: The impact of European Structural Funds in Objective 1 regions. *Regional Studies, 38,* 97–113. doi:https:// doi.org/10.1080/0034340031000163226

Short, J., & Knopp, A. (2005). Transport infrastructure: Investment and planning. Policy and research aspects. *Transport Policy, 12,* 360–367. doi:https://doi.org/10.1016/j.tranpol.2005.04.003

Stephan, A. (2000). Regional infrastructure policy and its impact on productivity: A comparison of Germany and France. *Konjunkturpolitik: Zeitschrift für angewandte Wirtschaftsforschung, 46,* 327–356.

Tanzi, V., & Davoodi, H. R. (1997). Corruption, public investment, and growth (IMF Working Paper, 97/139). Retrieved from https://ssrn.com/abstract=882701

Tanzi, V., & Davoodi, H. R. (1998). *Roads to nowhere: How corruption in public investment hurts growth.* Economic Issues: No. 12. Washington, DC: International Monetary Fund. Retrieved from http://www.imf.org/external/pubs/ft/issues12/

Turano, G. (2011, November 24). Salerno-Reggio, ci mancava la maxi-multa [Salerno-Reggio, only the fine was missing]. *L'Espresso.* Retrieved from http://espresso.repubblica.it/dettaglio/ salerno-reggio-ci-mancava-la-maxi-multa/2167177

van den Heuvel, G. (2005). The parliamentary enquiry on fraud in the Dutch construction industry collusion as concept between corruption and state-corporate crime. *Crime, Law and Social Change, 44,* 133–151. doi:https://doi.org/10.1007/s10611-006-9009-5

Vickerman, R. W. (1995). The regional impacts of Trans-European networks. *The Annals of Regional Science, 29,* 237–254. doi:https://doi.org/10.1007/BF01581809

Vickerman, R. W. (2007). *Recent evolution of research into the wider economic benefits of transport infrastructure investments* (OECD/ITF Joint Transport Research Centre Discussion Papers, 2007/09). doi:https://doi.org/10.1787/234770772187

Wachs, M. (1989). When planners lie with numbers. *Journal of the American Planning Association, 55,* 476–479. Retrieved from http://hdl.handle.net/10822/833099

World Bank (2011, June). *Curbing fraud, corruption, and collusion in the roads sector.* Washington, DC: The World Bank Group. Retrieved from http://siteresources.worldbank.org/INTDOII/Resources/Roads_Paper_Final.pdf

Chapter 12
Globalization and Institutional Change in Italian Industrial Districts

Harald Bathelt and Nicolas Conserva

Industrial Districts and Globalization Processes

During the 1980s and 1990s, Italian industrial districts and their internal economic structure became a major field of academic inquiry in the social sciences, receiving a lot of attention as an alternative regional industry configuration that successfully resisted the trend toward mass production and large-firm dominance during the Fordist era. Especially the so-called Third Italy was celebrated for its ability to achieve growth on the basis of an agglomeration of small and medium-sized firms that were closely linked through regional production networks (Becattini, 1990; Becattini, Bellandi, & de Propris, 2009; Belussi & Pilotti, 2002; Brusco, 1982), characterized by localized learning processes and specialized institutional settings (Amin & Thrift, 1995; for an overview of developments and debates see, Bathelt, 1998; Bathelt & Glückler, 2012).

With globalization processes intensifying since the 1980s and pressure on firms and regions to become better integrated into the global economy, new challenges to growth have arisen in these industrial districts. The fundamental question raised by these developments is whether localized learning systems can survive in an era of increased global competition (Belussi & Sedita, 2012; Camuffo & Grandinetti, 2011; dei Ottati, 2009a, 2009b; Lan, 2015; Rabellotti, 2004; Whitford, 2001; Whitford & Potter, 2007). In other words, how can the institutional settings of industrial districts and the mechanisms in place to support localized production and learning be modernized to enable economic growth in a globalizing world?

H. Bathelt (✉)
Department of Political Science and Department of Geography and Planning,
University of Toronto, ON, Canada
e-mail: harald.bathelt@utoronto.ca

N. Conserva
Department of Political Science, University of Toronto, ON, Canada
e-mail: nicolas.conserva@mail.utoronto.ca

J. Glückler et al. (eds.), *Knowledge and Institutions*, Knowledge and Space 13,
https://doi.org/10.1007/978-3-319-75328-7_12

To answer this question in this chapter, we employ a case study of the Canavese district in northern Italy, north of Turin. The region has an interesting economic structure in that it is characterized by two interlinked organizational fields (DiMaggio & Powell, 1983), with a concentration of key suppliers, users, regulatory agencies, and other organizations in both the automotive–metallurgical and electronics–mechatronics industries. Canavese is home to the automotive producer Fiat and the electronics and minicomputer firm Olivetti that dominated the development of the two organizational fields. While somewhat different from other industrial districts that do not specialize in capital-intensive and technology-based industries, Canavese also established a localized production and learning system with a division of labor that was centered on the two lead firms (e.g., Albino, Garavelli, & Schiuma, 1998; Giblin, 2011). With increasing global competitive pressure on Fiat and Olivetti, the entire region had to go through extensive restructuring processes beginning in the 1980s. Interestingly, both organizational fields underwent a similar institutional change, evolving from a context characterized by localized learning and a distinct regional manufacturing culture to a more global, open-learning based and interactive system, while maintaining regional linkages and reference points.

In this chapter we use the example of Canavese to show that it is advantageous from the perspective of regional economic development to employ a hybrid mix of elements combining institutional change with continuity to cope with the challenges of globalization. It is argued that successful regional restructuring of a localized production system cannot be based on radical technological and institutional shifts alone. While such restructuring requires that some fundamental institutional adjustments be initiated to encourage the formation of global linkages and new technological trajectories, the process also needs elements of continuity to support established industries and prior competitive advantages. In the context of this volume on knowledge and institutions, we demonstrate in this chapter how an institutional perspective is crucial in understanding spatially differentiated processes of economic and social change.

In the next section, we develop our conceptual argument and present a model that relates regional restructuring outcomes to different types of adjustments in the localized institutional context and the industry structure. This is followed by brief comments about the methodology applied and a description of the socioeconomic context of the Canavese region with Fiat and Olivetti. The analytical part of our study presents a systematic discussion of how the regional production system developed from a setting of localized learning into an open economic system, providing support for the conceptual model of industrial, institutional, and regional change. We conclude by considering policy implications.

Regional Growth and Institutional Change

In conceptualizing the process of how localized learning systems can adjust to globalization pressures and successfully restructure, we develop a perspective that pays particular attention to the role of the regional institutional context and its adjustments. This perspective links to other work in economic geography that has dealt with the dangers of regional lock-in and the challenges of maintaining regional resilience. There is a now broad literature on regional lock-in processes emphasizing the threats to innovation and economic growth that result if institutional settings become too rigid or are over-embedded in hierarchical power structures with few dominant actors (e.g., Hassink & Shin, 2005; Martin & Sunley, 2006). This literature focuses on ways to explain and avoid institutional rigidity. Other, more recent work has focused on the economic resilience of regions that experience external shocks. Related studies have investigated how regions are able to withstand or overcome such ruptures and return to their former growth paths (e.g., Hassink, 2010; Martin & Sunley, 2015; Pike, Marlow, McCarthy, O'Brien, & Tomaney, 2015). Although the studies on lock-in and economic resilience emphasize the importance of institutions in economic development, their analytical focus is on preventing interruptions to economic growth patterns, rather than on investigating the interdependencies between corporate adjustments and regional institutional change in generating a new regional development path. Especially in the context of fundamental ruptures, when localized learning systems are threatened by globalization processes, the institutional perspective applied in this chapter may be useful in exploring the potential for successful regional restructuring and discussing alternative scenarios of development (Bathelt & Glückler, 2012; Glückler & Bathelt, 2017).

Institutions and Institutional Context

An institutional perspective is crucial when analyzing regional economic development as a collective process because institutions enable economic actors to develop expectations of the behavior of other actors and reduce uncertainties in economic life (e.g., Hodgson, 1988; North, 1990). Firms will find it less risky to engage in collaborative practices, in particular when certain types of behavior can be enforced and deviations sanctioned. Like the "tricks of the trade" of how to behave in a certain environment, specific institutional settings are a prerequisite for the development of any sort of social division of labor. Therefore, when analyzing coherent economic structures, such as localized learning systems, special attention must be paid to the role of regional institutions that enable coordinated interaction and generate the conditions for the reproduction of such patterns (e.g., Rodríguez-Pose & Storper, 2006). If such institutional settings are replaced by new types of institutions, learning processes that rely on a regional division of labor may change substantially and localized interaction patterns may disappear.

While most researchers in economic geography would agree with the above logic (e.g., Boschma & Frenken, 2009), the understanding of institutions is often vague and the term *institution* used unspecifically to refer to all sorts of government influences on economic development. This causes misunderstandings as to how institutions operate (Bathelt & Glückler, 2012, 2014). If, for instance, an established government initiative in a region introduces a new policy to stimulate economic growth, the question arises as to whether this is a case of institutional persistence (because it is carried out by an established organization) or institutional change (because of the introduction of a new policy). Our answer would clearly depend on the understanding of institutions applied. In the following, we argue for a careful and explicit definition of institutions.

We suggest looking at institutions in terms of how they shape economic interaction. In some studies, governments, banks, or pension funds are viewed as institutions (e.g., Clark & Monk, 2013). However, in our perspective these are organizations, not institutions. A ministry for economic development, for instance, does not have an immediate impact on economic interaction. Nevertheless, it may decide upon and create new rules, regulations, and policies that are relevant for the firms in a region because these are intended to guide their behavior. In economics, institutions are therefore widely understood as rules and regulations (Gertler, 2010; North, 1991). In our view, however, such rules and regulations are not yet institutions. They establish a framework for actions but do not determine a specific form of action and interaction. For instance, a new regional start-up policy providing financial incentives may lead to innovative firm start-ups from local universities or it may trigger vertical disintegration in existing industries. In the first case, this may generate a regional context of individualistic technology start-ups; in the second, a trust-based division of labor in established industries may develop. This example suggests that rules and regulations can be interpreted differently by firms and may have a completely different outcome in terms of the unfolding regional practices and patterns of interaction. It is these latter patterns of correlated behavior (Setterfield, 1993) or planned and unplanned stabilizations of economic interaction (Bathelt & Glückler, 2014) that we refer to as institutions in a narrow sense.

For an institutional analysis of regional economic change, it is clearly not enough to focus on only one of these institutional building blocks. As suggested by DiMaggio and Powell (1983, p. 147), "highly structured organizational fields provide a context in which individual efforts to deal rationally with uncertainty and constraint often lead, *in the aggregate*, to homogeneity in structure, culture, and output" [emphasis added]. When investigating the dynamics of organizational fields within a framework of regional change, it is therefore necessary to consider all levels of what we refer to as the *institutional context*, as well as their interplay (Glückler & Bathelt, 2017): the role of and linkages between institutional actors (individuals and organizations that generate rules), the rules and regulations that are created by them (and act as a framework for interaction), and the patterns of economic interaction that develop in practice (i.e., the institutions in a narrow sense). While these interconnections between organizations, rules, and practices have hardly been systematically studied in broader conceptual and empirical investigations, some extreme scenarios seem intuitively clear when considering the consequences of globalization processes. It is likely, for instance, that existing firms operating according to long-term rule systems with established practices may have a hard time adjusting to abrupt changes caused by globalization. Conversely, a large number of young firms that engage in emerging technology fields driven by new rules and regulations may develop flexible interaction patterns that make it quite easy to adjust to new

Table 12.1 Regional restructuring scenarios as a response to globalization pressures

Regional restructuring scenarios		Adjustments in the regional institutional context		
		Persistence	Hybrid change	Fundamental change
Adjustments in the regional industry and corporate structure	Persistence	- Loss of corporate competitiveness - No effects of regional learning - Regional decline	- Institutional stimulus unsuccessful - Stagnation of regional learning base	- New institutions do not match - Loss of regional learning base - Regional crisis
	Change	- Limited new learning patterns develop - Hollowing out of regional learning platform - Slow regional change	- New and old industries integrated in new and established learning cycles - Growth in global economy consistent with localized learning	- New industries supported by new institutions - Established industries left behind - Bifurcated regional structure

Source: Design by authors

global structures. Nevertheless, the institutional context cannot exclusively concentrate on such young firms and emerging technologies. The challenges of globalization in the localized learning context of an industrial district also have to be met by existing firms operating in established technologies according to long-established practices of production and marketing. It is therefore fundamental to develop bridging and connecting capabilities between established and new practices to trigger broader, more inclusive regional change.

Industrial, Institutional, and Regional Change

To discuss the institutional context of regional economic change in more detail, we introduce a simple model that can be applied to the situation of a localized learning system, which is challenged by globalization processes. The model, summarized in Table 12.1, presents different scenarios of regional economic change in relation to two factors: (i) adjustments in the regional industry and corporate structure and (ii) adjustments in the regional institutional context. We assume that these two types of changes can originally occur independently but that at later stages industrial change can influence or trigger institutional adjustments and vice versa (Glückler & Lenz, 2016). Inspired by the studies of Douglas and Hargadon (2017), Scott (1998), and Streeck and Thelen (2005), which point at the importance of hybrid or mixed scenarios, the following analysis investigates how different combinations of corporate and institutional changes in a region will influence the outcome of regional restructuring processes in response to increasing globalization.

Table 12.1 refers to a specific regional context, such as an industrial district, that has developed a coherent industry structure characterized by localized learning dynamics and self-sustained innovation. As this regional context is challenged by a wave of globalization processes associated with widening markets, new international competition, and newly emerging technology centers, both industry and corporate structures in the region and the institutional context are put under pressure. Table 12.1 pictures six possible scenarios.

In a first set of scenarios, we assume that core parts of the corporate structure in the region do not respond adequately to globalization forces, continuing instead to collaborate with the same set of regional or national partners and relying on the same technologies as before. Although such an extreme scenario of industrial persistence may be hard to find in pure form, the Barletta footwear district in southern Italy illustrates a similar situation in which industrial structures have remained largely unchanged and challenges have not led to substantive innovation (Boschma & Ter Wal, 2007). In such a case, a positive regional outcome cannot be expected, no matter what changes are implemented or occur in the institutional context. Indeed, the case of Barletta shows how a regional government has struggled to identify appropriate policies to support regional change in the face of a largely unresponsive industry structure (Rosati, 2016). If the institutional context in this situation largely persists, a loss of corporate competitiveness can result, with remaining regional learning processes unable to fundamentally solve globalization-related problems as actors lack access to wider knowledge ecologies. Such a situation could be related to institutional hysteresis (Setterfield, 1993) or regional lock-in (Martin & Sunley, 2006) and result in regional decline. If such a situation is coupled with efforts to radically change the institutional context, for instance, by generating new research organizations and establishing a fundamentally different set of support policies, the outcome may not be much different because the new institutional conditions are not likely to match the preexisting corporate structures persisting in this scenario. In the end, this can threaten the regional learning basis and result in a regional economic crisis.[1] Hybrid institutional change would have a similar effect since the industry structure is persistent and does not adjust to globalization pressures.

The outcome is fundamentally different if core parts of the regional economy recognize the opportunities and threats associated with globalization and engage in corporate restructuring processes, for instance, by investing in new technologies and linking with international markets and technology centers through foreign-direct investments (e.g., Cantwell, 2014). Two cases that illustrate this situation are the Fermano and Riviera del Brenta footwear districts in the Third Italy (Buciuni & Pisano, 2016; Cutrini, 2011; Rabellotti, 2004). In contrast to Barletta, these two districts underwent successful industrial reorganization and innovation processes,

---

[1]An example of such an outcome is the unsuccessful implementation of a science park and a related start-up strategy. It has long been known (e.g., Massey, Quintas, & Wield, 1992) that such initiatives often only stimulate a limited response and little regional change, especially if public policies do not systematically link preexisting industries with the new developments.

which were supported by regional policies and led to a changing institutional context. In our model, the precise outcome in a situation of substantial industrial and corporate change depends on the nature of the institutional adjustments that occur or are implemented, as indicated in Table 12.1. We distinguish three ideal-type situations:

(i) If the institutional context in terms of practices, regulations, and policies remains largely the same, new learning patterns may apply to those firms that engage in restructuring but exclude other regional actors.[2] This may result in a progressive weakening of the regional learning platform and in a hollowing-out process (Bathelt, 2009, 2013), resulting in slow regional change, limited economic growth, or even stagnation.

(ii) If radical changes are implemented within the institutional context by, for example, providing incentives for fundamental organizational shifts and introducing policies targeting new industries and start-up processes in new technology fields, the effects may be more promising, although the overall outcome may still be slow regional change and a bifurcation of the regional economic structure as traditional industries with persistent product and technology structures may be left behind.

(iii) The scenario is quite different, however, if one considers a hybrid structure of institutional adjustments involving, for instance, new policies directed, on the one hand, at modernization and adjustment processes in traditional industries and, on the other hand, at discontinuous technological change and the establishment of new industries. The example of the city of Prato pictures a similar situation, in which new Chinese entrepreneurs with novel manufacturing practices have entered the field of ready-to-wear fashion (*pronta moda*) and coexist with older Italian producers and their established manufacturing culture (Lan, 2015). It is through such hybrid settings that both established and new industry structures can be supported simultaneously and become integrated in overlapping learning cycles. This new structure then has the potential to transform existing learning patterns by integrating external actors and technological developments while encouraging localized feedback loops. It is such hybrid institutional change that may have the potential to preserve localized learning dynamics in the context of the global economy by combining fundamentally new institutional elements, which open up regional dynamics, with preexisting ones that encourage coherent regional linkages.

The importance of hybrid institutional change has also been pointed out in other literature on regional and national economic restructuring processes (e.g., Evenhuis, 2015; Streek & Thelen, 2005). In their political economy analysis, Mahoney and Thelen (2010), for instance, identify multiple institutional strategies that link

---

[2] Although such an extreme situation may not be typical, it can occur when, for instance, regional policies and industrial practices focus on the traditional industry structure and do not support the development of or shift to new technologies. The case of Barletta (Rosati, 2016), but also the chemical industry regions in East Germany (Bathelt, 2013) may illustrate such a scenario.

preexisting with new economic structures. These hybrid institutional adjustments range from displacement strategies (in which new institutions challenge and replace older ones) to conversion (in which established institutions are redesigned to new purposes), but also include strategies of layering (linking new elements to existing ones) and drift (where active adjustments are made to existing institutional settings). Pike et al. (2015) emphasize that such processes are not one-time adjustments but involve repeated restructuring and institutional calibration over an extended period. Which strategy is appropriate in a specific situation depends on the conditions of the challenges and the nature of the preexisting institutional context.

In sum, the argument behind the six regional restructuring scenarios in Table 12.1 suggests that the chances for successful regional economic change are best if, on the one hand, open and flexible adjustments in corporate structures occur and if, on the other hand, these are coupled with hybrid changes in the institutional context that address both the need for fundamental restructuring and the importance of securing regional coherence related to pre-existing competencies. Of course, the reality is more complex than expressed in this model because institutional contexts involve multiple levels consisting of organizations, rules, and stabilized practices. There is no guarantee that changes of these three levels will always be directed toward the same outcome. For the sake of our overall argument, we do not investigate the potential contingencies between these levels but focus on the entirety of the institutional context and on those changes with the most notable impact.[3] Much research is still necessary to investigate the relationships that exist between the different levels of the institutional context.

Methodology

In this research we used the Canavese district in the Piedmont region of Italy as a theory-confirming typical case (Seawright & Gerring, 2008; Tokatli, 2015) to investigate the restructuring processes in a region subjected to globalization processes that have challenged the sustainability of its localized learning system. Canavese, located north of Turin, can be viewed as a typical case because the region with its two organizational fields was able to successfully adjust to globalization pressures in a process enabled by hybrid institutional change, as we illustrate in the empirical part of our chapter. In the 1990s and 2000s, the region's dominant industries that developed historically around its two lead firms, Fiat and Olivetti, were challenged by new international competition from both highly developed industrial regions and low-labor-cost locations. At the same time, markets opened up and massive foreign-direct investment processes were undertaken by regional firms that developed a multinational structure with access to international markets and technologies. The

---

[3] Such contingencies are important, as illustrated by Glückler and Lenz (2016), who identify four different types of connections between the levels of interaction practices and rules and regulation in the institutional context: reinforcement, substitution, circumvention, and competition.

Table 12.2 Economic demography of Canavese by industry groups; 1991, 2001, and 2011

	1991	2001	2011
Economic indicator	Industry total		
Firms	20,150	24,350	23,450
Employees	95,800	102,100	87,000
	Industries related to Olivetti and Fiat[1]		
Firms	2,050	2,500	3,250
Employees	31,400	28,350	31,000
Firms (% of industry total)	10.1	10.3	13.8
Employees (% of industry total)	32.8	27.8	35.6
Employees in firms related to Olivetti & Fiat with 250 or more employees (%)	38.4	20.1	17.4
Employees in firms related to Olivetti & Fiat with less than 250 employees (%)	61.7	79.9	82.6

Note.[1] Electronics, mechanics, steel molding, and components
Source: Computed from ISTAT (1991, 2001, 2011) for the local labor market areas of Cirie, Ivrea, and Rivarolo Canavese

Canavese district managed these challenges quite well compared to other Italian regions (e.g., Buciuni & Finotto, 2016). Between 1991 and 2011, the number of firms in the district increased from 20,150 to 23,450, while employment experienced a modest decline from 95,800 to 87,000 jobs (Table 12.2). Remarkably, the historically dominant automotive–metallurgical and electronics–mechatronics industries were able to restructure quite successfully and avoid a deeper regional crisis. In fact, employment in these industries remained constant between 1991 and 2011, at about 31,000 employees, and the number of firms increased by more than 50%, from 2,050 to 3,250. As a result, the regional share of these industries in employment and firm population increased during the 1990s and 2000s. This was due to tremendous start-up and growth processes of small and medium-sized firms (less than 250 employees) and declining employment in large firms (250 or more employees).

We used an institutional perspective in our empirical analysis to investigate the successful restructuring processes in Canavese, applying a mixed-methods approach. On the one hand, this involved the collection of data, prior academic work, and policy reports, as well as the analysis of media and published interviews with key entrepreneurs and experts. We also conducted 18 semistructured interviews in "close dialogue" (Clark, 1998; Yin, 2009) with regional firms, planning authorities, institutional actors, and observers during the summer of 2015 to systematically collect information about the industrial and institutional adjustments that took place. We began the interviews with questions about the early development of the district and the institutional context that formed in terms of decisive organizations, policies, and interaction practices, and followed by questions about the role of globalization processes and the resulting threats to the competitiveness of local industries. Finally, interviewees were asked to compare today's industrial structure and institutional context with the earlier ones and to identify the changes that occurred.

Interviewees were selected initially by contacting significant firms, policy and planning authorities, and university researchers, and subsequently through a snowball method. In the end, the various sources of information were triangulated with each other (Miles & Huberman, 1994) in an attempt to reinterpret the regional restructuring process from an institutional perspective consistently across these various sources. Our methodology did not permit the direct study of interaction patterns between firms and their dynamics. Instead we based our implications on an interpretation of interview data and prior descriptions in the literature. The results presented in the following sections allowed us to draw conclusions about the different levels of the institutional context and their changes.

The Socioeconomic Context of Canavese

Historically, the Canavese region developed a spatial division of labor shaped by the two lead firms, Fiat and Olivetti. The region's northeastern part, around the city of Ivrea, Olivetti's headquarters location, specialized in electronics, information and communication technologies, and fine mechanics; the southern part near Turin in automotive manufacturing; and the northwestern part in mechanics and steel molding (Confindustria Canavese, 2015; Demetrio & Giaccaria, 2010). The organizational fields surrounding Fiat and Olivetti and their respective institutional context are investigated in separate subsections below.

Fiat and the Automotive–Metallurgical Industry

Fiat was originally established in 1899. The firm developed a network of production facilities in Turin and adjacent areas. Not only did Fiat become a major automotive producer in Europe, but the growth of the industry also spawned a broad network of local suppliers and service providers in western and southern Canavese. These suppliers were largely oriented toward Fiat, which purchased 70 to 80% of their products, and thus quite dependent on the automobile producer (Aimone Gigio, Cullino, Fabrizi, Linarello, & Orame, 2012). Although Fiat had begun establishing international linkages to some European markets as early as the 1920s, these were mainly sales-oriented and focused on market integration. Global knowledge acquisition practices and international partnerships were seemingly less important. However, intense rationalization and cost-cutting pressures in the European automobile industry during the 1980s and 1990s led to international mergers and acquisitions (Hudson & Schamp, 1995), exerting strong competitive pressures on Fiat. The consequences were restructuring processes and successive downsizing exercises aimed at cutting costs (Whitford & Enrietti, 2005). The impact of these pressures on the supplier sector in the Canavese district was severe. Between 1991 and 2007, employment in car manufacturing decreased by over two-thirds—although component production did recover from an initial decline (Aimone Gigio et al., 2012). Resulting job losses were largely outweighed by the growth of other segments of the sector (Table 12.2). Despite this downturn, the automotive industry kept a strong foothold in the region. By 2009, 355 of Fiat's tier-1 suppliers were still located in the province of Turin, indicating that there was still a substantial local production system (Aimone Gigio et al., 2012).

Overall, the automotive–metallurgical production system in the Canavese region was highly dependent on Fiat. The firm had established a hierarchical division of labor and more or less dictated the conditions of producer–user relationships and the direction of technological change. Underlying this institutional context was a Fordist political economy with centralized capital-labor relations and strong unions (Bagnasco, 1986; Whitford & Enrietti, 2005). Overall, disadvantages of the large-firm dominance in this industry were visible in the institutional context, which remained focused on the role of Fiat, with no particularly strong initiatives to support restructuring or the development of new industries.[4] This part of the regional economy was clearly locked into the value chain of Fiat. Although specifically attuned to the context of the global automobile industry with linkages to international markets, the institutional context was fundamentally characterized by linkages within the regional production system and localized learning processes that were the drivers of regional growth.

Olivetti and the Electronics–Mechatronics Industry

Similar to Fiat, Olivetti was established as a family business in 1908 and developed a strong reputation as a producer of typewriters—a relatively new technology at that time. Olivetti internationalized its activities early on, exporting products to other countries and setting up market-related branches in Barcelona (1929) and Buenos Aires (1932). In the 1940s, Adriano Olivetti took control of the firm at a time when it had begun producing mechanic calculators and would soon develop electric typewriters (1950s). From these activities, the firm moved into technologically related segments of the electronics industry. Olivetti produced Italy's first electronic mainframe computer in 1959 and the first desktop computer worldwide (Programma 101) in 1965 (Brilliant, 1993; Olivetti, 1978–2009; Radogna, 1960). It also focused on electronic calculators, which were very successful. Olivetti eventually developed into a major player in the fields of electronics and office equipment with a total of 73,300 employees in 1970 (47% of whom were in Italy) and a strong international presence (Barbiellini Amidei, Goldstein, & Spadoni, 2010; Castagnoli, 2014).

---

[4] Interestingly, Fiat became a shareholder of Olivetti in 1964. The firm viewed this engagement primarily as a portfolio investment, rather than a strategy to develop competencies in the electronics sector. Later, when Olivetti ran into problems, Fiat used its ownership share in the firm to push for a sale and disintegration of the electronics division with the idea of strengthening other business segments of Olivetti (Gallino, 2003).

By that time, the eastern part of Canavese had developed into a distinct electronics–mechatronics district. One interviewee who had experienced this process described in 2015 how there had been and still was a specific atmosphere in this district. Olivetti had a strong presence in the region, especially in Ivrea, and many families had members that worked for Olivetti. The firm also introduced an extensive corporate welfare system and supported employees' education programs. All this led to the development of collaborative capital-labor relationships in the region, strong employee loyalty, and high levels of social trust (Arrigo, 2003).

In the 1970s and 1980s, the firm continued to internationalize its activities through takeovers and partnerships and established research and development centers in leading high-technology regions such as Cupertino and New Canaan in the United States and Cambridge in the United Kingdom (Castagnoli, 2014). Canavese itself never developed into a similarly vibrant hot spot because it lacked, as our interviewees indicated, the necessary variety of competitors and technology leaders. Although Olivetti recognized the importance of being located close to leading-edge technology clusters, the establishment of research and development subsidiaries in such regions was not a substitute for a strong, localized knowledge ecosystem around its innovation and production base in Ivrea. One observer explained in an interview that there had been attempts to sell activities to and closely collaborate with another technology leader that could have provided better access to leading technology clusters, but that these attempts ultimately failed.

By the 1990s, Olivetti had lost its leading edge and was unable to cope with the technology dynamics driven by leading regions such as Silicon Valley. Like the minicomputer industry in Boston's Route 128 region (Saxenian, 1994), it ran into problems, leading to a shift toward telecommunications equipment. Not only did the firm lose its leadership, it also came under huge financial pressure as a result of problematic management decisions and its extensive corporate welfare system (Gallino, 2003). The firm had always been focused on hardware rather than software development and observers argued that Olivetti eventually failed because it was unable to exploit its first-mover advantages over American competitors and shift from electronics to computers in the early 1970s (Gallino, 2003; Perotto, 1995; Soria, 1979).[5] Eventually, after a merger–takeover deal with the Telecom Italia group in 1999, the Olivetti brand name was marginalized and the firm's global leadership ultimately gone.

The regional impact of Olivetti's growth was just as significant as that of Fiat, albeit in a different way. Olivetti shaped a regional production system involving more interactive, trust-based collaboration than the one surrounding Fiat. Firms in this production system continued to be innovative in order to maintain their competitiveness. Olivetti supported university programs, professional schools, and even high schools to generate new talent and sustain existing capabilities (Arrigo, 2003). As pointed out in our interviews, the firm had developed a local supplier network somewhat like Fiat's but not nearly as large, with some 80% of it consisting of small

---

[5] It was no longer possible to exploit these advantages after Olivetti's electronics division was sold to General Electric in an attempt to overcome financial difficulties.

family businesses (Michelsons, 1990). In contrast to Fiat, the supplier network was not structured hierarchically, instead being more open and based on interactive learning processes. Networks, as one expert told us, were often made up of former Olivetti employees who had gotten to know each other while working at that firm. These networks strengthened regional capabilities and led to the development of new technologies through firms such as Manital, CTS, ASIC, or Logitech—in other words, developments related to former innovations by Olivetti.

The corporate culture of Olivetti produced an interactive and open learning network based on trust. Early on, Adriano Olivetti developed strong linkages between the firm and the local community and pushed for active knowledge exchange and the idea of free knowledge access. In this spirit, the firm organized events with international designers to broaden its knowledge base beyond purely technical skills. Olivetti also established programs for its employees to regularly visit other production facilities and research centers. One of the interviewees suggested that because of these practices "Ivrea engaged with globalization [even] before globalization existed". These kinds of practices also made it possible for employees in the local production system to develop broad competences and contribute to the reproduction of innovation dynamics—albeit not quite at the level of diversity and competition as in leading technology clusters. When Olivetti finally faltered, extensive early-retirement programs were negotiated with the national government. Although publicly funded, these programs were in line with Olivetti's practice of providing extensive corporate welfare to its employees (Arrigo, 2003; Censis, 2001; Provost & Lai, 2016). The downside of these programs was a massive loss of local talent due to retirement. A consequence of this was that a local start-up boom, such as that seen in regions such as Boston or Silicon Valley, did not happen (Bathelt & Glückler, 2012).

Although the context of the electronics–mechatronics district differed in important ways from the automotive industry in that it was less hierarchical, more open, and oriented (as early as the 1960s) toward international linkages, there were also fundamental similarities. Both organizational fields had a strong regional technology orientation, important localized learning processes, and were embedded in their respective localized manufacturing culture with limited linkages to global technology dynamics.

From Localized Learning to Open Systems

Having characterized the structure and evolution of the localized production and learning system in Canavese, we explain in this section how the region was able to overcome the threats and challenges accompanying economic globalization processes in the 1990s and 2000s. It is argued that this was possible because new economic activities were established and existing structures upgraded to meet the demands of open markets and international competition. This went hand in hand with fundamental changes across the entire institutional context as new players introduced new economic models, new policies were established, and practices evolved from localized learning to open systems integration. This process was also linked to and built upon existing institutional settings and former business legacies, enabling the inclusion of traditionally operating firms in the overall restructuring and modernization process. Interestingly, such hybrid institutional change occurred in both the automotive–metallurgical and electronics–mechatronics industries of the Canavese region. It enabled a push from localized learning and interaction toward open systems and global networks while actively embedding prior structures and competencies.

Internationalization of Fiat

Ongoing competitive pressures in the automobile industry during the 1990s led to further downsizing at Fiat but also supported opening up the industry's structure, which became more internationalized. Local supplier linkages substantially decreased, although some continuity remained, with about 30% of Fiat's supplies still originating from the surrounding region (Aimone Gigio et al., 2012) in 2007. Suppliers reacted to the overall decline in orders from Fiat by actively strengthening other business segments and developing new customer relations beyond Turin and Canavese. In fact, significant internationalization processes gradually emerged in the supplier sector. This was also accompanied by efforts to move vigorously into new technology fields and to develop new products. Former Fiat managers also got involved in start-up processes, while building upon and strengthening preexisting network relations. One could say that the highly localized Fiat district was transformed into a more open and internationalized automobile district (Aimone Gigio et al., 2012; Whitford & Enrietti, 2005). Automobile suppliers continued to collaborate locally with each other, albeit less so with Fiat. As one interviewee emphasized, "firms learned they have to collaborate to survive."

In contrast to Olivetti's strong social and cultural impact on the electronics industry and its labor force, the influence of Fiat was different and focused on the production system, being less concerned with the promotion of local socioeconomic development. Fiat's presence and its impact in the region continued to decline after the 1990s (Confindustria Canavese, 2015; Demetrio & Giaccaria, 2010), with its headquarters eventually even moving to the Netherlands after Fiat took over Chrysler. Despite this, the firm maintained key research centers and university linkages in the region. Existing local research capabilities also attracted new firms from other regions and countries, including General Motors, which established its local Powertrain Europe research center in 2005 as a result of a partnership with Fiat and continued its activities in the area even after this agreement ended. Public policies supported the regional transformation of the automotive sector, although they were not decisive in triggering it. For instance, regional initiatives like the Aerospace Platform were established to strengthen the development of engine technologies in different applications. Other policies were put in place to manage areas with discontinued production, in particular through the regional agency Torino Nuova Economia, a public-private consortium that included Fiat (Torino Nuova Economia, n.d.).

It appears that crucial elements of this institutional change resulted more from bottom-up processes than from top-down policies—as firms realized the significance of establishing new external markets, oriented themselves to their peers' strategies, and recognized the importance of regional networks. This went along with a decline of Fordist production structures, while preserving a distinct regional production context and building upon existing competencies. The process of hybrid institutional change was also supported by new firms and organizations and through government programs that introduced new policies.

Institutional Legacy of Olivetti and Arduino

In the electronics–mechatronics industry, Olivetti's legacy was just as important as that of Fiat in the automotive–metallurgical industry, although in different ways. Despite the fact that many employees went into early retirement and were no longer available in the local labor market when Olivetti downsized in the 1990s, start-up processes of new firms in related electronics fields were substantial (Ronca, 2015; Vanolo, 2008). Former Olivetti employees were heavily involved in such start-up processes, which benefited from these individuals' experience in the industry and their network linkages to other employees and firms in the region around Ivrea. One observer confirmed in an interview that new firms were often established by "sons of ex-Olivetti workers [on the basis of] inherited software skills." Through these processes, the regional industry opened up and became more diversified. The electronics sector expanded its basis (for instance in software development) and strengthened its established competencies in industrial design. Our interviewees often emphasized that Olivetti's prior activities had inspired the mindset of free knowledge and open exchange was now shared by so many people.

The firm Arduino, a pioneer in open-source technology, is a good example of the effects of Olivetti's institutional legacy of freely accessible and available knowledge. Arduino is a world-renowned producer of a programmable logic controller by the same name (Arduino, 2016; de Paoli & Storni, 2011; Stückler, 2016) that permits its users to interact with their environment. The firm's economic success is based on the development of flexible, high-performance technologies available at a low price. Produced according to an open-source concept, the Arduino controller has become a worldwide standard for prototyping tasks applied in all sorts of electronics applications. Users of this technology form a diverse group made up of electronics firms and professionals, as well as hobbyists. The components can either be purchased as a package and assembled by the user or acquired as a preassembled product. In the latter case, the board carries the Arduino trademark. Interestingly, Arduino, a new player in the region, is directly linked to Olivetti's former activities and has benefited from that firm's previous regional research and labor market competencies. The Arduino technology was originally developed by the Interaction Design Institute that was linked to Olivetti and Telecom Italia's former CSELT laboratory.

One former manager in the region described in an interview that "the Institute . . . captured the entire innovative atmosphere [of the district]."

The firm Arduino is widely linked to its global user community that provides crucial input into product development but also promotes knowledge-sharing with the local district and thus supports local cohesion. While the trademark guaranteed local production in the Canavese region, the firm's open-source philosophy broke with the area's traditional localized division of labor (de Paoli & Storni, 2011). Despite its success, the size of the firm and its direct regional impact via supplier relationships have remained limited. As one insider specified during our interviews, Arduino sold about one million boards and had an annual turnover of €15 million in 2014. Local supplier linkages during the time of our research were not extensive, consisting of about 10 firms directly involved in production with a total of about 80 employees. New hardware and software development largely took place in-house, while bug-fixing and learning relied on the global virtual user community. Still, local identification was apparently strong, with the firm achieving close to cult status in the region—as well as among community members worldwide.[6]

Altogether, these and related shifts generated the conditions for the former district to develop into a successful, more diverse information technology cluster. As argued above, the competencies of this cluster are associated with earlier technological successes but are also linked today to other information technology developments in the Turin region and have opened up spatial knowledge ecologies even further internationally than Olivetti's prior operations.

While Olivetti was still a leader in technology development, other information technology firms were attracted to the region (de Paoli & Storni, 2011). They embedded their activities locally and established corresponding supplier linkages. This development contributed to the overall strength of the cluster and actively supported its renewal. These processes continued thereafter. New and existing research institutes in the region in fields such as engineering and industrial design produced new technologies and further improved the localized skill basis. Related innovations from firms such as Arduino became reference points in technology development and strengthened the local labor market. One interviewee emphasized that, as a consequence, "competencies are still in the territory [today]" and another observer added that "there is a specific cultural milieu in the field of coding [that has developed]". Overall, it seems that the local industry structure is still strong and develops international linkages, while district-like divisions of labor based on localized learning are somewhat weaker (see, also, Demetrio & Giaccaria, 2010).

As in the case of the automotive–metallurgical industry, the electronics–mechatronics district benefited from hybrid institutional change supportive of a shift

---

[6] Despite this success, the future of Arduino is open at this point as the founders have been involved in an internal dispute since 2014 about the future development of the firm. As Arduino has increasingly come under cost pressure, some of the founders suggested shifting production to China while others insisted on preserving the local trademark. This dispute resulted in a lawsuit that was settled in October 2016. However, it remained unclear whether the production of boards will remain in Canavese (Simonetta, 2016).

toward open learning and global knowledge circuits that built upon rather than giving up the distinct regional manufacturing culture and localized reference points. This shift affected the entire institutional context. Aside from new organizations, such as Arduino, that have pushed for institutional change and new economic practices, policies have been introduced to support and strengthen regional technological capabilities (Censis, 2001; Confindustria Canavese, 2015; Consorzio Aaster, 2013; Vanolo, 2008). For instance, the regional government founded research and development facilities in technologically related fields to establish an information technology innovation pole, and policies were introduced to strengthen the localized learning system by providing incentives for interfirm collaboration. In addition, university departments in engineering and communication technology were temporarily shifted from Turin to Ivrea, supporting the restructuring process. At the same time, diversification policies in the region attempted to link new initiatives to the institutional legacy of the region, by, for example, establishing a new biomedical technology park in buildings of the former Olivetti laboratories, thus linking the new development to the innovative spirit of Olivetti (Ronca, 2015). Despite such top-down shifts at the level of organizations, regulations and policies, important shifts in the institutional context occurred especially at the level of interaction and learning practices in a more bottom-up fashion.

Conclusions and Policy Implications

Using an institutional perspective to analyze regional economic change, we have suggested in this chapter that successful economic adaptation to external pressures can best be accomplished if industry and corporate restructuring processes are coupled with hybrid institutional change. Such hybrid adjustments combine new institutional settings to support new technological developments in certain fields with institutional continuity in others to actively integrate established industries and former corporate structures into the restructuring process. This theoretical claim has been justified through an ideal-type model of regional restructuring that is subject to adjustments in the institutional context and in industry and corporate structures as depicted in Table 12.1. The northern Italian district of Canavese, which is characterized by two organizational fields around its automotive–metallurgical and electronics–mechatronics industries, is used as a typical case to provide empirical support for this argument. Since the 1990s, the region experienced periods of economic turmoil and strong globalization pressures that threatened the cohesion of its economic structure and learning dynamics (dei Ottati, 2009a; Whitford, 2001). Although these organizational fields were characterized by dominant players, in other words, Fiat and Olivetti, the importance of both firms sank drastically over time as Fiat began to wind down its regional production system and Olivetti's activities faded away. Globalization pressures brought into question the value of the dominant localized learning models that had been so successful in previous periods. As a consequence of the decline of the lead firms, new innovative projects were initiated, regional networks cut, and new global knowledge linkages established.

Interestingly, the shifts in the two organizational fields went along with similar hybrid adjustments in the institutional context that involved organizations, rules and regulations, and durable economic practices.

With its open-source philosophy, Arduino was a role model in generating virtual links with global user communities (Arduino, n.d.). The region's automotive–metallurgical and electronics–mechatronics industries established new international linkages with suppliers and technology partners and diversified their markets more than in previous periods. This process was supported by an institutional context linked to former legacies and reference points, helping to integrate long-established industrial activities broadly into the new economic structures and to maintain localized knowledge dynamics. At the same time, incentives were provided for discontinuous start-up and innovation dynamics, supported by new specialized research, training, and education facilities.

Canavese is, of course, a specific regional case and the argument about hybrid institutional change, although supported by other work on institutional change (e.g., Evenhuis, 2015; Mahoney & Thelen, 2010), requires rigid empirical testing using a comparative approach. We therefore wish to exercise caution in drawing broad generalizations from this research. One could argue, for instance, that the specific structure of Canavese and the dominance of two large players make it difficult to transfer findings to other regional settings. While such implications would always be problematic, what makes the case of Canavese so useful and interesting is that it is much less homogenous than other industrial districts. It consists of two rather different organizational fields around the automotive–metallurgical and electronics–mechatronics industries, both of which had created a context of localized production and learning, as well as a specific local manufacturing culture. Remarkably, the challenges of globalization processes led to similar hybrid institutional adjustments. New firms and research organizations entered the regional economy and established new orientations and linkages. Existing firms opened up and engaged in new learning processes without giving up their former reference points and networks, with the automobile supplier industry, in particular, even strengthening regional collaboration. Regional change was driven by important bottom-up adjustments in the institutional context advanced by new firms and organizations, as well as by new support policies in a more top-down fashion.

In the end, however, in referring to a relational perspective of economic action and interaction (Bathelt & Glückler, 2012), it is necessary to emphasize that the outcomes of such institutional change are contingent in nature and that success eventually depends on whether economic actors can be activated to engage in new opportunities and make respective business decisions. In the case of the Canavese district, there is no guarantee for successful growth in the future, because new developments as in the case of Arduino may be threatened through corporate power struggles or other influences. However, the opening up of the learning system, successful industry restructuring, and strong new linkages supported by hybrid institutional change have put the region into a favorable position from which it can react to and even proactively prepare for future changes in the global economic and technological landscape.

Acknowledgements Some of the arguments developed in this chapter were initially presented in 2015 at the Global Conference on Economic Geography in Oxford and the Symposium on Knowledge and Institutions in Heidelberg. We are indebted to the participants of both events for stimulating discussions and suggestions. In particular, we would like to thank Johannes Glückler and Regina Lenz for including us in the Heidelberg Symposium and for providing detailed comments on an earlier draft. We also wish to thank James Bell and Daniel Hutton Ferris for superb edits and comments in the preparation of this chapter. This chapter is a revised and updated version of a *SPACES online* discussion paper by Bathelt and Conserva (2016).

References

Aimone Gigio, L., Cullino, R., Fabrizi, C., Linarello, A., & Orame, A. (2012, February). *Indotto Fiat o Motor City? La filiera dell'auto torinese di fronte alle nuove catene globali del valore* [Fiat cluster or Motor City? Turin's automotive industry and the new global value chains]. Paper presented at the conference *Le trasformazioni dei sistemi produttivi locali* [The transformation of local production systems] organized by the Banca d'Italia and Department of Economics of the University of Bologna, Bologna. Retrieved from https://www.bancaditalia.it/pubblicazioni/altri-atti-convegni/2012-trasform-sist-produttivi/Indotto_Fiat_o_Motor_City.pdf

Albino, V., Garavelli, A. C., & Schiuma, G. (1998). Knowledge transfer and inter-firm relationships in industrial districts: The role of the leader firm. *Technovation, 19*, 53–63. doi:https://doi.org/10.1016/S0166-4972(98)00078-9

Amin, A., & Thrift, N. (1995). Living in the global. In A. Amin, & N. Thrift (Eds.), *Globalization, institutions, and regional development in Europe* (2nd ed., pp. 1–22). Oxford, UK: Oxford University Press.

Arduino (n.d.). *What is Arduino?* Retrieved from https://www.arduino.cc/en/Guide/Introduction

Arrigo, E. (2003). Corporate responsibility in scarcity economy. The Olivetti case. *Symphonya, 1*(1), 114–134. doi:https://doi.org/10.4468/2003.1.10arrigo

Bagnasco, A. (1986). *Torino: Un profilo sociologico* [Turin. A sociological profile]. Turin: Einaudi.

Barbiellini Amidei, F., Goldstein, A., & Spadoni, M. (2010). *European acquisitions in the United States: Re-examining Olivetti-Underwood fifty years later.* (Quaderni Di Storia Economica No. 2). Retrieved from https://www.bancaditalia.it/pubblicazioni/quaderni-storia/2010-0002/Quaderno_storia_economica_1.pdf

Bathelt, H. (1998). Regionales Wachstum in vernetzten Strukturen: Konzeptioneller Überblick und kritische Bewertung des Phänomens 'Drittes Italien' [Regional growth in networked structures: Critical review and conceptualization of the phenomenon of the 'Third Italy']. *Die Erde, 129*, 247–271. Retrieved from http://www.digizeitschriften.de/dms/resolveppn/?PID=GDZPPN003001822

Bathelt, H. (2009). Re-bundling and the development of hollow clusters in the East German chemical industry. *European Urban and Regional Studies, 16*, 363–381. doi:https://doi.org/10.1177/0969776409340193

Bathelt, H. (2013). Post-reunification restructuring and corporate re-bundling in the Bitterfeld-Wolfen chemical industry, East Germany. *International Journal of Urban and Regional Research, 37*, 1456–1485. doi:https://doi.org/10.1111/j.1468-2427.2012.01194.x

Bathelt, H., & Conserva, N. (2016). *Globalization and institutional change in Italian industrial districts.* SPACES online, 2016–02. Toronto and Heidelberg. www.spaces-online.com. Retrieved from http://www.spaces-online.uni-hd.de/include/SPACES_2016-02%20Bathelt_Conserva.pdf

Bathelt, H., & Glückler, J. (2012). *Wirtschaftsgeographie: Ökonomische Beziehungen in räumlicher Perspektive* [Economic geography: Economic relations in spatial perspective] (3rd ed.). Stuttgart: UTB–Ulmer.

Bathelt, H., & Glückler, J. (2014). Institutional change in economic geography. *Progress in Human Geography, 38*, 340–363. doi:https://doi.org/10.1177/0309132513507823

Becattini, G. (1990). The Marshallian industrial district as a socio-economic notion. In F. Pyke, G. Becattini, & W. Sengenberger (Eds.), *Industrial districts and inter-firm co-operation in Italy* (pp. 37–51). Geneva: International Institute for Labour Studies.

Becattini, G., Bellandi, M., & de Propris, L. (2009). Critical nodes and contemporary reflections on industrial districts: An introduction. In G. Becattini, M. Bellandi, & L. de Propris (Eds.), *A handbook on industrial districts* (pp. xv–xxxv). Cheltenham: Edward Elgar.

Belussi, F., & Pilotti, L. (2002). Knowledge creation, learning and innovation in Italian industrial districts. *Geografiska Annaler, 84* B, 125–139. doi:https://doi.org/10.1111/j.0435-3684.2002.00118.x

Belussi, F., & Sedita, S. R. (2012). Industrial districts as open learning systems: Combining emergent and deliberate knowledgef structures. *Regional Studies, 47*, 165–184. doi:https://doi.org/10.1080/00343404.2010.497133

Boschma, R., & Frenken, K. (2009). Some notes on institutions in evolutionary economic geography. *Economic Geography, 85*, 151–158. doi:https://doi.org/10.1111/j.1944-8287.2009.01018.x

Boschma, R., & Ter Wal, A. L. J. (2007). Knowledge networks and innovative performance in an industrial district: The case of a footwear district in the south of Italy. *Industry and Innovation, 14*, 177–199. doi:https://doi.org/10.1080/13662710701253441

Brilliant, E. (1993). Theory and reality in the vision of Adriano Olivetti. *Voluntas, 4*, 95–114. doi:https://doi.org/10.1007/BF01398386

Brusco, S. (1982). The Emilian model: Productive decentralisation and social integration. *Cambridge Journal of Economics, 6*, 167–184. doi:https://doi.org/10.1093/oxfordjournals.cje.a035506

Buciuni, G., & Finotto, V. (2016). Innovation in global value chains: Co-location of production and development in Italian low-tech industries. *Regional Studies, 50*, 2010–2023. doi:https://doi.org/10.1080/00343404.2015.1115010

Buciuni, G., & Pisano, G. (2016, October). *Knowledge integrators and the survival of manufacturing clusters.* Paper presented at the iBEGIN conference on International Business, Economic Geography, and Innovation, Philadelphia.

Camuffo, A., & Grandinetti, R. (2011). Italian industrial districts as cognitive systems: Are they still reproducible? *Entrepreneurship & Regional Development, 23*, 815–852. doi:https://doi.org/10.1080/08985626.2011.577815

Cantwell, J. (Ed.). (2014). *Location of international business activities: Integrating ideas from research in international business, strategic management and economic geography.* Basingstoke: Palgrave Macmillan.

Castagnoli, A. (2014). Across borders and beyond boundaries: How the Olivetti company became a multinational. *Business History, 56*, 1281–1311. doi:https://doi.org/10.1080/00076791.2013.876534

Censis (2001). *Reinventare il Canavese: Strategie per il riposizionamento del sistema economico e sociale* [Reinventing Canavese: Strategies to readjust the economic and social system]. Milan: Franco Angeli.

Clark, G. L. (1998). Stylized facts and close dialogue: Methodology in economic geography. *Annals of the Association of American Geographers, 88*, 73–87. doi:https://doi.org/10.1111/1467-8306.00085

Clark, G. L., & Monk, A. H. B. (2013). The scope of financial institutiosns: In-sourcing, out-sourcing and off-shoring. *Journal of Economic Geography, 13*, 279–298. doi:https://doi.org/10.1093/jeg/lbs061

Confindustria Canavese (2015). *Strategie per il Canavese: Dieci anni di studi e ricerche sul territorio* [Strategies for Canavese: Ten years of studies and research about the territory]. Ivrea: Ivrea Grafica.

Consorzio Aaster (2013). *Strategie per il Canavese. Cosa sarà. Ipotesi di futuro e scenari di sviluppo* [Strategies for Canavese. What will happen. Hypotheses for the future and scenarios for development]. Canavese. Retrieved from http://docplayer.it/12780715-Strategie-per-il-canavese-cosa-sara-ipotesi-di-futuro-escenari-di-sviluppo.html

Cutrini, E. (2011). Moving eastwards while remaining embedded: The case of the Marche footwear district, Italy. *European Planning Studies, 19*, 991–1019. doi:https://doi.org/10.1080/0954313.2011.571062

dei Ottati, G. (2009a). An industrial district facing the challenges of globalization: Prato today. *European Planning Studies, 17*, 1817–1835. doi:https://doi.org/10.1080/09654310903322322

dei Ottati, G. (2009b). Semi-automatic and deliberate actions in the evolution of industrial districts. In G. Becattini, M. Bellandi, & L. de Propris (Eds.), *A handbook on industrial districts* (pp. 204–215). Cheltenham: Edward Elgar.

Demetrio, V., & Giaccaria, P. (2010). *Geografia del sistema manifatturiero piemontese: Nuove forme di organizzazione e coordinamento* [Geography of the Piedmontese manufacturing system: New forms of organization and coordination]. Rome: Carocci.

de Paoli, S., & Storni, C. (2011). Produsage in hybrid networks: Sociotechnical skills in the case of Arduino. *New Review of Hypermedia and Multimedia, 17*, 31–52. doi:https://doi.org/10.1080/13614568.2011.552641

DiMaggio, P. J., & Powell, W. W. (1983). The iron cage revisited: Institutional isomorphism and collective rationality in organizational fields. *American Sociological Review, 48*, 147–160. Retrieved from http://www.jstor.org/stable/2095101

Douglas, Y., & Hargadon, A. (2017). Domesticating innovation—Designing revolutions. In H. Bathelt, P. Cohendet, S. Henn, & L. Simon (Eds.), *The Edward Elgar companion to innovation and knowledge creation* (pp. 152–164). Cheltenham: Edward Elgar.

Evenhuis, E. (2015, August). *Path dependency across scales: Towards a more differentiated and multi-scalar perspective on regional institutional change*. Paper presented at the Global Conference on Economic Geography, Oxford.

Gallino, L. (2003). *La scomparsa dell'Italia industriale* [The demise of the industrial Italy]. Turin: Einaudi.

Gertler, M. S. (2010). Rules of the game: The place of institutions in regional economic change. *Regional Studies, 44*, 1–15. doi:http://10.1080/00343400903389979

Giblin, M. (2011). Managing the global-local dimensions of clusters and the role of 'lead' organizations: The contrasting cases of the software and medical technology clusters in the west of Ireland. *European Planning Studies, 19*, 23–42. doi:https://doi.org/10.1080/09654313.2011.530529

Glückler, J., & Bathelt, H. (2017). Institutional context and innovation. In H. Bathelt, P. Cohendet, S. Henn, & L. Simon (Eds.), *The Edward Elgar companion to innovation and knowledge creation* (pp. 121–137). Cheltenham: Edward Elgar.

Glückler, J., & Lenz, R. (2016). How institutions moderate the effectiveness of regional policy: A framework and research agenda. *Investigaciones Regionales—Journal of Regional Research, 36*, 255–277. Retrieved from http://hdl.handle.net/10017/28164

Hassink, R. (2010). Regional resilience: A promising concept to explain differences in regional economic adaptability? *Cambridge Journal of Regions, Economy and Society, 3*, 45–58. doi:https://doi.org/10.1093/cjres/rsp033

Hassink, R., & Shin, D.-H. (2005). Guest editorial: The restructuring of old industrial areas in Europe and Asia. *Environment and Planning A, 37*, 571–580. doi:https://doi.org/10.1068/a36273

Hodgson, G. M. (1988). *Economics and institutions: A manifesto for a modern institutional economics*. Cambridge, UK: Polity.

Hudson, R., & Schamp, E. W. (Eds.) (1995). *Towards a new map of automobile manufacturing in Europe? New production concepts and spatial restructuring*. Berlin: Springer.

ISTAT (2001). *8° Censimento Generale Dell'industria E Dei Servizi* [8th general census of industry and services]. Retrieved from http://dwcis.istat.it/cis/index.htm

ISTAT (2001). *8° Censimento Generale Dell'industria E Dei Servizi* [8th general census of industry and services]. Retrieved from http://dwcis.istat.it/cis/index.htm

ISTAT (2011). *9° Censimento Generale Dell'industria E Dei Servizi* [9th general census of industry and services]. Retrieved from http://dati-censimentoindustriaeservizi.istat.it/Index.aspx

Lan, T. (2015). Industrial district and the multiplication of labour: The Chinese apparel industry in Prato, Italy. *Antipode, 47*, 158–178. https://doi.org/10.1111/anti.12104

Mahoney, J., & Thelen, K. (2010). A theory of gradual institutional change. In J. Mahoney, & K. Thelen (Eds.), *Explaining institutional change: Ambiguity, agency, and power* (pp. 1–37). Cambridge, UK: Cambridge University Press.

Martin, R., & Sunley, P. (2006). Path dependence and regional economic evolution. *Journal of Economic Geography, 6*, 395–437. doi:https://doi.org/10.1093/jeg/lbl012

Martin, R., & Sunley, P. (2015). On the notion of regional economic resilience: Conceptualization and explanation. *Journal of Economic Geography, 15*, 1–42. doi:https://doi.org/10.1093/jeg/lbu015

Massey, D., Quintas, P., & Wield, D. (1992). *High-tech fantasies: Science parks in society, science and space*. London: Routledge.

Michelsons, A. (1990). Mercati, tecnologie e imprenditori nel Canavese [Markets, technologies, and entrepreneurs in Canavese]. In R. Maglione, A. Michelsons, & S. E. Rossi (Eds.), *Economie locali tra grande e piccola impresa: Il caso di Ivrea e del Canavese* [Local economies between large and small firms: The case of Ivrea and Canavese] (pp. 109–166). Turin: Fondazione Adriano Olivetti.

Miles, M. B., & Huberman, A. M. (1994). *Qualitative data analysis: An expanded sourcebook* (2nd ed.). Thousand Oaks: Sage.

North, D. C. (1990). *Institutions, institutional change and economic performance*. Cambridge, UK: Cambridge University Press.

North, D. C. (1991). Institutions. *Journal of Economic Perspectives, 5*, 97–112. doi:https://doi.org/10.1257/jep.5.1.97

Olivetti (1978–2009). *Olivetti: Storia di un'impresa* [Olivetti: History of an enterprise]. Associazione Archivio Storico Olivetti. Retrieved from http://www.storiaolivetti.it

Perotto, P. G. (1995). *Programma 101. L'invenzione del personal computer: Una storia appassionante mai raccontata* [Programma 101. The invention of personal computers: A fascinating story never described]. Milan: Sperling & Kupfer.

Pike, A., Marlow, D., McCarthy, A., O'Brien, P., & Tomaney, J. (2015). Local institutions and local economic development: The Local Enterprise Partnerships in England, 2010–. *Cambridge Journal of Regions, Economy and Society, 8*, 185–204. doi:https://doi.org/10.1093/cjres/rsu030

Provost, C., & Lai, S. (2016, April 13). Story of cities #21: Olivetti tries to build the ideal 'human city' for its workers. *The Guardian*. Retrieved from https://www.theguardian.com/cities/2016/apr/13/story-cities-21-adriano-olivetti-ivrea-italy-typewriter-factory-human-city

Rabellotti, R. (2004). How globalization affects Italian industrial districts: The case of Brenta. In H. Schmitz (Ed.), *Local enterprises in the global economy: Issues of governance and upgrading* (pp. 140–173). Cheltenham: Edward Elgar.

Radogna, P. (1960). Adriano Olivetti: Some notes on his contribution to planning. *The Town Planning Review, 31*, 182–186. Retrieved from https://www.jstor.org/stable/40178354

Rodríguez-Pose, A., & Storper, M. (2006). Better rules or stronger communities? On the social foundations of institutional change and its economic effects. *Economic Geography, 82*, 1–25. doi:https://doi.org/10.1111/j.1944-8287.2006.tb00286.x

Ronca, C. (2015). *Trasformazione di un sistema produttivo locale e linee guida per una 'mappa delle competenze': Il caso del Canavese* [Transformation of a local production system and guidelines for a 'map of competences': The case of Canavese]. Working Paper on Knowledge Society No. 08. Ivrea: Fondazione Adriano Olivetti. Retrieved from http://www.fondazioneadrianolivetti.it/_images/pubblicazioni/collana/032615060354WP_Trasformazione%20di%20un%20sistema%20produttivo%20locale_vers.pdf

Rosati, D. (2016). *Regional inequalities in the commodity of trust: The case of two industrial districts in the Italian footwear industry*. SPACES online, 2016–01. Toronto and Heidelberg. www.spaces-online.com. Retrieved from http://www.spaces-online.uni-hd.de/include/SPACES_2016-01%20Rosati.pdf

Saxenian, A. L. (1994). *Regional advantage: Culture and competition in Silicon Valley and Route 128*. Cambridge, MA: Harvard University Press.

Scott, A. J. (1998). *Regions and the world economy: The coming shape of global production, competition, and political order*. Oxford, UK: Oxford University Press.

Seawright, J., & Gerring, J. (2008). Case selection techniques in case study research: A menu of qualitative and quantitative options. *Political Research Quarterly, 61*, 294–308. doi:https://doi.org/10.1177/1065912907313077

Setterfield, M. (1993). A model of institutional hysteresis. *Journal of Economic Issues, 27*, 755–774. Retrieved from https://www.jstor.org/stable/4226717

Simonetta, B. (2016, October 2). Arduino, scoppia la pace: Raggiunto l'accordo sulla proprietà del marchio [Arduino, its reconciliation. Agreement achieved on the property of the trademark]. *Il Sole 24 Ore.* Retrieved from http://www.ilsole24ore.com/art/tecnologie/2016-10-02/arduino-scoppia-pace-raggiunto-accordo-proprieta-marchio-113139.shtml?uuid=ADIz2tUB

Soria, L. (1979). *Informatica: Un'occasione perduta. La divisione elettronica dell'Olivetti nei primi anni del centrosinistra* [Computers: A lost chance. Olivetti's electronics division in the first years of center-left governments]. Turin: Einaudi.

Streeck, W., & Thelen, K. (2005). Introduction: Institutional change in advanced political economies. In W. Streeck, & K. Thelen (Eds.), *Beyond continuity: Institutional change in advanced political economies* (pp. 1–39). Oxford, UK: Oxford University Press.

Stückler, M. (2016, July 31). Computer für Bastler: Was ist eigentlich ein Arduino? [Computers for hobbyists: What actually is an Arduino?]. *Spiegel Online.* Retrieved from http://www.spiegel.de/netzwelt/gadgets/arduino-erklaert-das-kann-der-microcontroller-a-1105328.html

Tokatli, N. (2015). Single-firm case studies in economic geography: Some methodological reflections on the case of Zara. *Journal of Economic Geography, 15*, 631–647. doi:10.1093/jeg/lbu013

Torino Nuova Economia (n.d.). Retrieved from http://www.torinonuovaeconomia.it/organigramma_eng.php

Vanolo, A. (2008). The electronic and mechatronics industry in Ivrea. In IGEAT–ULB, Politecnico di Milano, & UMS Riate (Eds.), *The impact of globalisation and increased trade liberalisation on European regions* (pp. 37–52). Study for the General Direction REGIO of the European Commission. Retrieved from http://ec.europa.eu/regional_policy/sources/docgener/studies/pdf/impact_liberalisation_a2.pdf

Whitford, J. (2001). The decline of a model? Challenge and response in the Italian industrial districts. *Economy and Society, 30*, 38–65. doi:https://doi.org/10.1080/03085140020019089

Whitford, J., & Enrietti, A. (2005). Surviving the fall of a king: The regional institutional implications of crisis at Fiat auto. *International Journal of Urban and Regional Research, 29*, 771–795. doi:https://doi.org/10.1111/j.1468-2427.2005.00621.x

Whitford, J., & Potter, C. (2007). Regional economies, open networks and the spatial fragmentation of production. *Socio-Economic Review, 5*, 497–526. doi:https://doi.org/10.1093/ser/mwm004

Yin, R. K. (2009). *Case study research: Design and methods* (4th ed.). Thousand Oaks: Sage.

Chapter 13
Studying Entrepreneurship as an Institution

Pamela S. Tolbert and Ryan Coles

Research on entrepreneurship, which became a key part of organizational scholarship in the late twentieth century, was initially dominated by studies of individual dispositions and attitudes that make a given person more or less likely to become an entrepreneur. This work gave little attention to the structural factors that might facilitate or inhibit the actual expression of such dispositions and attitudes in entrepreneurial activities (Aldrich & Wiedenmayer, 1993; Katz & Gartner, 1988). More recent research, however, has begun to redress this neglect, documenting the important influence of contextual conditions, such as kinship and friendship ties, and the size and sectoral location of former employers on individuals' likelihood of becoming an entrepreneur (Buenstorf & Klepper, 2010; Halaby, 2003; Kacperczyk, 2013; Sorensen, 2007). These influences operate by affecting both individuals' readiness to consider entrepreneurship as a viable employment option (Nanda & Sorensen, 2010; Stuart & Ding, 2006) and their possession of skills, knowledge, and resources needed to become an entrepreneur (Dencker, Gruber, & Shah, 2009; Gambardella, Ganco, & Honore, 2015; Hiatt & Sine, 2014).

While recent organizational studies thus have considerably expanded the view of the nature and determinants of entrepreneurship, they generally have maintained the focus of older work on the individual as the unit of analysis (for an important exception see Kwon, Heflin, & Ruef, 2013). Yet a variety of literatures, including work on racial and ethnic groups, gender studies, and economic geography, implicates characteristics of collectivities as determinants of entrepreneurship and suggests consequent group-level variation in both rates and forms of entrepreneurship. Hence, analyses focusing on the question of what conditions encourage and shape the form of entrepreneurial activities at the group or community level offer potentially important new insights for scholars interested in understanding such economic phenomena.

P. S. Tolbert (✉) · R. Coles
ILR School, Department of Organizational Behavior, Cornell University, Ithaca, NY, USA
e-mail: pam.tolbert@cornell.edu; rsc256@cornell.edu

© The Author(s) 2018
J. Glückler et al. (eds.), *Knowledge and Institutions*, Knowledge and Space 13,
https://doi.org/10.1007/978-3-319-75328-7_13

This paper seeks to spur research on this topic by identifying and discussing two key aspects of entrepreneurship that are likely to vary across collectivities: *modes of entry*, or common pathways to founding business enterprises, and *modes of governance*, or forms of ownership and hence decision making in new enterprises. Although there are other relevant dimensions that could be studied, these two tap ones that existing research has shown to be significantly related to group differences and are also likely to be influential in shaping critical organizational outcomes.

Our approach reflects theoretical arguments about the utility of examining entrepreneurship as an institution (Brandl & Bullinger, 2009; Tolbert, David, & Sine, 2010) and dovetails with recent work in institutional theory emphasizing the need to understand how a general institution may vary in specific ways over time and in different locations (Ansari, Fiss, & Zajac, 2010). We begin by briefly summarizing the logic of this broad theoretical framework and reviewing a number of independent streams of work on entrepreneurship with the aim of showing how an institutional perspective helps link these currently disparate streams. We then draw on existing research to suggest some of the key social conditions likely to predict variations in the two institutional dimensions that are the focus of our discussion, and offer a number of propositions to help lay a foundation for (and we hope, inspire) further research in this area.

Connecting Institutional Theory and Entrepreneurship Research

Because both *institution* and *entrepreneurship* are used in very different ways in existing work, we start by briefly clarifying our own definitions of these terms. In our use, similar to that of Meyer and Rowan (1977), an institution is a pattern of behavior (or an observable behavioral artifact—for example, a formal law or organizational rule) based on commonly shared beliefs and understandings that justify the behavior. The latter aspect, the justifying beliefs and understandings, represent what we refer to as an *institutional logic*.[1]

The term *entrepreneurship* suffers from the same sort of etymological problems as *institution,* as reflected in the wide array of definitions found in research on this topic (Aldrich & Ruef, 1999/2006). These definitions range from ones that, mirroring Schumpeter's (1911/1968) concern with the creation of new markets, reserve the term for new firms that introduce major innovations in products, services, or technology to those that focus on new firms in high technology industries (regardless of the novelty of the products or produced services) and ones that include all efforts to establish new, independent business organizations. The latter definition fits most closely with common measures used in empirical research, which often rely on self-employment, or actions designed to lead to self-employment, as an

---

[1] This is a slight variation on some standard definitions of the latter term, such as that offered by Thornton and Ocasio (2008).

indicator of entrepreneurship (e.g., Acs, Audretsch, & Strom, 2009). We follow the latter, *big-tent* approach to defining entrepreneurship as the act of creating new economic organizations. This approach seems preferable, because it is generally not possible to identify which innovations will lead to market destruction or creation, a priori, and we believe that limiting entrepreneurship research to a select set of industries or types of firms is unnecessarily confining.

Thus, treating entrepreneurship as an institution entails examining patterns of behavior involved in the founding of new economic organizations, specifically, patterns that are characteristic of a group and are based on commonly shared beliefs and understandings that support that behavior. In this context, seminal work in institutional theory explicitly recognized the utility the perspective provides for studying entrepreneurship, noting:

> The growth of rationalized institutional structures in society makes formal organizations … both easier to create and more necessary. After all, the building blocks for organizations come to be littered around the societal landscape; it takes only a little entrepreneurial energy to assemble them into a structure. (Meyer & Rowan, 1977, p. 345)

Our addition to this view is to focus on understanding existing differences in these *building blocks* among different social groups and in different time periods.

Despite the prominence that institutional theory has attained in contemporary organizational studies (Greenwood, Oliver, Sahlin, & Suddaby, 2008), its use by researchers interested in the problems of understanding the nature and sources of entrepreneurial activity has been relatively rare (see also Tolbert et al., 2010).

Prior Entrepreneurship Research: From Dispositions and Motives to Institutional Influences

This probably reflects, at least in part, the disciplinary dominance of economics and psychology in much of the work on entrepreneurship. Both disciplines encourage a focus on the personal motives and calculations of individual entrepreneurs in deciding to found a business (Kirzner, 1973; McClelland, 1965). And indeed, this emphasis is still prominent in some contemporary organizational literature on entrepreneurship (e.g., Gielnik, Spitzmuller, Schmitt, Klemann, & Frese, 2015; Shane & Nicoloau, 2015; Van Gelderen, Kautonen, & Fink, 2015).

Contextual Sources of Entrepreneurship: Recent Studies

As noted previously, a growing segment of entrepreneurship research highlights the importance of extraindividual, or contextual influences, on entrepreneurs. For example, early work in this vein provided evidence that self-employed parents often transmit entrepreneurial values to their children (Halaby, 2003; Miller & Swanson, 1958; though see a later study by Aldrich & Kim, 2007).

Current research suggests that a more proximal and powerful force on entrepreneurship is the context provided by individuals' own employment experiences—particularly the size and nature of previous employing organizations, and relationships with former coworkers. For example, a study by Sorensen (2007) of entrepreneurs in Denmark found that individuals employed in smaller and younger firms were more likely to become entrepreneurs than those employed in larger, older firms. He attributes this result to the greater opportunities to gain entrepreneurially relevant managerial experiences and knowledge provided by smaller and younger firms (see also Dencker et al., 2009). Kacperczyk's (2012) study of the career paths of employees in U.S. mutual fund organizations corroborates this argument by showing that individuals who founded new firms in this industry often came from smaller fund organizations. Similarly, another study by Özcan and Reichstein (2009) found that individuals employed in public sector firms in the United States were less likely to enter into self-employment than similar individuals employed in private sector firms.

As most authors acknowledge, selection effects may be operative in these studies as well: Individuals with inclinations to become entrepreneurs may seek employment that provides them with greater autonomy and opportunities to develop particular skills. Insofar as smaller, younger and less bureaucratic organizations attract entrepreneurial individuals, they are likely to provide a social environment that makes entrepreneurship more normatively acceptable. In line with this, studies of U.S. academics by Stuart and Ding (2006) and Kacperczyk (2013) indicate the importance of peer attitudes towards entrepreneurship in spurring faculty members' entry into new commercialized science firms.

Work in this tradition importantly extends understanding of the social forces that shape individual decisions to become an entrepreneur, but still neglects larger, more macrolevel influences on entrepreneurial activity that manifest in varying rates of new venture formation across geographical areas and in different time periods. A variety of research—by gender studies scholars, by sociologists studying race and ethnic relations, and by economic geographers—has amply documented group-based variations in rates and forms of entrepreneurship. This work provides a good point of departure for investigating entrepreneurship as an institution.

Group-Based Variation in Rates of Entrepreneurship

A long line of work by economic geographers has highlighted marked differences in the rates of entrepreneurial activities across regions, across countries, and across cities within countries (e.g., Acs & Armington, 2006; Acs et al., 2009; Ardagna & Lusardi, 2008; Breschi & Malerba, 2001; Glückler, 2006, 2014; Sternberg & Rocha, 2007; Vaillant & Lafuente, 2007). Although scholars often focus on economic and policy-level factors, such as tax rates and other governmental regulations, in explaining variation in entrepreneurship (e.g., Eesley, 2009; Torrini, 2005), evidence of the importance of cultural or normative sources can be found in a number of studies as well (Davidsson & Wiklund, 1997; Fairlie & Meyer, 1994). For example, Vaillant and Lafuente (2007) trace the relatively high rates of entrepreneurship in rural Catalonia (compared to other rural areas of Spain) to Catalonia's distinctive constellation of cultural values.

Likewise, the importance of group-linked, cultural influences can be adduced from research on gender differences in entrepreneurship. In general, women's rates of entrepreneurial activity roughly follow those of their male counterparts in a given country, but a persisting gender gap in both entrepreneurial attitudes and action exists within virtually all countries (Jennings & Brush, 2013; Kelley, Brush, Greene, & Litovsky, 2011). While lower rates of entrepreneurship among women are often attributed to gender-based variations in human and social capital required for business entry (Kim, Aldrich, & Keister, 2006), the inclusion of measures of such capital in models predicting self-employment does not eliminate gender differences (Budig, 2006; Thébaud, 2015). Thus, it seems reasonable to attribute widespread differences in men's and women's propensity to found new organizations, at least in part, to normative, collective understandings that commonly define entrepreneurship as less appropriate for women than men (Baughn, Chua, & Neupert, 2006; Elam & Terjesen, 2010). Hence, like the research from economic geographers, studies by gender scholars also suggest the utility of studying entrepreneurship as an institution—behavioral patterns driven by shared social understandings and norms.

Finally, research by U.S. sociologists on race and ethnicity has often implicitly investigated entrepreneurship as an institution that varies across identity groups (Aldrich & Waldinger, 1990; Light, 2003; Light & Rosenstein, 1995). Zhou, reviewing the literature in this area, notes, "It is generally known that certain groups of immigrant and ethnic minorities are more entrepreneurial and more likely than others to adopt small business ownership" (2004, p. 1041). She then lists Jews, Japanese, Koreans, Chinese, Iranians, and Cubans as examples of such groups. Just as in studies by economic geographers and gender scholars, such variations are often attributed to differences in both material and human capital resources (Light & Rosenstein, 1995), but it is important to note that, net of these influences, group-level patterns of social ties (Kwon et al., 2013) and norms supporting entrepreneurship (Raijman & Tienda, 2000) have been found to act as independent influences on rates of entrepreneurial activity.

Group-Based Variation in Forms of Entrepreneurship

There is also evidence of the role of normative influences on the forms that entrepreneurial activities take, as well as on rates. Work on ethnic entrepreneurs, in particular, has investigated how particular aspects of entrepreneurship vary across different nationality groups. Studies in this tradition have documented group differences in processes through which individuals acquire relevant skills and knowledge needed to found their own firms, differences in founders' aims for such enterprises, and differences in the structural arrangements that characterize the enterprises (e.g., Portes & Zhou, 1999; Raijman & Tienda, 2000; Zhou, 2004).

We note that these aspects are relevant to the distinction often drawn between opportunity and necessity (or voluntary and involuntary) entrepreneurship. This distinction explicitly taps the extent to which individuals' engagement in entrepreneurial activity is more or less by choice (Block & Wagner, 2010). It reflects, at least implicitly, the assumption that entrepreneurs with more resources and alternative employment options are more likely to be characterized by voluntary entry, while those with fewer resources and options are often driven into entrepreneurship, lacking alternative means of making a living. Some key sources of cross-national data on entrepreneurship, such as the Global Entrepreneurship Monitor, which has collected survey data regularly since 1999 on new business activities in a variety of countries, gather information on this by asking respondents about their dominant motives for undertaking such activities (Wennekers, van Stel, Thurik, & Reynolds, 2005, p 305).

We are sympathetic to the case for distinguishing different forms of entrepreneurship (this is quite consistent with the approach we take here), but this bifold distinction seems overly simplistic and hard to draw in practice. Many entrepreneurs have mixed motivations, regardless of their level of resources (Williams & Williams, 2014). Hence, like Katz and Gartner (1988), we argue that scholarship on entrepreneurship can benefit from focusing more on activities and behaviors associated with creating new economic organizations, rather than on differences in psychological motives. Although several survey and ethnographic studies have noted that the entrepreneurial process appears both complex and chaotic (Aldrich & Ruef, 1999/2006), greater attention to patterns that characterize particular social groups may reduce some of the seeming unpredictability of these activities. Viewing entrepreneurship through an institutional lens encourages greater attention to group-level variation in the processes and the context of entrepreneurial foundings than does a reliance on a simple necessity–opportunity distinction.

An Institutional Approach to Entrepreneurship

In sum, different lines of research have documented group-based variations in rates of entrepreneurship (regardless of whether the group is defined by geography, gender, or other social markers), and suggested the importance of cultural or normative sources of such variation. Conceptualizing entrepreneurship as an institution provides a vantage point for integrating much of this research. Again, in this conception, entrepreneurship entails a behavioral component, activities aimed at founding economic enterprises, and an ideational component, shared cultural understandings (logics) that define the general acceptability and desirability of such activities, as well as the typical form of enterprises.

This approach meshes well with recent organizational studies suggesting greater attention be given to understanding the way in which institutions may vary, depending on both time and location. This is in contrast to most early empirical work based on institutional theory, which typically focused on explaining the diffusion of particular institutions—whether a type of law, a personnel practice, or a newly formalized organizational position—over time and space (e.g., Davis, 1991; Fligstein, 1985; Tolbert & Zucker, 1983). Almost invariably, the diffusing institution was treated as being identical from one adoption to another. However, recent studies have drawn attention to the variable nature of institutions (Ansari et al., 2010; Colyvas & Jonsson, 2011; Hipp, Bernhardt, & Allmendinger, 2015; Kennedy & Fiss, 2009) and the need to understand factors that affect such variation.

One example is provided in a study by Fiss, Kennedy, and Davis (2012) of the adoption of severance packages—often referred to as *golden parachutes*—for executives of companies acquired by outside investors. Such arrangements emerged among large U.S. corporations in the late 1970s, and spread rapidly as an antitakeover measure, one promoted as enhancing shareholder value. While the original studies treated all adoptions as identical (Davis & Greve, 1997), closer examination by Fiss et al. (2012) revealed a number of ways in which the content of the packages varied across organizations, including the number of top-level managers who were covered, the conditions under which this measure would be activated, and the range of benefits provided. Moreover, such variations were found to be significantly related to both firm-level and temporal factors: Over time, adopters of golden parachutes expanded the range of benefits provided, but this was contingent on characteristics that affected organizations' visibility, including news media scrutiny of a firm, and how dispersed its stock ownership was. That is, the nature of this institution was dependent on both the time period and the conditions facing organizations that enacted it.

The study by Fiss et al., as well as a number of others (Ansari et al., 2010; Djelic, 1998; Zilber, 2002), helped illuminate the important insights that can be gained by exploring both the forms and sources of institutional variability. We think that empirical studies of entrepreneurship, in particular, can be enriched by this approach for several reasons. First, it provides a unifying framework for the varying definitions of entrepreneurship within the field. What have been treated as competing definitions can be viewed as simply tapping institutional variations, and the social, economic, or other conditions that give rise to these variations can become the focus of research. Relatedly, this approach facilitates the organization of past empirical work and, in guiding future work, allows theoretical insights to be more carefully explored.

A review of various streams of extant work suggests a variety of potential dimensions along which entrepreneurship may vary. These include processes of employee recruitment and selection (Baron, Burton, & Hannan, 1999), chances and criteria of receiving external support (Chen, Yao, & Kotha, 2009; Ding, Sun, & Au, 2014), and structural stability (Beckman & Burton, 2008; Boeker & Wiltbank, 2005), among others. However, to date there has been no systematic program of research on any of these dimensions. Below, we focus on just two dimensions that seem likely candidates for concentrated research, where findings could substantially advance both theoretical understandings and social policy decisions: modes of entry and modes of governance. We draw on existing work to propose specific variants within each of these modes.

Two Dimensions of Entrepreneurship: Entry and Governance Modes

Modes of Entry

Research on ethnic entrepreneurship in the United States, in particular, has drawn attention to distinctive paths leading to the formal founding of new businesses that typify different immigrant groups (Banerjee, 2013; Light, 2003; Raijman & Tienda, 2000). Although there is little or no cross-referencing of this research by studies of nonimmigrant entrepreneurs in Western countries, the latter provides some evidence of similar types of pathways (Baron et al., 1999; Sorensen, 2007). Based on our review of these literatures, we distilled three ideal typical modes of entry into entrepreneurship that vary in terms of the degree to which they are associated with prior experience relevant to the new enterprise, and the nature of that experience. We label one an *emergent mode*, a second as an *apprenticeship mode*, and a third as a *neophyte mode*, and discuss each in turn.

Emergent Mode

The emergent mode of entry is well-documented in the literature on ethnic entrepreneurship as a common route to self-employment. This route involves business activity that often begins in the informal economy—that is, economic activities that are not registered with or regulated by government (e.g., producing goods for local distribution at farmers markets, providing in-home services, etc.), and are often done on a part-time or casual basis. However, these activities can, over time, provide the basis for establishing officially recognized, ongoing business organizations, even if this was not the initial objective of the founders.

Raijman and Tienda's (2000) study of an immigrant neighborhood in Chicago suggests that this is a relatively common route into entrepreneurship among Hispanic immigrants to the United States, and more generally, among immigrants with lower levels of education and skills. Research on self-employment among nonimmigrant women also suggests this as a common path to entrepreneurship, both in the United States (Budig, 2006; Carr, 1996) and other countries (Kelley et al., 2011), particularly among nonprofessionals. When family responsibilities make participation in the formal economy difficult, women may turn to activities in the informal economy—for example, providing childcare and other personal services—that later receive licensing and become part of the formal economy.

This mode of entry provides would-be entrepreneurs with the gradual acquisition of experience in production and organizational activities and with opportunities to test the market for their product. Thus, it may be common among those who have been characterized as hybrid entrepreneurs (Raffiee & Feng, 2014), that is, individuals who hold regular paid employment while undertaking activities that ultimately lead to full-time self-employment. There is probably more variation among the individuals who take this route in terms of their initial commitment to creating an ongoing, formal enterprise, but if they experience some success we would expect them to be motivationally indistinguishable from other entrepreneurs who are characterized by different modes of entry (see also Williams & Williams, 2014).

Apprenticeship Mode

What we call the apprenticeship mode entails entry into entrepreneurship after having previously served as an employee of a firm in the same or a closely related industry. This is often discussed in the ethnic entrepreneurship literature in terms of coethnic employment (see also Light, 2003). In the latter case, a more established member of an immigrant group hires comparatively recent immigrants from the same national background, often providing relatively low pay and demandingly long working hours. Although this arrangement is exploitive in the short run, studies have pointed out that it enables the acquisition of knowledge, experience, and contacts required to start a business (as well as time to acquire new language skills and gain familiarity with customs). It is a common basis for the founding of new enterprises among Korean, Cuban, Indian, and other immigrant groups (Banerjee, 2013; Raijman & Tienda, 2000). The propensity of some groups to rely on this entry mode accounts, in part, for the concentration of ethnic groups in certain industries and businesses (Uzzi, 1996).

Other research has also provided evidence of the apprenticeship route by nonimmigrant entrepreneurs. A classic example is provided by the case of Fairchild Semiconductor, a company founded by eight former employees of Shockley Semiconductor Laboratory. Fairchild Semiconductor served as a jumping-off point of entrepreneurship for its employees, their newly founded Silicon Valley firms being referred to as *Fairchildren* (Lécuyer, 2006). This pattern, of former employees leaving a firm to found their own because of dissatisfaction with operations or concerns about the long-term survival of an employer, often characterizes industries based on new technologies, and a research literature on *spinoffs* has begun to explore the conditions that produce and shape it (e.g., Baltzopoulos, Braunerhjelm, & Tikoudis, 2015; Bathelt, Kogler, & Munro, 2010; Brittain & Wholey, 1988; Klepper, 2009; Klepper & Thompson, 2010). To date, most of this work has focused on questions about the kinds of firms that generate spinoffs, the role of universities in this process, and the relation of parent company performance to that of spinoffs.

Although related to our discussion of apprenticeship, this literature has not systematically examined questions about the kinds of industries, regional conditions or social groups that are most likely to be characterized by this mode of entry, relative to other modes. As noted, the literature on spinoffs has concentrated on industries with new technologies; but the literature on ethnic entrepreneurship suggests that spinoffs are common in other, low-technology industries as well. The juxtaposition of these two literatures highlights the utility of considering apprenticeship as a distinctive form of entry to entrepreneurship and examining the conditions under which it is most likely to occur. We underscore the importance of retaining a focus on entry into economic sectors that are related to prior employment, as part of defining this mode; this is what distinguishes it from other modes (for a related point, see Baltzopoulos, Braunderhjen, & Tikoudis, 2016).

The apprenticeship mode of entry offers would-be entrepreneurs the opportunity to gain critical experiential learning in a relatively protected context. It may foster the acquisition of relevant knowledge, ties, and other resources more quickly than an emergent mode of entry, but it is also apt to be associated with initial costs in terms of foregone earnings and promotion opportunities (Bidwell & Briscoe, 2010).

Neophyte Mode

What distinguishes this mode of entry from those previously discussed is that it entails little or no relevant industry-based production or management experience. It *may* result from the independent invention of a new product or service, which is then patented and developed, perhaps with the support of investors, and used as the basis for the founding of an organization to produce and sell it. This is what, we surmise, is imagined by most people in response to the term *entrepreneur*, and is an image often valorized in the popular press (e.g., depictions of Thomas Edison or Mark Zuckerberg). But it may also involve the founding of a quotidian enterprise in an existing industry, such as the opening of a bed-and-breakfast inn by a former programmer, or a firm producing improved headrests for infant car seats, developed by an end-user (Shah & Tripsas, 2007).

As indicated, the key feature of this entry mode, for our purposes, is the lack of strong connections between individuals' previous job history and the new enterprise. As a consequence, the ability to develop needed organizational skills and knowledge and to make adaptive changes in products and processes in response to market reactions are comparatively limited. This clearly has implications for the survival of new enterprises, although survival also may be affected by the presence of entrepreneurial infrastructures in a given industry that can provide support to nascent entrepreneurs.

Modes of Governance

A separate institutional dimension of entrepreneurship involves the various forms of ownership in new enterprises. As discussed below, although popular notions of entrepreneurship often conjure up the image of owners as solo pilots, braving both bumpy weather and mechanical failure alone, in reality entrepreneurial organizations are more likely to have multiple owners, in other words, founding teams rather than single founders (Ruef, 2010). Variations in ownership arrangements are likely to affect decision making, access to resources, and other organizational features; hence, we refer to these arrangements as modes of governance.

In this context, we argue that it is useful to distinguish first, between solo and team forms of governance as a broad cut, and second, between teams in terms of family and nonfamily membership. The latter distinction is not a clean one, since the governance arrangements in new firms can involve a mix of family and nonfamily members. However, extant work (e.g., Ruef, 2010, p. 67) suggests that such mixed ownership is a relatively uncommon mode of governance. Both because it appears uncommon and for the sake of simplicity, here we simply contrast teams made up of family members with those made up of nonfamily members.

Solo Entrepreneurs

Classic research and theory often implies a conception of the entrepreneur as a heroic loner (Harper, 2008; Schumpeter, 1911/1968). Shane and Venkataraman's (2000) seminal work, for example, argued that entrepreneurship sits at the nexus of two phenomena, the occurrence of opportunities for profit and the existence of individuals able and willing to pursue such opportunities. Likewise, Schumpeter's original theory on economic dynamism suggested the entrepreneurial actor as a solitary figure endowed with "pioneering vision" who disturbs the economic status quo through innovation (Harper, 2008, p. 615). Others have been even more explicit in insisting that entrepreneurship necessarily involves single individuals (see also Kirzner, 1973, 1979; Casson, 1982), because both the identification of opportunities and the ability to act freely to take advantage of such opportunities require independent actors, unhobbled by constraints and coordination costs of collaborative decision making and action.

However, research on entrepreneurship in the United States, using the same general definitional approach that we do, suggests that a little less than half of all entrepreneurial efforts involve a single owner (Ruef, 2010). While the advantages of sharing decision-making responsibilities, as well as financial risk, make the attractiveness of a team form of governance understandable, decentralized or shared decision making often entails problems of conflict and coordination, as classic organizational studies have amply documented (Scott & Davis, 2007; Tolbert & Hall, 2009/2016). This suggests there may be significant differences between firms led by solo entrepreneurs and those led by teams in both functioning and outcomes, but to date there has been little systematic study of such differences (for a notable exception, see also Ruef, 2010).

Family Teams

An additional, useful distinction can be drawn within team-led enterprises, involving a comparison between those constituted by family members and those based on extra-familial ties, such as shared occupational membership, common organizational history, and ethnic or national identity. Research on the United States suggests that between two-thirds and three-fourths of all new team-led enterprises are family based (Brannon, Wiklund, & Haynie, 2013; Ruef, 2010), but this may underestimate the true distribution because it is not uncommon for husbands to report themselves as the sole owners of new firms despite the critical contributions made by wives (Portes & Zhou, 1999, p. 151). Married couples and live-in partners constitute the majority of family-owned new enterprises (Ruef, 2010, p. 67).

Data on self-employment among different ethnic groups in the United States suggests that some are much more likely to rely on spouses and family members to create founding teams than others. For example, being married is a strong predictor of self-employment among Koreans in the United States; this is less true of white, native-born Americans, and it is unrelated to self-employment among U.S.-born blacks (Portes & Zhou, 1999). Likewise, some work also suggests international differences. For example, Cruz, Howorth, and Hamilton (2013) find that the percentage of family-based firms is relatively low in the United States compared to other countries.

Families are often assumed to represent a strong, closed form of network that enhances trust and ongoing commitment among members to one another (Coleman, 1990; Hurlbert, Haines, & Beggs, 2000; Uzzi, 1996). Insofar as family members' economic fates are tied together (Becker, 1981; Oppenheimer, 1997), conflicts of interest and self-serving motives are apt to be minimized (Lim, Busenitz, & Chidambaram, 2013), and this may ease some of the problems that are common to group-based decision making. These factors presumably facilitate entrepreneurial efforts by family-based teams.

Nonfamily Teams

On the other hand, ownership teams composed of nonrelated individuals can also offer some important advantages, including social ties to a wider network of potential resource providers, and recruitment of individuals with relevant technical knowledge and skills. This may account for Ruef's (2010) empirically based estimates that, among team-led enterprises in the United States at the turn of the twenty-first century, approximately a quarter to a third had owner teams composed of nonfamily members.

His work, as well as other studies (Saxenian, 2006; Sorenson & Audia, 2000), suggest that nonfamily teams typically exhibit a high degree of homophily in terms of gender, ethnicity, age, and/or professional membership. Such homophily may serve, at least in part, as a substitute for kinship-generated trust (Williams & O'Reilly, 1998). The strong tendency toward occupationally based similarity among team members, common in U.S. firms, could also partially reflect the fact that new firms frequently have their genesis within existing firms (Saxenian, 1994; Zucker, Darby, & Brewer, 1998). Members of a firm who interact frequently may develop the sort of social trust and norms that lower the risks of starting a new enterprise together (Zucker, 1986).

Data on startup firms in the United States also provides evidence of industrial-level variation in the reliance on nonfamily founding teams (see also Ruef, 2010, p. 69): startup firms in the wholesale and retail sector (including restaurants), for example, are much more likely to have family-based ownership than those in finance, real estate, and consulting. This may partly reflect differences among occupational groups. Some occupations cultivate strong shared identities among members that can serve as a basis for trust (Tanis & Postmes, 2005), thus facilitating collective decision making, which increases the viability of nonfamily governance. Insofar as occupations with strong shared identities are more prevalent in certain industries, this could produce industry-level differences in foundings by nonfamily teams. Likewise, if some ethnic groups are prone to use common ethnic identity as a basis for founding-team formation and are concentrated in certain businesses, this could also produce observed industry variations in nonfamily-team foundings.

Explaining Institutional Variations in Entrepreneurship

The preceding discussion cited research showing patterned differences in entrepreneurial activity across social groups in terms of modes of entry and governance. Understanding why one mode is more dominant among some social groups or in certain contexts is important to gaining a better theoretical understanding of entrepreneurship as a social phenomenon. In addition, from both a theoretical and a more policy-oriented perspective, linking these institutional variations to associated outcomes (e.g., probabilities of entrepreneurial persistence and enterprise survival) is an important task for entrepreneurship scholars.

Thus, we now turn to these issues, and offer a number of propositions concerning the kinds of community or group-level characteristics and social conditions that are apt to affect the predominance of certain modes of entry and governance in a given setting. In formulating these propositions, we have drawn partly on existing research, but we also rely on our own intuitions and understandings to suggest a variety of potential avenues for future research.

Sources and Outcomes of Different Entry Modes

Emergent Mode

As previously noted, research on immigrant-founded enterprises suggests that this entry route is more common among Hispanics than Koreans, a difference that is usually attributed to Koreans' preemigration experience with entrepreneurial ventures and to lower average levels of education and other resources possessed by Hispanics (Raijman & Tienda, 2000). This is also consistent with cross-national evidence from the Global Entrepreneurship Monitor's survey data, which indicates a noticeably higher rate of nascent entrepreneurial activity in *factor-driven* econo- mies (countries that are less developed in terms of technological capabilities, finan- cial institutions, etc.) than in more developed economies (Bosma & Levie, 2010).[2] Together, this work suggests emergent entry is likely to be a dominant mode of entry in social groups whose members typically lack access to formal employment, either because they lack necessary human capital (have limited education attain- ment, accumulated work experience, etc.) or because of an underperforming econ- omy. Of course, much nascent entrepreneurial activity does not result in the founding of formal business enterprises (Carter, Gartner, & Reynolds, 1996). However, we posit that the greater the amount of participation by a group in informal economic activities, the greater the chance that its members will become entrepreneurs via this route.

Note that the lack of access to formal employment may not only reflect general economic conditions or human capital but can also be due to the incompatibility of formal employment with other aspects of individuals' lives. In line with this, the Global Entrepreneurship Monitor data also show that, in both highly and less devel- oped economies, women are more likely to be among those in early-stage entrepre- neurship phases,[3] even though men are more likely to be established business owners (Kelley et al., 2011, p. 19, p. 31). The incompatibility of family and work roles may limit women's access to formal employment, thereby encouraging them to seek employment with more casual operations, at least initially (Budig, 2006; Thébaud, 2015). And again, the greater the proportion of a group engaged in activi- ties in the informal economy, the more likely its members will be characterized by an emergent entry mode. Thus:

Proposition 1: An emergent entry mode will be more common in geographical areas with lower levels of formal employment overall.

Proposition 2: An emergent entry mode will be more common among groups and communities whose members have less education, work experience, or other aspects of human capital.

Proposition 3: An emergent entry mode will be more common among women than men.

Moreover, insofar as greater regulation in a location presents fewer opportunities to undertake economic activities on an informal basis, this will inherently limit an emergent entry mode. (Note that this is not intended to imply that regulation neces- sarily limits new foundings or entrepreneurial opportunities overall; it simply restricts this particular mode of entry into entrepreneurship.) Therefore:

---

[2] In these data, *nascent entrepreneurs* are those actively involved in starting a business that has yet to pay salaries, wages or other financial returns to owners for more than 3 months.

[3] This includes both those classified as nascent entrepreneurs, and those who have succeeded in recording financial returns for more than 3 months, but less than 42 months.

Proposition 4: An emergent entry mode will be more common in communities with less stringent regulation of economic activities.

As noted, from the standpoint of founding a sustainable new enterprise, there are advantages to having had prior experience in a given area of production activity or service provision, and emergent entry into entrepreneurship will provide this. However, unless this activity involves collective production (i.e., multiple producers), individuals are less likely to acquire the skills of coordination and communication that are necessary for effective day-to-day operation and expandability of an enterprise (see also Block & Wagner, 2010, for related evidence). This is likely to disadvantage them relative to those entering via apprenticeships. Thus, we posit that:

Proposition 5: Groups and communities in which emergent entry is a dominant mode will have higher rates of failure among new enterprises, ceteris paribus, than those in which apprenticeship entry is dominant.

Apprenticeship Mode

Existing research suggests that the apprenticeship mode is common among ethnic entrepreneurs in small, service-sector industries, such as restaurants, information technology staffing, clothing, and beauty shops catering to ethnic clientele. Thus, it is more likely to occur in communities with greater numbers of smaller, service sector firms and in those with a concentration of individuals with distinctive tastes, in other words, in a niche market. It may also be the case that smaller, service sector firms have fewer pathways for upward mobility as an employee; thus, founding one's own business may become a logical option for employees of such firms who desire greater earnings and status.

It is important to note that an apprenticeship mode is not typical of all immigrant groups. Research by Raijman and Tienda (2000) found that it was very common among Korean immigrants to the United States but relatively rare among those from Mexico. Banerjee's (2013) research on information technology entrepreneurs indicated that it was more common among members of some Indian states than others. Clearly, flows of knowledge about who is looking to hire new employees and which employees are looking for work are critical for this mode to function (Fernandez & Fernandez-Mateo, 2006). Hence, it is more likely to occur in communities and groups characterized by comparatively strong network ties (Kwon et al., 2013). Such ties may be based on common ethnic identities, but occupational groups may also serve as the foundation for this sort of dense network (Barley & Kunda, 2004; Tolbert, 1996).

An apprenticeship mode often involves the creation of additional competitors for existing employers, because employees take the knowledge they have gained to found their own firms. In order to be sustainable, this pathway will likely rest on collectivistic norms that temper such competition by reinforcing a long-term view and expectations of quid pro quo relationships (Saxenian, 1994; Uzzi, 1996; Zucker, 1986). In this context, we suggest three more propositions:

Proposition 6: An apprenticeship entry mode will be more common in communities with a relatively high proportion of small, service sector firms.

Proposition 7: An apprenticeship entry mode will be more common in communities with denser social networks.

Proposition 8: An apprenticeship entry mode will be more common in communities with cultural norms that mitigate economic competition.

An apprenticeship mode of entry generally provides individuals with relevant industry knowledge and contacts, as well as knowledge of common management issues and pitfalls. This background is likely to enhance entrepreneurs' ability to cope with many of the challenges that face new organizations. Hence,

Proposition 9: Groups and communities in which apprenticeship entry is a dominant mode will have lower rates of failure among new firms than those dominated by other modes of entry.

Neophyte Mode

We suspect that a neophyte mode is a relatively uncommon pathway into entrepreneurship. In our conception, it is distinguished from other modes largely in terms of individuals' preexisting experience (or lack thereof) in the industry in which they found a new enterprise, or a closely related one.[4] Founders who base their business on genuinely new products or services necessarily become entrepreneurs via this mode (insofar as they create an industry as well as a new business), but we would characterize a person who quit (or lost) a job in a financial services firm and opened a restaurant as also representing the neophyte mode.

Taking this route into entrepreneurship is likely to require a more rapid acquisition of the resources needed for ongoing production by an enterprise because these could not have been gradually gained through previous employment, as in the case of emergent and apprenticeship modes. Moreover, insofar as it entails genuinely new products and services, this mode may rest on substantial preinvestment in innovation activities—the devotion of time, labor, specialized knowledge, and often financial capital to experimentation and the successive development of ideas. In consequence, we expect the neophyte mode typically to be found in more developed economies, and within those economies in wealthier communities.

While the lack of opportunities to gain relevant industry-based knowledge and contacts increases the risks associated with founding a new enterprise (Kirzner, 1973, 1979; Schumpeter, 1911/1968; Von Mises, 1949/1950), those risks can be reduced by the presence of an entrepreneurial infrastructure—the presence of advisors experienced in startup activities, arrangements for lending resources, and

---

[4] We recognize that how to decide whether an individual's former experience is in a *closely related* industry, and thus to distinguish between apprenticeship and neophyte modes empirically, will be challenging. Nevertheless, we think efforts to draw this distinction are useful for further entrepreneurship research.

strong and stable legal systems (e.g, with established patent laws and sanctions for their violation). This kind of infrastructure may be based on formal organizations (e.g., Silicon Valley), though it may also exist informally in some communities (Suchman, 2000). Hence, we propose:

Proposition 10: A neophyte entry mode will be more common in wealthier communities.

Proposition 11: A neophyte entry mode will be more common in communities with more developed legal and financial support systems for new ventures.

Because founders who enter entrepreneurship via a neophyte mode have less relevant experience and training, we expect this route not only to be rarer than others, but also more risky, all else being equal.

Proposition 12: Groups and communities in which a neophyte entry mode is dominant are more likely to have higher rates of failure among new enterprises than those dominated by other modes of entry.

Sources and Outcomes of Variation in Governance Modes

Solo versus Team-Based Modes

We expect that broad cultural values will be an important influence on the likelihood that new enterprises will have a single individual at the helm, rather than a team. In individualistic cultures, personal goals and achievements are valued above those of groups in which a person is a member (Hofstede, 1980; Rothwell, 1999/2010, pp. 65–84), and this is likely to enhance the attractiveness of solo entrepreneurship (Brandl & Bullinger, 2009).

Even within individualistic cultures, differences in attitudes and values associated with social class membership may affect preferences for solo entrepreneurship. Researchers have noted that self-reliance and self-direction are values most strongly held by middle and upper classes (Kohn, Naoi, Schoenbach, Schooler, & Slomczynski, 1990; Pearlin & Kohn, 1966; Ruef, 2010, p. 11).[5] These values are likely to be associated with individuals' willingness to—and even preferences for— taking on the responsibilities of managing an organization on their own.

Research suggests the form of governance in new enterprises may not only be affected by entrepreneurs' own values and preferences, but by their status within a community and, more specifically, social perceptions of them as an entrepreneurial team member. For example, a number of studies have suggested femininity is often negatively associated with entrepreneurial ability (Ahl, 2002; Henry & Marlow,

---

[5] Note that classic studies in this area (Kohn et al., 1990) used parental occupation—particularly that of fathers—to define social class, based on the assumption that higher status occupations permit and require members to exercise more autonomy and creativity at work, which in turn, shapes child-rearing practices.

2014), thus providing an explanation for Ruef's (2010) finding that in the United States women are much more likely to be solo entrepreneurs than their male counterparts. That is, such perceptions make women less likely to be considered in the formation of entrepreneurial teams, at least outside their immediate family, necessitating independent entrepreneurial efforts (Ruef, 2010). Similar social perceptions of other social groups not generally deemed to have characteristics required for entrepreneurship may limit their inclusion on founding teams, thus increasing their likelihood of solo entrepreneurship. Therefore, we posit:

Proposition 13: A solo governance mode will be a more common in groups with more individualistic than collectivistic cultures.

Proposition 14: A solo governance mode will be a more common among groups and communities with a high proportion of middle and upper class members.

Proposition 15: A solo governance mode will be more common in groups and communities who are perceived in the larger society as lacking entrepreneurial abilities.

Finally, we argue that the choice between a solo or a team mode of governance will influence the probability of new venture's survival and profitability. Not only does being a solo owner make great demands on individuals' decision-making skills, but shared ownership is likely to facilitate access a wider pool of resources required to keep firms going during often difficult startup stages (Harper, 2008; Packalen, 2007). Thus, we posit:

Proposition 16: Groups and communities in which a solo governance mode is more dominant are likely to have higher rates of new venture failure than those with team-based governance modes.

Family versus Nonfamily Team Modes

Much of the research on entrepreneurial teams thus far has focused on determining whether and when founding teams are more likely to form from strong or weak networks (homophilous versus heterogeneous ties) (see also Gedajlovic, Honig, Moore, Payne, & Wright, 2013; Ruef, 2010, pp. 60–84). Family and friendship or occupational ties are often lumped together in one strong-ties category, and scholars have yet to specifically tackle questions of why entrepreneurial teams may form along family or nonfamily bases.

As noted above, families are often typified as a strong, closed form of network, one that enhances trust and ongoing commitment to entrepreneurial activity (Coleman, 1990). However, the strength of norms of obligation to family members is a cultural variable (Altinay & Altinay, 2008; Bégin & Fayolle, 2014), and this variability is likely to affect the degree to which group members rely on family in forming an entrepreneurial team. In part, such variations are linked to the development of the state: Where governments play a bigger role in providing social safety nets for citizens, the economic success or failure of an individual will have relatively few repercussions for his or her family members (Barakat, 1993, pp .23−25), and normative obligations of family members toward one another are apt to be both more limited and weaker (Bégin & Fayolle, 2014). In addition, different religions and philosophical traditions vary in the weight they give to family obligations. For example, Confucianism attaches particular importance to family obligations (Fingarette, 1972). Thus, we posit that both state policies and cultural norms may affect the strength of family ties:

Proposition 17: Family teams will be a more common governance mode than non-family teams in communities and groups where state-based support systems are weaker.

Proposition 18: Family teams will be a more common governance mode than non-family teams in communities and groups in which cultural values emphasize family obligations.

In addition, reliance on family or nonfamily members in forming entrepreneurial teams is apt be affected by the existence of alternative trust-producing arrangements (Guseva & Rona-Tas, 2001; Zucker, 1986). These arrangements may be formal, including the development of organizations that certify claims of financial responsibility and enforce contracts. They may also be informal, including occupationally or ethnically based strong network ties that serve the same functions of certifying individuals and enforcing agreements.

We argued previously (see Proposition 11) that an entrepreneurial infrastructure—including rationalized, impersonal arrangements for lending resources, enforcing contractual agreements, providing business advice and guidance systems—can reduce risks and uncertainty associated with new foundings, and that this is likely to increase the likelihood of solo entrepreneurship. By the same token, such arrangements may make it easier to create trust among nonfamily members, who will most likely have a shorter acquaintanceship and familiarity with each other, compared to families. Strong and stable informal network ties, based on common membership in an occupational or ethnic community, may serve similar functions. These ties can provide in-depth information about individuals, as well as sanctioning power for norm violations through social ostracism. This suggests two additional propositions:

Proposition 19: Nonfamily teams will be a more common governance mode than family teams in communities and groups with more developed legal and financial support systems for new ventures.

Proposition 20: Nonfamily teams will be a more common governance mode than family teams in communities and groups with denser informal social networks.

Finally, we argue that the inherent longevity of family relationships (compared to nonfamily ones) is likely to have consequences for new enterprises. Some authors have argued that members of family firms are likely to have a unique stewardship perspective towards the organization, leading them to invest in the business as part of a family legacy (Miller, Le Breton-Miller, & Scholnick, 2008). In line with this, family-owned firms presumably seek to develop a community culture that results in loyal employees, and strong connections with other external stakeholders that may be especially critical during times of crises (Arregle, Hitt, Sirmon, & Very, 2007; Das & Teng, 1997; Davis & Greve, 1997; Tsui-Auch, 2004). Such an orientation is likely to contribute to the survival probabilities of ventures founded by family teams.

Proposition 21: Family teams will have lower rates of failure in comparison to other governance forms.

While the family-team mode of governance may lead to higher probabilities of survival, it may contribute to lower rates of growth. Some research suggests that family-owned firms are more likely to emphasize nonfinancial goals than others (Farrington, Venter, & Van der Merwe, 2011), and in some cultures, running a business is viewed as less desirable than pursuing a career in an established profession (Zhou, 2004). In this context, the goals are to create a business that supports one generation and underwrites the education and occupational transition of the next; maximizing revenues and growth are not paramount. Moreover (and in contrast to arguments about the dominance of a stewardship perspective in family firms), some work indicates that members of family firms may be less likely to distinguish the firm's resources from their own personal resources. Based on a survey of 673 family-owned businesses, Zuiker et al. (2002) concluded that, "The intermingling of financial resources ... leads to decisions that are good for the short-term but not for the long-term viability of the family business" (p. 69).

Finally, reliance on family members to help form a new venture is very likely to restrict the ability to tap specialized skills and knowledge that may be needed for new enterprises. This is likely to be a particular limitation for ventures that involve more innovative activities and thus require diverse training and expertise of members. Hence, we would expect ventures governed by nonfamily teams to be more likely to be engaged in developing innovations and to pursue risky capital structures to exploit potentially profitable opportunities (Mishra & McConaughy, 1999). Taken as a whole, these arguments suggest that:

Proposition 22: New ventures with family teams as a governance mode are likely to grow less and more slowly than nonfamily teams.

Conclusions

If entrepreneurship is to become a long-lasting field of research, a broader, more developed conceptualization of the phenomenon is required, one that will help unify the otherwise eclectic existing literatures that comprise entrepreneurship studies and provide a guiding framework moving forward. We have argued that treating entrepreneurship as an institution, that is, as patterned behavior reflecting social understandings shared by members of a particular group, provides such a conceptualization. With it, what are now viewed as competing definitions of entrepreneurship can be seen simply as institutional variations, and studies focusing on specific variations can provide knowledge of the social, economic, or other conditions that produce them. Furthermore, this approach facilitates the organization of past empirical work and, in guiding future work, allows exploration of new theoretical insights.

We note that an institutional approach to examining entrepreneurship has a long pedigree, traceable at least to Weber's (1919/1958) classic work, *The Protestant Ethic and the Spirit of Capitalism*, analyzing the impacts of Calvinist beliefs as a key influence on the creation of business enterprises in western Europe and the United States. In some ways, our proposed research agenda represents an extension and elaboration of this early work.

While there are a variety of institutional aspects of entrepreneurship that could be studied, in this chapter we highlighted two dimensions, modes of entry and modes of governance, which we discussed in terms of behavioral manifestations. The first refers to observed pathways that lead to the formal founding of new economic organizations. We identified three common pathways, or modes, including what we labeled emergent (foundings resulting from the evolution of part-time activities, often undertaken informally, into a business enterprise), apprenticeship (foundings by individuals based on expertise gained from employment in a particular industry), and neophyte (foundings involving entry into an industry with little or no prior experience in it). The second dimension, modes of governance, involves differing ownership arrangements that, we argue, are apt to be closely tied to decision making and risk sharing in new enterprises. We again identified three separate types, including solo entrepreneurs, family teams, and nonfamily teams.

Based on these distinctions, as well as our review of previous research streams on entrepreneurship, we generated a number of propositions concerning conditions that are likely to affect the likelihood that entrepreneurial patterns in a group along these dimensions will take a particular form. The logic of our propositions can be debated. And we would strongly encourage that, because the aim of the chapter is to generate further reflection and research on these dimensions of entrepreneurship, as well as others.

Our focus on pathways and governance reflects our belief that understanding variations in these dimensions is of both theoretical and practical importance, but we recognize that there are other dimensions of entrepreneurship that also could be explored in future research. Two additional dimensions we suggest include modes of financing and modes of exit. The first refers to the primary source of material resources used in initial stages of organizing entrepreneurial enterprises. Reliance on different sources is likely to affect the timetable of entrepreneurial activities as well as criteria used in evaluating continuance or discontinuance of entrepreneurial efforts. Contemporary research on entrepreneurial financing has investigated a variety of sources of financing, including banks, private investors, government agencies, family, and self (Pahnke, Katila, & Eisenhardt, 2015; Zahra & Sharma, 2004). However, treating this as an institutional dimension of entrepreneurship could provide a unifying framework allowing better integration of such work. Similarly, focused attention on identifying the conditions that shape different modes of exit (e.g., failure, acquisition, or *morphing*—a substantial transformation of goals, products, etc.) could lead to useful insights into another dimension that could be of general interest.

And while we have concentrated on behavioral aspects of entrepreneurship as an institution, the logics, or common beliefs and rationales that justify and underpin the behaviors, are clearly a necessary part of our proposed research agenda. A growing body of work has used the concept of logic to explain geographical and occupationally linked variations in organizational structures and practices. Pahnke, Katila, and Eisenhardt (2015), for example, argued that different logics held by different investor groups—venture capitalists, corporate venture capitalists, and government agencies—are the source of key differences among new ventures and their performance.

Much less work, however, has focused on the questions of how variations in logics arise and persist (or disappear) over time.[6] Some provocative work by Fairlie and Meyer (1996) provided evidence that variations in entrepreneurial propensities among immigrant groups to the United States persist over generations, suggesting that different logics can survive even in a similar, homogenizing environment. In contrast, work by Zilber (2002) showed that the existence of two competing logics in the same organization led to conflict and ultimately resulted in the dominance of one and the disappearance of the other. Not only do we need documentation of the nature of logics associated with variations in entrepreneurship, but we also need research on the question of what leads such logics to survive over time or to change. Thus, there is much work to be done in order to understand entrepreneurship as an institution. Our aim is to encourage such work, and thus, we believe, move scholarship in this area forward in an integrated way.

References

Acs, Z. J., & Armington, C. (2006). *Entrepreneurship, geography and American economic growth.* Cambridge; UK: Cambridge University Press.

Acs, Z. J., Audretsch, D. B., & Strom, R. J. (2009). *Entrepreneurship, growth and public policy.* Cambridge, UK: Cambridge University Press.

Ahl, H. J. (2002). *The making of the female entrepreneur: A discourse analysis of research texts on women's entrepreneurship.* JIBS Dissertation Series: Vol. 15. Jönköping: Jönköping International Business School.

Aldrich, H. E., & Kim, P. H. (2007). A life course perspective on occupational inheritance: Self-employed parents and their children. In M. Ruef & M. Lounsbury (Eds.), *The sociology of entrepreneurship* (pp. 33–82). Research in the Sociology of Organizations: Vol. 25. Bingley: Emerald Group.

Aldrich, H. E., & Ruef, M. (2006). *Organizations evolving* (2nd ed.). Los Angeles: Sage. (Original work published 1999)

---

[6]The notion of institutional entrepreneur is sometimes invoked to explain changes in established organizational practices and structures (e.g., DiMaggio, 1988), but this work seldom addresses how and when such change agents are likely to emerge (Hardy & Maguire, 2008.)

Aldrich, H. E., & Waldinger, R. (1990). Ethnicity and entrepreneurship. *Annual Review of Sociology, 16*, 111–135. doi:https://doi.org/10.1146/annurev.so.16.080190.000551

Aldrich, H. E., & Wiedenmayer, G., (1993). From traits to rates: An ecological perspective on organizational foundings. In J. Katz & R. Brockhaus (Eds.), *Advances in entrepreneurship, firm emergence and growth* (Vol. 1, pp. 145–196). Greenwich, CT: JAI Press.

Altinay, L., & Altinay, E. (2008). Factors influencing business growth: The rise of Turkish entrepreneurship in the UK. *International Journal ofEntrepreneurial Behavior & Research, 14*, 24–46. doi:https://doi.org/10.1108/13552550810852811

Ansari, S. M., Fiss, P. C., & Zajac, E. J. (2010). Made to fit: How practices vary as they diffuse. *Academy of Management Review, 35*, 67–92. doi:https://doi.org/10.5465/AMR.2010.45577876

Ardagna, S., & Lusardi, A. (2008). *Explaining international differences in entrepreneurship: The role of individual characteristics and regulatory constraints.* NBER Working Series: NBER Working Paper 14012. Cambridge: National Bureau of Economic Research. doi:https://doi.org/10.3386/w14012

Arregle, J.-L., Hitt, M. A., Sirmon, D. G., & Very, P. (2007). The development of organizational social capital: Attributes of family firms. *Journal of Management Studies, 44*, 73–95. doi:https://doi.org/10.1111/j.1467-6486.2007.00665.x

Baltzopoulos, A., Braunerhjelm, P., & Tikoudis, I. (2015). Spin-offs: Why geography matters. *Journal of Economic Geography, 16*, 273–303. doi:https://doi.org/10.1093/jeg/lbv006

Banerjee, M. (2013). *The origin of differences in immigrants' strategic choices: Job seekers and entrepreneurial firms* (Doctoral dissertation). ILR School, Cornell University.

Barakat, H. (1993). *The Arab world: Society, culture, and state.* Berkeley: University of California Press.

Barley, S. R., & Kunda, G. (2004). Gurus, hired guns and warm bodies: Itinerant experts in a knowledge economy. Princeton: Princeton University Press.

Baron, J. N., Burton, M. D., & Hannan, M. T. (1999). Engineering bureaucracy: The genesis of formal policies, positions and structures in hightechnology firms. *Journal of Law, Economics & Organization, 15*, 1–41. doi:https://doi.org/10.1093/jleo/15.1.1

Bathelt, H., Kogerl, D. F., & Munro, K. A. (2010). A knowledge-based typology of university spin-offs in the context of regional economic development. *Technovation, 30*, 519–530. doi:https://doi.org/10.1016/j.technovation.2010.04.003

Baughn, C. C., Chua, B.-L., & Neupert, K. E. (2006). The normative context of women's participation in entrepreneurship: A multicountry study. *Enterpreneurship: Theory and Practice, 30*, 687–708. doi:https://doi.org/10.1111/j.1540-6520.2006.00142.x

Becker, G. S. (1981). *A treatise on the family.* Cambridge, MA: Harvard University Press.

Beckman, C. M., & Burton, M. D. (2008). Founding the future: Path dependence in the evolution of top management teams from founding to IPO. *Organization Science, 19*, 3–24. doi:https://doi.org/10.1287/orsc.1070.0311

Bégin, L., & Fayolle, A. (2014). Family entrepreneurship: What we know, what we need to know. In A. Fayolle (Ed.), *Handbook of research on entrepreneurship: What we know and what we need to know* (pp. 183–212). Cheltenham: Edward Elgar.

Bidwell, M., & Briscoe, F. (2010). The dynamics of interorganizational careers. *Organization Science, 21*, 1034–1053. doi:https://doi.org/10.1287/orsc.1090.0492

Block, J. H., & Wagner, M. (2010). Necessity and opportunity entrepreneurs in Germany: Characteristics and earnings differentials. *Schmalenbach Business Review, 62*, 154–174. doi:https://doi.org/10.2139/ssrn.899968

Boeker, W., & Wiltbank, R. (2005). New venture evolution and managerial capabilities. *Organization Science, 16*, 123–133. doi:https://doi.org/10.1287/orsc.1050.0115

Bosma, N., & Levie, J. (2010). *Global entrepreneurship monitor: 2009 global report.* Babson Park: Babson College. Retrieved from http://www.babson.edu/Academics/centers/blank-center/global-research/gem/Documents/gem-2009-global-report.pdf

Brandl, J., & Bullinger, B. (2009). Reflections on the societal conditions for the pervasiveness of entrepreneurial behavior in Western societies. *Journal of Management Inquiry, 18,* 159–173. doi:https://doi.org/10.1177/1056492608329400

Brannon, D. L., Wiklund, J., & Haynie, J. M. (2013). The varying effects of family relationships in entrepreneurial teams. E*ntrepreneurship: Theory and Practice, 37,* 107–132. doi:https://doi.org/10.1111/j.1540-6520.2012.00533.x

Breschi, S., & Malerba, F. (2001). The geography of innovation and economic clustering: Some introductory notes. *Industrial and Corporate Change, 10,* 817–833. doi:https://doi.org/10.1093/icc/10.4.817

Brittain, J. W., & Wholey, D. (1988). Competition and coexistence in organizational communities: population dynamics in electronics components manufacturing. In G. R. Carroll (Ed.), *Ecological models of organizations* (pp. 195–222). Cambridge, MA: Ballinger.

Budig, M. J. (2006). Intersections on the road to self-employment: Gender, family and occupational class. *Social Forces, 84,* 2223–2239. doi:https://doi.org/10.1353/sof.2006.0082

Buenstorf, G., & Klepper, S. (2010). Why does entry cluster geographically? Evidence from the U.S. tire industry. *Journal of Urban Economics, 68,* 103–114. doi:https://doi.org/10.1016/j.jue.2010.03.005

Carr, D. (1996). Two paths to self-employment? Women's and men's self-employment in the United States, 1980. *Work and Occupations, 23,* 26–53. doi:https://doi.org/10.1177/0730888496023001003

Carter, N. M., Gartner, W. B., & Reynolds, P. D. (1996). Exploring startup event sequences. *Journal of Business Venturing, 11,* 151–166. doi:https://doi.org/10.1016/0883-9026(95)00129-8

Casson, M. C. (1982). *The entrepreneur: An economic theory.* Oxford: Martin Robertson.

Chen, X.-P., Yao, X., & Kotha, S. (2009). Entrepreneur passion and preparedness in business plan presentations: a persuasion analysis of venture capitalists' funding decisions. *Academy of Management Journal, 52,* 199–214. doi:https://doi.org/10.5465/AMJ.2009.36462018

Coleman, J. S. (1990). *Foundations of social theory.* Cambridge, MA: Harvard University Press.

Colyvas, J. A., & Jonsson, S. (2011). Ubiquity and legitimacy: Disentangling diffusion and institutionalization. *Sociological Theory, 29,* 27–53. doi:https://doi.org/10.1111/j.1467-9558.2010.01386.x

Cruz, A. D., Howorth, C., & Hamilton, E. (2013). Intrafamily entrepreneurship: The formation and membership of family entrepreneurial teams. *Entrepreneurship: Theory and Practice, 37,* 17–46. doi:https://doi.org/10.1111/j.1540-6520.2012.00534.x

Das, T. K., & Teng, B.S. (1997). Time and entrepreneurial risk behavior. *Entrepreneurship: Theory and Practice, 22*(2), 69–88.

Davidsson, P., & Wiklund, J. (1997). Values, beliefs and regional variations in new firm formation rates. *Journal of Economic Psychology, 18,* 179–199. doi:https://doi.org/10.1016/S0167-4870(97)00004-4

Davis, G. F. (1991). Agents without principles? The spread of the poison pill through the intercorporate network. *Administrative Science Quarterly, 36,* 583–613. doi:https://doi.org/10.2307/2393275

Davis, G. F., & Greve, H. R. (1997). Corporate elite networks and governance changes in the 1980s. *American Journal of Sociology, 103,* 1–37. doi:https://doi.org/10.1086/231170

Dencker, J. C., Gruber, M., & Shah, S. K. (2009). Pre-entry knowledge, learning and the survival of new firms. *Organization Science, 20,* 516–537. doi:https://doi.org/10.1287/orsc.1080.0387

DiMaggio, P. J. (1988). Interest and agency in institutional theory. In L. G. Zucker (Ed.), *Institutional patterns and organizations: Culture and environment* (pp. 3–22). Cambridge, MA: Ballinger Press.

Ding, Z., Sun, S. L., & Au, K. (2014). Angel investors' selection criteria: A comparative institutional perspective. *Asia Pacific Journal of Management, 31,* 705–731. doi:https://doi.org/10.1007/s10490-014-9374-z

Djelic, M. L. (1998). Exporting the American model: The postwar transformation of European business. Oxford, UK: Oxford University Press.

Eesley, C. E. (2009). Who has 'the right stuff'? Human capital, entrepreneurship and institutional change in China. *Proceedings of the 2009 Portland International Conference on Management of Engineering and Technology*, 1919–1944. doi:https://doi.org/10.1109/PICMET.2009.5261928

Elam, A., & Terjesen, S. (2010). Gendered institutions and cross-national patterns of business creation for men and women. *European Journal of Development Research, 22*, 331–348. doi:https://doi.org/10.1057/ejdr.2010.19

Fairlie, R. W., & Meyer, B. D. (1994). *The ethnic and racial character of self-employment*. NBER Working Series: NBER Working Paper 4791. Cambridge, MA: National Bureau of Economic Research. doi:https://doi.org/10.3386/w4791

Fairlie, R. W., & Meyer, B. D. (1996). Ethnic and racial self-employment differences and possible explanations. *Journal of human resources, 31*, 757–793. doi:https://doi.org/10.2307/146146

Farrington, S., Venter, E., & Van der Merwe, S. (2011). Organisational-based factors influencing the non-financial goals of family businesses. *Management Dynamics: Journal of the Southern African Institute for Management Scientists, 20*(3), 51–67. Retrieved from http://search.proquest.com/docview/1434982110/fulltextPDF/B60E0C8B11644FAPQ/1?accountid=10267

Fernandez, R. M., & Fernandez-Mateo, I. (2006). Networks, race and hiring. *American Sociological Review, 71*, 42–71. doi:https://doi.org/10.1177/000312240607100103

Fingarette, H. (1972). *Confucius: The secular as sacred*. New York: Harper & Row.

Fiss, P. C., Kennedy, M. T., & Davis, G. F. (2012). How golden parachutes unfolded: Diffusion and variation of a controversial practice. *Organization Science, 23*, 1077–1099. doi:https://doi.org/10.2307/23252450

Fligstein, N. (1985). The spread of the multidivisional form among large firms, 1919–1979. *American Sociological Review, 50*, 377–391. doi:https://doi.org/10.1016/S0742-3322(00)17003-2

Gambardella, A., Ganco, M., & Honoré, F. (2015). Using what you know: Patented knowledge in incumbent firms and employee entrepreneurship. *Organization Science, 26*, 456–474. doi:https://doi.org/10.1287/orsc.2014.0937

Gedajlovic, E., Honig, B., Moore, C. B., Payne, G. T., & Wright, M. (2013). Social capital and entrepreneurship: A schema and research agenda. *Entrepreneurship: Theory and Practice, 37*, 455–478. doi:https://doi.org/10.1111/etap.12042

Gielnik, M. M., Spitzmuller, M., Schmitt, A., Klemann, D. K., & Frese, M. (2015). "I put in effort, therefore I am passionate": Investigating the path from effort to passion in entrepreneurship. *Academy of Management Journal, 58*, 1012–1031. doi:https://doi.org/10.5465/amj.2011.0727

Glückler, J. (2006). A relational assessment of international market entry in management consulting. *Journal of Eonomic Geography, 6*, 369–393. doi:https://doi.org/10.1093/jeg/lbi016

Glückler, J. (2014). How controversial innovation succeeds in the periphery? A network perspective of BASF Argentina. *Journal of Economic Geography,14*, 903–927. doi:https://doi.org/10.1093/jeg/lbu016

Greenwood, R., Oliver, C., Sahlin, K., & Suddaby, R. (2008). Introduction. In R. Greenwood, C. Oliver, K. Sahlin, & R. Suddaby (Eds.), *Sage handbook of organizational institutionalism* (pp. 1–46). London: Sage.

Guseva, A., & Rona-Tas, A. (2001). Uncertainty, risk, and trust: Russian and American credit card markets compared. *American Sociological Review, 66*, 623–646. doi:https://doi.org/10.2307/3088951

Halaby, C. N. (2003). Where job values come from: Family and schooling background, cognitive ability and gender. *American Sociological Review, 68*, 251–278. doi:https://doi.org/10.2307/1519768

Hardy, C., & Maguire, S. (2008). Institutional entrepreneurship. In R. Greenwood, C. Oliver, K. Sahlin, & R. Suddaby (Eds.), *Sage handbook of organizational institutionalism* (pp. 198–217). London: Sage.

Harper, D. A. (2008). Towards a theory of entrepreneurial teams. *Journal of Business Venturing, 23*, 613–626. doi:https://doi.org/10.1016/j.jbusvent.2008.01.002

Henry, C., & Marlow, S. (2014). Exploring the intersection of gender, feminism and entrepreneurship. In A. Fayolle (Ed.), *The handbook of research on entrepreneurship. What we know and what we need to know* (pp. 109–126). Cheltenham: Edward Elgar.

Hiatt, S. R., & Sine, W. D. (2014). Clear and present danger: Planning and new venture survival amid political and civil violence. *Strategic Management Journal, 35*, 773–785. doi:https://doi.org/10.1002/smj.2113

Hipp, L., Bernhardt, J., & Allmendinger, J. (2015). Institutions and the prevalence of nonstandard employment. *Socio-Economic Review, 13*, 351–377. doi:https://doi.org/10.1093/ser/mwv002

Hofstede, G. (1980). *Culture's consequences: International differences in work-related values.* Beverly Hills: Sage.

Hurlbert, J. S., Haines, V. A., & Beggs, J. J. (2000). Core networks and tie activation: What kinds of routine networks allocate resources in nonroutine situations?. *American Sociological Review, 65*, 598–618. doi:https://doi.org/10.2307/2657385

Jennings, J. E., & Brush, C. G. (2013). Research on women entrepreneurs: Challenges to (and from) the broader entrepreneurship literature? *The Academy of Management Annals, 7*, 663–715. doi:https://doi.org/10.1080/19416520.2013.782190

Kacperczyk, A. J. (2012). Opportunity structures in established firms: Entrepreneurship versus intrapreneurship in mutual funds. *Administrative Science Quarterly, 57*, 484–521. doi:https://doi.org/10.1177/0001839212462675

Kacperczyk, A. J. (2013). Social influence and entrepreneurship: The effect of university peers on entrepreneurial entry. *Organization Science, 24*, 664–683. doi:https://doi.org/10.1287/orsc.1120.0773

Katz, J. A., & Gartner, W. B. (1988). Properties of emerging organizations. *Academy of Management Review, 13*, 429–441. doi:https://doi.org/10.2307/258090

Kelley, D. J., Brush, C. G., Greene, P. G., & Litovsky, Y. (2011). *Global entrepreneurship monitor: 2010 women's report.* Babson Park: Babson College.

Kennedy, M. T., & Fiss, P. C. (2009). Institutionalization, framing and diffusion: The logic of TQM adoption and implementation decisions among U.S. hospitals. *Academy of Management Journal, 52*, 897–918. doi:https://doi.org/10.5465/AMJ.2009.44633062

Kim, P. H., Aldrich, H. E., & Keister, L. A. (2006). Access (not) denied: The impact of financial, human, and cultural capital on entrepreneurial entry in the United States. *Small Business Economics, 27*, 5–22. doi:https://doi.org/10.1007/s11187-006-0007-x

Kirzner, I. M. (1973). *Competition and entrepreneurship.* Chicago: Chicago University Press.

Kirzner, I. M. (1979). *Perception, opportunity and profit: Studies in the theory of entrepreneurship.* Chicago: Chicago University Press.

Klepper, S. (2009). Spinoffs: A review and synthesis. *EuropeanManagement Review, 6*, 159–171. doi:https://doi.org/10.1057/emr.2009.18

Klepper, S., & Thompson, P. (2010) Disagreements and intra-industry spinoffs. *International journal of industrial organization, 28*, 526–538. doi:https://doi.org/10.1016/j.ijindorg.2010.01.002

Kohn, M. L., Naoi, A., Schoenbach, C., Schooler, C., & Slomczynski, K. M. (1990). Position in the class structure and psychological functioning in the United States, Japan, and Poland. *American Journal of Sociology, 95*, 964–1008. http://www.jstor.org/stable/2780647

Kwon, S. W., Heflin, C. M., & Ruef, M. (2013). Community social capital and entrepreneurship. *American Sociological Review, 78*, 980–1008. doi:https://doi.org/10.1177/0003122413506440

Lécuyer, C. (2006). *Making Silicon Valley. Innovation and the growth of high tech, 1930–1970* Cambridge, MA: MIT Press.

Light, I. (2003). The ethnic ownership economy. In C. H. Stiles & C. S. Galbraith (Eds.), *Ethnic entrepreneurship: Structure and process* (pp. 3–44). International Research in the Business Disciplines: Vol. 4. London: Emerald Group.

Light, I., & Rosenstein, C. (1995). *Race, ethnicity and entrepreneurship in urban America.* New York: Aldine de Gruyter.

Lim, J. Y.-K., Busenitz, L. W., & Chidambaram, L. (2013). New venture teams and the quality of business opportunities identified: Faultlines between subgroups of founders and investors. *Entrepreneurship: Theory and Practice, 37*, 47–67. doi:https://doi.org/10.1111/j.1540-6520.2012.00550.x

McClelland, D. C. (1965). N achievement and entrepreneurship: A longitudinal study. *Journal of Personality and Social Psychology, 1*, 389–392. doi:https://doi.org/10.1037/h0021956

Meyer, J. W., & Rowan, B. (1977). Institutionalized organizations: Formal structure as myth and ceremony. *American Journal of Sociology, 83*, 340–363. Retrieved from http://www.jstor.org/stable/2778293

Miller, D., Le Breton-Miller, L., & Scholnick, B. (2008). Stewardship vs. stagnation: An empirical comparison of small family and non-family businesses. *Journal of Management Studies, 45*, 51–78. doi:https://doi.org/10.1111/j.1467-6486.2007.00718.x

Miller, D. R., & Swanson, G. E. (1958). *The changing American parent: A study in the Detroit area.* New York: Wiley.

Mishra, C. S., & McConaughy, D. L. (1999). Founding family control and capital structure: The risk of loss of control and the aversion to debt. *Entrepreneurship: Theory and Practice, 23*, 53–64. Retrieved from http://search.proquest.com/docview/38791075?accountid=11359

Nanda, R., & Sorensen, J. B. (2010). Workplace peers and entrepreneurship. *Management Science, 56*, 1116–1126. doi:https://doi.org/10.1287/mnsc.1100.1179

Oppenheimer, V. K. (1997). Women's employment and the gain to marriage: The specialization and trading model. *Annual Review of Sociology, 23*, 431–453. doi:https://doi.org/10.1146/annurev.soc.23.1.431

Özcan, S., & Reichstein, T. (2009). Transition to entrepreneurship from the public sector: Predispositional and contextual effects. *Management Science, 55*, 604–618. doi:https://doi.org/10.1287/mnsc.1080.0954

Packalen, K. A. (2007). Complementing Capital: The role of status, demographic features, and social capital in founding teams' abilities to obtain resources. *Entrepreneurship: Theory and Practice, 31*, 873–891. doi:https://doi.org/10.1111/j.1540-6520.2007.00210.x

Pahnke, E. C., Katila, R., & Eisenhardt, K. M. (2015). Who takes you to the dance? How partners' institutional logics influence innovation in young firms. *Administrative Science Quarterly, 60*, 596–633. doi:https://doi.org/10.1177/0001839215592913

Pearlin, L. I., & Kohn, M. L. (1966). Social class, occupation, and parental values: A cross-national study. *American Sociological Review, 31*, 466–479. Retrieved from http://www.jstor.org/stable/2090770

Portes, A., & Zhou, M. (1999). Entrepreneurship and economic progress in the 1990s: A comparative analysis of immigrants and African Americans. In F. D. Bean & S. Bell-Rose (Eds.), *Immigration and opportunity: Race, ethnicity and employment in the United States* (pp. 143–171). New York: Russell Sage Foundation.

Raffiee, J., & Feng, J. (2014). Should I quit my day job?: A hybrid path to entrepreneurship. *Academy of Management Journal, 57*, 936–963. doi:https://doi.org/10.5465/amj.2012.0522

Raijman, R., & Tienda, M. (2000). Immigrants' pathways to business ownership: A comparative ethnic perspective. *The International Migration Review, 34*, 682–706. doi:https://doi.org/10.2307/2675941

Rothwell, J. D. (2010). *In the company of others: An introduction to communication* (3rd ed.). New York: Oxford University Press. (Original work published 1999)

Ruef, M. (2010). *The entrepreneurial group: Social identities, relations, and collective action.* Princeton: Princeton University Press.

Saxenian, A. (1994). *Regional advantage: Culture and competition in Silicon Valley and Route 128.* Cambridge, MA: Harvard University Press.

Saxenian, A. L. (2006). *The new Argonauts: Regional advantage in a global economy.* Cambridge, MA: Harvard University Press.

Schumpeter, J. A. (1968). *The theory of economic development: An inquiry into profits, capital, credit, interest, and the business cycle.* Harvard Economic Studies 46. (8th ed.; R. Opie, Trans.). Cambridge, MA: Harvard University Press. (Original work published 1911)

Scott, W. R., & Davis, G. F. (2007). *Organizations and organizing: Rational, natural and open system perspective*. Upper Saddle River: Pearson Prentice Hall.

Shah, S. K., & Tripsas, M. (2007). The accidental entrepreneur: The emergent and collective process of user entrepreneurship. *Strategic Entrepreneurship Journal, 1*, 123–140. doi:https://doi.org/10.1002/sej.15

Shane, S., & Nicolaou, N. (2015). Creative personality, opportunity recognition and the tendency to start businesses: A study of their genetic predispositions. *Journal of Business Venturing, 30*, 407–419. doi:https://doi.org/10.1016/j.jbusvent.2014.04.001

Shane, S., & Venkataraman, S. (2000). The promise of entrepreneurship as a field of research. *Academy of Management Review, 25*, 217–226. doi:https://doi.org/10.5465/AMR.2000.2791611

Sorensen, J. B. (2007). Bureaucracy and entrepreneurship: Workplace effects on entrepreneurial entry. *Administrative Science Quarterly, 52*, 387–412. doi:https://doi.org/10.2189/asqu.52.3.387

Sorenson, O., & Audia, P. G. (2000). The social structure of entrepreneurial activity: Geographic concentration of footwear production in the United States, 1940–1989. *American Journal of Sociology, 106*, 424–462. doi:https://doi.org/10.1086/316962

Sternberg, R., & Rocha, H. O. (2007). Why entrepreneurship is a regional event: Theoretical arguments, empirical evidence, and policy consequences. In M. P. Rice & T. G. Habbershon (Eds.), *Place* (pp. 215–238). Entrepreneurship: The Engine of Growth: Vol. 3. London: Praeger Perspectives.

Stuart, T. E., & Ding, W. W. (2006). When do scientists become entrepreneurs? The social structural antecedents of commercial activity in the academic life sciences. *American Journal of Sociology, 112*, 97–144. doi:https://doi.org/10.1086/502691

Suchman, M. C. (2000). Dealmakers and counselors: Law firms as intermediaries in the development of Silicon Valley. In M. Kenney (Ed.), *Understanding Silicon Valley: The anatomy of an entrepreneurial region* (pp. 71–97). Stanford: Stanford University Press.

Tanis, M., & Postmes, T. (2005). A social identity approach to trust: Interpersonal perception, group membership and trusting behaviour. *European Journal of Social Psychology, 35*, 413–424. doi:https://doi.org/10.1002/ejsp.256

Thébaud, S. (2015). Business as plan B. Institutional foundations of gender inequality in entrepreneurship across 24 industrialized countries. *Administrative Science Quarterly 60*, 671–711. doi:https://doi.org/10.1177/0001839215591627

Thornton, P. H., & Ocasio, W. (2008). Institutional logics. In R. Greenwood, C. Oliver, K. Sahlin, & R. Suddaby (Eds.), *The Sage handbook of organizational institutionalism* (pp. 99–128). London: Sage.

Tolbert, P. S. (1996). Occupations, organizations and boundaryless careers. In M. B. Arthur & D. M. Rousseau (Eds.), *The boundaryless careers: A new employment principle for a new organizational era* (pp. 331–349). New York: Oxford University Press.

Tolbert, P. S., David, R. J., & Sine, W. D. (2010). Studying choice and change: The intersection of institutional theory and entrepreneurship research. *Organization Science, 22*, 1332–1344. doi:https://doi.org/10.1287/orsc.1100.0601

Tolbert, P. S., & Hall, R. H. (2016). *Organizations:Structures, processes, and outcomes.*(10th ed.). Upper Saddle River.: Pearson/Prentice Hall. (Original work published 2009)

Tolbert, P. S., & Zucker, L. G. (1983). Institutional sources of change in the formal structure of organizations: The diffusion of civil service reform, 1880–1935. *Administrative Science Quarterly, 28*, 22–39. doi:https://doi.org/10.2307/2392383

Torrini, R. (2005). Cross-country differences in self-employment rates: The role of institutions. *Lobour Economics 12*, 661–683. doi:https://doi.org/10.1016/j.labeco.2004.02.010

Tsui-Auch, L. S. (2004). The professionally managed family-ruled enterprise: ethnic Chinese business in Singapore. *Journal of management studies, 41*, 693–723. doi:https://doi.org/10.1111/j.1467-6486.2004.00450.x

Uzzi, B. (1996). The sources and consequences of embeddedness for the economic performance of organizations: The network effect. *American Sociological Review, 61*, 674–698. Retrieved from http://www.jstor.org/stable/2096399

Vaillant, Y., & Lafuente, E. (2007) Do different institutional frameworks condition the influence of local fear of failure and entrepreneurial examples over entrepreneurial activity? *Entrepreneurship and Regional Development, 19*, 313–337. doi:https://doi.org/10.1080/08985620701440007

van Gelderen, M., Kautonen, T., & Fink, M. (2015). From entrepreneurial intentions to actions: Self-control and action-related doubt, fear and aversion. *Journal of Business Venturing, 30*, 655–673. doi:https://doi.org/10.1016/j.jbusvent.2015.01.003

Von Mises, L. (1950). *Human action: A treatise on economics.* New Haven: Yale University Press. (Original work published 1949)

Weber, M. (1958). *The Protestant ethic and the spirit of capitalism* (T. Parsons, Trans.). New York: Scribner. (Original work published 1919)

Wennekers, S., van Stel, A., Thurik R., & Reynolds, P. D. (2005). Nascent entrepreneurship and the level of economic development. *Small Business Economics 24*, 293–309. doi:https://doi.org/10.1007/s11187-005-1994-8

Williams, K. Y., & O'Reilly, C. A. (1998). Demography and diversity in organizations: A review of 40 years of research. *Research in Organizational Behavior, 20*, 77–140.

Williams, N., & Williams, C. C. (2014). Beyond necessity versus opportunity entrepreneurship: Some lessons from English deprived urban neighbourhoods. *International Entrepreneurship and Management Journal, 10*, 23–40. doi:https://doi.org/10.1007/s11365-011-0190-3

Zahra, S. A., & Sharma, P. (2004). Family business research: A strategic reflection. *Family Business Review, 17*, 331–346. doi:https://doi.org/10.1111/j.1741-6248.2004.00022.x

Zhou, M. (2004). Revisiting ethnic entrepreneurship: Convergences, controversies and conceptual advancements. *International Migration Review, 38*, 1040–1074. doi:https://doi.org/10.1111/j.1747-7379.2004.tb00228.x

Zilber, T. B. (2002). Institutionalization as an interplay between actions, meanings, and actors: The case of a rape crisis center in Israel. *Academy of Management Journal, 45*, 234–254. doi:https://doi.org/10.2307/3069294

Zucker, L. G. (1986). Production of trust: Institutional sources of economic structure, 1840–1920. *Research in Organizational Behavior, 8*, 53–111.

Zucker, L. G., Darby, M. R., & Brewer, M. B. (1998). Intellectual human capital and the birth of U.S. biotechnology enterprises. *American Economic Review, 88*, 290–306. Retrieved from http://digitalassets.lib.berkeley.edu/irle/ucb/text/irla0277.pdf .

Zuiker, V. S., Lee, Y. G., Olson, P. D., Danes, S. M., Van Guilder Dik, A. N., & Katras, M. J. (2002). Business, family, and resource intermingling characteristics as predictors of cash flow problems in family-owned businesses. *Journal of Financial Counseling and Planning, 13*, 65–81. Retrieved from https://my.afcpe.org/system/journals/vol1326.pdf

The Klaus Tschira Stiftung

The Klaus Tschira Stiftung was created in 1995 by the physicist Klaus Tschira (1940–2015). It is one of Europe's largest privately funded non-profit foundations. The foundation promotes the advancement of natural sciences, mathematics, and computer science and strives to raise appreciation of these fields. The focal points of the foundation are "Natural Sciences – Right from the Beginning," "Research," and "Science Communication." The involvement of the Klaus Tschira Stiftung begins in kindergartens and continues in primary and secondary schools, universities, and research facilities. The foundation champions new methods in the transfer of scientific knowledge, and supports both the development and intelligible presentation of research findings. The Klaus Tschira Stiftung pursues its objectives by conducting projects of its own but also awards subsidies after approval of applications. To foster and sustain work on selected topics, the foundation has also founded its own affiliates. Klaus Tschira's commitment to this objective was honored in 1999 with the "Deutscher Stifterpreis," the award conferred by the National Association of German Foundations.

The Klaus Tschira Stiftung is located in Heidelberg and has its head office in the Villa Bosch, once the residence of Carl Bosch, a Nobel laureate in chemistry. www.klaus-tschira-stiftung.de

J. Glückler et al. (eds.), *Knowledge and Institutions*, Knowledge and Space 13, https://doi.org/10.1007/978-3-319-75328-7

Fig. 1 Participants of the symposium "Knowledge and Institutions" at the Studio Villa Bosch in Heidelberg, Germany. © Johannes Glückler, Heidelberg

Fig. 2 Villa Bosch, the head office of the Klaus Tschira Stiftung, Heidelberg, Germany. © Peter Meusburger, Heidelberg

Index

Printed by Printforce, the Netherlands